# Countering the Counterculture

# Countering
# the
# Counterculture

*Rereading Postwar American
Dissent from Jack Kerouac to
Tomás Rivera*

## Manuel Luis Martinez

THE UNIVERSITY OF WISCONSIN PRESS

Publication of this book has been made possible in part by the generous support of the Anonymous Fund of the University of Wisconsin-Madison

The University of Wisconsin Press
1930 Monroe Street
Madison, Wisconsin 53711

www.wisc.edu/wisconsinpress/

3 Henrietta Street
London WC2E 8LU, England

Library of Congress Cataloging-in-Publication Data
Martinez, Manuel Luis.
Countering the counterculture : rereading postwar American dissent from
Jack Kerouac to Tomas Rivera / Manuel Luis Martinez.
p.     cm.
Includes bibliographical references and index.
ISBN 0-299-19284-9 (alk. paper)
1. American literature—20th century—History and criticism.   2. Beat generation.
3. American literature—Mexican American authors—History and criticism.
4. Literature and society—United States—History—20th century.
5. Counterculture—United States—History—20th century.
6. Mexican Americans—Intellectual life.   7. Mexican Americans in literature.
8. Social problems in literature.   9. Libertarianism in literature.
10. Dissenters in literature.   I. Title.
PS228.B6 M37 2003
810.9′358—dc21          2003005654

*To my father, Emanuel Martinez,*
*and to my mentor and friend, Albert Gelpi*

# Contents

viii • *Contents*

# *Acknowledgments*

I would like to thank the many people who gave me the benefit of their wisdom and advice in the writing and revision of *Countering the Counterculture*. Mike Davis, Michael Sprinker, Shari Huhndorf, David Halliburton, Ray Hedin, Jonathan Elmer, John Gonzales, Jose Limon, David Cantrell, and Eric Shockett. I am especially indebted to Albert Gelpi and Ramon Saldivar whose patience and good counsel were invaluable to me throughout this project.

Thanks to my editor, Mara Naselli, for her hard work and perspicacious editing. You've made this a better book.

Special thanks goes to the Stanford Humanities Center, the MacDowell Artists Colony, the Indiana University Minority Faculty Fellowship, and in particular to the Ford Foundation for encouragement and financial support.

I could not have finished this project without the support of my parents and my brothers and sisters who showed great faith in me and kept me going when I became discouraged and my energy waned. Special gratitude goes to Olivia Martinez whose faith and grace never lagged. Thank you from the bottom of my heart.

# Countering the Counterculture

# Introduction

## *Dissent and the American Culture of Mobility*

"But just what do migrant writers have to say to the Beats?" It is a question that was put to me by an incredulous colleague when I first began formulating this project. My answer begins with the ubiquitous American motif of "movement and mobility" that forms an important discursive site that I call "movement discourse." Movement discourse articulates social strategies and endorses various democratic frameworks and understandings of "liberty." Under this rubric, I examine the literatures of dissent in postwar America and the conversation created on the nature of participation, access, citizenship, and a slew of issues and elements that have defined the democratic debate. "Movement" as a subject and as a discourse has a number of permutations and connotations that, when juxtaposed, uncover important links between democratic, liberal, and leftist dissent in the postwar era.

In the texts I examine, "movement" takes on three main connotations that are underpinned by particular understandings of the ideal democratic form: movement as personal mobility, movement as neoimperialism, and movement as communitarian politics. This juxtaposition highlights the omnipresence of an American individualist atomism and isolation that cripples the democratic impulse and leads to political and theoretical dead-ends for those "countercultural" or dissenting movements that were influenced by the Beats. The migrant worker text, which I argue is truly countercultural in that it does not give in to or endorse the individualist version of democracy, retains a materialist understanding of mobility and its paradoxical nature, and thus is more capable of instituting a communitarian, participatory critique of individualism. Ultimately, it signposts the way to what I call an Americano strategy that is different from the other forms of movement discourse-oriented dissent (the Beats, their fellow travelers, and even the Chicano movement) that have been so susceptible to isolationism and atomism in the postwar period.

The key to our understanding of the "American ideal" is the positioning of the self and the community in relation to the ability to move at will. In our society, freedom and power are defined through "access." No group understands the concomitant paradoxes more profoundly than the twentieth-century Mexican/Mexican American migrant. No group of postwar writers explored the prerogatives of "mobility" more profoundly than the Beats. Therein lies the heart of my study: we cannot understand the so-called American ideal, its paradoxes, the culture it has shaped, or the dissent provoked by that culture, without examining the experience, literary production, and history of the postwar Mexican American subject in conversation with the literary and ideological production of the most influential "dissenting" writers. This study seeks to show that much can be learned from juxtaposing the work of the Beats and their fellow-travelers with the work of postwar Mexican Americans, not merely as opposing cultural productions, but as participating equally, fully, sometimes in complicity, at other times at odds, in the production of an "American" discourse.

We might in fact argue that postwar America can most effectively be understood through the dissent that periodically reached a critical mass. In this sense, in order to define the culture, one might begin by comparing it to the "counterculture." But this supposes that we should read culture through a series of oppositional moments, as a sort of crude dialectical process through which we can read the dynamics of culture and history as a binary defined as action and reaction: conservative movement, liberal movement; state power, social movement; hegemony, counterhegemony; power, resistance. As Michel Foucault, Louis Althusser, Antonio Gramsci, and Raymond Williams have demonstrated, this is a gross oversimplification. However, this is the way in which postwar dissent in general, and the American counterculture in particular, have been read: the so-called "conformity" of the 1950s was countered by the Beats, the military-industrial complex was challenged by the New Left, American imperialism was challenged by radical separatist movements, and so forth. This has produced, in most cases, not only inadequate readings of postwar protest and dissent, but an inadequate understanding of the democratic debate and civic discourse of the second half of the "American century."

Thus, this book is an intervention in reading practices that have operated largely in isolation from each other and therefore have not yet provided a full, complex understanding of this important American narrative. I'm speaking of an American studies project that continues to marginalize minority narratives, histories, literatures, and is especially ignorant of the Mexican American subject's role in the making of national culture and politics. By the same token, I wish to intervene in the trajectory of a Chicano studies that has allowed itself to be marginalized by working at so great a distance from "mainstream" history and literature, that it can perceive its own production only as "oppositional" or "resistant." This book is a call for both disciplines to broaden their perspectives and to understand the profound imbrication between the Chicano and the "American" narratives, making possible a more fruitful interrogation that we might call "Americano studies."

The quarter of a century following World War II presents a unique historical matrix that allows for a rich analysis of class, race, gender, and the cultural and political interstices through which they interact. The participation of African Americans and Mexican Americans in the war effort created a significant segment of marginalized citizens who felt that they deserved to participate fully in the American polity and economy. The large number of women who had entered the industrial force felt ambivalent about returning to the home, and they were increasingly unwilling to accept the prewar conditions of the domestic sphere. The upward mobility of America's workforce created the need for a cheap, mobile, temporary labor pool to satisfy the needs of Midwestern and Pacific agribusiness. The Bracero Program was designed to fill that need as cheaply as possible. The Southwest became the destination of Mexican immigrants, giving the United States new millions of Mexican and Mexican-descended residents, many of them undocumented. These men and women participated in the national economy, faced inequality in this and other spheres, and aspired to participate as fully as their white, male counterparts in the economy and within their society.

The institutionalization of corporate America and the organization of suburbia gave rise to a variety of grievances and fears in the minds of its subjects. This created a paradoxical desire to escape the constrictions of organization through a strategic appropriation of marginal positions and subjectivities, while at the same time erecting a defensive perimeter to hold off the growing demands of the previously marginalized. The company man, himself now a vagabond at the mercy of corporate dictates, looked back nostalgically to the time when self-determination was possible, when moving meant moving West, toward the frontier. William Whyte's interviews with corporate executives convey a new white migrancy: "We never plan to transfer, says a company president, and we never make a man move. Of course, he kills his career if he doesn't. But we never make him do it. The fact is well understood, it is with a smile that the recruit moves—and keeps on moving—year after year, until, perhaps, that distant day when he is summoned back to Rome" (Whyte 275). Ironically, the organization man did not see his forced movement as remotely parallel to the forced movement of the migrant in the 1950s; labor did not see itself as a commodity valuable most for its fluidity, that is, its ability to move where it was most needed. Such blindness testifies to the illusory ideals of movement and "individualism" to which white collar labor and the middle class subscribed while in the service of a corporatism they did not fully comprehend. The advantages that the middle-class laborer enjoyed provided him with an illusory differentiation from the immigrant, the migrant, the service laborer. But their social and economic positions would come much closer as the era of affluence came to an end and globalization gathered momentum in the 1970s. This could have been predicted reading Ernesto Galarza's *Merchants of Labor* in conjunction with J. Kenneth Galbraith's *The Affluent Society*.

The white male subject, confronted with a stultifying corporate structure, a carefully arranged suburban home, and challenges from minority workers and women, was compelled to protect his space of privilege (real or imagined). More often than not he did so at the expense of positive liberty (socially-oriented), rather than negative liberty (individualist-oriented). As Anthony H. Birch addresses this distinction: "On the one hand, liberty has been defined as freedom for the individual to do whatever he or she wants to do; in short, that liberty is the absence of restraint. This is the negative concept of liberty. On the other hand, liberty has been asserted to be freedom to do things that are worth doing, to engage in self-development, to have a share in the government of one's society. In Isaiah Berlin's terminology, this is the positive concept of liberty" (Birch 96).

In summary, a simplistic view of 1950s and 1960s America posits a binary opposition between the establishment culture and a dissenting counterculture. I suggest that this period saw the creation of a variety of social strategies, notably involving uses and appropriations of what I call the "migrant function" as a form of self-marginalization. These strategies have often been held up as a dissenting practice to right wing reactionary culture most frequently enumerated in studies of corporatism, consumer society, McCarthyism, conformism, and the military-industrial complex. In my view, both varieties of social strategies—dissenting, self-marginalization and "reactionary" conformism/corporatism—were manifestations of a fear of the growing visibility and demands of women and minorities, and of the restrictions inherent in organized life. Ultimately, both reactionary and radical strategies had in common the articulation of a neoindividualism, and the call for the creation of an individualist space protected from the demands of the "other." All these tendencies produced a society-wide discourse on the nature of democracy in this new era. The question of how to define citizenship, civil rights, community, individualism, liberty, social justice, racial equality, civic duty, "Americanism," society, gender, class, self-reliance, choice, participation, and egalitarianism took on new, but contradictory and contested, meanings.

I focus my critique on the "counterculture," defined broadly, not because it "failed" or was hypocritical, but because its effects have come under attack even though its strategies did not produce a long-lasting cohesive *communitas* or communal instinct.[1] A central reason for bringing the Chicano narrative and the American narrative together is to uncover the underlying ideologies that crippled the counterculture, creating not a radical *communitas* or radical collective alternatives, but instead a consensus model that ultimately seems to have been co-opted by the capitalist hegemony established after World War II. In short, much of the counterculture's activity was self-subverting subversion. A close analysis of the slippages, conflations, and elisions through an examination of the trope of "movement" in countercultural rhetoric bears this out.

I am largely concerned with the most fundamental of the social objectives of a particular Beat-influenced countercultural strain that ultimately disabled its own ability to effect a radical egalitarian alternative. I argue, along with Ernesto Laclau and Chantal Mouffe, that an egalitarian agenda was appropriated and rendered inoperative by a liberal-conservative agenda. A "democratic discourse" developed, masking a weak decisionism based on consumer culture and product choice with the illusion that a strong, "inclusive" market economy will bring about equality. "We are thus witnessing the emergence of a new hegemonic project, that of liberal-conservative discourse which seeks to articulate the neo-liberal defense of the free-market economy with the profoundly anti-egalitarian cultural and social traditionalism of conservatism" (Laclau and Mouffe 58). I argue that this liberal-conservative discourse emerged at the beginning of the postwar

American period with the creation of an effete pluralism and the institution of a corporate culture, and also resided in the very language and discourse of the most "radical" and "progressive" dissent the postwar era had to offer. Its fundamental ideology and strategy implied the reinstitution of an older American individualism, as revealed in the ways Americans talked and thought about movement and mobility. This postwar hegemonic project remains effective because it profoundly concerned the ways in which Americans wanted (and want) to think about themselves (mobile and progressive), and the social system in which they wanted (and still want) to live (open, but not radically so).

The defense of "individualism" that the Beats articulated in the 1950s became increasingly reactionary in the 1960s. At the core of this reactionary fear was the threat of absorption by a radical democratic impulse personified by civil rights activists, a "threat" that the Beats did not take seriously in the early 1950s as they appropriated ethnic personas in their search to escape conformism. Laclau and Mouffe define the threat from the New Right as follows: "A liberal-conservative bloc creates or has created an organic ideology which constructs a new hegemonic articulation through a system of equivalencies which would unify multiple subject positions around an individualist definition of rights and a negative conception of liberty" (Laclau and Mouffe 176). My contention is that the emergence of this hegemonic articulation can be seen in the earliest work of William S. Burroughs, Jack Kerouac, and Ken Kesey, and to some extent, Allen Ginsberg, and I will argue that this ideology is inherent in the principles and agenda of much dissenting rhetoric in the 1960s. Even the civil rights movement offshoots during that period would not be able to escape entirely the isolationist, atomistic logic at work in the rhetoric of American dissent.

If an unbridled, decadent individualism shackled and short-circuited various manifestations of countercultural Anglo dissent, what hampered the Chicano movement in its attempt to create a lasting, progressive, even radical, politics? Ultimately, its cultural nationalism and separatist tendencies, its identity politics, and its exclusive communality led to an isolationism that looked very much like the isolation created by Beat individualists. The Chicano movement, through its nationalist wing, rejected the possibility of a "national culture." This rejection is most visible in the disavowal of the Mexican American generation's faith in participatory politics as "assimilationist." The *movimiento* literature I examine articulates a practice of movement discourse that refused to operate within the national public sphere and democratic debate for fear of being absorbed or assimilated into "America." The movement created an enclosed cultural sphere that could not be penetrated by the non-Chicano Mexican American, and populated "Aztlan" with a fixed subject that was manifested through fixated forms: the *pachuco*, the *pinto*, and the *indio*. Ultimately, the movement, like its symbolic trifaceted subject, did not do much to undo the exclusion and immobilization that Mexican Americans had suffered, but rather in isolating themselves wound up in an eerily similar position to the self-isolated, atomistic Beats.

Ultimately, Migrant literature, viewed through movement discourse, can be read as undoing the immobilization and exclusion by insisting on a material reading of the paradoxes of American democracy. The Migrant narrative demonstrates the inadequacy of individualist-inflected dissent in countering a system built upon submissive individualism and consumerist-decisionist "democracy." Migrant movement discourse exposes the immobilizing nature of American mobility in the service of capital. Positioning it next to Beat, countercultural, and *movimiento* discourse puts into relief the limitations of the rhetoric of mobility and the underlying metaphysical faith in its inevitable progress. This "Americano" critique speaks to the different manifestations of exclusionist and separatist isolationism produced by individualist-inflected dissenting ideology. It points instead toward a participatory, egalitarian realpolitik that calls for a communitarian national culture.

Through the Migrant narrative, I argue that the only effective alternative to the neoindividualist logic is a renewed commitment to an egalitarian agenda, one that I will use to distinguish the "Americano" project (articulated by key Mexican American activists and migrant writers) from both the neoindividualist strain of the counterculture and the separatist version of *el movimiento*. I accept Laclau and Mouffe's argument that "The task of the Left isn't to renounce liberal-democratic ideology, but on the contrary to deepen and expand it in the direction of a radical and plural democracy" (Laclau and Mouffe 176). But we can only begin to deepen and expand liberal-democratic ideology if we recognize the inherent limitations of a liberal-progressive discourse fraught with the underpinnings of a neoindividualism that is difficult to reconcile with communality and positive liberty.

## Movement in the American Imagination

The paradox of Zeno's arrow describes the paradox of the American culture of mobility. The flight of an arrow, said Zeno, is an apparent example of motion. But at any given moment of its flight, the arrow is either where it is or where it is not. If it moves where it is, it must be standing still, and if it moves where it is not, then it cannot be there; thus it cannot move. Likewise movement in post–World War II American society has proven paradoxical: the subject moves constantly while existing in a state of immobility. The irony of "progress" was itself a long-standing topic of the twentieth century. The problem of whether the modern subject can actually progress, and how one defines progress in relation to how society-at-large defines it, has too often been reduced to a question of personal mobility in the face of constraining systemic forces or frameworks. Rather than seeking to analyze and ameliorate social or economic frameworks, the American individualist seeks to escape the "social" or the "communal" that becomes associated with systemic constraint. Progress is thus defined as individualist prerogative. The twentieth-century American writer departed in Odyssean fashion to map the boundaries that limit his potential. It is a question of probing the walls of the prison while using one's prerogative to move as an act of personal defiance to restraint.

In the romantic tradition, such defiance creates a metaphysical moment of transcendence for the erstwhile immobilized subject.

It creates, albeit as a fiction, a way in which to live within the social system while defying its demands and laws. This defiance creates illusory mobility; it is the narrative of the automobile commercial that promises freedom, a handsome driver taking in Big Sur's heart-stopping ocean views as he masterfully handles the road cutting through jagged cliffs, all the while ignoring the reality of the checkbook.

More accurately, postwar movement can be described as expatiation. The Latin root of "expatiate" is *exspatiatus*, meaning to wander as well as to digress. The analysis of movement discourse deeply engages both manifestations of expatiation. Writers of the American experience have long conflated the two meanings, combining the experience of moving at will with the sense of being tangential or existing in a state of irrelevance. Moving at will is achieved by becoming "irrelevant" in the sense of "marginal." Personal liberty is to be found by experiencing the liminality of the "other." Many of the writers this book consider movement at will an exercise of their liberty, and write their experience as an articulation of that liberty. In plainer terms, they mythologize movement. They digress as an escape from the imposition of structure, a digression into a periphery generally reserved for the marginalized subjects of American society. But there is a crucial difference: unlike the marginalized figure, these writers are assured of their ability to return to relevance. They are assured access despite their dalliance in the margins where the truly marginal are kept at bay.

Even the OED definition of "movement" reveals a slippage that I suggest is critical in our analysis of the various movement discourses and the social models that they seek to effect. Defining "movement" as "the action or process of moving; change of position; passage from place to place, or from one situation to another," the dictionary definition suggests an analogy between physical movement, spatial or personal, and the process of change itself. It equates the existence of an "open" system with the mobility of the system's elements. It is a slippage that links physical movement with social movement, personal movement with communal movement, digression with relevance, revolution (circular) with evolution (progressive). That a system's elements move does not necessarily mean the system is itself "open," or that the system is not dictating the nature of such movement. What is the nature of mobility in a system that allows only a dictated, plotted-out movement? It is the paradox to which Kerouac gives voice in his body of fiction.

I take seriously Theodor Adorno's description of the "proto-typical bourgeois individual" as a modern-day Odysseus, "originating in the consistent self-affirmation with its ancient pattern in the protagonist compelled to wander" (Horkheimer and Adorno 43). This evokes the American writer moving across a territorialized topos attempting to reinscribe the land so as to defend a type of personal agency that has been formulated around the figure of the self-subsisting individual. The illusion of personal mobility becomes the illusion of an independence apart from systemic constraint, an independence which seeks to render the system powerless to constrain.

Like Adorno's modern Odysseus, the American writer mythologizes movement as a strategic form of self-preservation, at voyage's end sure to be rewarded by his return home to his fixed (e)state. The voyage is undertaken through the land of the marginal, removed from the center and the gravitational pull it exerts through its hierarchical organization. Once that marginality is appropriated, and a liminal state achieved, the voyager may return to his place within the system, newly assured that he is not at all constrained. It is a most cynical use of "freeplay," a form of subversion that ultimately does not subvert. His "estate" is fixed, within the protected space which "society" has created for him. The "other" remains within his space, irrelevant, marginal, safely outside the gates, his access denied. The modern Odysseus reaches selfhood by "being an entity only in the diversity of that which denies all unity" (Horkheimer and Adorno 48).

Self-subsistence within a mobile corporatist society cannot participate within community, for community requires roots. The wandering American dissenting writer follows this pattern, expatiating, seeing himself as a modern Jeremiah, but a Jeremiah paradoxically concerned with defending his own individual space by writing it into existence. This is particularly true in post–World War II America, where all too often what is commonly thought of as the counterculture has come to signify simply a self-centered mobility that abhors communality as absorbing.

Historical currents and events present defining moments when cultural workers must provide cultural maps that reorient the writer and the reader living within the changing political/historical topos to past orienting mythologies/narratives that have established and explained subject positions before. This can be said to be the function of culture: it is an orienting force that positions the subject between ethos and worldview. In an Althusserian sense, culture is ideology, and in Fredric Jameson's formulation, the writer provides a cognitive map. Ultimately, the test of the countercultural must be the "map" it constructs. Does it reconcile the writer/reader to the conventional mythos and understanding of American society as "progressive" and ultimately "open," or does it challenge conventional narratives and mythologies? This is one of the central questions that our analysis of movement discourse will seek to answer.

In the introduction to his 1996 study, *The Death and Rebirth of American Radicalism*, Stanley Aronowitz states that American radicalism "has never enjoyed anything like success" (vii). His most trenchant observation is that such a failure is a result of a deep-rooted individualism that has acted against the impulse toward social justice: "In comparison to the idea of social responsibility through government intervention, the ideals of local control and individual initiative have as long and perhaps more powerful a history in American political culture and are shared widely, even among many who are otherwise socially liberal or radical" (16). This work examines the rhetoric of this "local control and individual initiative" as it has limited social activism on the left and made its way into even the most "liberal," "progressive" or "radical" social critiques. I seek to explain this lack of "success" as well as to suggest an alternative that can be found in the work of two migrant writers. The book is divided into two sections.

The first part, "The Roots of Postwar Dissent and the Counterculture," examines the advent of conformist and corporatist culture in the United States in the 1950s. I argue that this postwar American culture was driven by the fear of absorption that manifests itself in different ways: as a fear of "conformity" in the liberal imagination; as a fear of an encroaching red, black, and brown menace in the "conservative" imagination; and as a fear of a "castrating" femininity, figured as suburbia, in the masculinist imagination. Those fears motivate both the conservative and liberal agendas to react in very similar ways—by championing a submissive and atomistic individualism that ultimately ends in an isolationist defensive position precluding the formation of any kind of meaningful or progressive communalism.

In the first chapter I look at the work of William S. Burroughs and Allen Ginsberg, suggesting that their dissent seeks to create a "free" space by finding a new frontier, first in Mexico, then in South America, and later in Tangier. These "fellaheen" lands provide the embattled white male with a space free of women and free of a state power that is figured as a "welfare state." Ultimately, the self-marginalization the Beats utilize to great effect in order to remain outsiders is jettisoned in the new frontier, where the postwar male desire for a power free of "interference" and civic commitment can be enacted through what Burroughs called the "new imperialism."

In the second chapter, I take a close look at Jack Kerouac's literary production and find that his work can also be read as neo-imperialistic: its individualist program is evident in that each of his novels can be read as a denial of a different form of communal participation. His work is intensely hostile to anything resembling an egalitarian project. I then argue that this new interpretation, however, does not change his influence on the burgeoning countercultural movements. His neoindividualist narrative—imperialistic, misogynistic, and ultimately racist—deeply informs and shapes the nature of "mainstream" 1960s counterculture. I trace the lineage of his agenda through the work of Ken Kesey and Hunter S. Thompson, who is the subject of the third chapter.

In Thompson's narratives, we find both a deconstruction of the emptiness of the redemptive movement narrative in which the Beats were invested, as well as the "coup de grace" on the counterculture. While I argue that Thompson's insights into 1960s dissent are often accurate and trenchant, his ultimate position is to retreat into an isolationism reminiscent of the progressive and radical fronts he critiques. He argues that he has continued the legacy of the Beats, and I argue that he has done so in ways that are regressive and cynical. The legacy that these writers actually reproduce closely resembles nineteenth-century concepts about individualism, American exceptionalism, and manifest destiny. This is readily discernible in the valorization of physical movement and in the fashioning of a cult of decadent individualism. Nostalgia for the days of America as "nature's nation," in which one strikes west as an expression of progress, is thus manifested in Beat-inspired neoromanticism that elides the history and practice of conquest and exploitation, and, I argue, directly influences the 1960s counterculture. Thus these writers and activists popularized an entrenched commitment to an individualist ideology that was not at all "countercultural," in the egalitarian sense, but rather was a rehashing of an American "rugged individualism" that was ultimately hostile to a Rousseauean commitment to civic participation and radical egalitarian democracy — *civitas* if you will.

In part two, "The Americano Narrative: Postwar Mexican American Dissent and Community," I argue that Mexican Americans were participating in the remapping of American culture, and were forming answers to the questions facing all Americans in the thirty years following World War II: the relation of the individual to the community, the ability to participate in the shaping of a national culture, the viability of democratic participation, and other questions concerning the nature of cultural and national citizenship. In so doing, Mexican Americans were participating not only in the external or national political debate, but were fiercely engaged in an internal, intracultural democratic debate shaped largely by generational and civic orientations and aspirations. Mexican American, Chicano, and "Americano" views were articulated in response to each other and, taken together, form a microcosm of the larger sociopolitical debate.

In chapter four, I read Oscar Acosta's narrative as a template for the growing tension between Mexican American and Chicano identity, that also clearly engages with a Beat/mainstream countercultural ethos. His work is thus a locus of the negotiation between Anglo, Mexican American, and Chicano cultural and social politics. Movement for Acosta becomes the axis of tension between a personal, individualistic mobility *(movida)*, a pull toward a communally oriented "movement" (or *movimiento*) and the isolationist, separatist tendencies inherent in both cultural nationalism and Beat-like neoindividualism. Written at the birth of Chicano identity, Acosta's work articulates the tension between a Mexican American generational aspiration to become "American" and the price of repressing "Mexican" identity. However, Acosta finds that the Chicano identity he encounters in his *movimiento* activism is too narrowly constructed and requires him, in a complete reversal of the Mexican American generation's project, to suppress the "American" side of his identity.

Chapter five focuses exclusively on the Chicano movement itself, in particularly at the height of its separatist and nationalist activity. I investigate *el movimiento* as Chicano consciousness is radicalized and examine the after-effects of its realpolitik and ideology. Whereas the Beats and Thompson reject communalism and endorse a negative liberty by embracing atomistic individualism, the Chicano separatist instinct ultimately endorsed isolation as well, not by embracing individualism, but by suggesting that a national, egalitarian culture was impossible. I argue that like its counterparts in the larger counterculture, *el movimiento* failed to mobilize an agenda that might have affected a larger public sphere through an inclusive communality. Although the movement had a different agenda, the discourse it produced shows the same fear of "absorption" displayed in the work of the Beats, one that ultimately precludes wide-scale democratic participation. To this end, I look at the work of three influential *movimiento* writers, Raulsalinas, Jose Montoya, and Luis Valdez, whose work bears the mark of intergenerational conflict and political ambivalence signaling an isolationism as paralyzing as neoindividualistic atomism. This suggests that *el movimiento* created a narrow, exclusionary identity politics that fragmented its fragile coalition along the national culture and local culture fault line. The most tragic effect of the break-up of the Chicano movement was the sense that the Mexican American subject had only two choices: assimilation or a separation that abdicated an "American" identity. This, I argue, left a vacuum that a conservative, consumerist agenda filled over the next decade.

The final chapter suggests a new rubric not only for understanding a political alternative for the postwar Mexican American subject, but also for developing a template for a "counterculture" unified around a radical egalitarian agenda. It calls for the creation of an Americano identity, a coalition of Mexican Americans committed to social justice and full participation in the American political, civic, and economic spheres that might also function as a model for an inclusive, participatory national culture. In so doing, I revisit the most progressive countercultural instincts and objectives. I examine the work of Ernesto Galarza and Tomás Rivera and claim that they should be understood as prototypical "Americanos." Their work suggests a new direction for social criticism and provides new possibilities for American studies, or Americano studies, as I would like to term it. Rather than calling for Aztlan, these activists called for the creation of América, and advocated what I call "Americanismo" rather than "Chicanismo." Their work should also be recognized for its prescient description and critique of an emerging post-Fordist economy and the paradoxes of American individualism and its faith in an illusory mobility. I argue that their social criticism and cultural production are truly countercultural, for they offer examples of a postwar dissent that does not short-circuit itself.

Ultimately I wish to demonstrate that juxtaposing the dissent of Mexican American writers and Anglo writers is not merely an exercise in the analysis of opposition or even resistance, but that both groups participate equally and fully in the production of an American discourse on democracy, citizenship, and the shaping of a national culture. Read together, both groups can be seen to have remapped postwar society through a conversation still in progress. By examining these various works and groups through a common discourse, I hope to contribute to a more complex understanding of the American counterculture and its various conceptions of democracy, as well as to current work defining the Chicano narrative. I also hope to further the efforts of scholars working toward expanding and bridging the work comprising what we now rather narrowly think of as two separate critical and historical inquiries: American studies and Chicano studies.

This book, then, is in part an answer to Jose David Saldivar's call for a new approach to comparative cultural studies. In his book *Border Matters: Remapping American Cultural Studies,* he discusses the necessity of reading a transgeographical variety of literary works and social critiques under a common rubric: "Not enough has been done to bring these texts to bear on the same subject, and juxtapose social/political analysis in any direct way . . . In my view, the greatest shortcoming of the work being done on the American canon is not its lack of theoretical rigor, but its parochial vision. Literary historians (even the newer ones) and critics working on the reconstruction of American literary history characteristically know little in depth about the history, symbologies, cultures, and discourses of the Americas. One value of focusing on comparative cultural studies is that it permits us to escape from the provincial, limiting tacit assumptions that result from perpetual immersion in studying a single culture or literature" (5). My study is thus dedicated to the continuing project of a truly inclusive Americano studies that lives up to the potential of cultural, social, and political dissent in the academy and, more importantly, in our society.

# Part 1

# The Roots of
# Postwar Dissent and
# the Counterculture

# 1

# "No Fear Like Invasion"

*Movement, Absorption, and Stasis Horror in the Beat Vision*

> Old style imperialism is dead. . . . If you want to give yourself a chance to get rich and live in a style that the U.S. has not seen since 1914, "Go South of the Rio Grande, young man."
>
> William S. Burroughs in a letter to Allen Ginsberg, 1951

> The hippie movement . . . has its roots directly in the Beat Generation.
>
> Barry Miles, *William Burroughs*

In *William Burroughs: El Hombre Invisible* (hereafter *Burroughs*) Barry Miles, biographer of both Allen Ginsberg and William S. Burroughs, makes a typical interpretation of the Beat phenomenon's cultural and political significance: "The group was more of a fraternity of spirit and attitude than a literary movement, and their writings have little in common with each other; what they did have in common was a reaction to the ongoing carnage of World War II, the dropping of the A-bomb and the puritan small-mindedness that still characterized American life. They shared an interest in widening the area of consciousness, by

23

whatever means available" (5). I take issue with many of these assertions but regard the quote as significant not only for what it al-
leges about the Beat writers, but for the way it seeks to ascribe
Beat "reactions" to those events that are commonly maintained as
the most significant of postwar America. It suggests a monolithic
U.S. culture in the throes of a puritanical conservatism, which was
challenged by a group of heroic writers who countered the hypocrisy and blindness of the period by "widening the area of consciousness." One need only watch a documentary such as *The
Source* to understand that the central triumvirate of Beat writers,
Kerouac, Burroughs, and Ginsberg, are credited as "the source" of
all significant postwar dissent.[1]

The version of history that this implies is troublesome for
many reasons. First, it sets up an axis of historical relations that
posits conservative arbiters of bourgeois culture against a subversive group that saves the decade by presenting a liberating cultural
movement; this movement "widens" consciousness and sets the
stage for an even more "liberating" countercultural movement in
the 1960s. Second, by positing the military-industrial complex
("carnage" and "atom bomb") as the central impetus to which the
Beats react, it sets up a view of history in which a small, primarily
Anglo, elite class controls the action of history, resisted by an
equally small, elite Anglo group, in this case, the Beats. As David
Farber writes in *The Age of Great Dreams:* "The sharpest and, in
many ways, most prescient attack on the net worth of People's
Capitalism came from a small pack of self-proclaimed 'Dharma
bums,' a.k.a. Beats . . . who'd fled corporate suburbia for a life of
hard kicks and still minds. Poet Allen Ginsberg rammed home
the Beats' outrage at an America grown old at midcentury. . . .
The last had not been heard of Allen Ginsberg and his vision of a
blasted America lost in its lust for money and power" (23). However, this typical reading overlooks the possibility that the action
and reaction of these two Anglo groups were focused on other social and historical events and trends, which were very much affected by women, African Americans, and Mexican Americans.

This site of antagonism, Beats vs. Military/Cold War/ Puritan-
ical/Bourgeois bloc, ignores the role of other major social factors
such as the emergence of a civil rights movement, a broadening

participation of women in the workforce, encroaching suburban-ization, and a significant influx of Mexican workers. The so-called puritanical impulses in American society, the rise of the military-industrial complex, and the formation of the Beat Gen-eration may have been not opposed, but rather similar responses to the rapidly changing social and cultural landscape. To what ex-tent did the burgeoning countercultural movement that the Beats created, and the 1960s version they influenced, share similar ideo-logical underpinnings with the conservative, puritanical culture to which critics like Barry Miles put them in opposition? In other words, is it possible that the Beats were not so much pitting their worldview against a vacuous, rigid, bourgeois conformity, but echoing, albeit dissonantly, the same tune as the chorus of reac-tionary elements of America in the 1950s?

If there exist more similarities than differences between these two groups, then I suggest that both were reacting to a similar fear of absorption. The primary Beats—Kerouac, Burroughs, Ginsberg, and later, Kesey—describe a much clearer approxima-tion to those reactionary, nativist, and racist ideologies to which they have conventionally been contrasted. It is this notion of counterculture that must be reconsidered. My intent is to chal-lenge the understanding of the counterculture as the antithesis of something that might be conceived as the "culture of the 1950s." Rather, as various cultural theorists such as Michel Foucault *(His-tory of Sexuality)*, Stuart Hall ("Cultural Studies: Two Para-digms"), and Antonio Gramsci *(Selections from Prison Notebooks)* have argued, there can never be such a thing as a true "countercul-ture." The imbrication of events and sociocultural forces are never simply dichotomous.

Jack Kerouac's novel, *Vanity of Duluoz* (1968), the final install-ment of the *Duluoz Legend* (a collection of autobiographical nov-els which were to comprise a memoir along the lines of Proust's *Remembrance of Things Past*), represents the end point of a reac-tionary trajectory that his Beat cohorts either repeated or approxi-mated. It offers a stunning disavowal of the "spirit" of his previous work. He writes of the youth culture's fascination with the auto-mobile in the 1960s: "Has the automobile filled them with such vanity that they walk like a bunch of lounging hoodlums to no destination in particular? . . . Everybody drives a car and goes with stupid erect head guiding the idiot machine through the pitfalls and penalties of traffic. . . . [N]owadays no one walks with unconcern, head down, whistling; everybody looks at everybody else on the sidewalk with guilt and worse than that, curiosity and faked concern, in some cases 'hip' regard based on 'Dont miss a thing.' . . . Today we hear of 'creative contributions to society' and nobody dares sleep out a whole rainy day" (9–10). In a transparent reference to his carefree travels depicted in his many novels, notably *On the Road*, Kerouac suggests his antipathy to the countercultural movement's attempt to invoke the ethos of that book in order to radicalize democratic participation in the late 1960s. The hippie generation is criticized for its lack of clear destination, and indirectly, for its appeal to the masses of youth (now "everybody drives a car" aimlessly). Ten years after the publication of *On the Road*, Kerouac appeared to have done an about-face, becoming extraordinarily reactionary and staunchly anticommunist, vocalizing his intense hatred of the 1960s counterculture and its "socialist" inspiration.[2]

In 1957, to the enthusiasm of young readers and the disapproval of an older generation, Kerouac had described the liberating effects of improvisational wandering. *On the Road* celebrates the freedom of increasingly chaotic traffic as Sal and Dean move farther south, getting closer to the "edge of America." Anarchy is suggested as Paradise and Moriarty reach the Mexican side of San Antonio where "cars crash through from the dark around town as if there were no traffic laws" (272). But Kerouac reserves his most enthusiastic language for his description of Mexico City traffic. When compared to his diatribe against the automobile in *Vanity of Duluoz*, this passage from *On the Road* is remarkable:

> Mad barefoot Indian drivers cut across us and surrounded us and tooted and made frantic traffic. The noise was incredible. No mufflers are used on Mexican cars. . . . "Whee!" yelled Dean. "Look out!" He staggered the car through the traffic and played with everybody. He drove like an Indian. He got on a circular glorietta drive . . . and rolled around it with its eight spokes shooting cars at us from all directions, left, right, *izquierda*, dead

ahead, and yelled and jumped with joy. "This is traffic I've always dreamed of! Everybody *goes*!" An ambulance came balling through. American ambulances dart and weave through traffic with siren blowing; the great world-wide Fellahin Indian ambulances merely come through at eighty miles an hour in the city streets, and everybody just has to get out of the way . . . and flies straight through. (301)

If read as contrasting assessments of the proper form (lessness) of democratic participation in the United States, these passages suggest a Kerouac whose political direction has shifted dramatically. But I would like to question whether or not this shift is as dramatic or as sudden as it first appears. In fact, I suggest that the reactionary paranoia evident in his later work is typical of the direction that Beat countercultural ideology took when faced with a "too successful" radical democratic program. When confronted with an encroaching conformism in both the home and the workplace in the early 1950s, the Beats popularized a defensive individualist strategy for claiming an alternative space for individual, masculine, white power. The manifestations of this neoindividualism, with its ideological roots in nineteenth-century romanticism, varied in nature, appropriating marginalized identities, the mythos of the frontier, and a deferred, male-dominated domestic sphere. It is not enough to suggest that the counterculture, as exemplified by the Beats, rejected bourgeois vacuity, hegemonic suburbanization, or even Cold War conformism. Nor would it be completely accurate to say that the Beats were in part reacting to these factors. In fact, both the anticommunist hysteria in Cold War America and the Beat mythos of rootless liberty emanated from the central myth of American individualism. The anticommunist efforts, intensified by nativist and racist attitudes, exploited the myth of the self-reliant, atomistic individual as the target of encroaching foreign powers intent on absorbing the individual within a formless, undifferentiated mass.

At the same time, Mexican workers were allowed into the country in huge numbers to pick crops, while simultaneously, and most infamously, the federal government instituted programs such as Operation Wetback. Laws such as the McCarran-Walter

Act targeted "aliens" for deportation and was used to silence political dissent. The point here is that both the "red scare" and the "brown scare" were based less on "protecting" the United States from a foreign military-style takeover, than on protecting against infiltration, a conquest from within. The Beats, who have been seen as maintaining "disparate" social views, all privilege the individual and the search for a realm in which he (I use the masculine pronoun purposely) might be free of invasion from without or subversion from within.

The Beats appropriate (some more cynically than others) the figure of the Mexican and the African American because the ethnic subaltern represents a liminality. Identification with downtrodden ethnic peoples has been misread as a direct attack on middle-class, Anglo conformism. It is rather a maneuver useful for the Beats' own purposes: in Burroughs's case, it is a calculated continuation of colonial and laissez-faire exploitation; in the case of Kerouac, it is a nostalgic and romantic search for a cultural/social space as yet unterritorialized and regulated by external forces. When their vicarious empathy for ethnicized liminality encounters an actual civil rights movement for racial liberation, the individualism based on freedom of personal movement finds its antithesis in a political movement based in a communion of shared values and community of shared identity.

There was a fundamental ideological difference between, on the one hand, the rugged individualism that enabled the laissez-faire capitalism of free market and right-wing entrepreneurs and, on the other hand, the left-leaning communitarianism of the liberation movements of ethnic minorities and women. This tension between freedom and equality, between the claims and demands of the individual and the society, runs through the whole of American experience, from the debates that forged the Constitution to contemporary debates about personal rights and social justice. The Beats dissented from participation in the capitalist money making and bourgeois suburban domesticity, but their dissent was directed at recouping or preserving the prerogatives of the self-subsisting and alienated individual. Thus the Beats could not mount an effective challenge to the status quo because they shared its underlying ideology: they dissented within the system. One clear and dramatic indication of this affinity between the dominant culture and the Beat form of resistance is the logic behind Kerouac's seeming reversal in rejecting the movements of the 1960s. When the forces of protest claimed him and his Beat ethic in the name of a radical and inclusive new community and in the cause of a socialist restructuring of political and economic life, Kerouac realized where his basic allegiance lay and vehemently disassociated himself from hippies and revolutionaries and deemed them unpatriotic subversives. The appropriation of the Beat ethic signaled for Kerouac the original crisis that fueled *On the Road,* the threat of personal absorption.

I focus on the use of "movement" purposely to indicate that ultimately "movement discourse," as principally engaged in by the Beats, actually concerns the perpetuation of the central illusion of "movement." It nominally identifies movement with transformation, but actually resists and elides fundamental change or subversion through the *appearance* of transformative action. The "movement discourse" of the Beats reproduces a hierarchy of Anglo capitalist power. It naturalizes a laissez-faire individualism that proclaims negative liberty inexorably leads to the best-realized manifestation of positive liberty: laissez-faire individualism leads to a "better society" for all. In this sense, it is a particular appropriation of the typical language of liberalism, which performs the opposite of what it claims to make apparent. For Kerouac and Burroughs this illusory progress/movement is manifested in their theological and political convictions.

In "Beatific: The Origins of the Beat Generation," Kerouac rejects the "Lost Generation" and their cynicism, which he sees as wrongheaded, and prefers instead a "loving" indifference that he seemingly derives from Buddhist tenets. However, this indifference also closely resembles Thoreau's isolationism and especially Emerson's rejection of politics in the private and personal mysticism of the "transparent eyeball." For Kerouac too, an isolated, submissive individualism avoided civic agency in the form of the "eyeball kicks" of private vision, a quasi-imperialistic technique revolving around observation, sought after by the early Beats. This genealogy is stressed by Kerouac later in an attempt to play down any perceived responsibility on his part for the hippie generation, whose dangerous activism he found repellent and "delinquent."

It has been said that the Beat movement is not really a movement at all; it exhibits no real set of cohesive aesthetics or politics.[3] Yet I suggest that the major Beats exhibit a common fear of an infiltrating "otherness," which they saw as resulting in the immobilization of the subject by a state controlled by marginal forces. The most abhorrent characteristic of such a state is the possibility that this sort of communality might lead to egalitarian logics of social organization. While many Beat critics center their analysis on the Beats as nonconformists in a stultifying era,[4] I suggest that their responses to an encroaching threat on their civil liberties spring in part from similar principles of the decade's Far Right, that is to say, an isolationist libertarianism that accepted and even preferred inequality as its operating system. Where civil rights maintain a liberalized inequality (that is, equality of opportunity), civil agency requires an egalitarianism in which the person is equal to the law and where equality of outcome is guaranteed. Such a form of egalitarianism challenges the organizing principles of hierarchy, which in the end, is much too radical a position for the Beats.

Rather, the Beats operated under a form of a delimiting Emersonian liberalism, which Christopher Newfield describes as "corporate individualism." Newfield suggests corporate individualism has deep roots in American conceptions of the individual and democracy: "The major American tradition of moderation rests less on the much-discussed balance between individual autonomy and popular sovereignty than on a habit of submission to authority that weakens autonomy and democracy alike. . . . I will call this sensibility the Emerson Effect: individual autonomy and public authority vanish together before unappealable laws, but this leads to the enhancement of freedom. Emersonian liberalism does not so much invent the conceptual frame as develops the political sensibility that allows its loss of both private autonomy and public sovereignty to feel okay. This is at least as important a contribution as the conceptual frame itself" (4). So that in the end, the

"Emerson Effect[ed]" Beats did not seek to challenge the hierarchical nature of their own society as much as seek to find a space for their own individual "freedom," a freedom that demanded submission to corporatist socialization while offering a neutered form of individualist "freedom."

The shared fears of containment and infiltration, which fueled McCarthyism and fervid anticommunism in the 1950s, can be understood as a common fear of a truly radical democracy.[5] McCarthyism and Beat philosophy are dissimilar attempts to protect a liberty and freedom based on laissez-faire individualism: a liberty that combines a rigid hierarchy of competition with a market logic of exchange in which product choice is confused with true political and social agency, and personal movement is privileged at the expense of civic and social movement. This consumerist decisionism can be seen most clearly in the development of Sloanism by Alfred P. Sloan, the longtime General Motors leader who based his market strategy on three precepts: "'A car for every purse and purpose,' rapidly introduced styling changes, and a corporate structure that combined decentralized management with highly rationalized financial controls" (Farber 21). That this market logic was alive and well in the 1950s can also be seen in Richard Nixon's argument for American democracy in the famed "Kitchen Debate" with Nikita Khruschev in 1959: "To us, diversity, the right to choose, the fact that we have a thousand different builders, that's the spice of life" (Farber 15). David Farber has argued that consumer culture created the illusion of a "new kind of equality," which was essentially "the right of every American to push a shopping cart and to decide what brought happiness" (64). Much faith was put on the great equalizer of the laissez-faire market and its particular brand of individualism.

This desire to construct a defense for laissez-faire individualism manifests itself in the writing of the Beats, in their constant efforts to escape "boredom," or in the times in which "being bored" precedes a decision to "move on." Such is the nature of William Burroughs's "stasis horrors." Paralysis of the individual, the inability to "move," is brought into social-wide occurrence by the stultifying effects of a communalism that the Beats view as conformism. This vision of the social contract as a paralyzing communalism that directly challenges individualist imperatives dates back to the Constitutional Convention and it fuels Burroughs's desire to flee. The impetus of the convention was an attempt to hedge or control the revolutionary impulse, which might have brought about what was perceived as too much revolution, too much diversity, thus paralyzing the nation's body—an image that Burroughs returns to many times.

At the same time, "individuality" is a privilege of those already in a position to "move," but not of the "masses" whose expression of individual rights and entitlements might infringe on the personal and property rights of the elite. By this distinct logic, inequality is not an impingement on free movement, but the first principle of a system that sanctions such personal movement. Such an understanding of "movement" then supplants the need for equality by becoming the manifestation and social metaphor of liberty. This formulation of movement as liberty poses a problem for civic redressive action in that it discourages communal or collective action, and instead encourages a ceding of agency to a faith in the regulating power of movement, that is, a faith in the invisible hand to regulate the social structure as it does the "free" market.[6] In the era of the Beats and 1950s society, the threat to such a system came from racial minorities. The "Black Scare" was as potent as the "Red Menace," for civil rights activities were gaining momentum in the South at the same time as the rise of the specter of the communist menace.

While the postwar boom extended its benefits to a specific but large middle-class, it relegated a growing, "marginal" workforce to a "secondary labor market" with secondary citizenship, controlled by xenophobic and nativist containment strategies. Groups such as the National Association for the Advancement of Colored People (NAACP) and League of United Latin American Citizens (LULAC), first-phase civil rights organizations, attempted to attain first-class citizenship through many of the progressive means of the preceding generation: adjudication, populism, and the electoral process. Desegregation would provide the issue around which direct action and grassroots organization would move into a radicalized second phase of the civil rights movement.

The rise of the radical democratic movement culture of the 1960s resulted from a complex set of post–World War II events and antagonisms: union conservatism, anticommunist hysteria, growing divisions between union and nonunion workers, mass migration, and deepening racial conflict in the North, South, and Southwest, along with the growth of a small, patriotic, vocal ethnic middle class culminating in the first phase of civil rights victories. These actions were certainly as "frightening" to the white American subject as the communist threat.

Rosa Parks's refusal to sit in the back of the bus and the resulting bus boycotts brought to the forefront Martin Luther King and the formation of the Southern Christian Leadership Conference. The SCLC united black community leaders within the organization while simultaneously organizing the black masses by using the church as its base. The Student Nonviolent Coordinating Committee was formed with the intention of building a "redemptive community." As Stewart Burns suggests, the SNCC strategy "boiled down to the question of how change comes about. SNCC activists asserted that deep and lasting change can only come from empowering people at the grass roots, and that this takes commitment to local people over time—not to ephemeral media stars" (13).

The "freedom rides" of 1961 were organized by the Congress of Racial Equality, founded by James Farmer, a veteran of nonviolent direct action in the early 1940s. The rides resulted in the desegregation of southern transportation facilities and also "contributed to the development of a self-consciously radical southern student movement prepared to direct its militancy toward other concerns" (Burns 16). SNCC also organized voter registration drives in Mississippi, mobilizing local and out of state college students. "Freedom schools" were held to build a foundation for a statewide youth movement. Through increased demonstrations and grassroots participation, the Voting Rights Act was passed under the Johnson administration. SNCC organized against the draft, ran its candidates in Southern elections, and helped create the National Black Anti-War Anti-Draft Union. SNCC organizer Willie Ricks formulated the Black Power movement, which had affinities with older leftist theorists such as Paul Robeson and Richard Wright, but now found a readily mobilized young audience.

Radicalized by SNCC's militant stand and his realization that what was needed for social change was a grassroots, class-based, interracial alliance of the poor, King began to conceive of an alliance against poverty and militarism, but before being able to institute it, he was assassinated on April 4, 1968. Thus Black Power engendered a militant black nationalism represented by groups such as the Black Panther movement and the older Nation of Islam. White middle-class reaction manifested itself in the repression of these movements by federal and state agencies.

McCarthy's hearings in the House Committee on Un-American Activities (HUAC) took place at the same time that White Citizens' Councils were formed over the issue of school segregation and voter registration drives. As "commies" were hounded out of the civil service, the armed forces, and Hollywood, "Operation Wetback" operatives were deporting Mexicans and Mexican Americans alike. Popular culture was rife with images of invasion and infiltration by space pods, Russian spies, communists, and evil union organizers.[7]

An infiltrating and paralyzing "other" is institutionalized through the state in one of William S. Burroughs's most striking "routines" in which it becomes clear that invasion fear was often racialized. In a letter written to Allen Ginsberg in 1955, Burroughs recounts a sketch that would gain infamy in *Naked Lunch*. He writes

> Did I ever tell you about the man who taught his ass hole to talk? . . . This man worked for a carnival, you dig, and to start was like a novelty ventriloquist act. Real funny, too at first. . . . After a while the ass started talking on its own. . . . Then it developed sort of teeth-like little, raspy, in-curbing hooks and started eating. He thought this was cute at first and built an act around it, but the ass hole would eat its way through his pants and start talking on the street, shouting out it wanted equal

rights. It would get drunk, too, and have crying jags, nobody loved it and it wanted to be kissed same as any other mouth. Finally it talked all the time day and night, you could hear him for blocks screaming at it to shut up, and beating it with his fist, and sticking candles up it, but nothing did any good and the ass hole said to him: "It's you who will shut up in the end. Not me. Because we don't need you around here any more. I can talk and eat and shit."

After that he began waking up in the morning with a transparent jelly like a tadpole's tail over his mouth. This jelly was what the scientists call Un-D.T.—Undifferentiated Tissue—which could grow into any kind of flesh on the human body. . . . So finally his mouth sealed over, and the whole head would have amputated spontaneous (did you know there is a condition occurs in parts of Africa and only among Negroes where the little toe amputates spontaneously?) except for the eyes you dig? . . . It needed the eyes. But nerve connections were blocked and infiltrated and atrophied so the brain couldn't give orders any more. It was trapped in the skull, sealed off. For a while you could see the silent, helpless suffering of the brain behind the eyes, then finally the brain must have died, because the eyes went out and there was no more feeling in them than a crab's eye on the end of a stalk. (*Letters of Burroughs* 259–60)

Here Burroughs creates a grotesque but effective allegory to describe his libertarian paranoia of an alliance between the "Welfare State" and initially unspecified agents. It is a conspiracy theory that places him in the position of the colonized rather than the colonizer. As seen in his autobiographical novels *Junkie* and, to some extent, *Queer*, Burroughs's fictional persona takes full advantage of liminal positioning in order to create a place from which to observe, and thus remain "outside" the authoritarian social structure he bemoans. He takes great pains to remain the outsider whether it be by declaring his marginality through his position as a drug addict or through his homosexuality.

In this allegory Burroughs describes the process by which the literal body, and the body of the nation, are contaminated from within. The body is taken over by this commercially exploited orifice that learns to speak and then cries "for equal rights." It is the

call for egalitarianism that precedes the eventual isolation and immobilization of the white subject. Egalitarianism prohibits personal agency and eventually isolates the mind of the subject from
the rest of the body. We find that the locus of identity and, by syn-
ecdochical connection, of decision making, is not only located in
the mind, but is the position of the white male at the head of the
nation's body. In this allegory, the body is now colonized from the
"bottom." The "top" is now isolated and confined expressing Burroughs's own fear of immobilization, a phobia he termed "stasis
horror."

More significantly perhaps, is the concept of Un-D.T., or undifferentiated tissue, which is a form of "mongrelized" (undetermined source) flesh that then effectively seals over the subject's
voice; for it sheds light on how Burroughs defines the colonizing
bottom. Burroughs's parenthetical association of spontaneous
amputation as an African or Negro trait provides a connection between his fear of the encroaching state and its mongrelized, "undifferentiated" agent(s). For Burroughs, the paralyzing bureaucracy has much to do with race.

Burroughs's earlier letters, in which he expresses his political
opposition to what he calls bureaucracy and the welfare state, provide a hermeneutic base for finding a central Beat theme within
the allegory. In one of these letters, Burroughs begins a diatribe
against the encroachment of authoritarian-police state viruses
within the body politic in the United States, but pointedly aims
his critique at a potentially egalitarian democratic system as well:
"The end result of complete cellular representation is cancer. Democracy is cancerous, and bureaus are its cancer. A bureau takes
root anywhere in the state, turns malignant like the Narcotic Bureaus, and grows and grows, always reproducing more of its own
kind, until it chokes the host if not controlled or excised. Bureaus
cannot live without a host being pure parasitic organisms. . . . Bureaucracy is wrong as a cancer, a turning away from the human
evolution direction of infinite potentials and differentiation and
independent spontaneous action, to the complete parasitism of a
virus. . . . the renunciation of life itself, a falling towards inorganic
inflexible machine, towards dead matter" (*Letters of Burroughs*

260–61). The emphasis on the paralysis of the individual, as well as the depiction of the body politic at the mercy of the bureaucratic state are libertarian themes. But in the case of Burroughs, the remedy of continual movement is most significant in conjunction with the Beat invective to just "Go!"

The appropriation of Emersonian visions of the individual's infinite potential joined with the categorical imperative of "differentiation" takes on an added resonance with Burroughs's earlier expressed horror at Un-D.T. The association of immobilization with undifferentiation suggests Burroughs's conflation of liberty with competition. Paralysis is the result of equality, of the loss of hierarchy. The analogy between paralysis and equality sets up the paradoxical desire for a fixed hierarchical structure in order that the individual might have the freedom to move. The issue of individualism thus takes on a central emphasis, which is in direct opposition to, and most threatened by, the mongrelization of the body. In an earlier letter to Ginsberg he states, "the capacity for infinite differentiation is to my mind a hugely important attribute of the human species and one frequently overlooked by social planners" (*Letters of Burroughs* 68). The significance of emphasizing "differentiation" must not be overlooked in what it suggests for the matter of social planning. For Burroughs, the concept of "differentiation" does not signify pluralism or multiculturalism, but instead designates an exclusive individualism cultivated within a rigid hierarchy. Thus the allegory centers on the crucial conflict between the "head" and the "bottom," and the paralyzing "undifferentiation" at stake should the "head" lose the battle for supremacy. "Free competition" and a rigid hierarchy are necessary for protecting the individual from absorption into an undifferentiated egalitarian body.

The economic logic suggests the need for expansion and a vision of "differentiation" that in the 1950s extended to marketing techniques. Even "liberal" social scientists such as David Riesman were looking for answers to undifferentiation in the market. Riesman went so far as to suggest that the rise of the conformist personality could be reversed by better marketing and increasing product choice. He suggested a "children's world fair" in which producers would provide a vast array of toys and diversions that children could peruse and choose without peer pressure so that they could begin to develop a more distinct individual persona: "Such suggestions, for example the world's fair for children, may look simply like a shift from less expensive selling to more expensive "specialty" selling. The inference is correct; as our national income grows, this merchandising shift is needed and desirable (366)."

Riesman echoes Burroughs's call for diversity and his fear of undifferentiated tissue. Both can be seen as accepting that the answer to the danger of mass culture lies in the ability of capitalism to create more distinct divisions of labor and to invent more diverse forms of consumption. The underlying fear of a deadening and "undifferentiating" communalism is quite evident in Burroughs's unending desire to escape "boredom."

Burroughs values "independent spontaneous action," a celebrated founding principle for the Beats. It was the source of Jack Kerouac's poetic, and the only rule of his aesthetic strategy. However, "spontaneity" as opposed to "paralysis" is not merely an aesthetic preference. Its political valence is seen further in Burroughs's critique of encroaching statism, which conflates the cancerous "bureaucratic state" with the "welfare state." In a letter to Ginsberg, Burroughs writes that the "Welfare State is on the way to becoming a Communist State, and that means a *bureaucratic police state*" (*The Letters of Burroughs* 67). It is important to recall the pervasiveness during this period of the Red Scare, and the wide dissemination of the House Committee on Un-American Activities hearings. For this sheds some light on the paranoia of internal contamination.

Stephen J. Whitfield's *The Culture of the Cold War* documents the intense fear of communist "contamination" in the 1950s. A reading of the comments and attitudes of McCarthyites shows that the Red Scare was actually a fear that the American body was threatened by a virus, which was variously defined as communist, black, gay, or foreign. Social issues of racism, integration, political dissent, immigration, and sexual politics took on a tropic form based on viral imagery.

Most interestingly, communism and integrationism were conflated, and the connection between an economic infiltration and racial infiltration was couched in the language of infections and viral attacks. Whitfield documents that the FBI was especially quick to connect a commitment to racial justice with political subversion. The conflation of "communism" and "integrationism" takes on a singular character, poisonous to the "body" of the nation: "Senator James Eastland (D-Miss) was able to charge after *Brown v. Board of Education,* that the Supreme Court had dared 'graft into organic law of the land the teaching, preachings and social doctrines of Karl Marx'" (Whitfield 23).

Truman's health care initiative was killed by the American Medical Association's charge that there were communist backers for the plan. Even the polio vaccine elicited skepticism from Oveta Culp Hobby, the Secretary of Health, Welfare, and Education (a virulent anticommunist millionaire). "Such free dissemination would be tantamount to 'socialized medicine' by the 'back door' which she apparently dreaded even more than the epidemic itself" (Whitfield 24).

The image of the contagion of race and communism is evident in the judicial system as well: "As liberal impulses became suspect, as sensitivities to constitutional safeguards were coarsened, the axis of American politics spun toward the primitive, the intolerant, the paranoid. In 1952, for example, the Supreme Court upheld *Carlson v. Landon,* a lower court decision to hold five aliens without bail, while the question of their deportation was under review. None had been convicted of—or even charged with—any crime. Refusing to grant the aliens bail, the district judge explained, 'I am not going to turn these people loose if they are Communists, any more than I would turn loose a deadly germ in this community'" (Whitfield 33). One might even read the Truman Doctrine and the Korean War itself as Truman's attempt to fight off the virus and to keep our hemisphere under quarantine.

Whitfield gives examples of the paranoia engendered even by high school textbooks: "Bragdon and McCutcheon's *History of a Free People* (1954) . . . undoubtedly multiplied the number of suspicious minds: 'Unquestioning party members are found everywhere. Everywhere they are willing to engage in spying, sabotage and the promotion of unrest on orders from Moscow'" (Whitfield 33). There is also evidence of the conflation of homosexuality and communism, both "secret practices" capable of infiltrating government and society. As a 1950 Senate report noted: "One homosexual can pollute a Government office" (44). In a bizarre similarity to Burroughs, Billy Graham uses the same rhetoric to describe the threat of contamination, praising the FBI agents "who, in the face of public denouncement and ridicule, go loyally on in their work of exposing pinks, the lavenders, and the reds who have sought refuge beneath the wings of the American eagle" (45).

The censorship undertaken by the State Department, a directive prohibiting from its libraries "all materials, including painting, by any controversial persons, Communists, or fellow-travelers" (Whitfield 39), also takes on the character of preventative surgery. Such a metaphor assists in linking together the Smith Act, the first peacetime sedition act in U.S. history, with the other forms of cultural and social paranoia. The provision's "Custodial Detention Program" required the compilation of names, based not on previous criminal conduct but on beliefs and associations.

The public had to be convinced of the threat of infection of radicalism. Much as a community would mobilize for a quarantine, the Congress began to put into place a system that would arrest the "radical-virus":

> By the end of 1952, another thirty-three communists had nevertheless been convicted, three others had been acquitted, and further trials were scheduled. One hundred twenty six Party leaders were eventually indicted. . . . Other legislation was designed to weaken American Communism even further. Over a Truman veto in 1950, Congress passed the International Security Act, which established concentration camps in Pennsylvania, Oklahoma, Arizona, and California. A Subversive Activities Control Board was also charged with registering Communists and Communist fronts. The Communist Control Act of 1954 . . . deprived

the Party itself of "all rights, privileges, and immunities attendant upon legal bodies." (Whitfield 49)

Keeping the cultural-wide paranoia of "contamination" and "infiltration" in mind, it is only mildly surprising to see Burroughs, an
indicted drug trafficker, complain about the "police state" and yet
echo the rationale for HUAC in anticommunist rhetoric.

In a direct sense, Burroughs creates a sort of biological justification for laissez-faire capitalism. The cancerous growth of statism stagnates the growth of the body by replacing the diversity of
"natural" tissue at various specific but differentiated jobs. By extension, the body is at its best and most productive when left to its
own natural processes of growth and divisions of labor. It is the
bureaus and welfare state that interfere with and kill the organism
as they enact the demands of minorities (in the case of the "ass
hole" allegory, isolating and paralyzing the white head). It is a loss
of personal agency at the hands of the state agency.

Burroughs's emphasis on mobility as growth is a reaction
against what makes its appearance in these texts as "boredom,"
"stagnation," and "stasis." The connotations of these terms are
many, but they share a common discourse with notions of the
need to push out toward new markets in the most capitalistic
sense, as well as, in what is most evident in the work of the Beats,
a renewing of the "pioneer spirit." This theme was persuasively
echoed in David Riesman's lament at the death of that "spirit."
*The Lonely Crowd: A Study of the Changing American Character*
displayed a concern with the depletion of "inner-directedness"
necessary for innovation and progress. Riesman constitutes such
inner-directedness as indicative of an individualism that is fast
disappearing in the United States. The inner-directed person,
presumably the ideal Burroughsian differentiated individual, "is
able to see industrial and commercial possibilities and to work
with the zeal and ruthlessness required by expanding frontiers in
the phase of transitional growth of population. Societies in the
phase of incipient population decline, alternatively, need neither
such zeal nor such independence. Business, government, the
professions, become heavily bureaucratized, as we see most

strikingly . . . in France. . . . Social mobility under these conditions continues to exist. But it depends less on what one is and what one does than on what others think of one—and how competent one is in manipulating others and being oneself manipulated. . . . But the product now in demand is neither a stable nor a machine; it is a personality" (46). There is an important parallel here of settled frontiers to "other-directed" conformist communality. According to Riesman's model, the Beats have resisted "other-directedness" by reconstituting the frontier.

Like Burroughs in his asshole metaphor, Riesman argues the need for hierarchy, differentiation, and direction, which are intimately related, in his view, to notions of individualism, free market, and movement. The "other-directed" man is no longer conscious of which way is up. The need is for the recuperation of an inner-directed hierarchy so that a "real" differentiation, which Burroughs calls for in the body/nation, might be reestablished. This is made clear in Riesman's lament: "As recent *Fortune* surveys indicate, a safe and secure job may be preferred to a risky one involving high stakes. What is more, it is no longer clear which way is up even if one wants to rise, for with the growth of the new middle class the older, hierarchical patterns disintegrate, and it is not easy to compare ranks among the several sets of hierarchies that do exist" (49). Paradoxically, individualism can only exist within a strict hierarchy, or what Christopher Newfield terms "corporate individualism."

Hierarchical structures are preserved through overproduction, which in times of prosperity conceals inequities and creates the illusion of abundance for all. J. Kenneth Galbraith provided a contemporary critique of this logic of overproduction and its endorsements of both neoindividualism and expansion in a tautological relation that posits growth and consumption as social curatives. In *The Affluent Society,* Galbraith claimed that overproduction and expansion were used to avoid egalitarianism and redistribution.[8] Burroughs's economic reasoning for going South replicates the self-seeking, socially irresponsible expansionist tendencies of overproduction.

Furthermore, Galbraith argued that such an outlook is not limited to the right but is common to the left as well: "[T]he goal of an expanding economy has also become imbedded in the conventional wisdom of the American left. The beneficent effects of such an economy, moreover, are held to be comprehensive. Not only will there be material improvement for the average man, but there will be an end to poverty and privation for all. This latter, in fact, is suspect. Increasing aggregate output leaves a self-perpetuating margin of poverty at the very base of the income pyramid. This goes largely unnoticed, because it is the fate of a voiceless minority" (97). He correctly predicted the devastating effects of overproduction on the lower class, which (in contrast to Burroughs's fears of the talking asshole) is left marginalized and mute in the expanding wake of the economy. His critique can thus be read as a prescient understanding of the ultimate failures of a Beat-inflected counterculture that ignored material egalitarianism and emphasized a form of individualism based on consumerist logic.

In the famed *Yage Letters*, written to Ginsberg from South America during Burroughs's search for a mythic, telepathic drug, he defines the "stasis horrors" that push him on in his expedition: "At dinner got bad case of stasis horrors. The feel of location, of being just where you are and nowhere else is unendurable. This feeling has been with me all over S.A." (*Letters of Burroughs* 174). Here, the dread of being immobilized echoes Burroughs's fear of the paralysis of the body and mind. This definition of stasis horror adds an imperialist element: the cure for stagnation and *ennui* is to move on to a new southern location. The theme of discovery serves this purpose. In a sense, Burroughs's motivation to explore South America in search of a new product, yage, with its fabled power of creating telepathic ability, is an indirect attempt to create a nonthreatening community (one that makes no demands on the individual's ability to move) through an alternate form of expansion—an expansion of consciousness. But this undertaking acts out cynical, neoimperialistic fantasies: in South America Burroughs hopes to operate freely in a colonized space of managed inequality.

The argument does not have to be proven through metaphorical extension. Burroughs writes many times to Ginsberg and Kerouac of the excellent opportunities in South America for buying cheap land on which to grow crops with almost no outside (bureaucratic) interference. And, as he learned during his stint as a Texas farmer the year before, this land contained a cheap exploitable workforce. In a letter to Kerouac written at the end of 1949, Burroughs sells Kerouac on the positive aspects of coming to Mexico: "Be mighty glad to see you down here. You won't make a mistake visiting Mexico. A fine country with plenty of everything cheap. One of the few places left where a man can really live like a Prince" (*Letters of Burroughs* 56). As in an earlier invitation to Ginsberg, where he likewise suggests Ginsberg take advantage of this newly configured imperialism, Burroughs extols the virtues of living like a "Prince."

It is evident that Burroughs is no democrat, or rather that his version of "democracy" does not extend to egalitarian or populist concerns. In a Lockean vision of the proper role of the state as guarantor of property rights, Burroughs sees American democracy as failing in that most sacred of duties. Later that year, he writes to Ginsberg: "I think the U.S. is heading in the direction of a Socialistic police state similar to England, and not too different from Russia. . . . At least Mexico is no obscenity 'Welfare' State, and the more I see of this country the better I like it. . . . I hope you are not serious in this labor leader idea. My opinion of labor leaders and unions is very close to the views so ably and vigorously expressed by Westbrook Pegler [right-wing ideologue], the only columnist in my opinion, who possesses a grain of integrity" (*Letters of Burroughs* 57). Burroughs's chief and recurrent complaint is the infiltration of the state with a Rousseaun imperative for communal organization. Therein lies his enthusiasm for Mexico, which, if nothing else, did inspire both Kerouac and Ginsberg to make several extensive visits. But to return to the infamous allegory, Burroughs, at this earlier juncture, provided the connection between the perception of the "red menace" at least partially in racial terms.

While running a farm he wrote Ginsberg that the farmers "are doing pretty good in Texas, but we are having labor trouble. . . . Believe me socialism and communism are synonymous, and both unmitigated evil, and the Welfare State is a Trojan Horse" (*Letters of Burroughs* 58). The "labor problem" consisted of the attempts by Mexico to regulate the flow of braceros (legal Mexican guest-workers) to the United States in order to force American labor contractors to provide the agreed upon conditions. Mexico sought to reverse the wage erosion that resulted from the influx of "illegal" workers allowed into the United States by the Immigration and Naturalization Service (INS), which simultaneously deported "legal" and "illegal" workers in order to drive U.S. wages even lower.[9] The "Trojan horse" by turns emits cancerous cells of unionism, socialism and, in the case of the Mexican workers, union-susceptible subjects. To get an idea of Burroughs's understanding of the migrant labor situation, it is helpful to cull several passages from a series of letters written to Ginsberg in 1948.

Nov. 30 —
The line between legitimate and criminal activity has broken down since the war. Most everyone in business violates the law every day. For example, we farmers in the Rio Grande Valley depend entirely on Mexican laborers who enter the Country illegally with our aid and connivance. The "civil liberties" of these workers are violated repeatedly. They are often kept on the job by force of gun (at cotton picking time when delay may mean loss of the entire crop). Workers who try to leave the field are shot. (I know of several instances.) In short my ethical position, now that I am a respectable farmer, is probably shakier than when I was pushing junk. Now, as then, I violate the law, but my present violations are condoned by a corrupt government. *(Letters of Burroughs 25)*

Nov. 30 —
I am so disgusted with conditions I may leave the U.S.A. altogether, and remove myself and family to S. America or Africa. . . . It's almost impossible to get anyone to do anything. Unions! That's the trouble, Unions! *(Letters of Burroughs 27)*

Dec. 2—
Enclose article about the Texas labor situation. The Rio Grande
Valley is one of the few remaining areas of cheap labor in the
U.S.A. The only alternatives to cheap labor ($2.00 per 12 hour
day) is mechanization, requiring a large initial outlay for expensive equipment. . . . If Valley farmers had to pay a living wage for
farm labor they would be ruined. A farm worker's Union is the
farmer's nightmare. If anyone wants to live dangerously in a
noble cause let him organize farm labor in Texas. . . .

I do not mean to convey the impression that Kells and I sit
under a palm leaf sun shelter, rifle in hand, "suppressing" the
workers. The whole deal is handled by labor and vegetable brokers. For example, I will make a deal with a labor broker, pay-
ing him so much per lb. to get my tomatoes picked and delivered to the vegetable broker who buys them. . . . The broker
backs a truck up to the Rio Grande and loads it with Mexican
"Wetbacks" as they swim or wade across the border. He drives
them to the field and gets the job done. Some brokers go in for
rough stuff, some don't. I recall one broker mentioning casually
that "his foreman had to shoot 2 wetbacks last night." But like
I say, I don't have anything to do with it personally. *(Letters of
Burroughs 29)*

While Burroughs distances himself from the brutality from which
he and the coterie of his fellow Rio Grande farmers benefit, he
does not distance himself from the necessary exploitation of
cheap labor, as shown by his invective against the unions and the
"socialism" they represent. He pointedly suggests that his broken
ethical code is justified by the breakdown in ethics in business,
thus suggesting that such ethics are overwritten by the ethic of
survival, a curious but important misappropriation of Emerson's
invective that "No law can be sacred to me but that of my nature"
(Emerson 262). More significantly, Burroughs makes a political
allusion to Locke's justification for attaining property through
someone else's labor and for protecting private property and
rights, in this case from the claims of his "wetback" laborers.

In a final invective against the meddling bureaucrats that have
"colon-ized" the old America into a paralyzed, immobile entity,
Burroughs harkens back to the America of the past, an America

of frontiers, which he attempts to recreate: "What ever happened to our glorious Frontier heritage of minding ones own business? The Frontiersman has shrunk to a wretched, interfering, Liberal bureaucrat" (*Letters of Burroughs* 61). In rhetoric similar to contemporary debates on the proper role of government, Burroughs faults liberalism for its bureaucratizing tendencies, without defining the nature of "one's own business." The conflation of business and personal activity further illustrates the promulgation of an individualism dictated by market logic. Burroughs was about to undertake his journey south in order to find the "pioneer" spirit that was missing in modern America: a foray in which he would be joined, at various times, by Ginsberg and Kerouac. Burroughs, more clearly than either of his fellow travelers, understood the economy of movement. He understood it in the only way in which migrant workers could and did, and implemented it in the only way in which exploiters of migrants can, and do.

## Democratic Discourse and the 1950s: Conformity, Communalism, Corporatism, and the Individual

The civic tension between liberty and equality in the United States go back to the founding of the republic, and even further back to competing forms of liberal-democratic thought. As the modern democratic state attempted to negotiate between these dual tendencies through the creation of checks and balances, it set them in perpetual conflict. In the twentieth century, the logic of market competition set a higher value on individualist subjectivity, and has discredited the egalitarian instinct as an encroachment of the space of the individual.[10] This mistrust of communalism created an approved individualist liberty at the expense of an inclusive, egalitarian, democratic *civitas* that would challenge political and market hierarchies. As Christopher Newfield writes, "In the United States, nearly any attempt to increase equality in any area except a widely accepted formal legal equality . . . is considered an attack on the liberties of the people. . . . This conflict between liberty and equality comes as close as anything in American life to constituting a national consensus. The notion that equality impairs liberty unites what we call "liberals" and "conservatives" in an everyday way. . . . In short, actual equality means tyranny, or at best, mediocrity" (35). There is a marked contrast, however, between a vapid egalitarianism, which the Right claims results from a lack of competition, and an egalitarian impulse that affirms communal cooperation and is seen by the Left as countering the submissiveness that atomistic individualism produces. Liberty is sold as the ability to move, and equality is defined as mere legal access, without regard to outcome.

Both of these notions are insufficient and draw more from notions of negative liberty, which is defined as the absence of constraint on the rights and preferences of the individual. Positive liberty, according to Isaiah Berlin, encourages not just the development of the individual, but also the constructive participation in self-government (Birch 96). The underlying assumption in positive liberty is an advocacy in collective terms rather than in individualistic terms.[11] There is no denying that there is a strong resonance between negative liberty and the work of Burroughs and Kerouac. But that is only half of the equation in this chapter. I suggest that in these texts there is also an idealized desire to achieve a communal union, and in this sense, enjoy the benefits of positive liberty. And yet, the inevitable showdown between these competing inclinations is for the Beats already decided in preference of the negative formulation.

As Birch points out, a person constructed by negative liberty is an individual characterized "as essentially pleasure-loving, pain-avoiding . . . [and] this is a sadly inadequate understanding of the human condition." As the English Idealists argued, people are "not just prompted by appetite. They desire what they think is good, they wish not only to be satisfied in various immediate ways, but to be moral. They seek to improve" (Birch 103). Most important, a belief in positive liberty entails a rejection of the functionalist-mechanistic view of the state as projected through negative liberty ideology. As Birch comments, "Rather than to be regarded with suspicion, the State must be made by the people and be free of coercion due to the participation which the individual had in its making and organization. Ideally there should be a common will in society which the state should embody and express, recognition of which would lead the great majority of citizens to conform voluntarily with the law" (104). The state, in this view, is therefore made of the people, in Rousseau's sense of the Sovereignty.[12]

The common critical view that has the Beat tradition emerging against conformity posits a false dichotomy, or at least an incomplete one that does not examine the effects of their subversion.[13] The popular imagination was fired up with the fears of encroaching communism and creeping socialism and supported the anticommunist hysteria that created public and private forms of "patriotic" conformity. In short, the perceived challenge to individualism presented by communal activism resulted in an adherence to a submissive corporatism. In the same manner, the Beats, in constructing a consciously individualistic aesthetic and politic, a nonbourgeois ethic, created a libertarianism that precluded any meaningful communal effort, thus weakening any politically organized effort at society-wide change. The result is an endorsement of an atomistic individualism that must conform because its recourse against systemic forces is inadequate. The conscious decision to champion the "negative" libertarian aspect of a "free society" in fact played into the hands of reactionary politics in the same way the democratic theories and views of the individual that Emerson, Thoreau, and Whitman popularized were used to justify westward expansion and reckless laissez-faire capitalism, and much later, to argue against the so-called welfare state and its "liberal" policies. The same dynamic appears within Beat-influenced countercultures of the 1950s and 1960s, providing for a self-subverting subversion.

The denigration of egalitarian and communal strategies will continue so long as egalitarian and communal efforts remain in conflict with market democracy. As it must; true egalitarianism posits the equality of the self with the law, as not simply its subject, but also its creator. It threatens naturalized hierarchical organization because it provides for direct participation in the making of social relations. For Kerouac and Burroughs (as for many white, midde-class males), the encroachment of the communal threatened their privileged space. The Beats erroneously conflated the communal with corporate organization and discipline, and thus the libertarian and anticommunal system that equated movement with liberty became the best option. Their "rebellion" against the bourgeoisie and conformism endorsed competition as the best form of social organization, making democratic participation and coalition "unnecessary." This faith in competition assumed that positive liberty was simply a by-product of negative liberty: a trickle-down, safe egalitarianism based on the illusion of "equal opportunity" rather than on a destabilizing guarantee of equal outcome for equal effort.

Even much of the liberal social criticism of the period, though outspokenly focused on the problem of conformism, suggested a deep-rooted anxiety caused by the loss of a stabilizing hierarchy. Again, David Riesman's *The Lonely Crowd* is a classic example. While concerned with the tendency of "other-directed," conformist personality, Riesman laments the passing of the "inner-directed" personality that, through its more competitive and individualistic qualities, provides a social hierarchy needed for a healthy society, one whose chief ideal is what he terms "autonomy." "Autonomy in an inner-directed mode . . . is no longer feasible. To understand why this is so requires a glance at the powerful bulwarks or defenses for autonomy that an era dependent on inner-direction provided and that are no longer so powerful today. These include, in the Protestant lands, certain attitudes toward conscience, and everywhere, the bulwarks of work, property, class, and hierarchy as well as the comforting possibilities of escape to the frontier" (Reisman 296). Similarly, William W. Whyte, in the influential book *The Organization Man*, deplores the loss of true competitive hierarchy, which has been replaced by the "social ethic." Conformity is thus associated with the communal and the staid. A loss of competition suggests that cooperation and progress are incompatible. A strict hierarchy sets the stakes for which true individuals compete, the by-product of which is innovation.

Even Carl Jung, the psychoanalytic champion of the collective, in his *Modern Man in Search of a Soul* describes the ultimate inadequacy of social existence: "A man can hope for satisfaction and fulfillment only in what he does not yet possess; he cannot find pleasure in something of which he has already had too much. To be a socially adapted being has no charms for one to whom to be so is mere child's play. Always to do what is right becomes a bore for the man who knows how, whereas the eternal bungler cherishes the secret longing to be right for once in some distant future" (48). This logic can be used to justify Burroughs's desires to continue moving south, and is in fact a description of the imperial imperative.

Laclau and Mouffe suggest that "the neo-capitalist euphoria of the two decades after WWII . . . appeared to offer an unlimited capacity for transformist absorption on the part of the system, and showed a linear tendency toward a homogenous society in which every antagonistic potential would be dissolved, and each collective identity fixed in a system of differences" (157). By establishing a position that relied solely on a radical individualism, the Beats wound up endorsing the absorption of antagonistic potential that might have resulted from true egalitarian participation. Their form of "difference" lent itself to fixed positions within a hierarchy that allows for personal movement, product choice, and promotion for its approved agents, but not for challenges to the system or structure itself.

Unable or perhaps unwilling to make a distinction between communal egalitarianism and corporatist conformism, the Beats attempt to construct nonconformist communities based on marginalized identities—most often black identity and Mexican identity. But because ultimately true marginality is too radical a departure, in the midst of their own communal constructions, they begin to fear racial absorption, and so reject even this sort of communalism (with the exception of Ginsberg). This is the sort of isolationism, already seen in Thoreau and Emerson, results in a particularly "American" form of deconstruction that targets the communal instinct. Now whether one wants to associate this paranoia of the "absorption of self" with individualism, racism, capitalism, industrialism, or even modernity itself is a more complex question. I suggest it is a mixture of factors, with historical precedents that become increasingly complex and differentiated through the nineteenth and the twentieth centuries.

Beat responses to apparent conformisms and "absorptions," are varied and complex, and resonate with the contradictions and conflicts of the 1950s and 1960s. In their search to reinvent the "American Individual" the Beats profoundly encounter issues of race, the place of the white man in America, a desire to reinvent the self through self-marginalization, an attempt to re-form the patriarchy, as well as to return to the nineteenth-century political social forms in order to find the "true path" for the future. They replay old justifications for the "new form of imperialism" Burroughs trumpets in tempting his fellow writers to "go South."

## The Fellaheen Frontier

In an interview with Daniel Odier, William Burroughs distanced himself from the "Beat Generation": "I don't associate myself with it at all, and never have, either with their objectives or their literary style. I have some close personal friends among the Beat movement: Jack Kerouac and Allen Ginsberg and Gregory Corso are all close personal friends of many years standing, but we're not doing at all the same thing either in writing or in outlook. You couldn't find four writers more different, more distinctive. It's simply a matter of juxtaposition rather than any actual association of literary styles or overall objectives" (*The Job*, 37). In his book *The Beat Generation*, Bruce Cook echoes the same sentiment crediting the Beat movement's protest of "such rigid principles, inflexible forms, and enforced conformity" (166). Burroughs's work, which is more postmodern, is often held in higher critical estimation.[14] But despite the evident differences, they do indeed share and disseminate a unified ideology. In a 1970 interview with Bruce Cook, Burroughs distances himself from Kerouac's reactionism in responding to a question about Kerouac's right-wing politics. Burroughs goes on record as having warned Kerouac against supporting the Right, but exculpates Kerouac's later excesses by suggesting that "After all, there's no doubt that the Beats ultimately had terrific radical political influence" (Cook 181). Burroughs does not revisit his own reactionary past nor does Cook press him to define the reaches of that influence.

Indeed, in what is a typical interpretation of his work, especially in regards to *Naked Lunch,* Cook suggests that Burroughs is ultimately an equal-opportunity hater whose vision is Swiftian. Barry Miles gives what has become the typical understanding of *Naked Lunch:* "*Naked Lunch* . . . [is] a full-scale offensive against the deep-seated hypocrisy, arrogance, naïveté and mindless futility which characterized so much of fifties American consumer society. . . . It was an attack on . . . puritan ideology which caused Prohibition and persecuted homosexuality. . . . It was an American confessional: exposing everything from the mundane life of the fifties American housewife to the full horror of capital punishment" (Miles, *Burroughs* 100). But this notion is at odds with Burroughs's understanding of his cut-up technique, and his experience in Mexico, South America, and Tangier. What emerges from a reading of his work contextualized within the scope of a larger Beat politic is a project undergirded with the same limitations, rather than one that is radically "different" from the Beat agenda. In fact, his work is often constructed in direct opposition to any sort of progressive, liberal, or communal politics.

I would suggest that in the final analysis Burroughs's work carries the radical individualism of Kerouac and Ginsberg, which for them culminates in an affirmation of status quo stability, to an authoritarian end. As stated above, Burroughs's asshole allegory thinly masks a paranoia of the undifferentiated masses, so that his ostensibly "individualistic" cure, radical individuation, is really a call for a rigid hierarchy in which difference is not simply tolerated, as in pluralism, but rigorously enforced and regulated. It is a difference based on racial, economic, and gendered inferiority. Burroughs's misogyny is legendary, extending to the claim in *The Job,* that women were an "evolutionary" mistake. "I think they [women] are a basic mistake, and the whole dualistic universe evolved from this error" (138). The sense that unity can be found by erasing the duality of gender suggests that for him "differentiation" in its most privileged sense is the prerogative of a very narrow group: white males. His own communal impulse was manifested in an all-male coterie that stressed woman-hatred, a debunking of all forms of "love," and which coincided with Burroughs's most apolitical technique: the cut-up method.

To understand the cut-up method we must begin with the precept that it is an aestheticized response to Burroughs's "invasion fears." In his biography, Miles quotes Burroughs as saying that he feels he has been pursued by some agent throughout his life: "'As soon as you get close to something important,' he said 'That's when you feel this invasion, that's the way you know there's something there. . . . The last thing the invading instance wants to do is confront you directly because that's the end of it. But invasion is the basis of fear: there's no fear like invasion'" (*Burroughs* 248). Taken at his own logic, Burroughs's work can thus be read as a defense against such invasion. The logic of the cut-up is imperialistic: strategically offensive in a martial sense, and authoritarian in its politics.

Burroughs began his experiments with the technique of the "cut-up" soon after the publication of *Naked Lunch*. With Brion Gysin, an English painter whom he met in Tangier, he began to cut newspapers into long strips that he would then juxtapose in columns to generate new syntax and meaning. Adopting Gysin's technique, Burroughs began his cut-up trilogy, which would eventually consist of *The Soft Machine, The Ticket That Exploded,* and *Nova Express*. The logic of the cut-up allows anyone to become an "artist." The cut-up artist subverts the control of the print media, original author, and producer (the cut-up method was also used on film) by arrogating the production of words, spoken or written. Burroughs claimed this subversive act then freed the reader of the cut-up to make his own associations, producing one's own ideas, logic, and vision, without the manipulation of authorial intentionality: "*Naked Lunch* proposed the virus metaphor to represent control, or agents of control (church, state, police). In *Soft Machine*, there are many examples of virus invasion . . . a whole gamut of Burroughs characters all waiting to permutate. The only way to thwart the intentions of the controllers is to destroy their means of control: their language. The cut-up is a means of escape. 'Rub out the word'" (Miles, *Burroughs* 122). Rather than a strategic attack on authoritarian modes of control, what is evinced is Burroughs's desire to isolate the self and kill off the threat of absorption posed by sharing a common language with the parasites. What we find in his cut-up work, however, is a definition of parasite that is now extended to include fellow humans, figured as intruding "neighbors."

If we compare the use of a conventional realist narrative in *Junky* to the cut-up narrative in *The Soft Machine*, we find that the hope held out in *Junky* of finding a communal drug that will provide the "final fix" has disappeared. With it has disappeared Burroughs's attempt to participate within community, and his attack on syntax and context is a strategic subversion of a common language with shared connotations and assumptions to formulate and communicate meaning.

For Burroughs, despite the human desire to escape, control is a condition of life. The cut-up rewrites his *Junky* experience, quite literally and physically, by destroying the chronological order of things as well as symbolically by cutting the experience of addiction, and whatever shared context he experienced with friends in Mexico City, to shreds. His friends in the earlier novel are now juxtaposed with images of their deaths in a confusing but grim montage in "Dead On Arrival," the first chapter of *The Soft Machine:* Bill Gains "in a Mexico City room with his douche bag and his stash of codeine pills . . . The Consul would give me no information other than place of burial in The American Cemetery"; Sailor who "went wrong in the end, hanged to a cell by his principals"; his boy lover Kiki stabbed "with a kitchen knife in the heart" (Burroughs, *Soft Machine* 7–9). Community is dead. In its place are the images of meddling strangers who pass for "neighbors" in a reprise to the image of a screaming girl that plays through the chapter. Their description becomes increasingly caustic: "neighbors rush in," "vecinos rush in" and "Enter the nabors."

Also gone is the paradoxical notion that the individual can "shoot yourself to freedom"; instead Burroughs repeats the line "he cannot quit," as a listener repeatedly responds: "Imposible quitar eso" (impossible to kick the habit). Over and over, addict desires to quit, but fails to "do yourself a favor and stay off" (*Soft Machine* 8). Meanwhile, dark, bold letters spell an ominous message: "INVADE, DAMAGE, OCCUPY" (7). The only defense for Burroughs is heard in the comforting Spanish voice: "Quedesa con so medecina, William" (Keep up with your medicine) (10, 11). Community is impossible because of a human nature that ultimately cedes control to something other than itself, and cannot therefore be itself. The only response is to try and remain inviolable, a state facilitated analogously through heroin addiction and the cut-up. Heroin thus acts as a defense against the need to cede control to either the communal or the bureaucratic "virus." Since human nature is defined through its propensity toward addiction, literally, addiction to addiction, Burroughs opts to cede power to the pure product of heroin: "Junk is the mold of monopoly and possession. The addict stands by while his junk legs carry him straight in on the junk beam to relapse. Junk is quantitative and accurately measurable. The more junk you use the less you have and the more you have the more you use. . . . Junk is the ideal product . . . the ultimate merchandise. . . . Junk yields a basic formula of 'evil' virus: *The Algebra of Need.* The face of 'evil' is always the face of total need. A dope fiend is a man in total need of dope. Beyond a certain frequency need knows absolutely no limit or control" (*Naked Lunch* xxxvii). This addiction is quantifiable, producing a formula of need that paradoxically leads to the absence of limits or control; unlike bureaucracy and civic participation, the addict is "immobilized for lack of junk" not because of its presence (*Junky* 64).

Thus the cut-up serves Burroughs's intentions to hold off "invasion" and "control" at the hands of the invaders by destroying the conventional structures of connection and relation (grammar, syntax, word order, and so on) that "make" meaning and communication. However, the antiauthoritarian political connotation of the cut-up method diverts attention from Burroughs's desire to subvert communal structures as well, themselves reliant on shared symbolic and cultural codes. Language, which Burroughs presumes is manipulative and controlling, is the very medium of the social act. To subvert the intention of the word is to destroy the cohesion of the sentence and paragraph. The cut-up method operates on two levels. On the practical level, it denies the possibility of shared meaning. It seeks to hold off the invading, meddling "neighbors." On the metaphorical level, it associates the unity of the written work with the unity of the body politic, and desires to destroy the latter symbolically as it annihilates the former.

At the same time, Burroughs's use of the cut-up can itself be seen as a colonizing act, in that he arrogates the meaning, the logic, the intent from a "subject" text. Like the fragmented portrayal of Tangier in *Naked Lunch*, and its colonized and divided state in the 1950s, Burroughs's technique is a form of authorial power garnered from a power to divide. The notion that the body of the white male is threatened with invasion that will strip the body of "differentiation" suggests that the body as text must be rendered impossible to unify. As he writes in the introduction to the third British edition of *The Soft Machine:* "The soft machine is the human body under constant siege from a vast hungry host of parasites with many names but one nature being hungry and one intention to eat." The body as text is divided, cut-up, permanently differentiated. Better that it should be incomprehensible than that it should be invaded. But lest this seem a romantic fatalism, Burroughs does not intend to give up power by a recourse to a democratizing chaos. Arbitration of meaning remains in the hand that wields the scissors. Ultimately the cut-up is a way of subverting narratives he considers threatening. He absorbs them, using a form of literary colonialism that destroys their logic, in favor of his logic. This he makes clear in the introduction to the British edition to *The Soft Machine:* "Glad to have you aboard reader, but remember there is only one captain of this subway" (2).

The cut-up becomes the literary form of his fantasy of "schlupping," which first appeared in *Naked Lunch*. The act involves a parasitic symbiosis in which one human emits a jelly onto another human who is dissolved and absorbed. As Ginsberg described it: "Schlupp for him, was originally a very tender emotional direction, a desire to merge with a lover" (Miles, *Ginsberg* 155). This early attempt by Burroughs for a "telepathic union" ends not in communal merging, but in a colonial appropriation, in which the other is absorbed, or even consumed. Such is in fact the nature of the cut-up.

The spatialization of such an aesthetic is represented by *Interzone,* Burroughs's fictionalization of Tangier, itself a "cut-up" city. While Burroughs lived in Tangier, the city was a small strip of land ruled by a consortium of nine countries with equal privileges they divided between them: for example, the French controlled the customs, while the British and the Belgians controlled the police force. "The town was wide open to corruption and shady deals, and one boulevard in the newly built French section was reputed to have 600 banks in a 300-yard stretch. . . . smuggling was rife, which meant it was a very cheap place to live" (Miles, *Burroughs* 74). It might be argued that Tangier was literally the most colonized city in the world. As depicted in *Naked Lunch,* it is a maze of streets, a surrealistic city in which walking out of a door might lead to the old American South, some thinly disguised South American township, or a Caribbean-like island (Upper Baboonsasshole). "Interzone is very much modeled on Tangier in the old international days: it was an Inter-zone, it was no country. The jungle scenes come from my South American explorations. Upper Baboonsasshole is Upper Babanasa actually" (Miles, *Burroughs* 98). The lands Burroughs surveys belong to "no country." These lands make up the liminal space the colonizer desires, free of the laws and debilitation of the colonizer's homeland. Paradoxically, the colonizer retains privilege while he or she explores. In it all are subjected to a mysterious set of laws and practices that appear more anarchic than systematic. Only the white subject walks through this wasteland untouched, the only reflexive subject in the midst of a land populated by a mish-mash of Arabs, Indians, Latinos, and tribal peoples. The central trope of this fictionalized Tangier/ Interzone, as Burroughs makes clear, is exemption: "The special attraction of Tangier can be put in one word: exemption. Exemption from interference, legal or otherwise. . . . No legal pressure or pressure of public opinion will curtail your behavior" (*Interzone* 59). In this sense, "extraterritorial" rights signify the privilege of whiteness in a divided and effete third world land. Tangier becomes for Burroughs both a literal and a literary culmination of his search for the "perfect" place. Its aesthetic is the cut-up, its politics a noninterfering, obfuscated authoritarian government in the guise of a fetid anarchy, its history a series of conquests, its fate predicted by Oswald Spengler as fellaheen, its racialization indicative of the inferiority of the dark races, its allure the freedom of the privileged liminality of the white explorer. As Brion Gysin, Burroughs's collaborator in cut-up technique, expresses about Tangier in the 1950s: "Tangier was like heaven. It was paradise then, absolute paradise. Everything was free, everywhere, drugs, boys, everything. There'd be money floating up and down the street and the sun shone all day, and the sky was as blue as the sea" (Miles, *Burroughs* 74).

Kerouac wrote of Burroughs's behavior in Tangier in *Desolation Angels,* which contains an account of his visit to help Burroughs put together *Naked Lunch* in 1957:

> "How do you like the Arabs?"
> "Just push em aside like little pricks" and suddenly he walked right thru a bunch of Arabs on the sidewalk, making them split on both sides, muttering and swinging his arms with a vigorous unnatural pumping motion like an insane exaggerated Texas oil millionaire pushing his way thru Swarms in Hong Kong. . . . "Just brush em aside, son, dont take no shit from them little pricks." (Kerouac, *Desolation Angels* 306)

Burroughs playing the ugly American is characteristic not only of the role he and Kerouac, and to a certain extent, Ginsberg, shared, but is indicative of a way of seeing the racial other: "In fact it's exactly like Mexico, the Fellaheen world, that is, the world that's not making History in the present; making History, manufacturing it, shooting it up in H bombs and Rockets, reaching for the grand conceptual finale of Highest Achievement (in our time the Faustian 'West' of America, Britain and Germany high and low)" (*Desolation Angels* 305). Kerouac's conflation of the eastern and southern peoples goes a long way in suggesting that the "superior American" pose was a carefully thought-out historical telos. Thus my contention that Burroughs's work is imperialistic goes further than its metaphorical manifestation, which is complicated by my understanding of imperialism as itself partly metaphorical. If one examines the United States' own imperialistic past one is struck by the multifaceted understanding of imperialism: as a military exercise, as a market enterprise, as a representation of inevitable historical forces, and lastly as the "natural" dynamic of racial laws. Considering the creation of its own colonial system, the United States in the nineteenth century understood imperialism as both a particular militaristic endeavor with its logistical and practical problems, as well as a metaphor of the nation's and culture's greatness, all the while acknowledging the necessity of a new form of market conquest as an alternative.[15]

Burroughs's own consideration of a fellaheen South America, ripe for a "new imperialism" is thus not new in itself. Oswald Spengler's historical fatalism played quite well within the scope of American racialism, both past and present. By the 1950s, the American justifications for expansion into lands deemed mismanaged and populated by inferior races were over a hundred years old. Burroughs's understanding of imperialism and my use of it in describing his work and political vision are thus both literal and metaphorical.

However, I do not make the parallel between nineteenth century beliefs about race, expansion, historical mission, and conquest and the writings of certain twentieth-century postwar writers as a mere allegorical connection. As Reginald Horsman has shown, the myth of Anglo-Saxon superiority has been a force in racial beliefs since the eighteenth century, and became especially virulent in the middle of the nineteenth century in America. But Horsman demonstrates that the effects of such racialism were implemented as social and political policy. Racially informed policy had scientific defenders and wide cultural dissemination that still influences racial categorization. The belief in such a historical narrative allows Burroughs to feel that he is not responsible for his writing, but is in fact simply a recorder of a historical process, associated with Spengler, that actually went back hundreds of years. "There is only one thing a writer can write about: what is in front of his senses at the moment of writing . . . I am a recording instrument. . . . I do not presume to impose 'story' 'plot' 'continuity'. . . .

Insofar as I succeed in Direct recording of certain areas of psychic process I may have limited function" (*Naked Lunch* 200). What Burroughs does not acknowledge is that even the mere recording of the psychic journey (as he ostensibly sets out to do in his travels through South America as recorded in the *Yage Letters*) inevitably establishes a socio-political-aesthetic trajectory. In a sense, to read Burroughs's major works chronologically *(Junky, The Yage Letters, and Naked Lunch)* provides us with such a map. He moves aesthetically from a gritty realism, to an exploratory expressionistic documentarianism, and finally to experiments with surreal techniques culminating in the cut-up experiments. A geographical representation of the same period shows Burroughs moving from the East coast to Texas, Mexico, South America, and then Tangier. Politically Burroughs retains a libertarian individualism. But most impressive is that his search for a personal historical telos is demonstrated through the parallels between the depiction of his persona and the spatialization of the places it inhabits. The work's trajectory remains stable, the levels of meaning—geographic, political, historical, psychic—achieve a consistency, even approach a holistic vision of Anglo-American individualistic desire. In what Clifford Geertz refers to as "thick description" Burroughs produces both a worldview and an ethos that is illiberal, racist, undemocratic, and which fairly represents the Beat-inflected beliefs that partly crippled many of the strains of 1960s American countercultures.

Initially Burroughs's literary and geographic journey is a search for transformative power to renew, to escape boredom, to find the means to transmute the power of death into the power of life. Thus his exploration with drugs itself becomes an attempt somehow to transcend the self while remaining the self. *Junky* takes Burroughs from his urban landscape of New York to the Texas farmlands and finally to Mexico. But in his attempt to change and expand, he conflates the growth of the self and the growth of nation, the uses of personal movement with the imperative to expand the market, all fueled by the fear of invading foreign subjects. The liminal imperative becomes imperial liminality. These themes are most evident in his travel piece, *The Yage Letters*, and his correspondence with Kerouac and Ginsberg written during the same period.

Although Burroughs's travels were necessitated by his legal travails (drug indictments in the United States and a murder charge in Mexico), his writing suggests that there was much more to his movement than the desire to escape "justice." Burroughs, several years older than Kerouac and Ginsberg, had in the early New York and Columbia University days lectured his younger friends on his own literary and historical theories. His suggestion that they read Spengler's *Decline of the West* was instrumental in the construction of a Beat historiographical understanding. For the Beats, the West was on the verge of decline, but the southern climes had already fallen into decay. Burroughs was extremely interested in Mayan and Aztec history, studying at the University of Mexico City with a background in anthropology at Harvard. His own ruminations on Mexico do not hesitate to make some startling racial assertions: "Mexico is my place . . . I would not go back to the U.S. under any circumstances. . . . This is basically an oriental culture (80% Indian) where everyone has mastered the art of minding his own business" (*Letters of Burroughs* 69). His studies in ancient Indian culture confirmed his belief in Spengler's vision of the fellaheen, and were later confirmed for him by his experience in South America.

What is most interesting here, is that, unlike Kerouac, whose belief was that the fellaheen peoples served as living guideposts to the fate of the United States and other industrial countries, Burroughs's response to the "decay" of South America closely resembles the justifications that had played out one hundred years before in the war with Mexico.[16] Mexico was populated with inferior peoples, themselves an amalgamation of various races (as opposed to the purity of the white race) and thus incapable of developing the same systems of self-government or the sciences. Admittedly, Burroughs never wrote specifically on the superiority of the Anglo-Saxon, but he did not have to. The status of the American in the jungle, in his ethnographic letters to Ginsberg, assumes and insinuates the inferiority of the South Americans. Burroughs traveled with the Cocoa Commission and a group of

American bureaucrats whom he calls the "Point Four" people.[17] His call for a "new imperialism" was to take the same form as nineteenth century southern expansion: "Typical of the 1850s was the belief that commercial penetration and population growth were the keys to future American relations with the rest of the world. American economic growth and the new technology would prepare the way for the ever-increasing American population to thrust outward into the most distant regions" (Horsman 286). Burroughs's purpose is more specifically to guard against his own personal decline, but the personal for Burroughs includes, or perhaps is a metaphor of, the position of the national body itself. In a sense, his journey into the fellaheen world is to stake out a space that can be used to stave off the process of decline. The notion that constant expansion keeps off decline by consistently "progressing" was itself used as a justification for old style imperialism, and interestingly was being used by several social scientists as a prescription for the ills of the nation in the 1950s.[18] The irony of traveling with the British Cocoa Commission as well as American officials appears to be lost on Burroughs, even though he often posed as an oil company official in order to get special treatment. Their combined reasons for the expedition represent a concerted effort by the West to interfere in Latin America's politics, economy, and culture. Together, they seek to expand cocoa production, contain communism, and establish a new outpost for the besieged American individual: "I have about decided to move on South—probably to Panama or Ecuador . . . I will have to start operations on a shoestring and under real pioneer conditions. . . . I prefer to settle in a country where they want Americans to come in and farm (I intend to buy a ranch) and where there are no restrictions on ownership nor the consequent possibility of some politician expropriating your ranch" (*Letters of Burroughs* 77). And yet, one must not lose sight of the more "spiritual" reason for Burroughs's travels, which has been held as the redeeming facet: the countercultural mission of escaping restraint. Burroughs's search for yage, while in one sense hedonistic, is idealistically tinged as he makes clear at the end of *Junky:* "I decided to go down to Colombia and score for yage. . . . I am ready to move on south and look for the uncut kick that opens out instead of narrowing down like junk. . . . Kick is seeing things from a special angle. Kick is momentary freedom from the claims of the aging, cautious, nagging, frightened flesh. Maybe I will find in yage what I was looking for in junk and weed and coke. Yage may be the final fix" (*Junky* 152).

## The Search for Yage

*The Yage Letters*—written by Burroughs to Ginsberg in 1953 and then continued by Ginsberg in 1960 during his own search for yage in South America—idealize transethnic migration. The search for a liminality that can be provided artificially will allow for that temporary "freedom" without threatening permanent change to the taker's actual privileged status and class. Burroughs's experimentation with yage yielded a series of transethnic/trans-gender/transchronological experiences, as seen in passages from the original letters written to Ginsberg before being edited for publication by Lawrence Ferlinghetti:[19]

> I turned right into a nigger and then this blue spirit got to me
> and I was scared and took some codeine. . . .
> Complete bisexuality is attained. You are a man or a woman
> alternately or at will. . . .
> There is a definite sense of space time travel that *seems* to shake
> the room. . . . Yage is space time travel. The room seems to
> shake and vibrate with motion. The blood and substance of
> many races, Negro, Polynesian, Mountain Mongol, Desert
> Nomad . . . Indian . . . passes through your body. You make
> migrations, incredible journies through jungles and deserts
> and mountains. . . . across the Pacific . . . South Pacific . . .
> South America where all Human Potentials are spread out in
> a vast silent Market. (*Letters of Burroughs* 179, 180, 182)

For Burroughs, yage provides the entrance to the marketplace of "marginalized" identities, and into the world of the fellaheen, a passage into an alternate existence in which the white male can experience difference and its liberating side effects, without having to give up the privilege of whiteness.

However, Burroughs maintains his "American" perspective throughout, expressing his distaste and contempt for the natives: "To say the Colombians run a loose ship is an understatement. . . . Wouldn't surprise me to see someone shit on the deck and wipe his ass with the flag" (*Yage Letters* 28). Nor does his "transethnic" experience keep him from his constant search for child prostitutes to exploit. His fascination with native behavior constantly veers between admiration and revulsion. On Peruvians he writes, "They are the least character-armored people I have ever seen. They shit or piss anywhere they feel like it. They have no inhibitions in expressing affection. They climb all over each other and hold hands. If they do go to bed with another male and they all will for money, they seem to enjoy it" (*Yage Letters* 42). Nor does he cease his racial theorizing. On the South American Indian he writes, "He is not, as one is apt to think at first, fundamentally an Oriental, nor does he belong to the West. He is something special, unlike anything else" (*Letters of Burroughs* 176).

Through the whole adventure Burroughs's greatest attraction to South America was the ability to experience such "freedom" while retaining the bourgeois privileges allotted to him in the West: "You can be a queer, or a drug addict and still maintain position. Especially if you are educated and well mannered. There is deep respect here for education, and correct behaviour in the sense of good manners" (*Letters of Burroughs* 185). Burroughs's wholehearted endorsement of going South had its effect on Allen Ginsberg. In the following year of 1954, Ginsberg traveled to Mexico to live amongst the natives and experience life on a Chíapas finca.

## Ginsberg's White Goddess

Throughout the 1950s and 1960s Allen Ginsberg remained perhaps the most public of the Beats, and his contribution to the counterculture of the 1960s was direct and active as opposed to

Kerouac, who withdrew during the 1960s, or as contrasted with Burroughs, whose influence was primarily in the avant-garde. Ginsberg became, along with Abbie Hoffman and Bob Dylan, one of the quintessential figures in the culture of the 1960s.[20] His work remained progressive, liberal, and critical of the status quo. One cannot discount the influence of *Howl* nor of his role in bringing forth the cause of peace, or of his role in assisting the cause of gay rights. Perhaps his marginalization as a Jew kept Ginsberg from the escape hatch that Burroughs and Kerouac used. Like other Jewish intellectual and political figures associated with the 1960s New Left, Ginsberg's personal history was profoundly shaped by mainstream American practices of sociopolitical exclusion and suspicion. Ginsberg's liminal identity was not a role he could drop if his position as a white male was indeed threatened. Ultimately, Ginsberg's Marxist roots and his experience as a gay, Jewish man proved to him the necessity for communitarian strategies.[21]

The young Ginsberg sought refuge from the frightening consequences of living life on the margins by playing the straight, white, middle-class family man (as he did with Elise Cowen in 1953 and Sheila Williams Boucher in 1954).[22] His relationships with women ended disastrously; his resolutions to live life as a straight man led to severe mental stress. Ginsberg seems to have understood societal, cultural, and ethnic borders in ways which Kerouac and Burroughs did not: as barriers that could not be used "strategically" by those immobilized within them (especially in 1950s America). In an early essay entitled, "Poetry, Violence, and the Trembling Lambs," he writes, "Recent history is the record of a vast conspiracy to impose one level of mechanical consciousness on mankind and exterminate all manifestations of that unique part of human sentience, identical in all men, which the individual shares with his Creator. The suppression of contemplative individuality is nearly complete" (*Deliberate Prose* 3). Ultimately Ginsberg, a persecuted homosexual, a child of radical, besieged Jews, and the son of a mentally ill mother, knew the consequences of transversing those imposed borders,[23] and the penalties enacted on those who crossed and were without the privileged haven of whiteness in America. But alive in this early essay is Ginsberg's anxiety over the threat of absorption by the "vast conspiracy" that seeks to impose a mechanical consciousness that obliterates individualism. Resisting "the suppression of contemplative individuality" meant finding a space to defend. There was a significant moment in his youth when finding that space took on neoimperial, neoindividualist characteristics shared by Kerouac and Burroughs. That moment saw him travel South and live with the white goddess, a moment in which as a young man, he was seduced by Burroughs's fellaheen vision of the imperial renewal that the magic South offered.

The motivation for Ginsberg's trip to Mexico in 1954 is manifold. Surely he was tempted by Burroughs's descriptions of his adventures in South America. He also indicates in letters to Neal Cassady that he needed a diversion after ending a trying romance with Burroughs who had recently left for Tangier. But more telling, and perhaps more compelling, are the journal entries written during his trip. In them, Ginsberg provides a motif for his journey: an explorer's narrative in which he revels in the role of the great white explorer. In the entries, he endorses Spengler's historiography and Kerouac's belief that Mexico and her people are fellaheen. Focusing on Mayan ruins, Ginsberg portrayed the people as living in antiquity, viewing their existence as a foreshadowing to the eventual desiccation of all Western civilization, and describing the sights as a "Spenglerian movie." The rejuvenation such exploration offered parallels Burroughs's purposes in South America and Tangier: creativity through new conquest, achieving liminality while retaining a personal space of power. In leaving the United States, Ginsberg supplants a powerless liminality (his identity as a homosexual in the 1950s) for a more powerful one.

At the beginning of his journey, he writes "Had thought yesterday despairing on bus, realized I was in Mexico in flight, no future, no past" (Ginsberg, *Mid-Fifties Journals* 33). His movement engenders a feeling that, while anxiety-provoking, also signals a sort of temporary freedom and sense of possibility. His fantasies are in fact predicated on the ability to move: "I want to escape to some great future with Bill Jack Neal Lucien, cannot do and in loneliness forming an imaginary movie-world without a plot—must make a great phantasy and carry it to Europe and throughout the world, traveling ever toward it" (Ginsberg, *Mid-Fifties* 34). In essence, this space provides the blank screen on which Ginsberg can project his movie-world. Such fantasy is only viable in a space that has no future or presence of its own, but offers only a past, dead and gone, and thus colonizable, even if only in fantasy.

Ginsberg spent a month at Chichen Itza, where the famed Mayan ruins were being excavated at that time. In the poem that describes this period in Mexico, "Siesta in Xbalba," Ginsberg sets the purpose to his visit by contrasting the "timeless" nature of the contemplation afforded to him by his surrounding at Chichen Itza with the profane time that is all too evident in New York City. The poem describing the ruins at Uxmal, a city that has seen the end of time, its existence and meaning comprehensible only in the past: "Late sun opening the book, / blank page like light, / invisible words unscrawled, / impossible syntax / of apocalypse—Uxmal: Noble Ruins." Ginsberg gives life to his title by immediately settling into the pensive mood provided by his surroundings; the pace and activity of New York cannot reach him in a country that is motionless and so he "succumb[s] to this / temptation—" (*Collected Poetry* 97).

The juxtaposition of his serenity to the frenetic lives of his friends in New York becomes characteristic of the dichotomy between the living and the dead civilization. The privilege Ginsberg retains, however, is that he is "alive" within the dead culture. He imagines his friends in a photograph, all at their different activities, and from his serene position in Mexico, he is able to pull them out of profane time and to capture their images so that they are mythologized: "all posturing in one frame, / superficially gay / or tragic as may be, / illumined with the fatal / character and intelligent / actions of their lives." (*Collected Poetry* 98).

The poem reveals a subtle dichotomy that Ginsberg had inherited from Burroughs: the notion that the fellaheen land lies outside of time and history. The warning that all civilization ends serves to suggest that temporality is itself a construct, or rather the product of historicity. The Mayans may be prologue to the future of the West, wherein that profane time itself eventually becomes sacred time in myth and legend. At the same time Ginsberg also suggests that such dead, "fellaheen" civilization (Mexico itself figured as a museum here) can provide a renewal for the deadened spirit of the West.

> blind face of animal transcendency
>           over the sacred ruin of the world
> dissolving into the sunless wall of a blackened room
>           on a time-rude pyramid rebuilt
>           in the bleak flat night of Yucatan
> where I come with my own mad mind to study
>           alien hieroglyphs of Eternity.
>                              (*Collected Poetry* 101)

In what is a spiritual version of Burroughs's more material regeneration, the fellaheen South lies outside of time, at least outside of profane, historical time, and is now a sort of sacred playground for the renewal of the northern civilized man. The scrap heaps of the past, of the fallen and decrepit, serve now to provide, to borrow a title from Lawrence Ferlinghetti, "a coney island of the mind." Interestingly, Ginsberg notes in his journal that reconstructing the entire city Uxmal, "they'd have a tourist attraction so vast and magical it would put their economy on a working basis" (*Mid-Fifties Journals* 41). The fellaheen culture becomes pure "past," no present and no future: the perfect ground for a spiritual imperialism.

> Pale Uxmal,
>           unhistoric, like a dream,
> Tulum shimmering on the coast in ruins;
> Chichén Itzá naked
>           constructed on a plain;
>
> ·  ·  ·  ·  ·  ·  ·  ·  ·  ·  ·  ·
> I alone know the great crystal door
>           to the House of Night,
> a legend of centuries
>           —I and a few Indians.
>                              (*Collected Poetry* 102–3)

The decay which is now Mexico, its past now its present and its future, serves as the site of a spiritual renewal for the souls living in "the motionless buildings / of New York rotting" (105). Chichan Itza is the fellaheen site of renewal, assuring a site for a redeeming movement: "there is an inner / anterior image / of divinity / beckoning me out / to pilgrimage" assuring for Ginsberg that past is not necessarily prologue. The west need not fall into decay; that there is indeed a future: "O future, unimaginable God" (106).

It is only then that he can return to the United States jumping "in time / to the immediate future" where he comes to the border "tanned and bearded / satisfying Whitman, concerned / with a few Traditions" (106, 110). Armed himself, now a prophet to

> The nation over the border
> [that] grinds its arms and dreams
>            of war: I see
> the fiery blue clash
>            of metal wheels
> clanking in the industries
>            of night, and
> detonation of infernal bombs
>
>            . . . and the silent downtown
> of the States
>            in watery dark submersion.
>                    (*Collected Poetry* 110)

His critique of American militarism has been prepared in the fellaheen land of Mexico that becomes a sacred colony, reduced to a sort of Club Med of Historical Lessons and Spiritual Renewal for the Dispirited Western Man. Sight is cleared, consciences restored, ancient Indian secrets revealed, cultures renewed. Barry Miles puts it much more succinctly: "He washed away ten years of New York soot in a tropical paradise" (*Ginsberg* 160).

Thus far I have addressed only Ginsberg's romanticization of Mexico and the historiographical aspect of such a vision. But Ginsberg's imperial metaphysics had imperial manifestations. Ginsberg quickly found himself taking on the persona of the great white explorer. On his arrival in Chiapas, ill-tempered because of the natives' failure to understand his faulty Spanish, Ginsberg met Karen Shields, who was known as the "White Goddess." She owned a local cocoa *finca* after starring in several Tarzan movies as "Jane." At first Ginsberg was interested in working with the Indians in the fields, but soon "found" himself leading an expedition to explore a nearby volcano. The transformation of Ginsberg's persona provides insight into the dynamic of the Beat in the fellaheen country. Apparently because of his whiteness Ginsberg is selected as leader and "most of the Indians followed him" (Miles, *Ginsberg* 163). Ginsberg's recounting of this period to Neal Cassady sounds much like Burroughs's own adventures in South America:

> It was a real great Life Magazine intrepid American adventure situation. I really was a great hero. . . . In Yajolon . . . I lived in the Presidente's house and strode the streets in my beard and all the Indians saluted me respectfully and asked me for volcano advice . . . and all the merchants invited me in back of their shops for coffee and the priest and I had many long afternoons over beer and theology and geology and I ate in the restaurant every evening and dined with the pilots of the crazy air service, heroes of the mountains. . . . my restaurant bills went to City Hall, and everybody in town loaned me mules and guides for further exploration, other caves came to me, I went to Petalcingo, Chillon, all the little villages and town in central Chiapas. (Miles, *Ginsberg* 163)

That Ginsberg was seduced by Burroughs's vision of the southern climes as open and utilizable is clear. Ginsberg, however, softened Burroughs's more material approach. He spiritualized it, gave it an aura of cosmic renewal, demonstrating the imperialist desire that underlies such romanticization. Imperial mysticism is soon followed by quasi-imperial action. Ginsberg found himself the leader of the Indians, the discoverer, explorer, the celebrated archetypal western man admired and desired by the fellaheen.

Of the major Beat figures, Ginsberg ultimately found, if not founded, a progressive communalism, however. As Burroughs continued to live an increasingly isolated existence in keeping with his brand of paranoid libertarianism and Jack Kerouac became increasingly paranoid and racist, never finding the refuge he sought so tragically on the road, Ginsberg seems to have realized that progress lay in a communal approach. But that would come later, after the triumvirate of Beat figures had already given powerful voice to a regressive individualism that would continue to hinder the realization of *communitas* in America.

# 2

# "With Imperious Eye"
## Kerouac's Fellaheen Western

I fly by with one quick Walt Whitman look . . .
*On the Road*

I'm an idealist who's outgrown his idealism.
35th Chorus, *Mexico City Blues*

"We laughed at how the Marxist society had finally arrived," one exec says, "but I think the real analogy is to the pioneers."
Business executive to William Whyte in his study of suburbia, *The Organization Man*, 1958

Jack Kerouac reached national recognition in the fall of 1957 with the publication of *On the Road*. The novel most resembled a draft that had been written in 1951 a few months after Kerouac returned from Mexico, as described in the book's final chapters.[1] Unable to find a publishing house that would take the risk of publishing a true-to-life account that might subject it to libel suits or obscenity charges, Kerouac increasingly lost hope of ever seeing it in print. The years between 1951 and 1957 were his most prolific period in which he wrote eight novels and four collections of poetry.

If one catalogs his novels by content, it becomes evident that while they are usually designated as "road" novels and "Lowell" novels (Kerouac's home town), they can also be seen as "U.S." novels and "travel" novels. Of these travel novels, *On the Road, Tristessa, Desolation Angels, Mexico City Blues* (poetry), *Lonesome Traveler* (a collection of separate pieces), and *Visions of Cody* all either take place in Mexico or deal extensively with Mexico as a setting. I would like to suggest that the Mexico/U.S. division is as important a symbolic binary as is the "road"/ "Lowell" division, and that the two are related in what they suggest about Kerouac's political vision and about the ideology of the Beat mission to reconstruct an American individualism against the "conformism" of the fifties.

In questioning the role of the individual within a perceived system of forced conformism and against the possibility of an egalitarian society, the Beat chose to reconstruct the individual in terms of a nineteenth-century ideology of the self that celebrated "self-reliance" as movement and expansion, personified by archetypal icons of individualism: the pioneer, trailblazer, and cowboy. The 1950s abound with these images in the popular media. The decade saw the rise of television and its most popular shows featuring westerns such as *The Rifleman, Gunsmoke, The Lone Ranger, Wagon Train, Have Gun Will Travel,* and Disney's *Davy Crockett.*[2] By 1959 there were thirty-five westerns on national television broadcast weekly. Eight of the top ten shows were westerns (Nachbar x). The movies of the decade were dominated by the genre of the western, as well as extremely popular films dealing with the legends of explorers Davy Crockett and Daniel Boone, the former beginning a nationwide trend of wearing "coon-tail hats." The novels of Louis L'Amour, Zane Grey, and Wayne D. Overholser sold millions of copies. Pulp fiction magazines devoted to western stories such as *Western Tales, Zane Grey's Western Magazine, Western Story Magazine, Blue Book, Ranch Romances, Frontiers West, Western Writers of America,* and *Roundup* were bestsellers.[3] Kerouac's use of the cowboy as a recurring image in his earlier works is not, therefore, an anomaly, but well in keeping with the 1950s popular imagination.[4]

Tellingly, television culture of the period is also marked by an abundance of family sit-coms that broadcast the image of middle-class stability and suburban civility. Through the well-known role models of Ozzie and Harriet Nelson, Robert Young in *Father Knows Best,* June and Ward Cleaver of *Leave it to Beaver,* and Ricky and Lucy Ricardo of *I Love Lucy,* to mention only the most popular of the decade, America learned that come what may, the patriarchal, bourgeois family structure was the avatar of stability and order, and that rebellion of any kind, inane as it might appear, would not, could not be tolerated. However, a juxtaposition of the domestic sit-com and the television western reveals a similar dynamic as Kerouac's road novels and his Lowell-home novels. The tension between conforming to a revitalized middle-class hegemony while attempting to keep the space open for males to expand their patriarchal reach is evident, although one might correctly argue that both the family sit-com and the western affirm a patriarchal hierarchy.

The end of the war with its attendant home boom and baby boom created the suburban space and a burgeoning crisis in the male, middle-class psyche, challenged as it was with the threat of being absorbed by domestic uniformity.[5] Its counteraction is a peculiar conflation of male domination exerted both in the home and in the projection of the male outside the home, whether in the business world, ranch, frontier, or battleground.[6] The causes of this anxiety are manifold and have been variously explained as a reaction to the perception of growing independence of women, who were entering the workforce as never before,[7] or as a reaction to the now pervasive corporate world. It was a world in which manual labor and factory work were being supplanted by white-collar work in an amorphous corporate structure that produced an alienated corporatist subjectivity, defined in part by the perception that the individual citizen had become irrelevant to the democratic process.

A critique of "normalization" in Daniel Whyte's *Organization Man* pointed to an industrialized effort to destroy the American "individual." This program was implemented through scientism, the social ethic, conformity, and testing. In *Organization Man,*

Whyte readily associates such normalization with any attempt at communal, radical democratic thought. The collective is always negative, easily manipulated as well as manipulative, conformist, and self-destructive. Whyte never seems conscious of the possibility that it is a specious individualism that allows for the formation of corporatism in the first place.

Whyte berates 1950s America for its "organization culture" and his critique approaches the technologies of "normalization" in much the same way as Foucault, twenty years later, in *Discipline and Punish*. Whyte's critique of the "social ethic" resembles the national fear of a creeping absorption of the individual. Sounding more like Ayn Rand than Foucault, Whyte writes that organization culture has given in to the social ethic that takes the creative room from the individual and cedes it to the practical, but uncreative group. In discussing the shortcomings of applying organization methods to science, Whyte uses the common language of exploration to describe the importance of the brilliant scientist working alone: "We urgently need . . . to create a climate in this country that will encourage basic discovery" (218). This climate is to be created by "the outstanding genius [who] would not prostrate himself before the group" (221).

Whyte's fear of encroaching conformity revolves around the threat to individual mobility as manifested by the ability to discover and use our American resources as opposed to foreign ideas and concepts (he writes that "we can no longer borrow ideas from abroad" [218]). Ironically, the climate of conformism, which Whyte feared was numbing Americans to the necessity of individualism, was actually very much in the public consciousness: in the writings of Kerouac and Burroughs, in the public obsessions with figures like Daniel Boone and Davy Crockett, in the mass-marketing of automobiles, and in the amusement parks such as Disney's "Discovery Land."

This dynamic was also expressed clearly in other best-selling liberal critiques such as C. Wright Mills's influential 1956 sociological study *The Power Elite* and David Riesman's *The Lonely Crowd*. In all these cases, the tension between domesticity and the projected desire to strike out for the frontier can be seen as a central antagonism between an individualism defined by personal, unrestricted movement and the forces of an immobilizing and effeminizing domesticity and bourgeois vacuity in the workplace and home.

What I suggest is that Jack Kerouac (and later Ken Kesey) gives voice to the 1950s impetus to move as the antidote to an encroaching domestic/conformist absorption of the self/individual. This threatened absorption takes on several social and political valences. While it appeared to resist conformism and domesticity, it actually resisted any kind of commitment to community and to the communal notion, and short-circuited direct forms of political participation. Thus the impetus to move provided a subversion to such conformity by taking on an isolationist and individualistic stance. The representations of these defensive stances manifest themselves in three major forms: an identification with a marginal ethnic group, an association with the myth of manifest destiny on the frontier, and a male-dominated domesticity forever resisted and deferred through the "freedom" of movement. Described in terms of concrete practice we can consider these manifestations as the construction of a liminal—and thus resistant—identity, a philosophy or ideology that formulates a land in need of a new colonization—land on which to claim a homestead—and an ideal vision of the workings of such a "home."

## The Multiplicity in Complicity

"One fast move, or I'm gone," Kerouac's persona in *Big Sur* repeats as his mantra. It is a central theme of his work. For it expresses the individual's fear of being overtaken and absorbed by the multiplicity. The multiplicity takes many forms in the work of the Beats: the family, the woman, the "wetback," the "other," the communist, the bureaucracy, an insect trust from another planet, undifferentiated tissue. Burroughs, in a mid-1980s interview, said "invasion is the basis of fear: there's no fear like invasion" (Miles, *Burroughs* 248). For Kerouac, it is a paradoxical reaction that transforms any communal action into encroachment. His reaction ("or *I'm* gone") is always to move on before his individual identity is threatened.

Consider *Big Sur*, one of Kerouac's later novels, in which he employs a Whitmanesque metaphor of "a creek having so many voices it's amazing." It is a celebratory naturalization of democratic multiplicity. But by novel's end, this vision is transformed into a terrifying cacophony of voices plotting against his sanity. The key to this horrifying vision is his emphasis on the "plot" that the voices suggest. The episode portrays not just a man going insane, as Gerald Nicosia suggests, but a growing paranoia of a conspiratorial multiplicity. In the course of the novel, the tension between the need for solitude and isolation and the attraction of society and the crowd becomes a paralyzing dread of invasion by the uncontrolled and riotous mob: "voices of the creek amusing me so much at first but in the later horror of that madness night becoming the babble and rave of evil angels in my head" (*Big Sur* 20). The political connotation suggests a fear of a radicalized democratic instinct amongst the masses.

Interestingly, because the multiplicity of voices is "irrational," one may infer a notion of rationality and a logic of the dominant through the ways that the marginal or "other" is in this instance naturalized as illogical: "soon my thoughts arent even as "rational" as that any more but become hours of raving—There are forces whispering in my ear in rapid long speeches advising and warning, suddenly other voices are shouting" (*Big Sur* 203). Kerouac's deepest moments of anxiety come from the absence of rationality; here these moments are marked with the sounds of multiplicity. Rationality is figured as univocal: peace and order established through the continued, and perhaps enforced, silence of other voices.

In the same novel, Kerouac seemingly comments on the negative impact of *On the Road*, as it has worked "too" well, having opened up a democratic vista that now invites too many participants: "No bitter complaints about society whatever from this grand and ideal man who really loves me moreover as if I deserved it, but I'm bursting to explain everything to him, not even Big Sur but the past several years, but there's no chance with everybody yakking — And in fact I can see in Cody's eyes that he can see in my own eyes the regret we both feel that recently we haven't had chances to talk whatever, like we used to do driving across America and back in the old road days, too many people now want to talk to us and tell us their stories, we've been hemmed in and surrounded and outnumbered — The circle's closed in on us the old heroes of the night" (*Big Sur* 67). Kerouac's regret stems from the growing number of voices that encircle him — suggesting restraint and immobilization — and threaten to drown him out — a threat to his individuality, a threat of personal dissolution: "I look at the moon it waves, moves, when I look at my hands and feet they creep — Everything is moving, the porch is moving like ooze and mud, the chair trembles under me." (*Big Sur* 200). Movement is here figured as lunacy, as a disease of the body, paralyzing the subject and in this sense constraining both the mind and the body.

Read as a depiction of democracy gone mad, of democracy infiltrated and made too radical and open, and thus paralyzing, this passage connects Kerouac's well-documented reactions to the 1960s counterculture to his not-so-well known sympathies with the Far Right in the 1950s. Kerouac's growing reactionism resulted from his perception that his "indifferent" (Kerouac's word for Buddhist detachment) individualistic principle had been distorted by the socially active, communal realpolitik, which he saw as residing in the "hippie" movement, a movement he associated with communism.[8]

As his hatred of communism became more and more pronounced throughout the 1960s, his racist and misogynist rancor grew increasingly virulent. Kerouac's forays into hate crime are well documented: cross-burning in Miami, Jew-baiting, increased public use of racist language. His support of Joseph McCarthy, documented from as early as 1953, four years before the publishing of *On the Road*, is particularly interesting. If McCarthyism is mass paranoia of infiltration or contamination by an inevitable communal authoritarianism, then Kerouac's defense of both McCarthy and William F. Buckley is not an aberration, but symptomatic of Beat romanticism itself, a shift that is borne out not only in the literature and the letters, but in the lives of these writers. I will concern myself with examining the defensive tactics created by Kerouac for protecting the "I" from the absorption and immobilization that threatened, both from within and abroad, the American individual in the 1950s.

Initially, we can read *On the Road* as a desire to rebuild a space for the individual man, and thus reestablish the strength of a threatened patriarchy, by going out to the frontier. This is not simply a metaphorical framing of the West or of Mexico and South America. For Kerouac, the southern lands were "fellaheen." Spengler's *Decline of the West* was a central text for him and his notion of the "fellaheen" was important in how he understood the third world. In his interpretation, the people who lived in these "primitive" and declining societies existed on the periphery of a fallen civilization waiting for its eventual recreation.

Kerouac's biographers, including Gerald Nicosia and Ann Charters, discuss Spengler's central importance to the making of a Beat historiographical logic: "Spengler's analysis of European history as occurring in cycles of cultural entropy contributed to the early Beat writers' apocalyptic vision of their times" (*Selected Letters: 1940–56* 65, n.1). Nicosia goes further, saying that Kerouac "often talked of Goethe's Faust and the way Spengler had used Faust to typify Western Man's endless reaching into space. To Jack, Spengler had found the essence of the western soul in Faust's craving for infinity" (204). It is significant that Kerouac's *Doctor Sax* is subtitled *Faust, Part III*, itself an apocalyptic vision of the old corrupt world, its civilization being swallowed up by an antediluvian snake that comes from the center of the earth. Its consumption releases doves, a symbol of cyclic renewal (its symbology borrowed from Aztec religion with which both Kerouac and Burroughs were fascinated). Carolyn Cassady describes the meaning of Spenglerian theory and its application to Mexico for Kerouac: "To him it seemed to represent a Utopian existence without hassles, a timeless peace. He and Neal favored Spengler's word 'fellaheen' to describe the culture, but since to them the term meant a people who weren't going anywhere but had already been and were resting before the next creative cycle occurred, it sounded to me like the impossible dream for these two men who loved dashing about looking for 'kicks'" (Charters 454).

As "Fellaheen Mexico" is more vividly described in Kerouac's novels, the purpose of the beat role as civilizers becomes more apparent. Kerouac and his coterie of fellow travelers serve as those who might bring the new civilization to pass. At the very least, they seek to become the prophets of an age yet to come. Whether one wants to read this literary/historiographical conceit as metaphysical longing or as political/social theory or both, it suggests that Kerouac, Burroughs, and Ginsberg were operating with a worldview that literally created lands waiting for renewal, revitalization, for cultural rebirth, views uncannily similar to nineteenth century foundations of manifest destiny.

In rejecting encroaching domesticity or "conformity," Kerouac, Burroughs, Ginsberg, and fellow travelers move in order to reestablish a strong patriarchy, create a colony and homestead in a "fellaheen" area for the purposes of establishing a male domestic sphere, itself liminal and "freewheeling," while establishing their independent identity through a self-marginalization that, more often than not, took its characteristics in appropriating ethnic or subaltern forms.

## Rancho Kerouac: Home of the New Male Domesticity

Kerouac's first novel, *The Town and the City,* later to be rewritten as *Vanity of Duluoz,* brought him an advance of one thousand dollars. He used the money to buy some land outside of Denver. His plan was to build a ranch for himself and his family: his mother Gabrielle, his sister Nin, and her husband and young son. His ambition, as Carolyn Cassady writes in her memoir *Off the Road,* was to "buy a ranch for all of us to share, and," she continues, "Neal answered with enthusiasm" (70). The correspondence regarding this ranch is interesting not only for what it suggests about Kerouac's desire to become a "westerner," but for what it portrays as an agreed upon ideal domestic arrangement. Neal Cassady describes the home he and Kerouac would build with the book advance: "for us to build a ranch, a great spread, together, would be better than renting rooms. . . . we had better start right now. . . . bring your buddies, we'll have a 7-8 bedrooms—your mother . . . and Carolyn are exactly alike—Carolyn's a great worker, and interior decorator. . . . And I'll get the money. A home—to go and come to—to grow old in—to make into a great place" (*Off the Road* 70). As early as May, 1948, Kerouac had rhapsodized to Cassady about his fantasy of living in the west. He wrote, "By Jesus Christ, I'm going to become a rancher, nothing else. I've made up my mind to become a rancher, I've learned all about it in books. . . . All I want is about 300 head, a spread that cuts enough alfalfa for them, a winter pasture, two houses for me and whoever joins me in partnership, etc. etc. . . . .And proceed to live a good life in the canyon countries, lots of forage, trees, high sharp mountain air . . . and marry a Western girl and have six kids" (*Selected Letters: 1940-56* 149). Cassady's reply gave specific shape to the growing fantasy.

> I envision Holmes, Bill Tomson, and . . . one Allen G[insberg], grubbing, scrubbing to aid, for they come in as they wish. No hard and fast, naturally, rules or obligations or expectancies or any such bourgoise [*sic*] strains in our veins toward them. The nucleus of our family then . . . : you, your mother, Paul, his wife and child, me, Carolyn and our offspring (*and* your wife?). That totals to 8 or 9, all living, striving. . . . Allen, Holmes, Tomson, and dear beautiful brother Herbert Huncke. This may seem to be becoming overdone, but, to continue, I don't really mean to include Burroughs. . . . but I do love him and Joan so much you know . . . pure speculation, but maybe visits at any rate. So, that's another 9 counting Julie and Bill junior. That makes a house that, at one time or another, ought to hold 18 people. How many rooms is that? Anywhere from 10 to 13. Kitchen, living room . . . , dining room, figure about 7-8 bedrooms. . . . Huge garden . . . Well, I'll stop. (Cassady, *Off the Road* 71)

Cassady might have gotten the idea of such a ranch from Burroughs's Texas spread he had visited the year before with Ginsberg. There Burroughs had a farm and ranch house complete with hired hand and long-standing personal friend Herbert Huncke, imported from New York City, and "wetbacks" to pick the crops.

Although its location would change throughout the years, Kerouac and Cassady continued to plan an eventual ranch-commune. When Kerouac's dream of a ranch in Colorado failed because of his mother's displeasure with Colorado and his sister's complaints, Kerouac sold the land at a loss and returned to the East Coast. Three years later, he wrote Cassady again, this time discussing the possibility of forming a communal homestead in Mexico. Influenced by Burroughs's suggestions that Mexico held cheap land and easy living, Kerouac wrote Cassady, now settled in Los Gatos, California. Kerouac's vision of Mexico as "fellaheen" began to take shape:

> We'd hang on to every cent, give the Mexicans no quarter, let em get sullen at the cheap Americans and stand side by side in defense, and make friends in the end when they saw we was poor too. Comes another Mexican revolution, we stands them off with our Burroughsian arsenal bought cheap on Madros St. and dash to big city in car for safety shooting and pissing as we go; whole Mex army follows hi on weed; now no worries any more. Just sit on roof hi enjoying hot dry sun and sound of kids yelling and have us wives and American talk of our own as well as exotic kicks and regular old honest Indian kicks. Become Indians. . . . I personally play mambo in local catband, because of this we get close to them and go to town. Wow. How's about it? Hurry to N.Y. so we can plan and all take off in big flying boat . . . across crazy land. (Charters 211)

Although Kerouac and Cassady never realized their plans, they did share a household. Carolyn Cassady describes the zeal with which Neal enticed Kerouac to come and live with them in 1951. He wrote to him:

> . . . but listen now, you'd have perfect freedom, great place in which to write, car to cut around in . . . a spot with absolutely everything you could need already set up for you. . . .and Al Hinkle and maybe Bill Tomson and whore houses . . . and freedom, man, freedom, no bull, Carolyn loves you, be like your mama without you having any need to cater like to her. . . . Carolyn wants to try and make it up to you. We could try by way of a few group orgies or whatever, although this might be sensibly be

postponed until after Oct. [Carolyn's due date] because she's as big as our house. . . . Incidently when all is lost you and I will go to Morocco and build railroad for a thousand a month. All we do is ride while African coolies dump ballast over roadbed. (*Off the Road* 146–47)

At this point, Kerouac was attempting to finish *On the Road*. This is significant for what Kerouac and Cassady's shared domestic fantasies suggest in reading a work written during Kerouac's most "optimistic" period, and for what it reveals about a novel that already contained the seeds that would subvert any subversive context to which Kerouac's readers would lay claim. In *On the Road*, Kerouac essentially writes a modern western in which the "heroes of the American night" set out to reestablish a clear connection to a patriarchal past, and lay claim to a frontierland in which they may then live without constraint of a perceived controlling matriarchy. Their liminal status is confirmed by a self-marginalization gained through appropriation of ethnic identity.

Through its racist conception of the "negro" as a psychotic figure, Norman Mailer's essay on Beat appropriation of black culture—"The White Negro"—points to the use of the ethnic figure as somehow outside of the quotidian, stultifying, middle-class landscape. Of course, Mailer does not make clear that such appropriation is made upon false premises (the ethnic "other" is somehow "naturally" violent or liminal), nor does he fault the "hipster" for his bad faith (since the hipster is always able to renounce his self-marginalization and join the mainstream, an option not open to "Negroes" or "Mexicans"). In regard to civil and economic rights, the 1950s offered the ethnic person no such freedom. Yet, despite Mailer's profound lack of understanding of the "mind" of the racial other, he does clearly articulate the uses of such an appropriation on the part of the hipster. In the case of Kerouac, I would claim that he more often imagines himself as "Mexican," although at times he pursues very specific "Negro" cultural attributes as well as "Indian" characteristics.

The writing of *On the Road*, in both its drafts and publication drafts, was quite a complex process. The novel was rewritten several times; one draft ultimately became the impressionistic and experimental *Visions of Cody,* and *Pic,* published posthumously, constitutes a final version in which Sal Paradise and Dean Moriarty are transformed into two Negro brothers. The version finally published as *On the Road* in 1957 was written by Kerouac in 1951 about his real-life travels across the country and into Mexico with Neal Cassady between 1947 and 1951. Much has been written about the futility of the travels chronicled in the novel. Even Burroughs wrote Ginsberg that Cassady and Kerouac's trips were "pointless and selfish." However, what has been overlooked is that the plot that revolves around frenzied movement is actually thematically fueled by the search for a both a literal father (Mr. Moriarty) and an archetypal father. Sal Paradise (Kerouac), who has no father and lives with his aunt, is immediately taken with the desire to go west and find Dean Moriarty (himself already a father) and to assist him in his search for his alcoholic, vagabond father.

This search takes on a spiritual dimension in the novel, establishing a motif of father/son figures as Paradise makes his way to Denver to join Moriarty. As he hitchhikes through the Midwest he meets a vagabond named Mississippi Gene, who has taken a young boy under his wing and is teaching him the ways of the road. Aside from its sentimental valence, Kerouac suggests that the ultimate father figure is the itinerant, the "bum" who travels unencumbered, thus conflating patriarchy with personal negative liberty, and with wanderlust, central to reconstituting male power in the face of a domineering feminine suburban creep.[9]

Moriarty sees his father "everywhere," as Carlo Marx (Allen Ginsberg) suggests to him: "remember, you pointed out the old bum with the baggy pants and said he looked just like your father?" (*On the Road* 48). The figure of Mr. Moriarty thus becomes emblematic of an archetypal patriarchal wanderer. Upon arriving in Denver, Paradise tours the streets where Moriarty senior and junior lived, noting that "It seemed to me every bum on Larimer St. maybe was Dean Moriarty's father . . . I went in the Windsor Hotel, where father and son had lived . . . " (58). Paradise's journey becomes a pilgrimage to uncover the genealogy of his "sideburned hero of the snowy West" who signifies "a new kind of American

saint." For Moriarty, his desire to find his own sense of independence and power is embedded in tales of his childhood mission,
which then becomes the "mission" of the book: "I had to find my
father wherever he is and save him . . . " (184).

The statement combines the past tense with the present and
implies the future. The pattern of the novel and of the lives of the
central characters is to find and save the "father" in themselves. In
his desire to emulate Moriarty, Paradise must also align himself
within this genealogy, and as he travels under the tutelage of Moriarty, he begins to assert his patriarchal lineage: "I saw myself in
Middle America, a patriarch" (*On the Road* 179). Ultimately Moriarty's "father" is the truly free man, the hobo, and since when he
"thinks about his father . . . and where he might be, which could be
anywhere," the father is in fact "everywhere" (232). Kerouac thus
establishes a ubiquitous patriarchy that takes as its central characteristic personal liberty, liminal and not constrained to any one
place. Moriarty and Paradise discuss the virtues of being "bums":
"'Why not, man? . . . There's no harm in ending that way. You
spend a whole life of non-interference with the wishes of others,
including politicians and the rich, and nobody bothers you and
you cut along and make it your own way.' I agreed with him. . . .
'What's your road, man?—holyboy road, madman road, rainboy
road, guppy road, any road. It's an anywhere road for anybody
anyhow. Where body how?'" (*On the Road* 251). Ultimate freedom
begins with asserting a male mobility.

This patriarchal impulse, however, must have a space in which
it can ultimately settle, that is, colonize. For Kerouac, as well as
Burroughs and Ginsberg, this is theorized as "fellaheen." Paradise
begins to see the fellaheen on his first cross-country trip where he
sees immobile, sullen "Indians": "Here Eddie stood forlornly in
the road in front of a staring bunch of short, squat Omaha Indians who had nowhere to go and nothing to do" (*On the Road* 21).
For Kerouac, his travels over the years would be in lands that he
continued to describe as fellaheen. Since by definition, the fellaheen are people living not only in the margins of society, but in
the margin of history, in becoming fellaheen Kerouac attains a
space outside the social structure he fears: feminine, domestic,
rooted, threatening to male wholeness.

In language that combines religious fervor with an imperial imperative reminiscent of Manifest Destiny, Paradise looks over Denver as the "Promised Land . . . and I could see the greater vision of San Francisco beyond, like jewels in the night" (*On the Road* 16). As he continues to wax poetic about the West, he conflates his life with the life of early America: "I was halfway across America, at the dividing line between the East of my youth and the West of my future" (17). The language of national expansion, becomes his own personal metaphor. It alludes in many ways to Whitman's "Song of the Open Road" as well as to Whitman's call for a poet who will expand with the nation.[10] Kerouac had a vision of Dean Moriarty as the hero of this expansion, an outlaw whose "criminality was not something that sulked and sneered; it was a wild yea-saying overburst of American joy; it was Western, the west wind, an ode from the Plains, something new, long prophesied long a-coming" (11).

The novel takes Paradise to California where he becomes a police guard assigned to a Sausalito workers' camp. According to his biographer Barry Gifford, Kerouac enjoyed carrying a gun, going so far as to take it with him during drinking binges in San Francisco where he would occasionally use it to scare homosexuals. However, Sal Paradise is more concerned with the hope that California will provide the culmination for his moving "spiritual" quest: "Somewhere along the line I knew there'd be girls, visions, everything; somewhere along the line the pearl would be handed to me" (*On the Road* 11). However, the allure of California proves to be illusory. Paradise reflects on the tawdriness of Los Angeles, and in a 1947 letter to Allen Ginsberg, Kerouac proclaims that California "is a shallow place. It's all show. There is nothing substantial. It hasn't got the beautiful spirituality of the South, nor the brooding Eastern qualities, nor even the good health and vigour of a Kansas City—it's got nothing" (*Selected Letters: 1940-56* 131). The restlessness, the "boredom" with California, prompts Paradise into leaving, in the same way that Kerouac and Burroughs continued to move. "Movement" itself is the cure for stagnation and boredom. Paradise foreshadows Kerouac's eventual desire to go to Mexico and Burroughs's travels in South America. "Here I was at the end of America—no more land—and now there was nowhere to go but back. I determined at least to make my trip a circular one; I decided then and there to go to Hollywood and back through Texas to see my bayou gang" (*On the Road* 78). This frames his spiritual quest in terms of finding more land. Because coming to the "end" imperils his ability to move, he must now travel in a circle, at least until he discovers other lands.

In Los Angeles, Paradise enacts his first attempt at self-marginalization through sexual relations with the "other," in what, I would suggest, provides a provisional manner of vicarious "movement" through the "other's" culture, enacting, in different form, the principle of travel. In a pattern to be repeated, Paradise's affair with the "Mexican girl" enacts the "conquest" of a woman of color, using her as a sexual conduit into a vicarious ethnicity while simultaneously exercising a form of domination over the feminine.[11]

Kerouac repeatedly had affairs with women of color and then wrote a novel or long piece in which he would agonize over his desire to enjoin the culture that the woman represented: his affair with Bea Franco is told in *On the Road,* his infatuation with Esperanza Villanueva is the subject of his Mexican novel *Tristessa,* and his affair with Alene Lee, a black woman he met in New York, is the subject of *The Subterraneans.*

In *On the Road* Paradise sees a young Mexican woman on a bus, and decides to strike up a conversation with her. He is "tired of himself," and the "strange girl" may hold new adventure for him. After a bout of paranoia in which he imagines that the woman, Terry, is a prostitute, he decides that he will accompany her to the Salinas Valley and become a crop picker long enough to save money for his trip back east. In a very revealing allusion, Paradise imagines himself and the woman as Joel McCrea and Veronica Lake in *Sullivan's Travels,* Preston Sturges's 1942 classic film that follows a wealthy movie director as he dresses like a hobo in order to find out how the "other half lives." The film's message concludes that social problems cannot be alleviated through "understanding" them, or through charity (Sullivan is nearly killed when handing money out to the "bums" who have been kind to him during the course of the film); the only option is to "make them laugh," a universal salve to the eternal problem of poverty. In much the same way, Paradise travels, deciding that the real problem is mortality, and thus not ameliorable.

As they undertake the journey to central California, Paradise takes on the persona of the subaltern: "We stood under a road-lamp, thumbing, when suddenly cars full of young kids roared by with streamers flying, 'Yaah! Yaah! we won!' they all shouted. . . . I hated every one of them. Who did they think they were, yaah-ing at somebody on the road just because they were little high-school punks and their parent carved the roast beef on Sunday afternoons?" (*On the Road* 88). This passage underscores his desire to find a space from which to critique the domestic, suburban sphere of roast beef and Sunday afternoons, by using the role that Terry proffers to him as her lover. With her and her brother, a "wild-buck Mexican hot cat with a hunger for booze," Paradise is able to pronounce that he has become "other": "They thought I was Mexican, of course, and in a way, I am" (*On the Road* 97).

Kerouac romanticizes the reality of migrant labor, desiring in-clusion into the communal existence of the poor, valley migrants, while such inclusion remains abstract or romantic. Paradise en-counters the rigors of picking: "I knew nothing about picking cotton. . . . Moreover, my fingertips began to bleed; I needed gloves. . . . My back began to ache. But it was beautiful kneeling and hiding in that earth. If I felt like resting I did, with my face on the pillow of brown moist earth (*On the Road* 96). Paradise's ideal-ization of the labor, which is performed by Terry and her family, transforms it from the back-breaking task that it is into a form of restful avoidance. The "brown moist earth" offers the "rest" that ethnic liminality provides the white male under assault. Here, this temporary escape into the world of the Mexican migrant figures as primal, simple way of life that no longer exists for the postwar American male and the confusing state of modernity that awaits in the city. Kerouac's romantic desire for a primal connection to the earth, *"tierra,"* is provided through the eroticized figure of "Terry," who is reduced to a sexually utilized function of other-ness. However, the real work of survival continues around him, as

Terry and her child pick "twice as fast" as he can and go on ahead leaving "piles of clean cotton to add to my bag" (*On the Road* 97).

Paradise soon feels that he cannot provide for Terry and her child and decides to leave. Although Kerouac suggests that Paradise is leaving because he feels guilt, I suggest that it is also a response to the reality of migrant work, the underside of a mobility that does not allow for free movement and fuels his desire to leave: "I hid in the grapevines, digging it all, I felt like a million dollars; I was adventuring in the crazy American night" (*On the Road* 101). The threat of being absorbed into a ready-made family—Terry, her child, and her extended "fellaheen family"—would spell the end of his "American adventure" (98). In this affair Paradise has managed to live as ethnic other, on the move, living for mañana, a philosophy he attributes to the Mexican. More important, by leaving when it appears his mobility may be threatened, he is able to recreate the most liberating of moves—escape. In language that alludes strongly to Hemingway's stories of men leaving women, Paradise has the sense, as he looks back at Terry waving sadly, that "this is the end of something" (101). However, for the privileged mobile subject like Paradise, it is also the beginning of something else.

Once freed from the danger of familial restraint, Paradise once again begins to bemoan the lack of experience that society affords the white man. While wandering alone in Denver, he begins to reflect on his desire to join the subaltern:

> At lilac evening I walked with every muscle aching among the lights of 27th and Welton in the Denver colored section, wishing I were a Negro, feeling that the best the white world had offered was not enough ecstasy for me, not enough life, joy, kicks, darkness, music, not enough night . . . I wished I were a Denver Mexican, or even a poor overworked Jap, anything but what I was so drearily, a "white man" disillusioned. All my life I'd had white ambitions; that was why I'd abandoned a good woman like Terry in the San Joaquin Valley. I passed the dark porches of Mexican and Negro homes. . . . I was only myself, Sal Paradise, sad, strolling in this violet dark, this unbearably sweet night, wishing I could exchange worlds with the happy, true-hearted, ecstatic Negroes of America. (*On the Road* 180)

The position of the "white man" is made tragic, the position of the ethnic other, as long as it remains abstract, romantic.

The language of exchange is here also important in understanding Kerouac's basic economy of movement not only as a metaphor, but more fundamentally as an endorsement of the equally romanticized free market. Kerouac's facility for taking on liminal identities is based on his assumed right to trade, to exchange, to try before he buys. Although in this passage he feels the burden of his whiteness, it does not last long, for as he moves within and without these various strata, Kerouac establishes the necessity of a sort of consumption and appropriation of various identities and ethnicities. Yet those shifts are never dangerously liminal, for they become products, merchandise for which Kerouac advertises. Much as the logic of 1950s merchandising replaced freedom with product choice, liberty for Kerouac is trying on different ethnic garb.

This disabling of the possible redressive action entailed in "difference" minimizes the possibility that the black subject might want to exchange places with the white subject. Instead of the more dangerous aspects of difference (which might be addressed and corrected in a radical "equalizing" move) such danger is replaced by a seemingly but deceptively benign consumerism: difference as mere choice — *not* unstable, competitive class and racial hierarchies. As long as this liminality is maintained as a consumable product, it is kept safe. An illusory egalitarianism of white subjectivity is established at the cost of objectifying ethnic identity for consumption. Thus the white outsider can experience a community without joining it. This results in two very different understandings of difference. For the marginalized and appropriated ethnic person marked by color, difference is a fixating hierarchy of power and agency; for the white subject, difference is an exercise of choice for those lucky enough to have the power of agency.

As Paradise finds his way back east, with his newfound patriarchal strength, he is able to associate with the east (that is the "east of his youth" and the youth of the nation) and its imperial past.

I thought all the wilderness of America was in the West till the ghost of the Susquehanna showed me different. No, there is a wilderness in the East; it's the same wilderness Ben Franklin plodded in the oxcart days when he was postmaster, the same as it was when Washington was a wild-buck Indian fighter, when Daniel Boone told stories by Pennsylvania lamps and promised to find the Gap, when Bradford built his road and men whooped her up in log cabins. There were not great Arizona spaces for the little man, just the bushy wilderness of eastern Pennsylvania, Maryland, and Virginia, the backroads, the black-tar roads that curve among the mournful rivers like Susquehanna, Mononga- hela, old Potomac and Monocacy. (*On the Road* 105)

Paradise, finds the father in the nation's history, in its mythos of the founding fathers, and in the commonality of pioneering movement, which he has had the courage to emulate. Kerouac as- sociates the real man, the moving man, with the American arche- types of the Indian-fighter, explorer, colonialist, and trailblazer. Much like the settlers of the eighteenth century, Kerouac sees a wide-open frontier populated only by fellaheen subjects waiting for a new era. Paradise establishes a genealogy that connects him directly to the fathers of the past, and suggests for him a future as prophet. Just as Whitman found in Emerson's "The Poet" the call to "write" America, Kerouac finds his calling to write anew that frontier spirit that has been settled, suburbanized, feminized, and domesticated, and finds that the hope for revitalizing masculine individuality lies in the mythos of a still-vigorous and resonant imperialist, masculine imperative.

## Mexico: A Fellaheen Western

The novel's climax is the trip that Paradise and Moriarty take to Mexico. There, Paradise finds that the search for the father must culminate in the reconstruction of the spirit of the father. In an ironic movement toward submission to the law of the father, Ker- ouac ultimately suggests that radical individualism must culmi- nate in submissive individualism. This form of individualism submits passively while projecting an illusory self-reliance and rebelliousness.

Mexico for Paradise and Moriarity is not only a land of liminal play, but also the space where the serious business of forming a visual imperialism must take place. Shortly before Paradise leaves for Mexico, he confides in Carlo Marx that he is being haunted by a "Shrouded Traveler": "It haunted and flabbergasted me, made me sad. It had to do somewhat with the Shrouded Traveler. Carlo Marx and I once sat down together, knee to knee, in two chairs, facing, and I told him a dream I had about a strange Arabian figure that was pursuing me across the desert; that I tried to avoid; that finally overtook me just before I reached the Protective City" (*On the Road* 124). The dark figure pursues the lone traveler, which puts Paradise in danger not of an encroaching conformity, but of the forces of the marginal. White man is threatened by black man. The price of wanderlust, of identifying too closely with the liminal ethnic, is perhaps conquest, absorption, even the death of white identity. The pursued Paradise must return to the isolated Protected City of Kerouac's dream. The appropriation of ethnic identity is thus shown to be only a temporary, liberalizing moment, from which the white Beat may retreat into the structure of white patriarchy, a privileged position that ultimately provides stability and a segregation from marginal forces.

The trip is figured as western man's archetypal journey: the men leave maternal, castrating women behind in search of more worlds to conquer. Paradise finds Moriarty in San Francisco and "rescues" him from the "sewing circle" of women who steal his joy. The "two broken-down heroes of the Western night" make a pact that the ultimate goal of their wandering is to find the father: "I think he's in Denver—this time we must absolutely find him, he may be in County Jail, he may be around Larimer Street again, but he's to be found. Agreed?" (*On the Road* 191). Thus the Mexican trip serves many purposes. It provides the occasion for the continuation of the mythic journey after Paradise has reached the West Coast and found that he must keep moving, since "our one and noble function of the time" is to *"move"* (133). The nobility of their actions has to do with finding that which eludes the grasp of the modern American male: mission, patriarchy, a sense of primal freedom.

When asked by an interviewer what poet he most admired and resembled, Kerouac replied that he had an affinity and sympathy for T. S. Eliot. The connection at first seems odd: Kerouac's manic improvisational poetry and Eliot's staid, carefully considered, academic verse.[12] But the comparison bears some examination when one considers that both Eliot's and Kerouac's work yearns for fragments to shore against their ruins. Both were religious (Kerouac French Catholic, Eliot Anglican), sympathetic to eastern metaphysics, and both sought a cultural and personal restoration through an ethnographic literary expedition that involved combing through "fellaheen" sites for valuable, meaningful material. Kerouac stated that the Beat movement rejected the Lost Generation for their cynicism, and claimed a lineage to the romantics and early modernists. The postwar literary movement of Kerouac, Burroughs, Ginsberg, and Kesey in a sense finds a patriarchal lineage that connects them to Eliot, Pound, Whitman, Emerson, and Thoreau. Kerouac's journeys to Mexico are, for him, a trip through the Waste Land where wandering like Eliot's Tiresias (see the final chapter of *Tristessa*), he attempts to find a restorative primal meaning.

Kerouac's mission is much more conservative than has been claimed by his more sympathetic critics. The Transcendentalist-Modernist-Beat lineage suggests a logic evident in American literature, by which the individual can act and move freely, yet craves ceding ultimate power to a stabilizing, regulating structure, whether it be Emerson's corporatist individualism and the Oversoul, Thoreau's pantheism and his eventual return to the city, Whitman's kosmic consciousness, Eliot's social and religious tradition, or Pound's artistic fascism and Confucianism. This tendency in Kerouac is manifest in the division between "Lowell" and "road" novels, and between his experience in the United States and Mexico. As in the westerns popular in the period, most notably *Shane*, Kerouac confronts the tension between a desire to create a homestead and an impulse to move on and avoid the stasis that threatens the masculine figure with domesticity. Thus the homesteading impulse is made imperialistic in order to resist feminization. The impulse toward personal liberty is structured and stripped of its revolutionary power by hierarchical racialization, which allows for a temporary liminality while keeping a rigid differentiation between the races as protection against absorption.

In *On the Road* this delicate balance is achieved by being "Mexican" in the United States, and by becoming "white" in Mexico. This biracialization results in some astonishingly clever shifts in what I call Kerouac's "Fellaheen Western." That Kerouac intends his most famous novel as a sort of western is made clear as Paradise and Moriarty sleep in an all-night movie house: "The picture was Singing Cowboy Eddie Dean and his gallant white horse Bloop, that was number one; number two . . . was a picture about Istanbul. We saw both of these things six times during the night. We saw them waking, we heard them dreaming, we sensed them dreaming, we were permeated completely with the strange Gray Myth of the West and weird dark Myth of the East when morning came. All my actions since then have been dictated automatically to my subconscious by this horrible osmotic experience" (*On the Road* 244). The scene is an extraordinary revelation of the instillation of an imperialist imperative in the subconscious of the American mind. Yet Kerouac does not reject the colonialist mindset even while recognizing its effect on his behavior and the critique it levels at America's history. Rather, he recognizes it as metanarrative, inescapable and pure, as founding myth, and a cultural necessity. It is this restorative project, in some sense akin to restoration of the father, to which the road of the title leads.

The foray south of the border begins with an enthusiasm reminiscent not simply of a tourist or traveler, but of a more ambitious project: "Do you know there's a road that goes down Mexico and all the way to Panama? . . . Yes! You and I, Sal, we'd dig the whole world with a car like because, man, the road must eventually lead to the whole world" (*On the Road* 231). Although Dean Moriarty's use of "dig" is colloquial, its archeological connotation suggests a deeper need to find a primal truth and appropriate its "vitality." Going south was often conceptualized as an anthropological or archeological project by the Beats: aside from legal and economic reasons, Burroughs sees his search for yage as a scientific expedition, Ginsberg's trip into the Yucatan jungles results in the "discovery" of a huge cavern in which he fantasized himself as a German geologist; and Kerouac's "research" into Aztec myths influenced his writing of *Doctor Sax* and the structure of its apocalyptic conclusion. The excursions into Mexico and South America represent a considerable shift from the self-marginalization that the Beats underwent in the United States. Once outside of American borders, the need for artificial liminality is unnecessary. Kerouac does not need to be "Mexican" or "black" in order to defend himself against encroaching domesticity. In Mexico and in South America, the Beat can once again be white, and in fact, must be white to protect his identity. In Mexico, Burroughs's bohemian sensitivities shift quickly toward the squeamish histrionics of a pampered American tourist: "There are no sidewalks, people shit all over the street then lie down and sleep in it with flies crawling in and out of their mouths" (*Letters of Burroughs* 63).

In Mexico, the association with the marginalized, operating in California in the novel's first half, is jettisoned as quickly as Kerouac/Paradise jettisons the Mexican girl, her family, and his wish to be Mexican when a communal domesticity threatens. It is in these moments of ethnic appropriation and disappropriation that the "core" identity of Kerouac and company is most clearly understood. In the allusion to the dream of the pursuing Arab and the walls of the Protective City, we find that its foundation is white, American-made, and ultimately impermeable.

I am not claiming that the imperialist imperative takes the same form as its more martial manifestations in the nineteenth and twentieth centuries. Rather, it takes the form of the visual, a technology of cultural evaluation and appropriation; it takes shape as the "eyeball kicks" about which Kerouac writes so enthusiastically. And yet, this "new" cultural imperialism, while less aggressive, serves much the same psychic and nationalist purposes as the Mexican-American War or the wars against Native American tribes. It provides Kerouac and company with a sense of power, of being in a land where he is superior, knowledgeable, and at the top of an intercultural hierarchy. Mexico is incapable of challenging his individual sovereignty in the way it is threatened in his own land.

With Moriarty figured as "mad Ahab at the wheel," and Paradise as the sidekick taking in the sights "with imperious eye," the expedition begins with a candid expression of the aggression with which this southern movement is fueled. "Suddenly I had a vision of Dean, a burning shuddering frightful Angel, palpitating toward me across the road, approaching like a cloud, with enormous speed. . . . I saw his huge face over the plains with the mad bony purpose and the gleaming eyes . . . I saw the path it burned over the road; it even made its own road and went over the corn, through cities, destroying bridges, drying rivers. It came like wrath to the West. . . . Everything was up, the jig and all. Behind him charred ruins smoked" (*On the Road* 259). This passage raises key questions as to what the "mad bony purpose" reflected in Moriarty's eyes means. Unlike the claim by Burroughs that Neal Cassady and Jack Kerouac had no purpose or logic in their travels, the "heroes of the Western night" do have a rationale. What Moriarty and Paradise flee is as important as what they are seeking in the "magic south." The emphasis on the force of Moriarty's will making its own road and laying waste to the surrounding countryside links the idea of pioneering with a scorched earth policy—a literal trailblazing.

Ironically, the path of destruction devastates those very structures that institutionalize patriarchal individualism: the city and its corporatist discipline, the farm with its idealized domestic space and work ethic. The destruction of the civilized reaches biblical proportions as Dean Moriarty, the harbinger of liberating individualism, brings a "purifying" destruction to the West. The "jig" is brought to an end, which signifies a beginning whose meaning can "only" be found in Mexico: "I couldn't imagine this trip. It was the most fabulous of all. It was no longer east-west, but magic south. We saw a vision of the entire Western Hemisphere rockribbing clear down to Tierra del Fuego and us flying down the curve of the world into other tropics and other worlds. 'Man, this will finally take us to IT!' said Dean with definite faith. He tapped my arm. 'Just wait and see. Hoo! Whee!'" (*On the Road* 266).

The "IT" can only be found in the Fellaheen ruins, among the charred remains of an ancient primacy. Whereas the classic American western seeks to mythologize the struggle between nature and man, between the forces of nature and civilization, the fellaheen western dismisses the dehumanizing enervating forces of society and seeks to restore the potency of the masculine individual: the strong man, the father, a humanized sovereign. This is Kerouac in his most radical moment; his strength, and what is most alluring to the 1950s generation of readers and critics faced with the demands of corporatist conformity, is his ability as a general diagnostician. Where Kerouac fails is in making the distinction between "Organization Man" and "organizing," between bourgeois domesticity and communal participation and activism. And thus Kerouac's fellaheen western hero seeks not to attack the forces that divide and compartmentalize humanity (which would mean creating an egalitarian society), but instead to recreate an older "primal" masculinity: one that combats the feminization of society, sets a racial hierarchy in place, and answers the immobilization of corporatism with a demand for the freedom to move, an answer already endorsed, indeed developed through the market system to quell such dissent.

The search for such a masculine form begins with the will to move and culminates in the finding of the father: "Here were the three of us—Dean looking for his father, mine dead, Stan fleeing his old one, and going off into the night together" (*On the Road* 267). To seek and to find become therefore reliant upon a series of visual technologies: observation, analysis, objectification, and a double-perception of the self—the self as seen in the eyes of the other. The previously "Mexican" Paradise becomes profoundly white, male, and American. He also becomes an observer of the alien, himself a self-aware object of the alien other's gaze. Ultimately, he becomes a collector, "qualified" to find the authentic, the primal, the valuable. This position is predicated upon movement as a form of exchange and choice. This reservation establishes the extent and limits of the dissent that Kerouac and his fellow-travelers were willing to risk.

In Laredo, "the end of America" (*On the Road* 273), Paradise begins to sense the "chaos" in the land of liminality. The marginalization that has served to isolate and protect him in the United States becomes unnecessary. In the borderland, structure and authority fall away. Paradise assesses the border guards: "The Mexicans looked at our baggage in a desultory way. They weren't like officials at all" (274). It becomes apparent that for Kerouac liminality, borderland heterogeneity, is not a matter of moving beyond the impingement of authoritarian structure, but instead offers a space free of all authority, where every individual can become his own sovereign. It liberates, while calling for the strength of the colonizer. Mexico is here feminized as inviting and seductive, as soft and weak. It does not take long for the conversation between the men to turn toward the idea of conquest:

> "Now, Sal, we're leaving everything behind us and entering a new and unknown phase of things. All the years and troubles and kicks—and now this! so that we can safely think of nothing else and just go on ahead with our faces stuck out like this . . . and understand the world as, really and genuinely speaking, other Americans haven't done before us—they were here, weren't they? The Mexican war. Cutting across with cannon.
>
> "This road," I told him, "is also the route of old American outlaws who used to skip over the border and go down to old Monterrey, so if you'll look out on that graying desert and picture the ghost of an old Tombstone hellcat making his lonely exile gallop into the unknown, you'll see further." (*On the Road* 277)

This passage between Paradise and Moriarty reflects complex associations and transformations. The journey turns adventure (kicks) into a new phase of exploration. However, this exploration is undertaken with a certain "safety" associated with the fact that they no longer need a marginalized persona. In Mexico, appropriating a marginalized identity does not equal a defensive resistance to systemic forces. In a fellaheen nation, the resilient individual must demonstrate strength.

When Moriarty muses that no other Americans can understand the sense of vitality he feels in a fellaheen society, he stops short when he recalls that there are Americans who have felt as he does: soldiers in the Mexican-American War. Paradise's reply continues the train of thought, as he imagines them on the same "road" as the one taken by American outlaws. The comparisons complement each other perfectly. In Mexico, the true American is a conqueror; in the United States, the true American is an outlaw; in both cases, the masculine subject is on the move. But to continue with the figure of the conqueror and of the outlaw, Kerouac suggests that in the United States, the individual must defend himself by remaining outside the system, outside of structure. The outlaw is a liminal figure. He is not a criminal, subject to the law and to its transgression, but outside of the entire system of sociojuridical subjection. Likewise, the figure of the "other" retains similar qualities (although the similarity is only advantageous to the romantic Kerouac; when he is "Mexican" is always free to become "white"). The American in Mexico does not need to maintain an external relation to the law or society, but must become a soldier who in turn must either conquer or risk being absorbed into the masses of the powerless and weak.

Obviously, Kerouac's notion of conquest has no martial intent. The intent of the tour is restorative, its logic ethnographic, its purpose the recovery of a fully armored individualism. The ideology of exceptionalism behind the westward expansion included a superior national identity justified in exploitative colonization. Kerouac's form of imperialism also allows him to feel justified in pursuing an individualist identity through the appropriation of fellaheen inferiors.

So far I have suggested that the fellaheen western serves several purposes: it dismisses the need for "society," attempts to restore a masculine strength, seeks to protect the individuality of the hero, and it accomplishes these things through an imperial relation to the local fellaheen expressed through visual techniques of observation and evaluation. The traveler "sees" all that he can, freely observing and searching for the "truth" that is evident in the lives of the primal subjects of his gaze. As Paradise observes that their movement through Mexico is "[n]ot like driving across Carolina, or Texas, or Arizona, or Illinois; but like driving across the world and into the places where we would finally learn ourselves among the Fellaheen Indians of the world, the essential strain of the basic primitive, wailing humanity that stretches in a belt around the equatorial belly of the world" (*On the Road* 281). The essence of the fellaheen retains its primacy, its connection to the earth; his existence is *of* the earth. The observation by Paradise that the "Indians . . . were not fools, they were not clowns; they were great, grave Indians and they were the source of mankind and the fathers of it" (281) is not, misguided as that would be, a declaration of some direct lineage. It is an "empirical" statement of the unchanged relation between the indigenous peoples of Mexico to the "land" in its broadest archetypal connotation. When he claims that "they knew who was the father and who was the son of antiquity of life on earth, and made 'history' and the Apocalypse" (281), he does not claim the Indian as a true primogenitor: Indian "father" to Beat "son." Rather, it posits that the true individual may absorb the primacy of the fellaheen father, and thus became the father. For Kerouac, the search for the father is complete when the masculinized individual recognizes the unassailable father within himself.

This recognition has the potential to restore to the "outlaw" in his own country, the power of the conqueror. Of course, it does not. As Kerouac seems to understand, this is because reconciliation is achieved only in the gaze of the fellaheen, in their "earnest, big brown eyes," "their great brown, innocent eyes": "Look at those eyes! . . . They were like the eyes of the Virgin Mother when she was with child" (297, 298). The fellaheen wait on the margins of history, waiting for a messianic moment, for the coming of the last man and the advent of the superman father. A Nietzschean historiographical logic prevails in *On the Road*. And seen in this light, Kerouac's later reaction against 1960s counterculture as weak, feminine, and dangerously egalitarian is perfectly logical.

As Sal leaves Mexico after being deserted by Dean Moriarty, he takes the mantle from a literary father-poet who closely resembles

Walt Whitman: "a tall old man with flowing white hair came clomping by with a pack on his back, and when he saw me as he passed, he said, "Go moan for man," and clomped on back to his dark. Did this mean that I should at last go on my pilgrimage on foot on the dark roads around America?" (306). The answer is yes, and Kerouac/Paradise sets out to live out and write his own "Song of the Open Road."

The final lines of *On the Road,* testify to the ultimate failure of atomistic, masculine individualism. The "father" does not exist; he is never realized or restored. Instead Paradise mourns his loneliness, the loss of community. Paradise's final words echo Kerouac's own futile loneliness and his longing for companionship: "I think of Dean Moriarty, I even think of Old Dean Moriarty the father we never found, I think of Dean Moriarty" (310).

## Leaving Home Behind

In early January 1952, Kerouac arrived in Los Gatos, California to live with the Cassadys. This period has been well-documented in Carolyn Cassady's autobiography, Ginsberg's diary, and several biographies, as well as in the film *Heartbeat*. Yet the emphasis in each of these works has been on the romantic tryst that developed between Carolyn and Jack at the behest of Neal Cassady. However, Carolyn describes the affair as a gateway into inclusion in what had been until then, a strictly male camaraderie. She writes, "The hope that my gamble would change the pattern of our lives was well founded. Like night changing into day, everything was showered with new light. Butterflies bursting from cocoons had nothing on me. Now, I was a part of all they did; I felt like the sun of their solar system. All revolved around me. Besides, I was now a real contributor for once; my housework and childcare had a purpose that was needed and appreciated. I was functioning as a female and my men were supportive. . . . I never felt left out anymore. They'd address remarks to me and include me with smiles and pats or request my view" (*Off the Road* 168).

For a short time, Carolyn found satisfaction as an object of tri-angulated desire by Jack and Neal, in a "game" that Carolyn later described in terms of a power struggle between the two men. Nor was it the first or last time that Kerouac and Cassady would share lovers. Cassady encouraged Kerouac to have sexual relations with his first wife, Luanne Henderson (Mary Lou in *On the Road*), as well as with his later mistress in San Francisco, Jackie Gibson Mercer (Willamina "Billie" Dabney in *Big Sur*). While the "free love" aspect of Beat philosophy has been discussed as a precursor of the later "free love" aspect of the counterculture, this "sharing" of women in a domestic space of ultimate "freedom" requires a deeper discussion. As Cassady described it, it recreates the do mestic sphere into one dominated by males, in which women are shared as objects of possession, and in which the potential of im-mobilization by family and community is minimized.[13]

In Kerouac's domestic fantasy, there is always the tension between the desire for the security of a home, but one that is not dominated by women, or rather, in which women, like Bur-roughs's "wetbacks," provide labor, but have no voice, and play no part in the real intellectual and creative purpose of the ranch-commune. In *Jack's Book* (Gifford and Lee) Luanne Henderson describes her role in New York City in 1947 when she and Neal Cassady made their first trip east in the hope of his being admit-ted to Columbia. She worked as a waitress all night, providing the only income for Cassady, Ginsberg, and Kerouac, and whoever else decided to stay in her small apartment. After her shift, she was expected to come home and clean and cook for the men. After a few weeks, she tired of this and told Cassady that the po-lice had come looking for him. This lie prompted Cassady to va-cate the apartment and sent Luanne back to Denver, an event that marked the beginning of the end of their marriage.

This misogyny is well documented in the work of the principal Beat writers. However, the misogyny is usually attributed to the homosocial/homosexual nature of relations among Kerouac, Cas-sady, Ginsberg, and Burroughs (all of whom had sexual relations with each other at one time or another).[14] However true this might be, there is another aspect to the misogyny that bears analysis: the association of women with domestic routine, responsibilities, and ultimately, with a "rooted" or immobilizing connection to a fixating community. Kerouac's *The Dharma Bums* and its sequel, *Desolation Angels*, expresses this dynamic (as did his own personal life) with its continual struggle between a desire to live alone, isolated on a mountain top, practicing sexual abstinence, focusing on a Buddhist "indifference" (which Kerouac interpreted as a disavowal of one's connection to material existence and corporeality), and his need for community that this asceticism was designed to preclude. Kerouac's community is always limited to his fellow writers or his mother and sister's family and he associates participation within community to a Catholicism that demands an active engagement with the world and an acknowledgment, rather than a denial, of the body. In *Big Sur* Kerouac depicts the conflict between his desire to remain aloof and self-reliant, and his need for others. Community is represented as familial domesticity and feared for its potential to absorb the individual. The family is metaphorized as an encroaching communalism.

My aim is not to simplify *Big Sur*. It is in many ways a poignant journal of alcoholic despair, as well as Kerouac's heartfelt memoir of the rigors of an unexpected fame as "King of the Beatniks," a title he excoriated and was used to his derision. But to stop there fails to see this novel as Kerouac's final and most telling enunciation of a subversive Beat philosophy. Written before *Vanity of Duluoz*, *Big Sur* is his final attempt at finding a balance between the individual and communal participation. The novel portrays the forces of absorption to which the Beats reacted, and unwittingly exemplifies the ultimate failure of neoindividualism as a viable democratic form. Kerouac acknowledges the impossibility of an Emersonian self-reliance, of Thoreauvian retreat, while remaining ambivalent and paranoid toward inclusive participation within even the most intimate of communal forms, whether the couple, the family, or even a circle of friends. In the end, the subject chooses the ultimate of negative liberties because, as Kerouac suggests, the cost of inclusion—giving of oneself—leads inevitably to disintegration of the self, or worse, an absorption by a "babbling" multiplicity that only an evil Whitman could have imagined.

The novel is based on Kerouac's real-life journey to San Francisco in the summer of 1960. It was an attempt to escape his lonely, tired existence in Northport, Long Island, with his widowed mother. Kerouac arranged with Lawrence Ferlinghetti to come west to regroup in peace and quiet at Ferlinghetti's Big Sur retreat and returned to the Bay Area, site of his past glory. Rather than coming into town secretly as had been agreed upon, Kerouac appeared in Ferlinghetti's bookstore, City Lights, drunkenly calling attention to himself and immediately inviting several of his San Francisco friends to join him at the cabin at Big Sur.

Already suffering from acute alcoholism, Kerouac begins to repeat in desperation the theme of the novel: "One fast move, or I'm gone." He repeats this phrase time and again as he expresses the paradox of his desperation at dissatisfied rootlessness and the inevitable desire to escape any encroachment on his personal space. In *Big Sur* that encroachment is embodied in the family. Kerouac portrays the individual in the process of disintegration that results from the demands of a wife and child.

After deciding to retire to the solitude of Lorenzo's (Ferlinghetti's) cabin, Jack Duluoz (Kerouac) attempts to regain his equanimity as he stumbles through the dark path in frightened blindness. His harrowing walk to the cabin is a metaphor for his inability to find his way in the chaotic environs of his last years. Searching has become perilous; it has now taken on the objective that it did not have in his early years: finding rest and a home. In the morning he awakens to find that he crossed a perilous bridge in the fog and that below in the chasm lies the twisted wreckage of a car: "So that the sight of that simple sad mountain, together with the bridge and that car that had flipped over twice or so and landed flump in the sand with no more sign of human elbows or shred neckties (like a terrifying poem about America you could write)" (*Big Sur* 17). The collapse and destruction of the car signifies Kerouac's understanding of the failure of travel and movement not only on a personal level, but as a national motif. His impulse is to overcome the isolation of his alcoholism and the rootlessness that has garnered him nothing but loneliness.

Here, as in *Desolation Angels,* Kerouac decides to encounter profound solitude in imitation of Thoreau's *Walden* enacting an Emersonian self-reliance. However, much like Burroughs's "stasis horrors" that propel him to move on, Kerouac begins to feel "bored." Kerouac's boredom and restlessness signal his desire for human companionship, but also point to an ambivalence of necessary sacrifices that community represents. In staking out a role as an "observer" he is able to maintain a peripheral membership, involved but never responsible. In characterizing what the trip to the West Coast will gain him, he writes that he can at least come away with "pleasant mental movies brought up at will and projected for further study—And pleasure—As I imagine God to be doing this very minute, watching his own movie, which is us" (*Big Sur* 25).

Significantly, Kerouac constructs a telos with an indifferent God as the primary observer, legitimating an apolitical observer's role that he maintains as his ultimate defense against being implicated within the group. It also suggests a determinist vision of the universe (one about which he continually vacillated), which also makes attempts at amelioration "vanities." He expresses the more reactionary thoughts he would echo in *Vanity of Duluoz,* that death was the real enemy, and mortality could not be fought with "commie" or "hippie" politics. "[H]ere I am almost fainting only it isn't an ecstatic swoon by St. Francis, it comes over me in the form of horror of an eternal condition of sick mortality in me—In me and in everyone. . . . I see myself as just doomed, pitiful—An awful realization that I have been fooling myself all my life thinking there was a next thing to do to keep the show going and actually I'm just a sick clown and so is everybody else" (*Big Sur* 41).

When he decides to leave the Big Sur cabin to find companionship, it is not a desire for a communal inclusion but the hope that company will help stave off the boredom of solitude and relieve the pain of mortality. Kerouac hitchhikes back to San Francisco to find these comrades. In what prefigures his parody of the American family, Kerouac describes his final hitchhiking trip:

This is the first time I've hitch hiked in years and I soon begin to see that things have changed in America, you cant get a ride anymore. . . . Sleek long stationwagon after wagon comes steering by smoothly, all colors of the rainbow . . . the husband is in the driver's seat with a long ridiculous vacationist hat with a long baseball visor making him look witless and idiot—Beside him sits wifey, the boss of America, wearing dark glasses and sneering, even if he wanted to pick me up . . . she wouldn't let him—But in the two deep backseats are children, children, millions of children. . . . There's no room anymore anyway for a hitch hiker. . . . Tho he might have secretly wished just a good oldtime fishing trip alone or with his buddies for this year's vacation—But the P.T.A. has prevailed over every one of his desires by now, 1960s. . . . And if he thinks he wants to explore any of the silent secret roads of America it's no go, the lady in the sneering dark glasses has now become the navigator and sits there sneering over her previously printed blue-lined roadmap distributed by happy executives in neckties to the vacationists of America who would also wear neckties. (*Big Sur* 44-45)

Domesticity has impinged upon free movement. The American man has been transformed, to Kerouac's disgust, from an explorer into a tourist. In what amounts to a catalog of Beat disdain, Kerouac suggests the danger of feminine absorption. Linking corporate America, community participation (PTA), and the family as immobilizing forces, Kerouac describes the emasculation of the American man as a prescribed journey for a subjectified, witless automaton. Here movement is co-opted by forces of bourgeois vacuity, in much the same way that Burroughs conflates the paralysis of the body-state by forces of bureaucratic statism with the colonization of the body from within. Kerouac's charge against the American family echoes Burroughs's charge that "What every U.S. bitch of them wants [is] a man all to herself with no pernicious friends hanging about" (Burroughs, *Letters* 233).

Kerouac sees fit to charge that the failure of his own rootless wandering is not due to the inherent failures of radical individualism, but that the "real man" can no longer move freely in a space that has been mapped by controlling women and sinister corporate executives. He writes, "My feet are ruined and burned, [and] it develops now into a day of complete torture, from nine o'clock in the morning till four in the afternoon I negotiate those nine or so miles when I finally have to stop and sit down and wipe the blood off my feet" (*Big Sur* 47). Thus the physical torture that he must endure to travel becomes an indictment of systemic oppression rather than a reconsideration of the ideology of free movement or individualism. Kerouac is then able to maintain the role of persecuted individual, holding on to a liminal space, a self-indulgent marginalization that precludes any attempt he might make for finding an active role within family or community.

His growing paranoia of communal encroachment is made evident as he visits with Cody Pomeray (Neal Cassady) and (in the passage quoted earlier in this chapter) bemoans that with "everybody yakking" he can no longer be heard, for "too many people now want to talk." Kerouac tellingly portrays himself and Cassady as being "hemmed in and surrounded and outnumbered" (*Big Sur* 69). Kerouac's portrayal lends itself well to the melodramatic roles of Davy Crockett and Jim Bowie (broadcast to the nation on weekly television) protecting the Alamo against the forces of immobilization: "The circle's closed in on us, the old heroes of the night" (*Big Sur* 69).

His paranoia grows as he imagines that his closest friends are "all a big bunch of witches out to make me go mad" (*Big Sur* 115). In what Kerouac depicts as his last hope for companionship and inclusion, Cody Pomeray and his family appear, "suffused in a golden light" (*Big Sur* 128). The ideal family—a romantic projection by Kerouac, since the Cassady family was in turmoil—is described as "holy" by Kerouac as he decides that salvation might lie along that route. Pomeray introduces him to "Billie," a cast-off mistress with a young son.

After Duluoz invites Billie and her son to the cabin, the "rigors" of family life begin to take their toll on him and he describes himself in terms reminiscent of his parody of the American family in the hitchhiking scene: "I realize Billie is insane and I'm not as insane as I thought and there's something wrong—I feel myself skidding; also because during the following week I keep sitting in that same chair by the goldfish bowl drinking bottle after bottle of port like an automaton" (*Big Sur* 157). Duluoz emphasizes the feeling of the self slipping away. His drinking becomes a response to the encroachment of Billie and her child upon his ability to move ("sitting in the same chair") rather than a sign of his alcoholism. There is more here than simple self-delusion, for his assessment of his position signals the central Beat fear of immobilization in a feminized suburbia.

And yet Duluoz is not so self-deluded that he does not have flashes of insight into the source of his sense of alienation and rootlessness: "Always an ephemeral 'visitor' to the Coast never really involved with anyone's lives there because I'm always ready to fly back across the country but not to any life of my own on the other end either, just a traveling stranger like Old Bull Balloon, an exemplar of loneliness" (*Big Sur* 179). But despite Kerouac's seeming regret at his "ephemeral" status, his depiction of the communal state is one of horrific consumption. Ensconced once again at the cabin with Billie, her son Elliot, Duluoz's close friend David Wain (Lew Welch) and girlfriend Ramona (Lenore Kandel), he begins to imagine that the group is trying to poison his food. Paranoid fantasies that his friends are really a circle of "warlocks" out to make him insane drive him toward a nervous breakdown, and the pleasant multiplicity of voices that he heard in the babbling stream become the voices of insanity: "soon my thoughts aren't even as 'rational' as that any more but become hours of raving—There are forces whispering in my ear in rapid long speeches advising and warning, suddenly other voices are shouting" (*Big Sur* 203).

The "magical" suffusion that imbues the Pomeray (Cassady) family earlier is replaced with witchcraft performed by the family. The voices that drown out rationality and the voices that threatened to drown out Duluoz's voice earlier connect the threat of communal absorption with the threat of a familial incursion on the individual. As in Burroughs's metaphor of the brain isolated in the head by the Un D.T. of the colonizing asshole, Duluoz's mind is also threatened with a profound isolation as voices cut off his ability to reason and to control his subjectivity.

In trying to gain his composure, Duluoz struggles with his desire to function within some form of communal dynamic, but finds to his increasing anxiety that communal inclusion involves responsibility and the dissolution of a "pure" individualist identity, one that will transform his freedom to move, into what he has characterized earlier as a systemically directed movement—the movement of the automaton: "I have to get out of there—But I have no right to stay away—So I keep coming back but it's all an insane revolving automatic directionless circle of anxiety, back and forth, around and around . . . but now their heads are together and they're whispering" (*Big Sur* 199). Consequently, while he realizes that his behavior appears bizarre to his "family" and friends, he suspects them of plotting against him. The ultimate result of Duluoz's attempt at finding himself within the family-community is that his personal, negative liberty/movement is transmuted into the horrifying perceptions of madness quoted earlier in this chapter: "I look at the moon it waves, moves, when I look at my hands and feet they creep—Everything is moving the porch is moving like ooze and mud, the chair trembles under me" (*Big Sur* 200). The novel ends with Duluoz finding some solace in the sign of the cross, suggesting that "something good will come out of all this," and decides to return home to his mother and isolation, any hopes of communal or political solutions to be dismissed (*Big Sur* 216).[15] Thus the Beat rebellion against "conformity" is taken to an abysmal extreme, dooming the individual to an effete and barren solitude, lest he be absorbed and thus "lost."

## The Passing of the Torch

A fateful meeting took place in the summer of 1964. It brought together Kerouac, Ginsberg, Cassady, and Ken Kesey. Kesey had loaded up his bus, "Further," and brought his Merry Pranksters to New York to meet the progenitor of the Beat and now the hippie movement.[16] Kerouac mistrusted Kesey and was uncomfortable with the hippies and their disrespect for the American flag which they were using as a throw cover for a couch on the bus. Neal Cassady was a performer in Kesey's traveling psychedelic road show and, fittingly, driver of the bus. The meeting proved to be highly suggestive as a metaphor of the dynamic of which I have written: Kerouac and Kesey, avatars of the postwar cultural revolution, sitting together, while their mutual friend Neal Cassady, the driver, the personification of liberating movement and prince of drift, is caught in the middle. Kesey was at the height of his popularity, Kerouac at the nadir of his. Kesey saw his mission as a continuation of what Kerouac had set in motion in the 1950s. Kerouac saw the hippies as mindless, communistic, rude, unpatriotic, and soulless. It would be a mistake, however, to believe that Kerouac's bitter hatred of countercultural politics and the youth rebellions of the day were simply products of his anticommunal and communist paranoia. His reactions were, in part, as envy of the new generation.[17] Kerouac was also disturbed by the rampant commercialization and massification of the Beat image in the rise of hippie culture. His hatred of the hippies might also have stemmed from his racial attitudes as well as his fear of communism. But the discomfort that shows on Kerouac's face in the pictures of the meeting of the most famous countercultural literary figures of the period is due in large part to Kerouac's fears that his work was being seen as progenitive of the 1960s counterculture.

His fear, as he states numerous times in essays written in the late 1950s and throughout the 1960s, was that his work had been appropriated by the forces of lawlessness, communism, and "delinquency." In a sense, this can be read as Kerouac's fear that the communal and liberating aspects of his work might actually be revolutionizing American culture. But I suggest that Kerouac, accurate as his fears might have been in their appraisal of the parallel between his work and the work of 1960s "radicals," would have been closer to the truth had he recognized that there were close ideological parallels of a much more regressive and reactionary nature between his neoindividualist cant and the forms of counterculture that Kesey and his Merry Pranksters heralded.

As I have suggested, a cultural protest emerged in the 1950s in response to a conformity brought about through corporatism, suburbanization, and a "feminization," acting as a defensive self-marginalization against attacks targeting individualist mobilities. This entailed rejecting any form of political communalism that was deemed threatening—a form of absorption that could not be tolerated. This, I suggest, is the legacy that Ken Kesey and other 1960s countercultural figures, as well as the youth rebellion at large, took as their central issue. The 1950s emergence of civil rights movements quickly brought a momentous new dimension to the self-marginalization that the Beats used as a defense against bourgeois threats to the individual. It threatened to supplant white power, and to absorb the individuals within those marginal communities into a politicized communitas. And thus a schism formed that pitted one form of "radicalism" against another. A counterculture based on protecting the privileges of white, liberalized individualism found itself at odds with a counterculture based on communal identity, egalitarianism, and a recognition of the "other's" individuality. Kerouac's discomfort has its origin in his perception that Kesey and his coterie of hippies had given in to communal egalitarianism. But, I would also suggest, his discomfort has no real basis, for Kesey was as deeply committed to a self-interested individualism as any of the Beats had ever been. In one photo, Neal Cassady sits in between Kerouac and Kesey, the personification of the link between the movement(s) represented by the two writers: a personal, free movement designed to keep both civic and the domestic claims at bay.

In an essay written in 1958 entitled "Lamb, No Lion," Kerouac produced his definition of "beat," in order to defend the movement from conservative critics who suggested that it had served only to engender delinquency amongst the nation's youth: "'Beat' doesn't mean tired, or bushed, so much as it means *beato*, the Italian for beatific: to be in a state of beatitude, like St. Francis, trying to love all life, trying to be utterly sincere with everyone, practicing endurance, kindness, cultivating joy of heart. How can this be done in our mad modern world of multiplicities and millions? By practicing a little solitude, going off by yourself once in a while to store up that most precious of golds: the vibrations of sincerity" (Charters, *The Portable Beat Reader* 562). The assumption that the fruits of the spirit—endurance, sincerity, kindness, and joy—are somehow incompatible with, or at least challenged by "multiplicity" is central to my critique of the Beat text. For it posits individual wholeness and growth as constantly endangered by a multiplicity that places demands against individual "sincerity"—the ability to be "true" to oneself and to the "other." The solution in Kerouac's works is to move—to "go off by yourself." I have already shown how this dynamic functioned in the work of the Beats, but as a segue into the next chapters, I will show that the same dynamic is in operation in Ken Kesey's work, and by extension, in the works of other countercultural writers of the 1960s.

Kesey's 1963 novel, *One Flew Over the Cuckoo's Nest*, provides the link between 1950s cultural protest and the "more radical" protest movements of the 1960s. In his novel, the threat to the individual comes from the institution. Whereas Kerouac and Burroughs suggest more oblique, insidious forces, Kesey places the individual at the mercy of systemic institutionalization that, as Althusser suggests, interpellates the subject into a self-subjectifying automaton. This is a standard reading of the novel. However, the parallels between Kesey and the Beat fear of absorption, paranoia of feminization, and fear of the minority, as well as the appropriation of ethnicity, are all operational in this neobeat, proto-countercultural novel.

Kesey's novel has rightly been celebrated as an exposé of the uses of discipline, order, observation, and the discourse of psychology—an early critique of panopticism and systemic interpellation that predates the work of Foucault and Althusser. But what has not been noted is Kesey's vision of the institution as a site of the individual male's castration, where masculine will is sapped. Kesey posits a matriarchal institution whose "muscle" is provided by black sodomites. Perhaps most alarming is that it is an opaque and ubiquitous "system" that creates community. Community is here portrayed as forced, immobilizing, effete, and castrating. It is singularly incapable of transforming itself into *communitas,* or of becoming "communal." The communal here is by its very nature authoritarian, susceptible to the will of the minority, of the woman, and is threatening to the power of the white male. The politics of the ward are a sham democracy, the suggestion being that democratic participation is itself impossible, or at least suspect. Kesey ultimately suggests that the solution to institutionalized immobility is a self-initiated, lone movement.

Although Chief Bromden is overshadowed by the colorful antihero McMurphy, his role as the narrator and eventual lone escapee is central in understanding the complex relations between movement, community, the individual, the institution, and techniques for combating the castrating matriarchy. Kesey's strategy is to use the Indian narrator, who pretends to be deaf and dumb, as a liminal figure characterized by ethnicity and mental state. As a large man made "small" by the institution, the chief represents the large penis made small in the presence of the castrating mother. McMurphy portrays the role of the father whose strength and indomitable will give the chagrined children the strength to resist matriarchal domination and grow large.

McMurphy's strength has its source in his recognition of two "truths": his sexual prowess that recognizes only two sorts of women, the "bitch ball cutters," and the fun girls, or prostitutes; he avoids the power of the combine "by never giving them a chance by always moving, a moving target is hard to hit" (63). But as Kesey only seems to recognize the two types of women (the vast majority of the former type), he also posits two forms of ethnicity, both of which reduce racial ethnicity to a function, and both of which correlate to the uses of this "ethnic-function" by the Beats. There is the ethnic as liminal space. This serves as a sort of observation point from which the marginalized subject can observe unnoticed as Chief Bromden does—silent, "deaf and dumb," with second sight. This is ultimately Kesey's understanding of authorship. The second function of ethnicity is that of colonized subject in the service of systemic power: the black attendants are described as sodomites and embittered agents of hatred. They are nothing more than "black machinery. . . . they hate," and function through ". . . wires in their head that lead directly to the nurse and work by rote instinct." Nurse Rachid is metaphorized as a mechanized spider whose web extends throughout the system, whose power is entrenched, as McMurphy finds out, because of her relation to the supervisor, also a woman.

But the novel is most often recognized for its critique of the techniques of discipline, observation, interpellation, and the effects of normalizing strategies enforced in the factory of Bromden's youth, in the suburbs glimpsed from the back of a bus, and embedded in racial and medical discourse. Kesey goes so far as to suggest through the ubiquitous presence of white, sterility, order, and uniformity are based on a racialized Anglo logic. But that is as far as his critique reaches. For his analysis of systemic oppressions places the white male in the role of victim. It places the white, masculine, mobile McMurphy as the bane of the institution, the free-thinking hero whose sacrifice is celebrated as a martyrdom for the cause of American individualism, whose example will give the Indian the courage to escape the control of the feminine and of the dark races. While it may seem a contradiction that the function of "Indian-ness" is used in opposition to the function of "blackness," I suggest that the Indian-function is not "ethnic" in the way that being black is "ethnic." The Indian represents the writer's liminal position; the black characters represent automated servility, perverse and simultaneously emasculated and emasculating.

The key to escaping the system for McMurphy is not through a communal effort. Time and again Mac's attempts to rally the men to his support, to get them to speak, to vote, to agree, are met with abject failure. Liberty is shown as the temporary release from the regulative power of the system, a release that can only be achieved through breach or violence by the lone provocateur. The final scene in which Bromden smothers the lobotomized McMurphy (the ultimate form of castration) and then rips the control panel from the ground and throws it through the ward window is suggestive in many important ways. It is the parallel liberating moment to McMurphy's attempted rape and murder of Nurse Rachid, a "successful" technique in that it strips her of her powerful aura in front of the men. Kesey links revolution against the system with violence against the matriarchal. Both acts emanate from the individual and not the community. The solution is escape, a liberating personal, solitary movement. McMurphy's communal urge at the novel's end (his decision not to escape, but to stay and avenge his protégé's death) results in his lobotomy—itself a representation of the ultimate form of de-individuation: mind becomes blank, personality destroyed.

The novel's theme suggests that the community is positively, but indirectly affected by the individual who acts truly for himself. The Chief's escape returns him to his old Indian haunts where he suggests that he will return to his "natural" state, a primal relation that Kesey can enjoy, as Kerouac did through the fellaheen, by voyeuristic appropriation. And so the Chief escapes at the sounds of "the running squeak of the black boys' shoes in the hall" (310). And the echoes of Kerouac, Burroughs, and Ginsberg are heard in Kesey's idealization of movement: "I ran across the grounds in the direction I remembered seeing the dog go, toward the highway. I remember I was taking huge strides as I ran, seeming to step and float a long ways before my next foot struck the earth. I feel like I was flying. Free" (310). In this light, Kerouac's rejection of what Kesey represented can only be interpreted as a peculiar misinterpretation that his philosophy of the self and the individual had been misappropriated in practice. Kerouac believed that Kesey and the Pranksters and the hippies had twisted his vision of the mobile subject into some strange, delinquent, perverse, communal effort designed to spread an absorbing, deindividuating egalitarianism. But it was a misinterpretation, for Kesey found in Kerouac the father for whom Paradise roamed the open road.

## Assessing the Beat Legacy

The Beat legacy is difficult to define. The recent retrospective, "Beat Culture and the New America: 1950–65," has toured the nation celebrating the liberating influence to which the movement gave voice. The Volvo company uses the cover of *On the Road* to sell its latest model, two aging hipsters reading passages to each other as they drive around in their forty-thousand dollar automobile. These are two drastically different interpretations of the Beat generation. Kerouac may have voiced the paradox of his legacy best in a 1969 essay written shortly before he died: "What am I thinking about? I'm trying to figure out where I am between the established politicians and the radicals, between cops and hoods, tax collectors and vandals. I'm not a Tax-Free, not a Hippie-Yippie—I must be a Bippie-in-the-Middle" (Charters, *Portable Jack Kerouac* 573). In the final assessment of his work—and of the work of his Beat colleagues—it may be that he is neither the voice of dissension as his most ardent readers claim, nor the violently reactionary racist he came to resemble in his final years. It may turn out that what the Beats most clearly signified was the tendency of American dissent to subvert its own countercultural instinct for the middle road, for stability, for the comfort of the status quo that promises a protective space for the individual. Even as Kerouac attempted to criticize political extremism in any guise, his most fervent and bitter criticism was saved for the "Flower Power Generation" and their protest against the "national right . . . of the United States to defend itself against its own perimeter of enemies . . ." (Charters, *Portable Jack Kerouac* 577). The title "After Me, the Deluge" can be read as the fear of a pursuing wave that threatens to subsume the individual. The title acts as an apt epitaph for his work and the character of such countercultural protest. In the end, the perimeter must be guarded against the "enemy," which threatens to close in on those "heroes of the American night." Kerouac's early radical energies were sapped because his ultimate belief that the individual must remain inviolate kept the radical potential of his project from extending and realizing itself in effective communal activity and purpose. The "middle" offered a space without any particular commitment other than to protecting one's "perimeter." For Kerouac, as for many before and many after, a narrow, protective, and exclusive individualism remained the final, pathetic refuge of American "dissension." And to use a Kerouac-like tone, there's nothing countercultural about that.

# 3

# *Civitas* and Its Discontents
## *The Lone Hunter Pleads the Fourth*

> I picked up the torch dropped by Kerouac and went on
> to become rich and famous . . . more or less.
> > Hunter S. Thompson, *Songs of the Doomed*

> If you were not before, you are now simply an an-
> archist. . . . Your desire to build a "personal fort" is, at
> best, infantile.
> > Oscar Acosta, in a letter to Hunter S. Thompson,
> > January 11, 1970

In the previous two chapters I leveled an inquiry into the pervasiveness of an individualist movement discourse within a particularly influential set of dissenting texts, arguing that a pervasive
(and persuasive) neoindividualism allowed for the ideology of
negative liberty to short-circuit burgeoning postwar commitments to positive liberty. We will soon see that the ideology of
negative liberty had a debilitating effect on the counterculture as
well. Stanley Aronowitz, in *The Death and Rebirth of American
Radicalism* argues that neoindividualism did indeed hold sway
during the 1960s, limiting the ability of the counterculture to coalesce and commit to a communitarian agenda. He argues that even
the New Left, the most communitarian of the countercultural

movements in the 1960s, strove to create a radicalism informed by a specifically "American" form of dissent that nevertheless owed much to an individualist ethos. While that form of dissent (characterized best in the work of Tom Hayden, C. Wright Mills, Staughton Lynd, and A. J. Muste) advocated a commitment to a communitarian and egalitarian radical democratic ethos, it could not escape the influence of what Aronowitz calls a "micropolitics of liberation." Thus the New Left, he argues, most aspired to create an "absolute sovereignty for the individual, whose power had been systematically undercut by representative government, trade union bureaucracies, and large impersonal institutions. The New Left intended to restore power to the *person* (which should not be confused . . . with 'power to the people,' a formulation of the black civil rights movement where the individual was subordinated to group interest)" (46). While we must be careful to distinguish the many strains that are generally brought under the rubric of the "counterculture," the individualist ethos Aronowitz exposes undercut egalitarian, communal tendencies by its repulsion of aggregative politics in the "mainstream" counterculture, defined here as a culture of dissent that emphasized negative liberty or the individualist prerogative. In his work, "gonzo journalist" Hunter S. Thompson uncovers this individualist tendency in the mainstream counterculture while falling prey to an individualism that was evident in the Beat ethos.

Thompson's acknowledgment of Jack Kerouac's work is significant not only for what it offers in a formal or aesthetic comparison, but also because it is helpful in tracing the development of a particular strain of movement discourse as it evolved from its 1950s origins to its 1960s versions. Initially Thompson replicates Kerouac's road romanticism in a reflection of America in the 1950s, portraying his early travels as explorations undertaken by a naive, idealistic journalist intent on writing a trenchant jeremiad. But Thompson soon moves beyond the early idealism of Kerouac's literature of expatiation. Thompson's idealism becomes cynicism, making him at once "post-Kerouacian" as well as an exemplar of America's move from the era of the "countercultural" to the era of the postcountercultural. In Thompson's work, the creation of left-wing paranoia becomes increasingly evident. The fear of deindividuation, which I claim was given voice in both the "culture" and "counterculture" of the 1950s, is now articulated from the "left" in the 1960s.

Insofar as 1950s cultural and social dynamics have been simplified by positing a reactionary element against a small, bohemian element, the sociopolitical conflicts in the 1960s have likewise been rendered.[1] It is not my purpose to rewrite the history of the 1960s, but to suggest that the decade's image as "countercultural" and the movements that rose to prominence during the period should be analyzed for the ideological and rhetorical traces of a neoindividualism that was so pervasive in the 1950s. My objective is to look at Thompson's work for such traces, and for the partial deconstruction of the notion of radicalism in the 1960s that his work provides. In essence, Thompson first replicates and then critiques the Beat movement narrative, but does it from a position that is more sympathetic to the "radical" positions of the decade. Finally, however, such sympathy does not keep Thompson from embracing the same isolationist conclusion that Kerouac, Kesey, and Burroughs suggest in their own work. Despite the different political orientations, the ideological strain of neoindividualism forces a choice between a commitment to positive or negative liberty. It is a conflict that is characteristic of the political and social movements of the 1960s. Rather than breaking from the 1950s and its "era of conformism," the 1960s must be read more complexly as a continuation of the previous decade's social and political debates. If the 1950s was a decade in which fear of encroachment directed public policy and influenced cultural production (both from the "right" and from the "left"), then the 1960s were also influenced by such fears and perceptions.

The 1960s opened with the lunch counter sit-downs in Greensboro, North Carolina.[2] Soon both white and black citizens were launching sit-ins in over one hundred fifty cities in both North and South. These courageous and effective sit-ins taught those who participated, as well as those who watched the protests on the nightly news, the value of organized public protest. Bourgeois belief in the power of the vote was challenged by the power of direct action. In this way, the margins had begun to challenge the center. It was this power to disturb the status quo that attracted the attention of middle-class youth looking for more direct, effective ways of rebelling against social and cultural standards. In this sense, there arose a contemporary understanding that the social movement launched from a position of marginality could be used for the purposes of securing individual mobility. This is a pattern that remains active throughout the 1960s, and can be used to differentiate and link various forms of countercultural activities as disparate as Abbie Hoffman's Yippies and *La Raza Unida*. The newfound power of marginality puts into relief the competing social strategies that undergird the movement culture of the 1960s.

Analogous to Beat exploitation of minority marginality, the social movement of "mainstream" counterculture of the 1960s borrowed its liminal status from the southern civil rights movement for its own purposes. The mainstream counterculture, defined here as countercultural groups most interested in creating and defending a culture of neoindividualism, did not seek to advance the cause of ethnic/racial equality so much as it sought to end the threat that the Vietnam War posed for individualist prerogatives. Once the war had ended, "radicalism" dissipated, as did the lip service paid to racial and class equality.[3]

As Thompson's work bears out, there is a traditional valorization of individualism that led not to communal alternatives, but to the conservative era of Reagonomics and the "me decade" materialism of the 1970s and 1980s. The conflicts in Thompson's work between the desire for isolation and the need for interaction can be read as a microcosm of 1960s struggle to define "community" and "citizen," which ultimately proved to be a ritual of reintegration rather than one leading to lasting, radical alternatives.[4] Thompson demonstrates a central reason why the counterculture failed to coalesce in a lasting and effective way.

His work bears the ideological and philosophical inconsistencies, which in the end, much like Kerouac's work, create a self-subverting subversion. As Sacvan Bercovitch claims about an earlier group of American writers: "The radical energies they celebrate serve in complex, contradictory, volatile but nonetheless compelling ways to sustain culture" (170).[5] Ultimately, Thompson's work demonstrates a more general principle of how the ideal of democracy, both in its liberal and conservative forms, is defined by the limits of individualism. Thompson's narrative is in many ways the narrative of the limitations imposed by neoindividualism on progressive and countercultural movements of the 1960s, and can be understood through the discourse of movement it produces.

## Defining the Counterculture: Two Models

Stewart Burns makes crucial distinctions between the New Left's commitments to communal-social alternatives and the "counter-culture's" ultimate reliance on "rugged individualism":

> Both New Left and counterculture were influenced by black consciousness, and constituted interwoven strands of a broad-gauged youth revolt. Yet each had a distinct core of values, motives, and aspirations that set it apart. The New Left was a bona fide social movement. The counterculture incurred no less of an upheaval, but was far more spontaneous, amorphous, and by and large, unorganized. . . . Much of the counterculture had little in common with the New Left and even felt alienated from the radicals, seeing their self-righteous seriousness as re-producing the social neurosis it rejected. And the "do your own thing" ethic of self-reliant independence that overshadowed the counterculture's communitarian urges was a far cry from the black church, which provided the protective, nurturing sanctuary of a real-life "beloved community" in the heat of struggle. When the going got tough, the New Left had no such shelter from the storm—only the survival tools of rugged individualism. (Burns 101)

This critique is not to denigrate middle-class 1960s radicalism, but only to suggest an answer to why middle-class youth rebellion, and for that matter, movement culture in general, dissipated as quickly as it appeared. It is an attempt to delineate what was, and is, often uncritically blurred: the politics of the individual and the politics of community. To be sure, the various civil rights movements were mobilized to demand that their members be recognized as full rights-bearing citizens. Certainly, this assertion relies on the sanctity and constitutional status of the individual. But affecting such social and political policy requires a commitment to a particular social strategy.

While there were movements that organized around communal alternatives, others were vested in maintaining an ideal open system in which its elements might more easily—and "independently"—move. In both cases, a ubiquitous but ill-defined "system" was at fault. Coalitions built to protest the "system" therefore had little else in common. Because of the uncritical blurring between individualist and communal strategies, they often seemed to work toward the same end, and in fact sometimes did. There was a dialectical relation between what I call middle-class youth rebellion and civil rights movements. But the result was more synergy than synthesis. The end of the Vietnam War and the creation of the Good Society were largely a result of the critical mass of protesters in the streets. But the 1970s proved that the primary commitment of the counterculture had been the push to legislate an inviolable space for the individual rather than the commitment to seeking social alternatives and what can be loosely called social justice.

In February 1966, General Hershey, commanding officer of the draft, declared that draft boards could begin inducting male college students of lower standing as determined by class, rank, and national examinations. Draft calls approached forty thousand a month, leaving middle-class students no longer insulated from military service. Students for a Democratic Society (SDS) organized the growing discontent into widespread protest. As a metaphor of enforced consensus, the armed forces and their role in Vietnam demonstrated to middle-class youth not only the inconsistencies in U.S. democracy, but demonstrated the lengths to which the government would go to enforce its will.

The leaking of a Selective Service memo on "channeling" caused outrage at its insidious machinations, but more importantly demonstrated the subtle social planning at work in the modern industrial, democratic state. The document asserted that the agency's purpose was only in part to induct men into the military. Its main function was "pressurized guidance," using deferments and the "club of induction" to force young men into occupations in the national interest (the defense industry, for example) that they might not otherwise select. As Stewart Burns asserts: "This strategy provided the benefits of totalitarian control without the moral or financial costs" (76). The memo stated "The psychology of granting wide choice under pressure to take action is the American or indirect way of achieving what is done by direction in foreign countries where choice is not allowed. Here choice is limited but not denied" (Burns 75). The purpose of such strategic guidance was aptly called "participatory totalitarianism" by draft resistance organizer David Harris.[6] It demonstrated the theories of C. Wright Mills and Herbert Marcuse in practice.[7]

Although the civil rights movements in the South had already begun to question second-class citizenship, the furor over "channeling" spoke to the question of white citizenship in modern America. It provided proof that the "citizen" in the United States was "one-dimensional," perhaps suffering from false consciousness, and provided evidence for the growing suspicion that the university produced what Marcuse called the "oppression of tolerance," an ineffectual liberalism, that facilitated "the manipulation of the 'trainees' of the 'new working class'" (xiii). All these formulations were direct outgrowths of 1950s concerns over standardization, conformity, suburban creep, and the creation of the organization man. Mills's own work had achieved some prominence in the 1950s with the publication of *The Power Elite.* The outrage over channeling was a direct manifestation of the furor over the power of the modern industrial-military complex to dictate the nature of white citizenship.

The desire to fight the "establishment's" insidious institutional influence was in part the need to defend the myth of white self-determination as well as an urge to construct a unified front against social and racial inequality. In this way, middle-class youth protest can be read in part as a reaction to both the overt and covert power of the state to "channel" free, middle-class youth by means such as the draft. The agitation over the Vietnam War was in large part motivated by the coercion to which citizens felt they were being subjected. The short-lived coalescence between white, middle-class rebellion and the civil rights movements in the 1960s was due to a shared interest in reasserting individual rights in America. The process of redefining "citizenship," which had intensified in the twenty years following World War II, was energized in the 1960s and underwent its most intense scrutiny of the twentieth century. The position of the individual in relation to the community was in a process of clarification; the algebra of utilitarianism and pragmatism failed because the presumed terms were in intense contestation. To be sure, protest movements of the 1960s had common interests, and both white protest and civil rights protest gained from cooperative efforts. Participation of white progressives in the civil rights struggle, some of whom gave their lives for the cause,[8] shows the communitarian strains of the 1960s counterculture did not break down along color or class lines. Ultimately, the differences in aims and motivations appear along these binaries: access/mobility, the community/the individual, egalitarianism/laissez-faire. These oppositions within the "movement" do not only describe the divergence between civil rights and white protest, but describe a divergence within civil rights movements as well as between the New Left and the mainstream counterculture that focused on individualist self-expression.

Thompson's early years serve as a template for the 1960s generation: the need or desire to rebel coupled with the drive to attain or retain privilege. His childhood and adolescence reveal a youth conflicted between the desire to fit into the genteel southern society of Louisville, Kentucky, and the desire to rebel against its outdated, classist code of chivalry and southern grace. Described as "multilevel," a young man who "hobnobbed with several cliques," and was drawn to the "greaser element," Thompson, due to his own humble origins, soon found the value in being able to move between cliques, classes, and ethnicities (Carroll 50).

While described as always a gentleman within polite society, Thompson found an outlet for his pent-up frustration in iconoclastic and destructive behavior. Even while still a student at Male High School, Thompson was arrested for vandalism and destruction of private property.

A friend theorizes that Thompson reverted to destructive behavior because of bitterness at his status in a community that was quite class-conscious: "Hunter's circumstances were such that the family simply couldn't afford to send him away to college anywhere . . . He was frustrated. . . . I think that he saw his contemporaries carrying on [going to Harvard and Yale] and he was unable to do so himself. And this turned from hurt and disappointment to anger and rage and frustration. I think that accounts for some of the violence and vandalism, too" (Carroll 56). Other friends see his rebellion and violence as pure iconoclasm: "I think Hunter always hated what Louisville stood for. What it stood for then and what it will always stand for. It's a boring, provincial, middle-class, family-oriented town. . . .The bottom line is Hunter would not have wanted to fit in. . . . Hunter couldn't wait to get out of there" (Carroll 57). Thompson's youth offers a general representation of middle-class youth disdain for a less formal, but even more pervasive, form of "channeling." Thompson's experience growing up in the 1950s was typical for a middle-class youngster, conflicted by his desire to subvert the well-established social landscape of the middle-class environment. Like Benjamin Braddock in the 1967 film *The Graduate,* there was a desire to escape a carefully plotted fate, but a hesitation to leave the bourgeois comfort represented in the film by the parents' suburban house and protective swimming pool. The 1960s social landscape of this middle-class ennui was superimposed with the political resistance of blacks and Chicanos, and most significantly for the Hunter Thompsons and Benjamin Braddocks, protestors of the Vietnam War.

Thompson's reaction to middle-class vacuity, like that of many of his brethren of the 1960s generation, was to replicate a Beat expatiation that either consciously or unconsciously pinned its hopes on a strategic negative liberty.

## Road Tales of the Doomed: Traveling through the American Century

In *Songs of the Doomed,* Thompson edited a collection of previous writings that included journals, an early attempt at a first novel (later published as *The Rum Diary*), and his first journalistic pieces. Interspersed with new essays written for the book's publication, the collection provides a series of links between Thompson's reactionary tendencies and his fascination with the centrality of the individual in the American *mythos* and its place within his own personal narrative.

It is a book ghost-written by Jack Kerouac, a series of Road Tales in which Thompson sets out to roam the by-ways and highways in search of new lands to conquer. As it partakes in the discourse of movement, *Songs of the Doomed* portrays a writer caught up in the romantic promises of expatiation. Thompson, like his predecessor, goes native in order to find a liminal space in which he can construct a detached persona, a facade through which he may safely observe.

Like Kerouac, Hunter Thompson spent a short time in the armed forces before being discharged. He also did a tour in the Peace Corps. Thompson portrays that period in his life as a struggle between a discipline to which he could not submit, and the desire to perform his civic duty in the spirit of John F. Kennedy's commission to "ask not what your country can do for you, but what you can do for your country." In the first section of *Songs of the Doomed,* the character Welburn Kemp, from the then unpublished *Rum Diary* Thompson wrote in the 1960s, appears as a young idealistic journalist who has left the service, worked on several small-town newspapers and has now come to New York to break into the professional ranks. Kemp/Thompson refuses to fit into the stifling faux-cosmopolitan mindset characteristic of the Manhattan/Columbia law school crowd of the 1950s. As an individual trapped amongst conformists, Thompson carefully crafts a persona that must search out the painful truth.

In a telling scene, he finds that his brand of truth telling is not appreciated by the generation of conformist urbanites. Welburn

Kemp carries a bag of lime, which is mistaken for lye, into a disco bar and immediately "poisons" the patrons and is publicly "flogged." The well-intentioned harbinger of truth destroys the "party," is accused of bringing poison and cast out, punished by truth-hating hedonists. Welburn Kemp, in the image of the journalist, desires to observe and participate, but is punished for the potential damage he might cause by describing those observations. He is therefore cast "outside" the community, becoming a lonely, liminal figure. The opposition between archetypal asocial genius whose brilliance is not recognized by a philistine but conformist community frames the conflict that directs Thompson's work. Like Kerouac, he desires to participate within community but is either misunderstood or eventually comes to understand that such participation will put his self-subsistence at risk. To be welcomed at the "party," he must leave his lye (ironically, his "truth") outside the door.

Thompson leaves Manhattan to go on the road. As a truth-telling journalist, his vocation depends upon finding a community of readers. However, these readers are constructed as heathen, and Thompson as their missionary, the proselytizing prophet of a doomed generation. Incessantly quoting the scripture, especially the *Book of Revelation*, Thompson's work takes on the urgency of the jeremiad; he becomes the prophet in the wilderness. He finds that his life's work will be to preach a firebrand religio-politics to the unconverted. As such, Thompson can quell the desire for interaction with a community, while remaining outside of its regulation. In Puerto Rico, he can live in the land of the liminal and rail against the conformists and the "channeling" culture.

As Mexico did for Kerouac, Burroughs, and Ginsberg, Puerto Rico serves as the fellaheen land for Thompson. The self-marginalization practiced in the United States (truth-teller cast out to wander alone) is jettisoned once he finds himself living in a land populated by marginals. In Puerto Rico, Thompson travels with his friends, acting brutish and getting into confrontations with the locals. Arrested for fighting in a restaurant, Thompson is quick to assert his citizenship, thereby gaining special privileges. Thompson demonstrates that his liminal status is voluntary. Read against his Chicano friend Oscar Acosta's experience in Mexican and U.S. courts, Thompson's "identity" is always secure as a white male. He is ultimately free to walk away, or at least to enjoy a legitimacy that Acosta demonstrates the "other" cannot.[9] For Thompson, marginalization is simply a strategy through which he can freely move between and within communities and groups while holding their demands at bay. For the "other," marginality provides no such opportunity to move.

The predicaments of the stoic Kemp recall Harry Morgan in Hemingway's most conflicted novel, *To Have and Have Not,* where class consciousness comes into direct tension with the racist theme of the white man's burden. Here too, Thompson's anticapitalist critique of U.S. investment in Puerto Rico is mediated by his fear of the "primitive." When Kemp visits the other side of the island, he and his friends visit a local club where Kemp begins to feel uncomfortable: "It was all exactly the same except that every head in the room was black. . . . I felt anxious and looked for a corner in the room where I could think unseen" (Thompson *Songs* 97). Uncomfortable with the "overwhelming" presence of blackness, Kemp retreats into the observer's role. Kemp becomes an ethnographer anonymously observing the "other." In a reversal that follows the pattern of the Beat explorer, the white radical jettisons his self-marginalization, taking on the role of the dominant observer in the land of the fellaheen when that fellaheen populace appears to threaten the observer's perch.

As Victor Turner explained in his work on the social drama and the liminal process, the threshold stage is the most dangerous to the social structure.[10] It holds the most subversive potential. Thompson's reaction to the appearance of such a moment is racially inspired. "I remembered that old saying that 'all niggers look the same,' a foul and callous outlook generally attributed to white trash. But when I looked into that room full of black dancers I saw that it was true—they all looked the same. And this man in front of me looked like all the others. . . . I got extremely nervous, standing there on the terrace and trying to deny to myself that 'all niggers look the same'" (*Songs* 97). Thompson fears a racialized loss of identity. He feels the potential for an erasure of whiteness through the "browning" the crowd represents. This epiphany reveals a central fissure in the white/ethnic radical coalescence of the 1960s. If the ultimate end of civil rights was genuine equality, white rebels such as Thompson were not about to sign on. In the end, the terror felt at seeing the white self absorbed by blacks "who look the same" proves to be a destructive force to any unified countercultural movement. Thompson's observation describes a deep fear of multicultural pluralism and the sort of radical communal alternatives it might engender.

Even while he denounces capital's neoimperial activity in the Caribbean ("I remembered Zimburger, and Martin, and the Marines—the empire builders, setting up frozen-food stores and aerial bombing ranges, spreading out like a piss-puddle to every corner of the world") Thompson is not able to separate himself from its racialism (*Songs* 102). Using a Marlow-like persona, he plays the white man revolted by the imperialist undertaking of his brethren, but at the same time revolted by the "primitive spirit" of the black man: "Behind us the music was growing wilder. . . . They had made a big circle, and in the middle of it Chenault and the small, waspish black man were doing the dance" (*Songs* 99). Falling "helplessly into a trance," Chenault strips, hypnotized by the primitive, sexual music: "She looked small and naked and helpless." Her white protector is beaten down as he struggles, "finally going down under a wave of black bodies" (*Songs* 101). In what reads like a gang-rape, the white man's most prized possession, his woman, is taken from him and he is left powerless, absorbed by a black mass, no longer visible or in control.

He leaves the territory, claiming that "the pattern [in Puerto Rico] is no longer Boom or Bust, but more along the lines of Organize and Solidify" (*Songs* 103). In what is an interesting, although indirect conflation of forces, Thompson seems to refer not only to capitalist organization and segmentation, but to the absorption, which the now-menacing black masses threaten. Once he can no longer enjoy the relative liberty that is at risk, he decides it is time to move, citing the Odyssean need to "seek what might be called 'the challenge of the uncertain'" (*Songs* 95). He recalls "that I read that experience makes the man and that he should push into unknown worlds and plum their meanings" (*Songs* 95). Ever the white liminal figure, he retains the privilege of moving on.

Thompson's work continues to reflect the tension between a desire to return to the age of independent American individualism, and a fear of dissolution into a civic-oriented coalition that embraces an egalitarian ethic—an ethic that acknowledges difference without establishing a "stabilizing" hierarchy. Thus "community" becomes coded as "politics." The fear of the masses requires the dismissal of *civitas* as the quaint ideal of participatory democracy:

> I think it's important not to avoid the ideal that reality in America might in fact be beyond the point where even the most joyous and honorable kind of politics can have any real effect on it. And I think we should also take a serious look at the health/prognosis for the whole idea of Participatory Democracy, in America or anywhere else.
>
> That to me is an absolutely necessary cornerstone for anything that we might or might not put together—because unless we're honestly convinced that the Practice of Politics is worth more than just a short-term money that power pimps pay for hired guns, my own feeling is that we'll be a lot better off avoiding all the traditional liberal bullshit and just saying it straight out: that we're all just a bunch of fine-tuned Political Junkies and we're ready to turn Main Street into a graveyard for anybody who'll pay the price and even pretend to say the Right Things. (*Songs* 157)

The public, gullible and ignorant, cannot be trusted to choose.

The flip side of Thompson's cynicism was a desire to practice an activist participatory politics. In *Songs of the Doomed*, Thompson discusses his "Iguana Project," an early plan for influencing mainstream politics by forming a coalition of the youth and "freak" vote. "If we can put together a platform that speaks not only for the new eighteen-to-twenty-one year olds but also the 11 million or so who turned twenty-one since '68, and also the Rock vote, the Drug vote, the Vet vote, the Hippie Vote, the Beatnik Vote, the Angry Liberal Vote—if we can do all this, we can force at least one candidate for the Democratic nomination to endorse our position and sink or swim with it" (*Songs* 133). His plan in 1971 co-opted the infrastructure of the American Independent party to push through a populist-liberal agenda that could then be used as leverage against the Democratic Party, a strategy that most third party campaigns have used since the nineteenth century. Nothing came of the "Iguana Project,"[11] but it sheds light on Thompson's highly publicized campaign to become sheriff of Aspen, Colorado: an election that almost succeeded and relied on a carefully managed grassroots coalition composed of local liberals: "druggers," anarchists, the poor, and citizens who resented land developers. In writing about his failed bid for office, Thompson reveals the impact of his loss on his vision of communal politics: "It occurs to me now that I could have left it all alone, and—except for my role as a journalist and all the constant action it plunged me into—my life would not have been much different, regardless of who won or lost any one of the myriad clashes, causes, confrontations, elections, brawls, chases, and other high-adrenaline situations that I found myself drawn to" (*Songs* 114). His admission signals his commitment to the role of observer. However, this focus was apparent even in his populist candidacy. Ultimately, as seen in his sheriff's platform,[12] the sphere that he is most interested in protecting is not the public realm, but the private; the site of political action shrinks from Aspen to his own Owl Farm, and shifts the emphasis from positive liberty to negative liberty, in which he stresses the imperative of noninterference. Like his literary mentor Kerouac, Thompson ultimately chooses to align himself with a decadent individualism.

## The End of American Individualism

"He who makes a beast of himself, saves himself from the pain of being a man." This epigram opens *Fear and Loathing in Las Vegas* and suggests an almost existential approach to the malaise of modern society, but it also reveals a misanthropic strain in Thompson's work that focuses on the predilection of the human toward bestial behavior. He suggests that a crude utilitarianism directs the human, an essentially pleasure-loving, pain-avoiding creature. Like Burroughs, Thompson's pessimistic view of human nature precludes, at the very least, an effective communal structure, and might in fact necessitate a coercive civic structure. For Thompson the desire to live within community is in constant tension with his disgust for the primal urges that no human can avoid. A Hobbesian vision of society results. Community serves only to protect the rights of the self-interested, and society constructs a rigid system to enforce stability. His work denies the understanding of *communitas* as mutually beneficial and democratic.

We might begin to analyze these tendencies by dividing his work into Road Tales and Aspen/Woody Creek Activism. This opposition exposes the tension for Thompson between the individualist and civic roles he found himself playing. Hunter Thompson's trip to Las Vegas, which he undertook with Oscar Acosta, was an attempt to write a new kind of novel. "My idea was to buy a fat notebook and record the whole thing, as it happened, then send in the notebook for publication—without editing" (*Shark Hunt* 107). Borrowing Kerouac's spontaneous prose method, he chooses to evoke the truth by going on the road, thus recreating an esthetic and personal liminality.

In the Road Tales the conflicts between unity/community/meaning and individual/fragmentation/meaninglessness/shallowness becomes apparent. Thompson moves from place to place, looking for the edge, for the speed freaks, for danger while also looking to subvert the system. But in so doing, he takes on the persona of the explorer, of the returning conqueror (as in *Lono*), the twentieth-century embodiment of the Emersonian "representative man."

*Fear and Loathing in Las Vegas: A Savage Journey to the Heart of the American Dream,* is Thompson's clearest, most penetrating exposé of modern American culture. In a parody of westward migration the great "red shark" loaded with supplies and illegal drugs (calling to mind the wagon trains loaded with provisions) roars toward the ultimately corrupt apotheosis of American ingenuity.

However, the novel is not simply an indictment of gauche materialism. Thompson reveals his contempt for the technology that has transformed humans into grotesque automatons, and in depicting the reification of "movement" into pure product, also a nostalgia for a time when Emerson could imagine great individuals moving with force and purpose. But Thompson's disillusion with Emersonian idealism demands a necessary isolationism in the midst of technological alienation. Community is made impossible, because human beings are revolting.

A parody of the western, the novel opens with Thompson and his faithful sidekick, "Samoan" attorney Oscar Acosta, heading toward Las Vegas. Thompson's instinct toward movement provides an ironic counterpoint to the westward expansion of the century before. Although his nominal purpose is to cover a little-known dirt bike race called the Mint 400, Thompson claims that he is really in search of the American dream: "What was the story? . . . Horatio Alger gone mad on drugs in Vegas" (*Vegas* 12). Thompson expects to find that American individualism has been packaged and sold. But he soon comes to the further realization that the systemic forces have tamed real individualism by constructing a self-enclosed, and perhaps inescapable public space. Las Vegas is the material embodiment of the sorts of fluidity that the market has substituted for actual liberty: "Stand in front of this fantastic machine, my friend, and for just 99¢ your likeness will appear, two hundred feet tall, on a screen above downtown Las Vegas. Ninety-nine cents more for a voice message. "Say whatever you want, fella. They'll hear you, don't worry about that. Remember you'll be two hundred feet tall . . ." Nobody can handle that other trip—the possibility that any freak with $1.98 can walk into the Circus-Circus and suddenly appear in the sky over downtown Las Vegas twelve times the size of God, howling anything that comes into his head" (*Vegas* 47).

Thompson's depiction of Las Vegas invokes the mythos of the open west, but exposes the reality as only deceptively open. Individual movement has been insidiously and intoxicatingly replaced with technological manipulation. Thompson disputes the claim of the democratizing benefits of modern technology.[13] The democratization such technology breeds is a blasphemy against the nature of the Real Individual, the "God" to which Thompson refers, and the only god Thompson accepts. Like Burroughs, Thompson reveals a terrified contempt for the "other's" voice. What happens if "anyone" can be heard? A mechanically and grotesquely magnified image does not make "anyone" into a "True Individual," but instead projects his vacuity for all to see, or at least for Thompson to see with disgust. As in Alan Trachtenberg's description of the vertiginous rise of potential Algers,[14] the average "man on the street" may now rise, but here the rise is only of a technologically engorged psyche. The reification of the ego has been exacerbated by commercial technology. Thompson portrays the move "up" as a deliberate and systemic deception in which the "individual" willingly participates.

Thompson's critique examines the ways in which technology has recreated effective and progressive movement. He finds his most striking image in the revolving barroom of the Circus-Circus, which takes its patrons in complete circles. The idea of "revolution" is itself compromised severely within the Circus-Circus, entrapping its subjects even while they aimlessly circle. In the interior of Circus-Circus, the subject is given the impression of unlimited opportunity, but the patron revolves in circles and is transformed from participator into spectator. To "entertain" suggests to "engage" or "involve" but it also connotes a superficial engagement that deflects or subverts serious consideration. For Thompson, the Circus-Circus is "the main nerve . . . the vortex of the American Dream" (*Vegas* 47). In the spinning vortex Thompson finds the free American individual immobilized and impotent in the seductive circulations of consumer capitalism. Thompson discovers that a center of the old West colonial-frontier mythos has given rise to an ironic effect: it is both the ultimate result of American individualism and the breeding ground for the interpellated, effete American individual he scorns. The entertainment state has co-opted liminal spaces, sponsoring money-making carnivals where its subjects can temporarily feel liberated.[15]

The implications of such a construction are grim: the transfixed automaton cannot achieve historical agency. Thompson demonstrates his own paralysis, able to sleep only with the white hiss of a television set, revealing a modern dependence on techno-logical mediation for an illusion of control that actually prevents awareness and action: "I walked over to the TV set and turned it on to a dead channel—white noise at maximum decibels, a fine sound for sleeping, a powerful continuous hiss to drown out everything strange" (*Vegas* 62). This desensitization not only trans-fixes the automaton within this revolving, all-encompassing, "en-tertaining" space, but also paralyzes both individual movement and political activity.

For Thompson, the inefficacy of communal movements is symbolized in the hippie obsession with drugs. Like the inertia that Raoul/Thompson experiences at the Circus-Circus, so too does the drug "trip" incapacitate. Getting "higher and higher" be-comes the all-consuming goal and perhaps the only option in the closed, mediated spaces of a deadened America where volunteer-ism is impossible. The goal is no longer to go farther, but is now to reach the ultimate high. Vertical societal movement is sup-planted by a specious, individual movement: "Let it roll! he [Acos-ta] screamed. Just as high as the fucker can go! And when it comes to that fantastic note where the rabbit bites its own head off, I want you to throw that fucking radio into the tub with me. . . . Just tell them I wanted to get *Higher*!" (*Vegas* 60). The endemic use of drugs replaces the socio-political space with one that is impervi-ous to "real" change, conducive only to entropy.

Thompson's own drug use becomes central to understanding his ambivalence toward the possibility of communality. At his most optimistic, Thompson suggests drug use itself constitutes the potential for a counterculture. Drugs seem to function not so much in misshaping reality, but rather to reveal the underpinnings and interiors of reality, the reality that exists "below" false con-sciousness. A chemical form of psychotherapy, drugs reveal the true psyche. The resulting distortion reveals darkened, personal interiors. This artificial "double-consciousness" is subversive be-cause the interpellated subject's sight is temporarily liberated.

On the other hand, Thompson's drug use grounds his theory that gonzo journalism is truer than mere "fact." Thus drug use and gonzo journalism simultaneously provide insight into that which lies beneath the veneer of society while providing an escape from the strictures of that society. It is this drugged, hallucinatory state that allows Thompson to see the subjects populating Vegas as surrealist grotesques (Ralph Steadman, the illustrator of the novel, draws monstrous humans).

Yet Thompson calls the socio-political efficacy of such "sight" into question. Ultimately his "pioneering" of interior space proves to be mere introspection, which results in nothing more than deeper physical, spiritual, and political immobilization. When Thompson takes a drug made from the adrenal gland, it results in terrifying paralysis: "I was so wired that my hands were clawing uncontrollably at the bedspread . . . My knees locked . . . I could feel my eyeballs swelling, about to pop out of the sockets. . . . It was hard to move my jaws; my tongue felt like burning magnesium. . . . I couldn't move. Total paralysis now. Every muscle in my body was contracted. I couldn't even move my eyeballs, much less turn my head or talk. . . . Death. I was sure of it. Not even my lungs seemed to be functioning. I needed artificial respiration, but I couldn't open my mouth to say so. I was going to die. Just sitting there on the bed, unable to move. . . . At least there's no pain" (*Vegas* 133). The drug-created liminality does not lead to any form of agency nor does it lead to *communitas*. Its only beneficial quality is as an escape from pain. He later alludes to Oedipal self-blinding by printing the newspaper account of a drug user who gouges out his own eyes while on a hallucinogenic trip. This form of introspection is not revelatory, but merely blinding.

This effectively declares the "freak movement" dead. The political potential of drug use is co-opted by the market that capitalizes in escapist entertainment: "The big market these days is for downers. . . .What sells, today, is whatever fucks you up—whatever short circuits your brain and grounds it out for the longest possible time" (*Vegas* 168). Thompson treats drug culture as a symptom of the dystopic reality dissipating utopian potentialities. His assessment of the counterculture's failure to reinvent American democratic ideals reads like a postmortem and is well worth quoting at length:

We are all wired into a *survival* trip now. No more of the speed that fueled the Sixties. . . . This was the fatal flaw in Tim Leary's trip. He crashed around America selling "consciousness expansion" without ever giving a thought to the grim meat-hook realities that were lying in wait for all the people who took him too seriously. . . . No doubt they all Got What Was Coming To Them. All those pathetically eager acid freaks who thought they could buy Peace and Understanding for three bucks a hit. But their loss and failure is ours, too. . . . A generation of failed seekers who never understood the essential old-mystic fallacy that somebody—or at least some force—is tending that Light at the end of the tunnel. . . . First gurus. Then, when that didn't work, back to Jesus. And now, following Manson's primitive/instinct lead, a whole new wave of clan-type commune Gods like Mel Lyman, ruler of Avatar, and What's His Name who runs "Spirit and Flesh." (*Vegas* 178–79)

Thompson enumerates the failure of radical groups to find an ideological center around which to unite except the solipsistic and narcissistic individual, doomed to fragmentation and paralysis: "The realities were already fixed; the illness was understood to be terminal, and the energies of the Movement were long since aggressively dissipated by the rush to self-preservation" (*Vegas* 180).[16] The Manson "family" recurs as a grotesque and criminally insane—but sympathetic—parody of domesticity and community indicative of alternative forms of *civitas*.

Attempting to leave Las Vegas in a paranoid frenzy, Thompson finds that he is unable to escape. The city has only one highway and circumstances conspire to return him despite his running from Las Vegas at high speed. "This is how the world works. All energy flows according to the whims of the Great Magnet. What a fool I was to defy him. He knew. He knew all along. It was He who sacked me in Baker. I had run far enough, so He nailed me . . . closing off all my escape routes, hassling me first with the CHP and then with this filthy phantom hitchhiker . . . plunging me into fear and confusion. . . . I was going back to Vegas. I had no choice" (*Vegas* 95). Faced with no choice as to living within the confines of a closed system, Thompson retreats to an individualism that promises to secure movement within this systemic enclosure, a retreat his fellow traveler, Jack Kerouac, and many middle-class youth rebels made.

What Thompson does not seem to acknowledge is that the failure to cohere, to construct a viable *communitas,* has more to do with the superficial nature of the appropriation of marginal identity without a profound commitment to struggles at the periphery. This failure to form a lasting alliance with racial struggles facilitated later reintegration into the mainstream for student and middle-class rebels, an option not open to their counterparts of color. Thus the barrier to a long-lasting social alternative was based in large part on the commitment to individualism rather than to civil rights and a communally based egalitarianism.

The search for the "American Dream," the initial rallying cry and Holy Grail of the novel, yields an old bar that was earlier converted into a psychiatrists' club, now toppled to make way for a "nut house." Its reality is neither romantic nor inspiring: "a huge slab of cracked, scorched concrete in a vacant lot full of tall weeds . . . which burned down about three years ago" (*Vegas* 168). Thompson subverts the physical and even spiritual place for which Americans have long searched. Even the individual seeker, the one legitimate pioneer, a Kerouacian backpacker who lives simply and unselfishly, is arrested and abused by corrupt police. Thompson uses this episode as the epithet for the "movement." The state frowns upon "real movement" outside its prescribed spaces. "To hell with the American Dream," Thompson mutters returning to the only place in which the pervasive system sanctions movement, the Circus-Circus (*Vegas* 190).

He attacks modern American culture by suggesting that its politics of entertainment and its political identity are one and the same. The Edenic garden Whitman saw is now but a corrupted desert. Vegas is not a naturally settled town, but an "artificial" city, constructed for the purposes of consumption and expenditure, the complete commodification of a space. Ultimately, the American dream's modern reality is a rampant perverse commercialism. In response, even the observer-critic must render himself "insane" in order to differentiate himself from the masses of animalized robots populating the terra firma of what is accepted as reality in Vegas. "The main story of our generation" turns out to be the empty repetitious "entertainment of the Mint 400." Where Thompson fails, however, is in penetrating the gaudy exterior of Las Vegas to examine the effects of the individualist strain in American democratic discourse that has rendered its subjects vulnerable to the rampant commercialism he detests. Instead, the drug-addled ethnographer establishes an "objective" distance by observing from a "higher" platform.

The issue of individualism undergirds all of Thompson's work.[17] He rails against the aggrandizement of the ego, which he sees as the center of rampant commercialism, while longing for the age of the great individuals (Captain Cook, Lono the Hawaiian god, H. L Mencken, and so on). Thompson's solution to the vacuity of late capitalism depends upon reconstructing the Great Man. As in Kerouac's 1950's version, Thompson's Road Tales seem to suggest that if the modern American is to escape the fate of becoming one of the mass of techno-mata running in circles, he must retreat into an isolated, protective atomism. Rather than overturning the system, he aims only to resurrect the principles of rugged individualism. Such a move takes no account of collective agency and political change, and in fact serves as a requiem for the freedom, hippie movement.

In the epigraph for *Songs of the Doomed* Thompson quotes the famous passage from *The Great Gatsby* in which Nick Carraway contemplates the failed ideal of the United States, and adds his own lament for the demise of the age of true American individualism. Thompson's frequent collaborator, artist Ralph Steadman, describes Thompson's vision: "Hunter may be the reincarnation of LONO—the God returned after 1500 years of wandering like a lovesick child to save his people—and his beloved American Constitution. . . . he sees inside the blackness of those silhouettes searching for the soul of a nation, united only in its desire to seek individuality in a melting pot" (*Songs* 33). Like Nick Carraway, whose search for true individuation ends in a dream of a lost America, Thompson turns his disillusionment into nostalgia for the ideal past. Like Jack Kerouac returning to the East Coast rhapsodizing about the forefathers of the nation, Thompson returns time and time again to analyzing the root of "our doomed generation" as a failure to live up to the spirit of democratic individualism.

## Visions of the Great Individual

Thompson's novel *The Curse of Lono* reveals the antagonism between exploitative liminality and the fear of true radical alternatives by once again positing the "great individual" against the commitment to *civitas.* The novel follows the same pattern as his exposés of the Hell's Angels, Las Vegas, and the 1972 Campaign Trail: the lone traveler "seeking for what he has never found," finding drug induced "adventure" as he reports on a competitive event (a marathon, a race, a campaign, the Superbowl, the Kentucky Derby).[18] In this way, Thompson suggests that the American character is defined by competition and danger in search without conclusion. Thompson reserves his highest admiration for events in which a sole survivor is crowned champion, and reserves his greatest scorn for the marathon participants who are satisfied with "Finishers" T-shirts. He and his friends do not enter the race but, as passive spectators, "heap abuse" on the runners:

> "You're doomed, man, you'll never make it."
> "Run you silly bastard."
> "You'll never make it back. You won't even finish! You'll collapse!" (*Lono* 51)

Thompson demonstrates that merely finishing is failure. Initially, Thompson's contempt is for a generation of "competitors" who transformed a "progressive" political movement into the pointless, circular movement, similar to the marathon. He observes cynically that the radicals of yesteryear are mere "runners" today:

> The same people who burned their draft cards in the Sixties and got lost in the Seventies are now into *running*. When politics

failed and personal relationships proved unmanageable; after McGovern went down and Nixon exploded right in front of our eyes . . . after Ted Kennedy got Stassenized and Jimmy Carter put the fork to everybody who ever believed anything he said about anything at all, and after the nation turned en masse to the atavistic wisdom of Ronald Reagan.

Well, these are, after all, the Eighties and the time has finally come to see who has teeth, and who doesn't . . . Which may or may not account for the odd spectacle of two generations of political activists and social anarchists finally turning—twenty years later—into *runners*. (*Lono* 55)

Thompson's critique stops short of examining racial and economic factors in the dissolution of 1960s radical movements. For him, the reason can be found in the lack of individual grit and determination. They simply lacked the "teeth" to compete effectively.

Thompson rightly suggests that the return of the Far Right is in part a reaction to the disillusionment of Watergate, while questioning the level of commitment to radical alternatives. But what Thompson cannot grasp is that true radicalism was rejected for the atavism of Ronald Reagan, and not for lack of competitive edge (individualistic killer instinct), but because of it.

## The IV Amendment: Defending the Perimeter

Like Jack Kerouac, Thompson in his late career has been most concerned with a reaction to perceived attacks on personal liberty. In *Songs of the Doomed*, Thompson angrily denounces capitalist materialism but stops short when confronted with the necessity of a communal counteraction. Rather, he conflates the invasion of "greed-head" land developers (the capitalist forces) with a xenophobic paranoia of a new threat: the invasion of a Latino menace. "There is a whole new ethic taking shape in South Florida these days, and despite the rich Latin overlay, it is not so far from the taproot of the old American Dream. It is free enterprise in the raw, a wide-open Spanish-speaking kind of Darwinism, like the Sicilians brought to New York a hundred years ago and like the

Japanese brought to Hawaii after World War II, and not really much different from what the Israelis are bringing to Lebanon today. The language is different, the music is faster, the food is not meat and potatoes, but the message is still the same. Rich is strong, poor is weak, and the government works for whoever pays its salaries" (*Songs* 193). Thompson spends much of his essay describing the Mariel Boat lift in which Fidel Castro sent convicted criminals to the United States, paralleling it with Latin "infestation" of boat people and drugs; corruption is portrayed as the external invasion of the American landscape. It calls to mind Burroughs and Kerouac's "invasion fear."

For Thompson, the corruption of the 1980s is mirrored in the corruption of the Mariel boat lifts in Florida, in which the "American Dream" of coming to this land is transmogrified into an invasion by insane criminals lusting for the profits of drug use. Immigrants are not the hardworking people we find in the works of Tomás Rivera, but corrupted "lepers" and "crazies," bringing their "dirty money to the new heartland" (*Songs* 222). Thompson refutes the possibility of honest or effective communal politics in the face of such corruption. Thompson shifts his political focus to the negative liberty of the individual due to the despoiled tendencies of the "new" American polity. Thompson trades this impossible social movement for a visceral and personal movement: a negative liberty in isolation.

Consequently, Thompson's last section in *Songs of the Doomed* deals with his personal court battle and his defense of the Fourth Amendment. The section is entitled "Welcome to the 90s: Welcome to Jail." Thompson sees the encroachment of a repressive state as the main threat to individualist prerogatives and thus goes on a battle to defend the Bill of Rights, specifically the Fourth Amendment against unreasonable search and seizure, quoting Justice Brandeis's warning against erosion of civil rights by "zealous, well-meaning men" who "are without understanding." Having lost faith in the power of communalism, he ends by battling the encroaching courts and "cheapjacks" trying to infringe on his rights to privacy and security. His latest work, *Better Than Sex: Confessions of a Political Junkie*—inscribed with the Fourth

Amendment—is an extended indictment of the infringements that all political processes impose on the rights-bearing subject.

Thompson's commitment to negative liberty no longer seems conflicted by an idealistic desire to participate communally: "There are a lot of ways to practice the art of journalism, and one of them is to use your art like a hammer to destroy the right people—who are almost always your enemies, for one reason or another, and who usually deserve to be crippled because they are wrong. . . . Mencken understood that politics—as used in journalism—was the art of controlling his environment, and he made no apologies for it. In my case, using what politely might be called "advocacy journalism," I've used reporting as a weapon to affect political situations that bear down on *my* environment" (*Better Than Sex* 16-17). Yet Thompson follows up this claim to individual self-determination by reprinting a letter written to the people of Aspen during his campaign for sheriff in 1970: "despite the natural horror of seeing myself as the main pig I feel ready. And I think Aspen is ready . . . for a whole new style of local government—the kind of government Thomas Jefferson had in mind when he used the word 'democracy.' We have not done too well with that concept—not in Aspen or anywhere else—and the proof of our failure is the wreckage of Jefferson's dream that haunts us on every side, from coast to coast, on the TV news and a thousand daily newspapers. We have blown it: that fantastic possibility that Abe Lincoln called "the last, best hope of man" (*Better Than Sex* 18). Thompson's own subversive critique of postwar American capitalism and political corruption are themselves undercut by his insistence on negative liberty as the first principle in the defense of his "environment."

Thompson's ultimate battle is one engaged within the system, demanding justice according to America's promise, in essence demanding that America live up to "America." Bercovitch's assessment of American Renaissance dissenters holds true for Thompson and much of countercultural rhetoric: "It seems a telling sign of cultural hegemony that even America's prophets of doom have played a part. In spite of themselves, they too helped transform what might have been a revolutionary threat—the experience of communitas issuing in genuinely alternative models—into a model of consensus" (188). In this model, consensus is paradoxically an atomistic individualism that in its obsession with resisting the 'participatory totalitarianism,' embraces isolationistic negative liberty and articulates a denial of the potential of *civitas*. Such a move resembles Kerouac's own tragic deconstructions of all possible communal structures. Both men retreat, fearing encroachment, all the while desiring community. This was not only their struggle, but the struggle of 1960s dissenters who desired to change the world so long as *the* movement did not threaten *their* movement.

# Part 2

# The Americano Narrative
*Postwar Mexican American Dissent and Community*

# 4

# Historian with a Sour Stomach

## Zeta's Americano Journey

> To understand where I am you have to understand how
> the Chicano movement has developed.
> Oscar Acosta, "Autobiographical Essay"

> All the guys I work with down here are either lily-
> livered liberals or loud-mouthed radicals . . .
> Oscar Acosta in letter to Douglas Empringham, 1970

One key characteristic of the countercultural, dissenting text is to interrogate the extent and nature of the rights-bearing subject's political and institutional access. The work of Oscar Acosta does so by uncovering strategies of immobilization erected to subjugate the postwar Mexican American subject. Depicting the biases of the law in dictating material relations and conditions, limiting access, curtailing mobility, and defining citizenship, he displays a keen understanding of both the ideological and repressive components of juridical power. As a Mexican American operating on the crest of a new, more "radical" consciousness (Chicanismo), Acosta not only writes about the complex negotiations undertaken in the interstices of shifting legal definitions of citizenship, but also about the shifting definition of "Brown-ness" with all of its social and civic implications. His interrogation peers inward as well as outward, at the self and the community, examining white America and brown America by the same token. Thus Acosta's movement narrative creates a useful template for understanding the complex, but exceptionally narrow alternatives faced by Mexican Americans living between the affluent society's 1950s and the tumultuous 1960s.

Precisely what this template indicates, however, has been a disputed issue amongst Chicano scholars. Acosta's work has been read (and often dismissed) as a parody of the Chicano movement. He is often written off as an interesting but irrelevant megalomaniac. Critic Juan Bruce-Novoa calls him a "Chicano Kerouac," portraying his work as a palimpsest of the Beat text ("Fear and Loathing on the Buffalo Trail" 41). Ramon Saldivar suggests that his narrative can be read as a chaotic search for identity that ultimately lacks direction. His lone biographer, Ilan Stavans somewhat dismissively suggests that Acosta's work is most useful as a paradigm of lost potential: "I see Zeta [Acosta], not without reason, as a collective paradigm, a useful pattern, a metaphor of millions that are dissipated, without coherent and cohesive guidance" (8). Taken together, these readings form a dismal portrait of the man and his labor, suggesting that Acosta was simply lost, unable to commit to *el movimiento,* perhaps too much influenced by Beat precursors: a derivative Chicano Beat, a caricature of diffuse individualism, a stand-in for a Chicano "lost generation" of sorts.

That Acosta explored a number of roles and identities will not be denied here, but I do take issue with the characterization of his movement (and movement narrative) as erratic or ultimately diffuse. His is much more than a cautionary tale and I argue that Acosta systematically, or at the very least, purposefully and consciously, explored the gamut of roles allowed to the postwar Mexican American. What makes his narrative an important literary and social document is that he investigated the limitations raised not only by the dominant white culture, but also by the Mexican

American generation that preceded him and the burgeoning Chicano Movement through which he created a brief, tempestuous identity. Acosta's "road" would take him from migrant roots, to Beat-inspired road romanticism, to radical Chicano *movimiento* politics, to an ultimate state of anarchistic isolation. Acosta's movement narrative—his journey from migrant, to *movimiento*, to *movida*—provides a powerful and informative case study that reveals the confining roles and restrictive boundaries faced by the Mexican American subject in search of full civic and political participation. In so doing, Acosta's movement narrative carefully charts the limits of both a postwar progressive-liberalism and a countercultural radicalism in creating a fully participatory, fully functioning, fully inclusive citizenship for its people of color.

## Americano Desire

The phrase "Americano," fraught with ambiguity and a good deal of controversy, signifies the ability of the American of Mexican descent to enjoy a full array of social and political alternatives. It signifies full participatory access to this nation's institutions, cultural and political, public and private. "Americano" signifies the right of the American of Mexican descent to retain, to practice, to *live* his or her cultural identity without being penalized, excluded, or isolated. It is largely an unrealized ideal. But I argue that the possibility of its realization drives the Mexican American narrative. It pushed the Mexican American generation (1920–1960) to fight for reform while convincing many that reform through assimilation was the only answer. I argue that the puncturing of that ideal led to the rise of nationalism and separatism that characterized a large and influential faction of the Chicano movement. Acosta's narrative is also inspired by this ideal, and his journey, in its routes, detours, and dead ends, maps the shape and trajectory of that Americano desire.

Although many have argued that Acosta's life was a model of inconsistency, the one constant theme that runs through his books, letters, and legal work is his desire to fully participate, to be a part of the legitimate "scene." It is telling that the definition of legitimacy and its stage of enactment (the scene) are constantly in flux. Acosta's story follows the marginalized and excluded subject, the American noncitizen-citizen, through the confusing and frustrating flux. But whether the scene changes from the courtroom, to the classroom, to the annals of literature, to the protest in the street, or whether legitimacy is to be measured in the eyes of young "white girls," or measured materially, or politically, Acosta never stops searching for a true, concrete, material measure of inclusion.

Acosta makes clear that the roots of his Americano desire for inclusion are planted by his father's generation: the patriotic Mexican American generation with its somewhat naïve hope that it would be allowed to participate if only it could assimilate fast enough, and memorize and practice the "rules" precisely enough. Practicing a similar faith, young Acosta played football, joined the Air Force, went to college, endeared himself to the leftover remnants of the San Francisco Renaissance poets and artists, became a lawyer, campaigned for John F. Kennedy, fought the good mainstream political fight. When these attempts were either met with indifference or failed, Acosta too went on the road, creating a relationship with the alternative press, Rolling Stone crowd that featured Hunter S. Thompson as its most visible practitioner.

Still dissatisfied, Acosta, feeling even more alienated and powerless (impotence is another powerful and consistent theme in his work), gave up on the individualist motif and returned to his *patria*, Mexico. When the inefficacy of this enacted nostalgia played itself out, Acosta took on the role of the Chicano radical, but quickly discovered the limitations of *el movimiento* at the same time that he discovered that the law was itself unable and/or unwilling to bestow upon him a "legitimate" and just role. Acosta's narrative comes to a disturbing realization: Mexican American participation in America remained, and was likely to remain, limited legally, economically, and socially. Acosta decided that the mainstream and alternative mainstream (middle-class counterculture) would not let him participate fully, or at least not as a *Mexican* American; he learned that the Chicano movement wanted to exorcise and erase his American participatory desire, to force him to jettison the *American* component of his Mexican American identity. So he quit on both sides, retreated into isolation, and disappeared off the face of the earth in 1973.

The above narrative sketch, wistful and brief as it may be, attempts to drive home the complex shifts and turns that Acosta underwent, and which I believe are emblematic of the postwar Mexican American search in all its intricate frustration. By the early 1960s, young Mexican Americans had begun to question the presumptions of their parents' generation on the possibility and desirability of assimilation. Race, they began to argue, played too deterministic a role in American society and could not be "overcome," to paraphrase the civil rights movement's ideal. As playwright Luis Valdez wrote from the vanguard, "Most of us know we are not European simply by looking in a mirror—the shape of the eyes, the curve of the nose, the color of skin, the texture of hair; these things belong to another time, another people. . . . [T]hey fill our Spanish life with Indian contradictions. It is not enough to say we suffer an identity crisis, because that crisis has been our way of life for the last five centuries" (*Chicano: The Beginnings of Bronze Power* 53). In a sense, if the "identity crisis" had been caused by the dominant society's extirpation of "Indian" existence (both literally and as cultural properties), then an acceptance of the "Indian-ness" inherent in Mexican American identity could provide for a powerful strategy against the crisis of self-doubt and exclusion. The Mexican American, it followed, created his or her own authentic identity that required its own sphere of legitimacy separate from the racist American nation. The result was that Valdez's indigenous/western binary defined "American" identity as European, Chicano identity as *"mestizo"* and ironically reinforced the racist discourse it sought to delegitimize.

Acosta's narrative exposes the self-limiting action of such a one-dimensional identity nexus in *Autobiography of a Brown Buffalo* (hereafter *Buffalo*). As the "Brown Buffalo" or the "Indian run amok," Acosta acknowledges his indigenous roots (*Buffalo* 41). Yet his identity, he realizes, is multidimensional, complex, impossibly imbricated. His view of himself naked in the mirror suggests a desire to create a unified, fully functioning entity of those diverse facets. He catalogs his body literally and metaphorically in Valdez's symbolic mirror: "brown belly," "two large hunks of brown tit," "sunbaked face," and "large, brown ass" (11). All are surveyed critically "every morning of my life" (11). Acosta's view of the fragmented self fuels his search for a form of social and political and personal agency that neither restricts or denies those different facets of his being.

Thematically Acosta's search for the self operates between two powerful poles of influence: the impulse toward forming personal identity through a process of individuation and the impulse toward forming a communal identity. As in Kerouac's movement narratives, this dialectic is articulated through the rhetorical interplay of "movement" as neoindividualist search and "movement" as communally undertaken political struggle. However, unlike Kerouac, Acosta's search is complicated by his desire to find or create a sphere of influence in which an amalgamation of both his "Mexican" and "American" identities can operate fully. While Keroauc, Burroughs, and Ginsberg went in search of ways to "disengage" from an "America," which they saw as threatening to individualist, Anglo, male prerogatives, Acosta's purpose (and the postwar Mexican American/Chicano's) is to find a way to successfully *engage* within an America that he sees as marginalizing and that seeks to render both him and his community irrelevant.

## The Mexican American Father

An early, Chicano-era essay by UCLA sociologist Fernando Penalosa suggests that the Mexican American subject must not collaborate with the dominant Anglo power by accepting barrioization. His essay was criticized at the time for denying that there was such a thing as a "Mexican American culture," and because it actively endorsed assimilation. That critique aside, however, we can also read into this essay an anxiety stemming from social and racial stratification: the very real possibility of being relegated to the narrow confines of the barrio or the picking fields. Penalosa recognized, and invoked, a paradigm that held sway as the Chicano movement emerged: the choice facing the Mexican American was to either *move* as an individual, which meant to assimilate and become "American" (as he advocated), or to join the movement, assert a Chicano identity, resist "Americanization," and lay a claim to Aztlan (both a symbolic and literal Chicano nation that Chicano activists argued was occupied territory). This was a limited choice, for in the former case what was required was a jettisoning of Mexican cultural identity, in the latter, a jettisoning of American identity.[1]

In a short piece titled "Autobiographical Essay," first published in 1971 and later compiled in *Oscar "Zeta" Acosta: Uncollected Works* (hereafter *Uncollected Works*), Acosta recognizes the stratification that shaped his worldview and fueled his rebellion: "The towns there were all the same, built around the railroad tracks. On one side of them you had the Mexicans; on the other side you had the Okies and then further out you had the Americans. Where I grew up, the world was composed of that—Mexicans, Okies and middle-class Americans—and nothing else" (*Uncollected Works* 5). Read as a spatial metaphor, Acosta's personal identity is overlaid with the same socio-racial divisions, a sort of internalized segregation of the psyche. To cross into the "wrong" side of town is to commit the transgression not only of invading the racial-ethnic other's space, but an act against one's own kind. Staying where one belongs geographically enacts the policing of "minority" identity; the accusation of "assimilationist" or *"vendido"* works as a persuasive cultural border patrol. An acceptance of either situation (psychic or social segregation) means living in a socially enacted, but partially self-enforced isolation.

The Mexican American generation sought to break out of that isolation at any price. Although they would be pegged later as "accommodationists" by certain Chicano militants, this postwar Mexican American generation, argues Mario Garcia, "realized better than any previous political generation of Mexicans in the U.S. the contradictions between American ideals and practices. However, they believed that these contradictions could be overcome or tempered until a later and more propitious time for greater fundamental change through peaceful reforms" (*Mexican Americans* 20). Since the end of World War II, the rise of a small, but growing Mexican American middle class had agitated for social and economic inclusion swelling the ranks of grassroots political organizations throughout the Midwest, Southwest, and California. A number of groups—the League of United Latin American Citizens (LULAC), *El Congreso del Pueblo de Habla Española* (Spanish Speaking Congress), the School Improvement League of San Antonio, the *Asociacion Nacional Mexico-Americana* (ANMA), the American G.I. Forum, union organizers, and various intellectuals—formed a varied and vocal vanguard that called for equal opportunity in America.

Mario Garcia writes that the "Mexican-American Left shared with middleclass liberals a reformist character within the boundaries of New Deal welfare capitalism" (*Mexican Americans* 33). And as David Gutierrez has shown, the Mexican American generation had a vocal and active socialist and labor-oriented faction.[2] Scholars may debate the nature and legacy of the Mexican American generation, but what cannot be denied is its strong determination to be included, to be relevant on the national scene.

Acosta describes his parents as quintessential members of the Mexican American generation, their identity tempered by their immigration experience and their desire to assimilate. His father's tour of duty as a sailor during World War II leads to a feeling of patriotism and loyalty to an idea of an America that has yet to materialize. As Mauricio Mazon shows in *Zoot Suit Riots: The Psychology of Symbolic Annihilation,* the patriotic fervor shown by loyal Mexican American citizens during World War II was never returned, repaid, or even much acknowledged by mainstream Americans.[3] Acosta's *"indio"* father's reliance on the Seabee's manual for its broad, efficient "know how" instruction suggests a central contradiction in the American myth of inclusion: his father's faith in Yankee ingenuity and self-reliance must be utilized in the junkyard, itself a symbolic site of the makeshift citizenship the Mexican American endured in postwar society: "We'd take a truckful of junk to the dump and spend the entire morning searching through the rotting, burning piles of trash, broken furniture, old clothes, busted tools and old family items, all of us in search of things that the horsetrader [father] thought could still be saved under the rules of the *Seabee's Manual"* (*Buffalo* 74). The *Seabee's Manual,* symbolic of the rules of inclusion and participation, does not contain and magic procedure devised to legitimate the Mexican American or his community. It is with some bitterness that Acosta recalls that he was prevented from playing with "the gang gathering behind the grocery store to smoke cigarette butts," but instead, in an act of futility, "had to shine our shoes and read the *Seabee's Manual"* (*Buffalo* 75). And yet, his father's faith in the manual instills, despite Acosta's frustration, a strategic openness to appropriating the material and social elements at hand found in a largely indifferent, sometimes hostile America.

In "Autobiographical Essay" Acosta discloses this inherited desire to participant in the broader social stage: "Between the ages of eight and eighteen, I hadn't spoken Spanish or hung around with the other Chicanos because, especially in high school, they stood off on the sidelines while I went ahead to do other things" (*Uncollected Works* 6). Acosta suggests that sitting on the periphery, even as a matter of strategic separatism, is not acceptable. It is an Acosta trademark, this penchant for direct engagement within the "mainstream," even as he associated politically with Chicano separatism. His growing childhood bitterness directed at the war effort ("FDR was as much my enemy as were the Japs") expresses frustration at being prevented from participating fully and equally as an "American," as much as it confronts misguided Mexican American patriotism (*Buffalo* 76).

The fact that his father's induction into the navy does not translate into first-class citizenship leads to a prescient awareness of the power of the state and of class politics. It leads to Oscar's first overt act of rebellion, spitting on "the picture of my father's flag" (*Buffalo* 76). It is a symbolic moment signifying not only Acosta's punctured idealism, but also the growing restlessness of a new generation of activists.

In a telling moment, young Acosta's inclusionist naïveté is further dispelled. As a young boy, he develops a crush on a young Anglo girl. He carves a tattoo on his hand and shows her that it bears her name. Although the girl ignores him for two years, he tries hard to impress her, going so far as to fight an "Okie" gamely. Believing that his beloved has taken notice, he waits breathlessly in class as she raises her hand: "'Yes, Jane, what is it?' I hear my teacher say. Silence, my heart flutters butterflies. My God! 'Will you please tell Oscar to put his shirt on . . . He stinks!' The room is filled with laughter. My ears pound red. I am done for. My heart sags from the overpowering weight of the fatness of my belly. I am the nigger, after all. My mother was right, I am nothing but an Indian with sweating body and faltering tits that sag at the sight of a young girl's blue eyes. I shall never be able to undress in front of a woman's stare . . . I might have my jersey ripped away from me in front of those thousands of pigtailed, blue-eyed girls from America" (*Buffalo* 94). Acosta is forced to see himself as he is seen in the "blue eyes" of an Anglo hegemony. Acosta associates his marginality or "otherness" as a part of his body ("fatness of my belly") that is unacceptable but ineradicable. This unacceptable part of him, as seen by Anglo eyes, relegates him to permanent outsider status in the most brutal of all terms: as a "nigger" and "indio."

It was this deepest fear of the Mexican American subject—the fear of exclusion—that the Chicano generation recognized clearly and rejected as a servile assimilation. The Chicano generation would not accept inclusion through a self-imposed eradication of one's Mexican-ness, one's brown-ness. Hence an important part of the generational dialectic was the evolution of a performative brown pride. Through his mother's use of "Indian" as a derogatory term for her children, Acosta depicts the Mexican American paranoia of a separate melting pot for the dark-skinned ethnic—one brewing a "colored" racialization—which prevented an earlier commitment to a unified civil rights cause. Thus, the main failure of the Mexican American generation was to create a communalism that made direct inroads into the mainstream while repressing its brown-ness for fear of being seen as racial "other." As Arnoldo De Leon shows in his study of the racial perceptions of Anglos, *They Called Them Greasers*, the distinction between white and black was carried over by Anglos in making the distinction between white and brown, especially in the Southwest, so that Mexican Americans were especially conscious of the "need" to distance themselves from a colored identity that read them as "black."[4]

Acosta recognizes that while being "white" allows for an individual identity apart from a cultural or social orientation, being "brown" places the Mexican American within a segregated community. His search for legitimation turns toward a personal separatism, a neoindividualist search for the self apart from his brown community, and thus from a colored racial affiliation. It is a strategy that takes him on the road where he will enact a Beat-inspired rootlessness.

## The Limits of the Road

Early in *Autobiography of a Brown Buffalo* Acosta writes, "I speak as a historian, a recorder of events with a sour stomach. I have no love for memories of the past. Ginsberg and those coffee houses with hungry-looking guitar players never did mean shit to me. . . . And the fact of the matter is that they got what was coming to them. It's their tough luck if they ran out and got on the road with bums like Kerouac then came back a few years later with their hair longer and fucking marijuana up their asses, shouting Love and Peace and Pot. And still broke as ever" (*Buffalo* 18). It is a somewhat bitter disavowal of the Beats that reveals his disappointment with a poetics of liberty that ultimately excluded him. After taking a job as a "functionary" in Lyndon B. Johnson's "War on Poverty" he judges it as simply a form of effete gradualism. Acosta charges that mainstream liberalism has failed to integrate American life: token efforts that only defuse social tensions and that do not undo cultural and institutional segregation only perpetuate inequality.

Likewise, the "voice" of Mexican American reformism, for Acosta, is effectively silenced by the machinations of a feckless, irresponsive liberal gradualism blind to its own inherent racism and exclusion: "Doesn't LBJ know Watts is burning in '65? . . .

Am I to prevent all this with a carbon copy of a court order that compels a Negro janitor to pay child support for his nine kids? Does anyone seriously believe I can battle Gov. Reagan and his Welfare Department even with my fancy $567 red IBM? . . . Will it really help turn the tide in our battle against poverty, powdered milk and overdrawn checks?" (*Buffalo* 28). Like Kerouac, Acosta takes off from the Bay Area, travels to Colorado, and then moves south through Texas into Mexico. His Bay Area experimentation with creative writing courses at San Francisco State included time with Mark Harris, Timothy Leary, and Ken Kesey. He writes of "entertaining them with my stories" (100). His dissatisfaction with liberalism and his ineffectual role inspire him to go on the road: "I definitely must run. I've got to hide, to seek my fortune in the desert, in the mountains. Anywhere but here" (*Buffalo* 67).

From the vantage point of making important connections and inroads with major figures of the counterculture and alternative press, Acosta's journey was a success. While in Colorado, he met Hunter S. Thompson and the two established a friendship that would prove mutually beneficial. Thompson was instrumental in procuring a publisher for Acosta's two novels, and Acosta gave Thompson much of the inspiration for *Fear and Loathing in Las Vegas* in which he appears as Thompson's drug-crazed lawyer.[5] A few years later, Acosta would follow Thompson's lead in running for public office. Thompson had run for sheriff in Aspen on the "Freak Power" ticket; Acosta ran for sheriff of Los Angeles County on the La Raza Unida Party (LRUP) ticket. But his Colorado experience and his brief but telling encounter with the mainstream counterculture (Acosta attended demonstrations and "be-ins"), proved inadequate to Acosta for several reasons, the most important of which centered on his growing awareness that he remained an exotic figure, accepted *because* of his difference.

Acosta's journey provides him with the opportunity to mix easily within pockets of a white society heretofore closed off to him. The time he spends in Aspen with "King," the Thompson-inspired character, enacts an acceptance of his "brown" identity, in which his "Aztec" persona performs unfettered before an Anglo gaze that does not reject him as it did during his childhood. It is during this time that Acosta comes to realize that Mexican American assimilationist-oriented inclusion is self-defeating. "Who are these strange people, these foreigners that don't understand me? Friends all, yet they bring me memories of pain and long suffering" (*Buffalo* 62).

In a scene that evokes a trip into Hades, Acosta is "reborn," and thereafter a new sense of purpose inspires him to work his way to Mexico: "[King] left me in my dungeon. I sat at the edge of the bed and tried to come to terms with it. A negotiation of sorts. But how does a man deal with fantasy? When you're in a dungeon all by yourself, a giant Doberman guarding against your escape . . . to whom do you turn? You got your palm read for free, you took her advice and look where it's gotten you? Salvation turned into damnation" (*Buffalo* 164). Acosta's epiphanic allegory reveals the inadequacy of both a Mexican American fantasy of eventual inclusion (it is here depicted as a "dungeon"), as well as insight into the pitfalls of a neoindividualism that undergirds the American libertarian impulse.

It might be argued that Kerouac, Acosta, and Thompson are linked in a symbolic patriarchal triad: Beat father, Beat sons. Thompson acted as a faithful torch bearer who attempted to transform a Beat-inflected neoindividualism into a radical politics; Acosta ultimately rejected the Beat ethos, deciding that its atomistic individualist identity would not fulfill the communal desire that still pulled at him. As he wrote to his estranged wife, Betty in 1959: "Not to overdo it, but I believe that because I have not had a country or a people with which I can fully identify myself, I have been so lost. More than anything else . . . I want to . . . find my peace with society. . . . I am speaking of my peace with the people around me" (*Uncollected Works* 72). This early desire to "arrive" (as Tomás Rivera would depict in the migrant's deepest hope for communal stability and inclusion) becomes more apparent as Acosta realizes that his own experimentation with rootlessness betrays the Mexican American's idyllic dream of inclusion. He remains mindful, however, that such arrival is closed off to him in America: "I had minded my p's and q's and I had committed *The Seabee's Manual* to heart. What else in God's name could they expect of me?" (*Buffalo* 135). It is at this point where we might begin to understand Acosta as the "anti-Kerouac." As Kerouac, Ginsberg, Thompson, and Kesey critique the failings of American democracy based on an idealized past of democratic perfection (a system populated by a narrowly conceived essential rights-bearing subject—the male, Anglo individualist), Acosta writes a stridently antiessentialist critique of modern America meant to revise the pervasive, constricted conception of the "American."

His narrative refutes the empty promises and principles of an American heritage that does not recognize him. His Beat-inflected road romanticism is over before it really starts as he recognizes that even "on the road," an oppressive, intolerant past still has the power to circumscribe his identity. Minding his "p's and q's" has not resolved the on-going contradictions of a liberalism that allows exploitation to flourish. Acosta cannot find a place in America, even within the alternative cultural sphere because of the preconception of the essential universal rights-bearing subject as white, male, and Anglo. This presumptivist liberalism does not allow for the possibility of effecting a revised democratic subject, nor is it up to forming a wide-scale reformist strategy.[6] It is a form of liberalism catering to an existing, narrowly conceived, and privileged citizenry. Neither Keroauc (as evidenced by his naïve pining to be "black" or "Mexican") nor Thompson seemed to understand the impact of racialism on the liberalist front. As Acosta wrote Thompson, "You think you know about the issue of race in this country, which has led you to conclude that it is not really an issue at all, and so when you read a play that deals with the issue of race . . . you consider it irrelevant. . . . Quite a neat trick if you can pull it off" (*Fear and Loathing in America* 281). Essentially, Acosta realizes that he does not fit into Thompson and Kerouac's nostalgic, idealized notion of an American nation populated by rugged individualists. Neither Thompson's Jeffersonian nation nor Kerouac's Whitmanian exuberance figure in the issue of race in a meaningful way. For Kerouac, race is simply a strategic pose to be utilized for his own temporary escape from the clutches of an American mainstream culture of containment. For

Thompson, Acosta suggests, race is something that will simply be overcome on the way to a more radically atomistic liberalism.

Finding that the "salvation" of neoindividualism has led him into a dungeon of deeper, more profound alienation, Acosta leaves Colorado, convinced that the cure to his identity crisis may reside not in overcoming "brown-ness" but in redefining it. In a move calculated to undo the extirpation of his Mexican roots (his father's Americano desire having led him to deny his children their mother tongue), Acosta heads south: "I stuck it out until I'd saved enough to get out away from those senseless drugs, those lifeless hippies and those tourist funhogs who clearly didn't have the answers for my ulcers or limp dick. . . . I decided to go to El Paso, the place of my birth, to see if I could find the object of my quest. I still wanted to find out just who in the hell I really was" (*Buffalo* 184).

## Returning to La Patria

Upon his arrival in El Paso, Acosta returns to his old neighborhood and upon seeing "his people," reflects on the different forces that have combined to strip him of his ethnic inheritance: "they all are speaking in that language of my youth; that language which I had stopped speaking at the age of seven when the captain [his father] insisted we wouldn't learn English unless we stopped speaking Spanish; a language of soft vowels and resilient consonants, always with the fast rolling r's to threaten or to cajole; a language for moonlit nights under tropical storms, for starry nights in brown deserts and for making declarations of war on top of snow capped mountains; a language perfect in every detail for people who are serious about life and preoccupied with death only as it refers to that last day on one's sojourn on this particular spot" (*Buffalo* 186). While Acosta's nostalgia appears to be a romanticization of his first language, it is actually an expression of his desire to recoup the Mexican part of his identity that the Mexican American generation felt needed to be repressed. It is here that Acosta articulates his sharpest censure of Mexican American assimilation.

When he finds that he is lost in the country of his father and cannot speak the language, Acosta imagines that his identity crisis is a function of cultural amnesia. His sexual hunger turns toward Mexican women for "the first time," where sexual conquest seems to give him the power he has lost in the "blue eyes" of Anglo women he is not allowed to possess. "If you want an exact date, you can say that I became a true son of the *indio* from the mountains of Durango on Jan 9, 1968. With fiery tequila and Country Joe and the Fish, with colored lights dancing in my brain, with more beautiful, voluptuous women at my disposal than I could have imagined in a month, I felt like a man should feel when he's on the lam, on the loose in search of his fucked up identity. We ate tacos and carnitas till they fell out my ears, we danced and drank and made love for a week until my money ran out" (*Buffalo* 190). Predicated on such visceral desires, Acosta's early enthusiasm for all things Mexican is cut short when he is arrested for fighting and must defend himself in a Mexican court. Unable to speak Spanish, he cannot defend himself. His legal skills have no bearing in the Mexican court and Acosta realizes that central to the exercising of political-juridical rights is a sanctioned civic space in which the subject has specific claims. His legal dilemma—the concepts of rights, territory, citizenship—makes for an epiphanic moment as he realizes that Mexico cannot be the site in which he builds a whole and effectual identity. He writes, "I've checked it all out and have failed to find the answer to my search. One sonofabitch tells me I'm not Mexican, and the other one says I'm not an American. I got no roots anywhere" (*Buffalo* 196). Acosta recognizes that he must return to the United States if he is to rectify the statelessness with which his father's generation unsuccessfully contended. Only in the United States can he attempt to create a "whole" identity, a fully functioning sense of self. His strategy will be structured around civic rights, brown-power, and social protest enacted in a radically reconfigured notion of America: Aztlan.

In a complex rereading of American-ness that incorporates Chicano nationalism and American constitutional law, Acosta attempts to synthesize a radically new sense of self that in a direct inversion of neoindividualist isolation, coheres communally. Imagining himself addressing a crowd of both Anglos and Mexican Americans he acknowledges "that unless we band together, we brown buffaloes will become extinct." For Acosta, this communalism must be structured not around a one-dimensional "Mexican" identity that denies him his Americano self, nor can it be built on an "American" identity that denies him his "brownness." He argues that "I am neither Mexican nor an American. . . . I am a Chicano . . . and Brown Buffalo by choice" (*Buffalo* 199). Invoking the right of choice is a complex but ingenious move. Acosta performs his due democratic prerogative by invoking his racial and cultural identity and enacting it on a juridical front. For Acosta such a practice brings together his father's Mexican American desire for inclusion with an ethnic and racial dimension that was often feared and discouraged by that generation.

## From Movement to *Movimiento*

*The Revolt of the Cockroach People*, Acosta's second autobiographical novel, attempts, as did many Mexican Americans in the 1960s, to form a cohesive communalism through Chicano identity. Having acknowledged the influence of his Mexican American father, a Beat ethos, an "American" upbringing, Mexican cultural traces, and his *indio* skin, Acosta plans to deploy fully this multipart identity within the U.S. public social sphere. Initially, his hope is that this multiplex personality is fully operative and demonstrable through Chicano consciousness, a movement that calls for inclusion and an expression of selfhood authenticated through the community. Renaming himself "Zeta," Acosta decides to make Los Angeles the site of his revolutionary objectives.

Several radical and revolutionary events in Chicano and American society marked the year 1968. In March Sal Castro led the Los Angeles high school blowouts in which thousands of high school and middle school students went on strike for a better education. Sal Castro and twelve other Chicano leaders would be indicted in June for conspiracy in a highly publicized trial in

which Acosta acted as counsel for the defense. The arrests demonstrated a new emphasis by J. Edgar Hoover's FBI on cracking
down on Chicano militantism.[7] Later that month, Chicano students at San Jose State walked out of commencement in what was
the first organized Chicano protest at a university. November of
1968 saw at San Francisco State a third world student strike which
would become the most protracted student strike in American
history. The second takeover of local government by Chicanos in
Crystal City, Texas, occurred in that same month and became a
model of political organization that employed local civic action as
the impetus for a national political agenda.

In a sign of Acosta's evolution, he goes from seeking legitimation in the "blue eyes of Anglo girls," to seeking legitimation for
*la causa* in the eyes of the law. The chronology of *The Revolt of the
Cockroach People* (hereafter *Revolt*) follows the three most publicized trials involving Los Angeles Chicano militants. Acosta
acted as counsel for what he calls in his novel, the "East L.A.
Thirteen" (thirteen defendants accused of conspiracy in the Los
Angeles school blowouts), "The St. Basil Twenty-one" (conspiracy to riot), and the "Tooner Flats Seven" (among them activist-
leader Corky Gonzales, all arrested on weapons charges). These
events transpired between late 1968 and late 1970. Acosta depicts
this period as parallel to his own personal and political transformation from politician to revolutionary to anarchist. As countercultural politics reach their zenith, Acosta's persona, Zeta, "splin-
ters" into a revolutionary cell of one. His community dwindles to
a community of one lone individual as an increasingly splintered
Chicano Movement breaks up.

His exclamation that "No soy politico. I'm a revolutionary"
(*Revolt* 186), is a disavowal of the reformist politics of the past
generation in favor of a strategy of direct action central to radical
Chicanismo. However, Acosta's political participation will in fact
retain a reformist aura, taking place in the most reformist of sites,
the courthouse. His objectives, as he lists at the novel's start, are
not at all revolutionary, but are in keeping with his earlier idealistic, but quite reformist goals: "I will learn Spanish. I will write the
greatest books ever written. I will become the best criminal lawyer

in the history of the world. I will save the world. I will show the world what is what and who the fuck is who. Me in particular" (31). It is an ambitious list that is in keeping with a Mexican American participatory agenda that expressed the desire to achieve first class citizenship and equal opportunity.

While Acosta's exuberant rhetoric could easily be read as mere self-aggrandizement, there is also an underlying expression for inclusion that it expresses—the consistent Americano aspiration that links all the stages of Acosta's journey toward self-realization. *Revolt of the Cockroach People* opens with Acosta in the proverbial eye of the hurricane, literally at the center of a race riot, through which he makes a metaphor of his dubious position. Acosta stands within the fracas, yet remains outside its chaos, a participant-observer at ground zero of the Chicano Movement. Though this may indicate an ambivalence toward community, it is more accurate to read his liminality as one Mexican American's wariness of constrictive identity politics. Acosta's metaphor reveals a cautious ego uncertain of how it is most effectively and expressively constituted. Acosta's narrator, Zeta, sees himself as accosted by a communal absorption that threatens to force him to deny or suppress valued facets that make up the self. In this sense, Acosta shares at least one concern with the Beat writers he has disavowed: how does one maintain a protective perimeter around the self and still remain part of a community?

Acosta desires to find meaningful inclusion within a political-cultural formation. He finds his mantra in a recurring epigraph by Mexican revolutionary Lopitos, founder of Acapulco, Mexico:

> La vida no es la que vivimos,
> La vida es el honor y el recuerdo.
> Por eso mas vale morir
> Con el pueblo vivo,
> Y no vivir
> Con el pueblo muerto.

Acosta first sees the inscription while meeting with a fasting Cesar Chavez. Acosta translates the poem with a deliberate ambiguity in regards to the relation of the self to the whole:

Life is not as it seems,
Life is pride and personal history.
Thus it is better that one die
and that the people should live,
rather than one live
and the people die.
                                        (*Revolt* 47)
                    Lopitos
             Acapulco, Guererro, 1960

His translation emphasizes the martyr's role as sacrifice for the people, and as such reveals a certain anxiety regarding self-sacrifice. But what exactly constitutes the "self" is left unanswered by Acosta. Is it a self-centered, acquisitive, bourgeois self? Or can we read Acosta's "one" in the above poem as referring to those parts of the self he resists sacrificing for *"el pueblo?"* Acosta, like the postwar Mexican American, finds that membership has its restrictions and its costs. Chicano affiliation, like Mexican American assimilation, has its psychic and cultural price. And it is steep.

At this stage of the novel, Acosta seems still to believe in the power of reform and democratic participation associated with a brand of inclusive pluralism. Recalling this period in his "Autobiographical Essay," he writes, "Those walkouts were the first major activity by Chicanos as Chicanos in the history of this country. There had been labor groups and political-type groups, but there had never been any group organized to organize and politicize the community as Chicanos on broad-based issues" (*Uncollected Works* 9).

Early in the novel, Acosta attempts to toe the line, to bridge Chicano activism with Mexican American reformism. Both signify a participatarian agenda. Acosta makes clear that he is interested in affecting national politics in the belief (much as his Mexican American predecessors) that local action can and will effect the national scene. His political demands, as late as 1970, are argued on the basis of the right of the Mexican American subject to enjoy equal rights as full citizens of the United States: "we're the largest ethnic minority in the Southwest—certainly here in Los Angeles we are. Statistically, we're the lowest in education, with an eighth-grade education being the median, and we're the lowest in housing and jobs. We have the problems here in Los Angeles and the Southwest that the blacks have throughout the country. . . . [Anglos] tend to see us as immigrants, which is absolutely wrong" (*Uncollected Works* 9).

He suggests that in large part, reform is a matter of making the Anglo American aware of the Mexican American history of participation, contribution, and legal status: "This historical relationship is the most important part of the present day relationships, but it's totally ignored or unknown or rejected by the Anglo society" (*Uncollected Works* 9). Ultimately, Acosta is a radical making conventional demands; he is a Chicano with Mexican American desires; he is a Mexican American who longs to achieve success within a liberalized and inclusive America. Acosta's transformation from this state to one of cynical anarchism that ultimately results in individualistic isolation was occasioned by both an Anglo-American refusal to recognize the Mexican American subject, and more surprisingly, by the narrow confines of a Chicano identity politics. The latter gave up not only on the possibility of reformist, national politics, but also delegitimized the Chicano/Mexican American reformist who desired to participate within the domain of the national culture.

Jose Limon has recently argued that *el movimiento* was too narrow in its activist focus and that its myopic vision blinded it to many possibilities for progress. "I now sense that its emphasis on youth and the universities led us to ignore much that had been accomplished and was being accomplished within the larger Mexican American society beyond the universities, particularly in the 1950s, which provided the foundation for our own success. The movement's nationalism led us to imagine both the dominant society and our culture in monolithic and mythic terms, a worldview from which many have still not yet recovered. Its militancy, while often necessary, was sometimes keyed on a scale of oppression symbolized by the plight of farmworkers but belied, for example, by a steady expansion of Mexican American working, lower-middle, and middle classes" (*American Encounters* 133). A complex reading of Acosta must recognize two useful dimensions of his narrative: first, as a depiction of the postwar Mexican American subject as he or she attempts to navigate an identity nexus within American society; and second, as an accurate representation of a circumscribed identity that proves inadequate to the task of building a broad-based social movement.

Of course, it is specious to "blame" the failure of the Chicano movement on self-chosen separatism, as if such a "decision," or more accurately, drift, could have occurred in a contextual vacuum. There was reason for frustration and disillusionment on the part of Mexican American activists, Chicano or not. Acosta voices his displeasure not only at the Anglo population and an effete gradualism, but also at a broader countercultural movement that he charges with self-interest and a dismissive posture toward racial politics: "we know that no other aspect of the broad movement is going to do shit for us. They'll pay us lip service, they'll condescend to us, but basically they're just as paternalistic to us as the white racist pigs" (*Uncollected Works* 10).

And while he charges the broader civil rights movement with integrationism—"I don't think even they know what they're fighting for because they're integrating into the society that they despise as fast as that society allows them to" (10)—he reveals his own integrationist yearning in a letter written to California politician Willie Brown: "All American is divided into three parts, white, black, and yellow . . . what about me?" (*Uncollected Works* 114).

It is this sense of being dismissed by not only Anglo mainstream politics, but also by the mainstream counterculture and a broader civil rights coalition that drives Acosta toward cultural nationalism. His criticism extends to Cesar Chavez. "Chavez is like a grandfather to the Movement . . . but we don't feel that his progress, his ideology, *is Chicano enough*. Cesar used the *white liberal population* quite a bit and, more than anything, this offends the *average* Chicano" (*Uncollected Works* 10, emphasis added). Acosta's disapproval of a broad-based, interracial coalition reveals much about the nature of cultural nationalism. It sets up an ambiguous, but nonetheless exlusionary criteria for what qualifies the individual as Chicano "enough." It also posits an "average Chicano" whose political reactions are prescribed. Lastly, it disparages the "white liberal population" predicating a monolithic mainstream to which the average Chicano is in direct opposition.

This form of cultural nationalism allows for no interplay of identity whether it be racial, ethnic, or regional. It precludes the possibility of political coalitions based on shared political orientations and class solidarity. Most damagingly perhaps, it suggests the impossibility of a reformed, inclusive, and fair America. "Aztlan is the land we're sitting on now. The land where my forefathers lived hundreds of years ago before they migrated to the valley of Mexico. The Aztecs referred to the entire Southwest as Aztlan. Now the Chicano movement has no need for anyone else's ideas but our own" (*Uncollected Works* 11). In a final, decisive rejection of reformist possibility, he writes, "We don't kid ourselves anymore. We know we're headed for a head-on collision with the rest of society. We're absolutely convinced of it and we're not being paranoid or nothing. We know that the main thing we want now is not better education or better jobs or better housing, because we know that they are not possible to achieve. It is not possible as the result of the history of human nature and the animal instinct against the races integrating in the liberal sense of the word" (*Uncollected Works* 12).

## From *Movimiento* to *Movida*

Unable to enact his communalist instinct in the service of creating an egalitarian national culture *(civitas),* Acosta turns toward Chicano efforts to build a separatist movement *(communitas).* His outright renunciation of mainstream politics protests the modern version of decisionism.[8]

While witnessing the Los Angeles high school blowouts, Acosta answers the call to join *el movimiento:* "Hey ese, come on, carnal. Join up with us!" In deciding to become "Chicano," he recalls a childhood racist incident in which his school principal refuses to allow Mexican children to dance with Anglo children: "The school board told me, instructed me not to let Mexicans march with Americans. . . . I'm sorry boys. But them's my orders"

(*Revolt* 30). In joining the movement, Acosta attempts to heal the rift created by the denial of his right to participate as an "American," a desire that has driven the narrative but has yet to be realized. Chicano community redresses the historical and psychological exclusion, offering Acosta respite from a rootless individualism: "Is this the place for a lone buffalo? . . . I am divided against myself, torn in two" (*Revolt* 42).

This "divided self" is in part a projection of Acosta's struggle to negotiate among the individualist strains of his brown buffalo identity—the misunderstood misfit uneasy with the assimilation of the Mexican American generation, the alienating Anglo-directed counterculture, and the call of Lopitas's poem to forsake the self for communal identity. His decision to enter the march represents his entry into the fray, the "hurricane" that threatens the dominant social structure that has denied him a place while perpetuating the illusion of inclusion.

In what amounts to a militant redefinition of "movement" by these young Chicanos, Acosta acknowledges the discursive struggle that pits an illusory and deceptive sense of movement (the illusion of eventual inclusion for which his father labored), against an invigorated *movimiento,* which aims to restore an analogous relation between "move" and "change." It is a "move" that is undertaken *en masse.* However, in taking this step, Acosta did not count on a growing separatist sentiment that would exclude his "Americano" aspirations by defining them as "selling-out." The price for Acosta, as well as for thousands of Mexican Americans, was a form of self-abnegation that denied critical elements of their "American" cultural persona, and in effect insisted on their living as stateless subjects: cultural nationalists opting for a mythical Aztlan.

This burgeoning separatism arose partially in response to the mistrust of Anglo, liberalist, and radical agendas that historically ignored Mexican American interests. In a speech delivered at a student protest attended mostly by young, white "radicals," Acosta takes this audience to task. "You don't know what you're screaming! You don't know what you're asking for! Do you realize that when it comes down to it . . . and it will come down, believe me . . . When the fires start up, when the pigs come to take us all, what will you do? Will you hide behind your skin? Behind your school colors? Will you tell the arresting officer that you are with the rebels? Will you join up with the Chicanos and blacks? Or will you run back to the homes of your fathers in Beverly Hills, in Westwood, in Canoga Park? Will you be with us when the going gets rough? . . . I doubt it seriously" (*Revolt* 179). Acosta, like many in the ranks of the radical ethnic movements, lost faith in mainstream or middle-class agents of reform, and this disillusionment did not bode well for democratic forms of redress. As Victor Turner notes, social breach (dissent and action) is followed by crisis through which systemic reparation often results in schism rather than reintegration. The nationalist *movimiento* opted for a militant and isolating separatism because it no longer believed in the possibility of a transformative politics.[9] "At that point [1968] I think that most of us believed we could integrate into the society and get a piece of the action. . . . But now, three years later, there have been few changes. . . . [Now] we have chosen a name— Chicano" (*Uncollected Works* 9). For Acosta and many others, Chicano identity has shifted and narrowed. It drifted toward isolation first dictated by an Anglo majority, but now created an empowerment through a cultural and political nationalism.

The separatist strategy did not develop in a vacuum. Early in the trial defense of Corky Gonzales, Acosta attacked the system of grand jurist selection as racist. In so doing, Acosta confronted squarely the inability of the democratic process to afford adequate protection and offer equal rights to people of color. In this most crucial of matters Acosta argued that full, equal, inclusive citizenship was not on the legal, liberal, or radical agenda. It was a disillusionment that was being felt in the ranks of a growing Chicano separatist constituency.

As the narrative continues, Acosta reveals a growing pessimism that this architecture of containment is not simply ideological. The jailhouse holding mainly prisoners of color, the material, concrete manifestation of legal and ideological immobilization, may be impossible to overcome through reformist measures. For Acosta, the vision of the Mexican American subject isolated and imprisoned permanently, kept from participating in the good life and its "democratic" process, spurs his separatist imagination:

> I follow Lieutenant Simpson and Sgt. Lovelace into the gray complex my hands still handcuffed behind me. The New County Jail is a monstrous structure, a square block of granite and concrete and steel. You enter through the back, with iron at your wrists, and the door clanks shut behind you and you are in an *institution,* a world unto itself. The floors are slick cement. The bars on all doors are painted gray. The prisoners are dressed in dark or faded blue jeans and pale blue work shirts. The shirts are stenciled across the back shoulders with the words, "LA County Sheriff—Prisoner." At the entrance, men are jammed into holding cells. They stand back to back, face to face. These men are still in regular street clothes. They have just come from various courts throughout the county and are now being processed and booked, fingerprinted, scrubbed and deloused before being given their new garb and a bed. Deputies in pressed khakis and short-sleeved shirts strut around and shout orders. Prisoner are lined up, fifty at a time. (*Revolt* 150)

In contrast to an earlier description of the "Glass House," the prison with a curiously transparent façade (implying the material repression that underlies the false promise of equal protection and the "pursuit" of happiness), Acosta here confronts the very real physical restraint and immobility of the actual prison. The transformative possibilities left open in an Althusserian recognition of ideological and hegemonic constructs are here closed off. Acosta provides an adroit but chilling metaphorical procession that leads from a repressive, but readable (and thus vulnerable) ideology of (im)mobility to the irremediable material truth of concrete and steel. In contrast to Ken Kesey's use of the mental asylum as the castrating mother institution to which prisoners have willingly given up their freedom, Acosta's prisoners are victims who have been strong-armed and immobilized, covertly and overtly, against their wills. They cannot escape through the appropriation of a marginalized persona like Kerouac, Burroughs, and Ginsberg. Rather, the Chicano is immobilized *through* his marginalization, not freed by it.

Acosta does not simply "regress" into separatism and then anarchic isolationism, but that there are clear and compelling factors that drive his eventual *movida*. These factors are not limited to Chicano separatist sentiment, but include the failure of U.S. liberal-reformism, and the indifference of the broader, middle-class Anglo counterculture mostly concerned with testing the limits of a decadent individualism and the avoidance of Vietnam. When Gilbert, Acosta's *vato loco* sidekick expresses dismay that "those putos are always gonna move us around when they want," it is a critique aimed specifically at the representatives of 1960s progressivism, Robert Kennedy and George McGovern, "liberal Anglos" who are trying to win the support of the Mexican American community for the upcoming election. For Gilbert and Acosta, these are bald-faced attempts to exploit the "Latino vote" that are similar to the south Texas party machine election day "patronage" of the Mexican vote in which votes are bought.[10] "Inclusion" is only a chimera, an empty promise aimed at getting votes. Behind the transparent ideology of natural rights, lies the immobilizing reality of steel and concrete.

For Acosta radical Chicano politics was a rejection of the mainstream. As the definition of the mainstream became broader, the tight circle of authentically revolutionary Chicanos became all the more exclusive. For the radical Chicano, recasting his identity along these lines was necessary not only for resisting a generalized Anglo repression, but also for rejecting the effete gradualism in which the assimilation-oriented Mexican American generation had faith. Thus separatism cut both ways and increasing cynicism had a steep price: "Fuck those college sellouts!" shouts Gilbert in reference to the more cautious Chicano college activists. Gilbert's particular configuration of militant identity has no room for the Mexican American, nor for an "Americano" identity retains its Mexican culture, its faith in reformist social justice, and its aspiration to participate fully in American society. The reality of mainstream indifference (including the mainstream counterculture) and continuing repression pushed some Chicanos to cut ties with Mexican Americans who had participatory aspirations and hopes of creating an inclusive national culture.

Acosta presents his case to the reader as he presents the case to the judge overseeing the Tooner Flats Seven trial. Acosta argues that the fundamental check in a democratic society, the jury system, has never been inclusive or egalitarian. On the basis of the impossibility of fair and objective hearings before the law, the law is invalid and democracy farcical. A relevant scene preceding the Tooner Flats trial follows Acosta's attempt at getting a coroner's inquest to rule "murder" in the apparent "suicide" of a young *vato loco* while held in the custody of the Los Angeles Sheriff's department. Despite the overwhelming evidence that the Fernandez death was a murder, the case is dismissed. An actual autopsy of Fernandez conveys Acosta's sense of futility as well as the fragmentation, indeed dissection, of the larger Chicano body at the hand of a corrupt judicial system and an indifferent American polity. This sets the stage for the trial in which Acosta has already given the reader ample evidence that the nature of the law is not to provide justice or equality but to protect the interests of those in power.

In the face of mainstream social indifference, Acosta takes violent action that not only rejects the legal system and the democratic process it crafts, but ironically also rejects membership in the larger Chicano movement. "You mean a *movida*?" asks Gilbert when Acosta, outraged and discouraged by the inability of the court to render justice, discusses taking violent action. Aside from venting his frustration at the inefficacy of liberal-democratic institutions, the *movida* is also Acosta's way of expressing his disgust with the futility of Chicano politics in the face of societal neglect. After much debate in choosing a political target, Acosta firebombs a Safeway to show support for the United Farm Workers. The target has particular relevance to Acosta's conflicted identity; an action in support of the farmworkers reveals his continued longing for an effective social role.

Within the tension that builds between his attempts to procure a social redress of Chicano grievances and his desire to act alone through unilateral acts of violence, there exists the doubt that radical change can be effected by any of the alternatives he has undertaken. His terrorist activity is not simply born out of a desire to separate completely (there is no actual Aztlan to retreat to or a territory to fight for). Rather it is an expression of a frustrated desire to be included as a fully functioning citizen-subject, a desire that was increasingly unpopular amongst the ranks of cultural nationalists and separatists. Thus this complex interplay of cultural and political identity produces conditions that make retreat into a defensive isolationism seems to Acosta the only possible reaction.

Acosta's loss of faith reflects, in part, the failure of the social contract. For if the makeup of the Grand Jury is itself prejudicial, there is no chance for a democracy to function equitably. To prove this to the jury in the Tooner Flats case, Acosta subpoenaed every judge in the Los Angeles County system. Through their court room testimony he was able to find ample evidence of racism in the grand jury selection. In finding that there has been a breach, he uses Locke's formulation of the fundamental right of the citizen to revolt when the social contract is abrogated by the Sovereign.

However, Acosta's claim that Chicanos are not willing citizens, and are in fact a conquered people of an unjust war, is at odds with his demand that the state admit Mexican Americans into the ranks of the *demos*.

While invoking Locke's argument that the children of a conquered people have the right to renounce any allegiance to the state,[11] Acosta's argument paradoxically calls for state acknowledgment of the Mexican American's citizenship. That contradiction reveals the vestiges of Acosta's Americano desire:

> As Cortez had done before, through modern warfare, through politics and diplomacy, the new white barbarians invade the land and subdue it. They inform the people that they now have a new government and a new religion—Christianity. . . .
>
> "But we are not Mexicans" the people cry out. "We are Chicanos from *Aztlan*. We have never left our land. Our fathers never engaged in bloody sacrifices. We are farmer and hunters and we live with the buffalo."
>
> But they are wrong. They are now citizens of America, whether they like it or not. And we'll call them Mexican Americans. But if they want to be Americans, they'll have to give up their slave name.

A hundred years later, the Chicanos turn to the government and to the priests and ask for justice, for education, for food, for jobs, for freedom and the pursuit of happiness. . . . And when they entered they were told: There is NO Room. Leave, or we'll kill you. Or jail you. Insult you. Mace you. Kick and bite. Scream and holler while the choir sings "Oh come all ye faithful." (*Revolt* 161)

This argument speaks specifically to the promises in the Constitution and to the viability of the American social contract. In this final speech in front of the court, Acosta reveals a struggle to find a viable synthesis, an "Americano" identity, which might legitimately and fully join together the multiple elements of postwar Mexican American experience within the context of full citizenship. He returns to the Mexican American generational demands for egalitarian treatment: education, economic opportunity, freedom, and civil rights. His commitment to cultural nationalism masks a deep desire for participatarian and inclusionary rights. Acosta argues for the acceptance of the positive liberty model of democracy. For Acosta, systemic redress is preempted because the model is already corrupt. Mexican American progressives and gradualists are already doomed because of the historical exclusion of the Mexican subject. In his own words the "Anglo is trying to exterminate the cockroach" and the only way to survive is to create a homeland. "There is only one issue: LAND. We need to get our own land. We need our own government. We must have our own flag and our own country. Nothing less will save the existence of the Chicanos" (*Revolt* 201). Yet, Acosta does not have much faith in that possibility, for the Chicano movement had already failed to build an inclusive community due to its own brand of restrictive identity politics and that fragmentation was already threatening the *movimiento's* cohesion.

Acosta's final act in *Revolt of the Cockroach People* is to plant a bomb in the courthouse that kills one man, ironically, a Chicano. He acts alone and no one is privy to his plan. Soon after, he leaves the *movimiento* behind to write his novel. In considering his *movida,* he writes, "Somebody still has to answer for all the smothered lives of all the fighters who have been forced to carry on, chained to a war for Freedom just like a slave is chained to his master. Somebody still has to pay for the fact that I've got to leave friends to stay whole and human, to survive intact, to carry on the species and my own Buffalo run as long as I can" (*Revolt* 257). Acosta's decision to act alone in pulling a *movida* (a Chicano colloquialism meaning "slick move") has important significance. It announces a break with *el movimiento* and a Chicano identity that is ultimately too narrow. His *movida* indicates his loss of faith that the broader countercultural movement will acknowledge the legitimate claims of the "cockroach people" as well as to effect radical change. Ultimately, for Acosta, it signals an end to the possibility of democratic reform and the sought after inclusion.

Acosta's rejection of the *movimiento* in all its forms (reformist, cultural nationalist, separatist) resembles Hunter S. Thompson's pessimism and paranoia that ultimately led political action to the claustrophobic space of atomistic individualism. While the references to "slavery" might at first suggest an overriding concern for personal liberty, as does his concern for carrying on his "own Buffalo run," at a deeper level it is also a rejection of an identity politics that does not recognize or enable his deepest personal, political desires: both *el movimiento* and mainstream America deny him his Americano identity. Unlike Thompson, Acosta's retreat into isolation does not result from a libertarian impulse so much as from both the loss of faith in a system that he sees as inherently and irretrievably racist, and a Chicano cultural identity that proves myopic. And so Acosta packs up and leaves his "friends" behind. Thus Juan Bruce–Novoa's contention that Acosta's political failure is a reflection of "the failure of the 1960s ideal of the grand coalitions," is only partially right ("Fear and Loathing on the Buffalo Trail" 48). It is also the inability of the Chicano movement to imagine a radical egalitarian, national culture, and the Americano subject that might give it shape.

Acosta's unfulfilled Americano journey had dire implications for *el movimiento* as well as for the fragile union that feared risky democratic debate and inclusion. Faced with the systemic, cultural, and social limitations of the U.S. democratic system, Acosta and the Chicano movement moved toward a separatist position that did not challenge two-tier citizenship (segretation). Ironically, separatism and cultural nationalism signaled a bizarre cooperation that threatened to make the limitations of American democratic participation permanent.

In this sense, Acosta became a victim of his own separatism, for in drawing the circle so tight, he cut off much of what made up the core of his identity. It was a process that proved to be too much of a sacrifice. Unable to continue as a Chicano nationalist, and unable to practice his identity as an amalgamation of American and Mexican elements, he was unable to enjoy a satisfying synthesis that might indeed given rise to a radically new citizen-subject. Ultimately, Acosta resembled the sad, isolated figure against, which he warned Hunter S. Thompson from becoming in a letter written in 1970: "If you were not before, you are now simply an anarchist, the lowest form of politics. It is easy, simplistic and totally without value to merely curse the darkness. . . . in fact, you remind me of the hippie and the militant. The former wants to be left alone and the latter, to destroy, so he can be alone. Your desire to "build a personal fort" is, at best, infantile" (*Fear and Loathing in America* 255). However, Acosta's "failure" is not so much a personal failure, but a failure of viable alternatives. It's a narrative of how a narrowly conceived individual identity, exclusionary communities, and an American political and civic landscape combined to immobilize the Americano dream.

# 5

# Mapping *el Movimiento*

## *Somewhere between América and Aztlan*

> I continue to mull over the social and personal signifi-
> cance of the Chicano movement beyond a close reading
> of texts to a larger reading of American society and
> Mexicans in the United States.
>
> Jose Limon, *American Encounters*

> I look at myself . . . who . . . dissolves into the melting
> pot to disappear in shame.
>
> Corky Gonzales, "I Am Joaquin"

Oscar Acosta is a case study of one Mexican American's conflicted response to the paradoxical nature of the "affluent society." Now we turn to an examination of the internal conflicts in
the making of the Chicano movement itself. Doing so requires
an analysis of how a closing of participatory potential was in
part, a result of isolationist tendencies within *el movimiento*. In
rejecting the imperialist and exploitative past of America, and
what they saw as the complicity of their parents' generation, the
Chicano generation sought to eradicate the pernicious influence
of Anglo culture. Chicanos defined themselves in a new way. No
longer Mexican American, the personal and communal "self"
would be purified of its "American" element. It was an attempt to

circumvent the process of oppositional identification through which the Mexican American subject was forced to reference his or her selfhood, position, and history in relation to mainstream, dominant history and social structure. But what many of the Chicano cultural workers failed to recognize was that in their efforts to define Chicano identity outside of Anglo history and culture, their version of "Chicano" identity continued to function in opposition (in a dialectical relationship) to "whiteness." The Chicano movement invoked white culture by its very attempt to render it invisible and irrelevant. Ignoring this sociocultural imbrication did not eradicate the existence of a shared reality, painful as many of its aspects were and continue to be.

Rather than drawing the struggle as a simple binary opposition between the "mainstream" and the "marginal," a more productive strategy might have been to think of the struggle as a full-on and continuous negotiation to create, and re-create, the national culture and its discourse. Instead, Chicanismo often settled for a facile dichotomy between the "assimilationist/accommodationalist sell-out" and the authentic "Chicano" subject. In attempting to hold that line, Chicanismo proved too limiting and damaged the broader Chicano movement as Mexican Americans saw the rigid choice between separatism and assimilation as untenable.

Examining the limitations of Chicanismo and *el movimiento* will help in an analysis of the emergence of the Hispanic generation (as Rodolfo Acuna has labeled post-Reagan, middle-class Mexican Americans). I use the terms "Hispanic" or "Hispanic generation" in a less judgmental sense than Acuna to refer to the Mexican American subject who readily identifies in this way. The term provides a way of "being" American that being "Chicano" has precluded. Thus when I write "Hispanic Generation" it should be clear that I do not intend it as a rubric under which all Mexican Americans fall, but rather as a term with which a growing number of Mexican Americans self-identify. Critics have treated the Hispanic Generation with a preemptory dismissal or veiled hostility because they assume the term simply designates right-wing affiliation or apolitical self-interest. However, this group's political and class aspirations, as well as the concept of "Hispanicization," should be examined in a fairer light.

"Hispanicization" is not simply a label imposed on Mexican Americans by the Reagan administration that must be "resisted." Nor does Hispanicization simply represent a creeping bourgeois worldview. These characterizations fail to recognize the intense political and economic desire for relevance and inclusion at work within the Mexican American polity and the individual Mexican American subject. It is not enough to dismiss "Hispanics" as victims of interpellation or false consciousness. Rather, Hispanicization functions, in part, as an alternative way of being "American" that answers a desire that was in operation long before the label "Hispanic" came "down from above." However, this study is far from an attempt to "rehabilitate" the term, but instead seeks to understand why Hispanicization has become an attractive alternative to so many, while it has also served a right-wing, conservative agenda rather than the progressive, egalitarian agenda at the heart of an earlier Chicano politics. It is an attempt to analyze why Chicano politics did not satisfy "Americano" desire, and how it failed to incorporate more Mexican Americans in its communal vision. An analysis of the ideological roots of "Hispanicization" must begin with a careful study of *el movimiento*.

The brutal police riot that ended what had been until then a peaceful protest of the Vietnam War organized by the Chicano Moratorium Committee in East Los Angeles on August 29, 1970, prompted an angry response. This letter to the editor of *La Raza*, a radical local newspaper, was published in the September 1970 issue: "Many Americans (of which I am one) are pretty upset, not only this episode, but the entire general attitude of most Mexican subjects whome [*sic*] we have allowed to come into these United States and ly [*sic*] on their dead ass'es [*sic*] and collect welfare or reap the benefits which our Gov. allows you. Most every Mexicano or Chicano illiterate is usually a liar, a cheat, a theif [*sic*] and for the most part very undependable. There are exceptions but dam [*sic*] few" (issue 3, 1970, 4). The letter is an extreme, albeit illiterate example of the more subtle and institutional manifestations of racism that Mexican Americans faced in the postwar era.[1]

The turmoil over the death of Ruben Salazar (two other Chicanos, Lynn Ward and Angel Diaz, were also killed by police in that riot) provides a microcosm of the obstacles facing Chicanos in attaining equal participation and protection under the law in postwar America.

During the Chicano Moratorium police riot, officers were told that "armed Mexican Americans" had been seen running into the Silver Dollar Bar. Eyewitnesses reported seeing nothing of the sort, and testified that three men who were unaware of any danger had in fact been forced back into the Silver Dollar Bar by the sheriff's deputies prior to their firing into the bar to "dislodge the barricaded gunmen." According to witnesses, the bar was not barricaded, and that in fact there was but a curtain hanging between the officers and the interior. The record states that no police officer called for the bar patrons to come out, but that a deputy instead proceeded to fire tear gas without warning.

Rather than using conventional tear gas canisters, which would have been sufficient since the doorway was open, the deputies used high-velocity tear gas missiles that were manufactured to pierce walls. Shooting point blank, at shoulder level trajectory, through an open doorway, the high velocity missile instantly killed Ruben Salazar, a popular and controversial Mexican American investigative reporter. The inquest held by the city was biased in favor of the sheriff's actions. The case was quickly dismissed as an "accidental death" even though there was ample evidence that sheriff's deputies acted improperly.

The case is interesting for many reasons. The killings and inquest convinced the Chicano community that their constitutional rights as citizens in the United States would be blatantly and viciously violated. The inquest demonstrated that their rights would not be upheld through legal recourse. Furthermore, the fact that an inquest was held only for Salazar's death exposed a classism on the part of the Los Angeles district attorney. No hearings were "needed" for the other victims of the police riots. More interestingly, in regards to democratic discourse is the response in the Chicano media to the hearings and the invasion of "peace" officers into the barrio.

In another telling letter to the editor also published in the September 1970 issue of *La Raza,* a reader writes, "My father told me 25 years ago when he was a sailor they beat the Living Shit out of your People. They called themselves "Pachuco's" but the Army and Sailors Made you guy's eat Shit. You know You would'nt [*sic*] do this thing in Texas, because they would Hang Your Chilli [*sic*] Ass." The invocation of the so-called Zoot Suit Riots of 1942 places the Chicano Moratorium murders in a telling and proper context. In both cases the state showed that it was willing to use force in the repression of Chicano/Mexican American cultural and political self-expression. The allusion to the Texas Rangers and their brutal repression of Mexican Americans made it clear to readers of that month's issue of *La Raza* that little had changed for the Mexican American subject since the nineteenth century. It was clear that lynching, beating, and murdering Americans of Mexican descent would be condoned.

The response of the Mexican American community to the violence and the farcical inquest was widespread and varied, but a survey of letters, essays, investigative reports produced by Mexican American citizens show an overwhelming sense of dismay. Letter and commentary alike express anger at the state's efforts to keep the Mexican American outside of the economic, juridical, social, political, and civic public sphere. This growing militancy was rooted in the increasing frustration of Mexican Americans confronted with second-class citizenship despite their contributions to the nation-state's economy, culture, defense, and history. Despite a growing nationalist rhetoric clamoring for a separatist-oriented "self-determination," Mexican American public opinion of the time suggests that what was most clearly and fundamentally at stake was the institution of a broad-based civil rights agenda.

Extracts from a survey of letters written during 1970 to *La Raza* shed light on the most pressing issue for Mexican Americans in that strife-filled year: "My hat is off to you, sir, for not letting anyone with the excuse of 'We do things in an orderly manner . . .' keep you from asking for your rights"; "The cynical attitude towards the witnesses . . . is unforgivable with respect to justice"; "[The inquest] displays a double standard of justice"; "I am very disgusted with the so-called law"; "I demand as a tax-payer, these officers be fully investigated"; "We have a war to fight against poverty, for equality, housing and many other things"; "Police and fireman must come from the very citizens they serve"; "We seek the real truth in our fight for equal justice in the Anglo society."[2] The preeminent sentiment is clearly one of frustration with outsider status; expressions of either revolutionary or separatist programs were represented, but not representative. This suggests that the heart of the matter for the Mexican American community remained the continual frustration of a participatarian desire that could not and would not be ameliorated by a form of Chicanismo that in many ways cultivated, and adhered to, an outsider status. This influential form of *movimiento* politics would formulate an isolationist agenda where there was no overwhelming separatist or indigenous sentiment or support in operation.

Some have argued that the rhetoric of "citizenship" and "rights" is produced by democratic discourse itself, and thus a "revolutionary" sentiment could not be truly or widely articulated. While this may be true to a certain extent, to dismiss the desire for full, equal, operative citizenship as simply a manifestation of false consciousness (or a deterministic democratic, liberalist discourse) is inadequate for understanding the complex political and cultural subjectivity of the postwar Mexican American. I intend to understand Mexican American yearnings and desires as expressed in material terms within the context of lived experience.

Many Mexican Americans sought a fairer, egalitarian America, a *civitas* that would amend the individualist, elitist drift that had excluded many Americanos from the political decisions and material successes that marked the affluent society. Reading Mexican American political and material aspirations demonstrates an immensely variegated constituency within the Mexican American community, many of whom felt alienated by the separatist and indigenous agenda of a vocal minority of *el movimiento*. Although this group consisted of multiple subjects, each a synthesis of multiple influences, all faced a common reality marked by material and experiential racism and economic exploitation.

Mexican American protest was then, as it had been for over a century, a unified, if amalgamated, response to a capitalist ethos constructed, in part, to repress a potentially dissident communal identity.

The Mexican American people were determined to hold the concept of American citizenship to its constitutional ideal, and were committed to practicing "democracy" by creating a *communitas* in opposition to the neoindividualism and racism that permeated American society. In short, to paraphrase one of Tomás Rivera's migrants using the discourse of movement, "they wanted to arrive," in its sense, in America.

Postwar Mexican Americans long immobilized within *barrios* and *colonias,* had been fixed in the social hierarchy through various strategies of containment that included inadequate education, institutionalized racism, exploitative labor practices, and legal and illegal statutes used to both restrain and force movement as needed. Now they confronted the necessity for a coherent, effective plan for implementing a national social strategy.

Many studies have shown that Mexican Americans—despite differences in social position, education level, gender, region, and even political affiliation—demonstrate a strong concern for their community (local and dispersed). Rodolfo de la Garza's 1983 study, conducted by the Southwest Voter Registration Education Project, indicates that despite mitigating differences in the above noted factors, that Mexican Americans shared "collective experiences" and should be considered a "cohesive electorate" (de la Garza et al. 8–9). In his incisive study, "The Many Faces of the Mexican-American," Carlos Gil suggests a strong communalist sensibility despite regional and generational factors. The Latino Cultural Studies Working Group, in *Latino Cultural Citizenship* edited by William Flores and Rina Benmayor also depicts a complex cultural communalism in full function despite an increasingly diverse and dispersed Mexican American community.

The Mexican American response to second-class citizenship had two crucial tendencies: a desire to maintain a united community and culture in the face of anticommunal strategies in the service of capital, and a wish to participate fully in the material and political culture of what was in fact "their" country. However, since "participation" in the American project meant taking part in an individualist democracy that enabled exploitative capitalism, and vice versa, the ability to both create and maintain a community while participating in the national democratic sphere lay in the reformation of capitalistic democracy through egalitarian practices. The answer to the American opposition between community and individual, between capitalism and egalitarianism, was not disengagement as advocated by separatists. Rather it was full engagement on the national and local levels. In his essay on the Mexican American postwar subject, Gil raises an important point: Mexican Americans have not only shaped U.S. culture and society, U.S. culture and society has shaped them as well.

The creation of a progressive, radical alternative to an American ethos of individuality and laissez-faire capital culture, was articulated through the radical democratic practice of transformative egalitarianism as seen in the efforts and works of several key Mexican American/Chicano activists and advocates such as Tomás Rivera, Ernesto Galarza, and Cesar Chavez.

While many efforts of the Chicano Movement made extraordinary and unprecedented strides in this direction, as a whole it fell short of creating an inclusive and nationally effective program. As John Garcia notes, "the primary focus of the Chicano Movement's activities and arenas were the barrio communities" (159). In "Backwards from Aztlan: Politics in the Age of Hispanics," historian Ignacio M. Garcia suggests that Mexican American politics in the 1990s have proven ineffective because "[t]heir agenda is tactically factionalized rather than based on a particular philosophical foundation, because they have no defined national leadership, and because, for all their national aspirations, they do not relate well to American history or Anglo institutions. . . . Their politics remain regionalized and nationally weak. . . . The Hispanic national leadership to date has been a transcendental leadership rather than an electoral-based one" (163). Despite his sympathetic view of *el movimiento,* historian-activist Juan Gomez-Quinones similarly suggests that the movement failed to coalesce lastingly or to produce a coherent national agenda. I would argue that these weaknesses are in part an inheritance from *el movimiento* politics. Relating to "American" history would prove to be exceedingly difficult for movement participants. With very good reason they narrativized the history of the Mexican American in the United States through an increasingly oppositional framework: be it through the lens of a vulgar Marxism, internal colonialist model, or postcolonial model.

Gomez-Quinones tends to put the blame for the dissolution of *el movimiento* on two groups: "the lumpen" (the *vato loco* and "extreme *indiginismo*") and the extremist left ("juvenile leftism"). He also suggests that the majority of students (a microcosm of the Mexican American community) was moderate: "The political fulcrum occurred in the middle; the right and the left extremes were marginal" (5). Taken together, what Gomez-Quinones suggests that a potentially cohesive, progressive, radically democratic, community did not cohere because of a failure of "leadership" to deal effectively with disrupting extremism (whatever its face). But why was the leadership ineffective? Certainly the leadership of the period was not weak. Cesar Chavez, Delores Huerta, Corky Gonzalez, Angel Gutierrez, Reies Lopez Tijerina, Oscar Acosta, Octavio Romano-V, and Juan Gomez-Quinones himself, are just a few of the bold, courageous, and effective leaders of different aspects of *el movimiento*. Individually and as a group, the changes that they helped institute were significant.

Rather, I contend that the movement's decline can be traced in part to a causal relationship between an inability to relate to "American" history and its "Anglo" institutions and what Juan Garcia suggests is a lack of "national" leadership and a "national" agenda: both are required to institute a radical social alternative. In essence, Mexican American/Chicano leaders often mistakenly framed the problems facing the Mexican American postwar subject.

In other words, so long as Mexican Americans were encouraged to see themselves in opposition to "American" history, "American" society, "Anglo" institutions, they tended to move toward an extremist cultural nationalism, separatism, *indiginismo,* and political isolation. While the Marxist contingent of *el movimiento* decried cultural nationalism, they did so in a way that proved ineffective at marshalling communal participation and support. In his analysis of the Marxist wing of *el movimiento,* Gustavo V. Segade recognizes that "the road to Aztlan" (cultural nationalism) led "directly away from fulfillment of the legitimate economic and political aspirations of the Chicano" (89). He suggests that the move from the "culture of politics" to the "politics of culture" stranded the movement. Although the aim of his essay is to historicize the 1970s Chicano Marxist intervention that emphasized class analysis, Segade demonstrates why the Marxist wing was not successful in creating as significant a following as the cultural nationalist contingency. Like the separatists and nationalists, Chicano Marxists ultimately discounted the progressive gains of the Mexican American generation to the extent that they worked actively to dismantle Mexican American studies programs by producing "revolutionary" demands that were dogmatic and even absurd. This transformation "from the politics of culture to the culture of politics," did not serve egalitarian and participatory aims and succeeded yet another set of exclusionary parameters that painted Americano desire cynically as "pragmatic," depicting participation in the "mainstream" as "making it in the system" (92). The Marxist rejection of liberalism through absurd forms of extremism was as destructive to radical democratic action as cultural nationalism.[3]

Likewise, the cultural nationalist wing of "Chicanismo" proved to be an inadequate model for challenging the status quo because it did not produce the vision of America that Mexican Americans time after time demonstrated they desired: potentially egalitarian, communal, inclusive. Gomez-Quinones notes that "gradually a perceptive development in political ideas occurred from protest over the denial of full and equal citizenship rights, to the rise of a vehement nationalism" (14). The push toward a vehement nationalism, which was not "marginal" but increasingly pervasive as the 1960s wore on, attempted to move Mexican Americans in a direction that they did not seem willing to go, if we judge by the movement's decline. This is a complex phenomenon;

the emergence of vehement nationalism did not occur in a vacuum, but was a response to brutal repression and unresponsive
government. Ideologically and materially, the inability, or even refusal, to project the Mexican American subject into "America"
had disastrous effects.

Cultural nationalism that exhorted Mexican Americans to
seek their past and future in Mexico and Mexican cultural and
political tradition was successful in refuting mainstream Anglo
racist views of the Mexican American heritage and culture. However, it was also successful in suggesting to Mexican Americans
that they had in effect, no real place within "American" culture. In
a move that ironically resonates with the racism the movement
challenged, "American culture" was relinquished to the Anglo.
American "democracy" was in many ways now viewed as an
"Anglo" institution. Part of the rejection of the Mexican American generation by the Chicano generation can be traced to the
former generation's pride and insistence on seeing themselves as
rightful participants in "American" culture.

The first issue of the landmark Mexican American journal, *El
Grito,* published in the fall of 1967, features a portrait of Theodore
Roosevelt with the Aztec eagle rather than the American eagle,
poised over his head. Below his ridiculously stern gaze, a floating
banner reads "El Presidente." Next to his portrait is the following
inscription of one of Roosevelt's speeches: "In the first place we
should insist that if the immigrant who comes here in good faith
becomes an American and assimilates himself to us he shall be
treated on an exact equality with everyone else. . . . But this is
predicated upon the man's becoming in very fact an American
and nothing but an American. . . . We have room for but one flag,
the American flag. . . . We have room for but one language, and
that is the English language . . . and we have room for but one
loyalty, and that is a loyalty to the American people" (vol. 1, no. 1,
5). The title above the piece reads "Keep Up the Fight for Americanism." Roosevelt's nativist, racist, jingoism aside, the composi-
tion of elements conflates the notion of "Americanism" with such
exclusivist nonsense. In essence, the implication is that Chicanos

must be willing to relinquish the definition of what it is to be American, and to abdicate the definition and practice of "Americanism" to dominant, racist, exploitative elements. Furthermore, the Aztlan fantasy created explicitly contradicts the vision of a heterogeneous America, creating in essence a "Chicano hegemony" that invokes a national origin that excludes Native American and African American claims (to name but two).

*El Grito* was relentless in its exposure of racist paradigms at work in the social sciences, humanities, media, political structure. The journal and its publisher *Quinto Sol* were major influences in Chicano publishing, giving voice to a distinguished and growing list of Chicano academics and writers. However, the seven-year history of the journal reveals a conflict among the Chicano/Mexican American intelligentsia between an urge toward a cultural separatism and a desire to participate fully and equally in the national academic and political arenas.

This struggle is evident in Octavio Romano's essay "The Historical and Intellectual Presence of Mexican-Americans." On the one hand, the essay is a prime example of the Mexican American's refusal to abdicate his or her rightful place in "American" society. It also reveals a vision of the Mexican American subject as complex and multifaceted and of a Mexican American community composed of complex individuals. On the other hand, the essay's taxonomy creates a subtly restrictive set of variations of Mexican American identity and ideology. "Indianist philosophy, Confrontationist, Behavioral Relativism, and Existentialism. Assimilation, Mexicanism, Realigned Pluralism, and Bi-Culturalism. Cholos, Pochos, Pachucos, Chicanos, Mexicanos, Hispanos, Spanish-surnamed people, Mexican-Americans. Many labels. Because this is such a complex population, it is difficult to give one label to them all. And probably the first to resist such an effort would be these people themselves, for such a monolithic treatment would violate the very pluralistic foundations upon which their historical philosophies have been based" (44). However conscious Romano's catalog is of difference within the Mexican American community, it does demonstrate that there existed a distinction between those who opted to remain within the

"American" framework (Pochos, Assimilationists, and so on) and those that had the "courage" and "foresight" to operate from a separating remove (Confrontationists, Chicanos, and so forth). The shift toward cultural nationalism simultaneously created a move away from anything that smacked of "assimilationism." We might read the steady shift from the journal's emphasis on social science toward a focus on literature to indicate a subtle rejection of participatarian political reform and a tacit, but consciously implied, endorsement of cultural nationalism.

Chicanos were insistent in writing poignant, forceful letters asserting their rights as Americans within a democratic state that they believed was as much theirs to shape as anyone else's. The majority of Mexican Americans did indeed want to assert their influence and participation in "America." They demanded change. The difficulty, of course, lay in how to affect this change, and even more fundamentally, what the nature of this change would be.

## Reconsidering *el Movimiento: Communitas* or *Civitas*?

The social movements of the 1960s have one thing in common. There was a tension between individualist-oriented political tendencies (the cultural side of the counterculture) and a desire to create a realpolitik aimed at achieving radical social justice. It is a choice that has fueled and bedeviled the American polity since its inception: the negotiation between positive and negative liberty, the dialectic between individual and community. Here, I will frame it as a choice between *communitas* and *civitas*—a distinction that plays on the difference between Victor Turner's description of *communitas* as a break-away community of dissidents aimed at protesting particular normative claims of the society at large (and which indicates the individualist-oriented agenda prevalent in the "mainstream" counterculture of the 1960s); and Rousseau's definition of *civitas* as a socially democratic community formed around an egalitarian logic. *Communitas* remains insular and is not particularly concerned with effecting wide-scale change, but often foregrounds an individualist agenda or single issue. The latter is inclusive and participatory, emphasizing an egalitarian civic sphere, its political topos, the nation-state.

The Chicano movement was faced with negotiating the choice between these two different notions of the political community. The tension between these alternatives was also central in the making of postwar American subjectivities, both "Anglo" and "Mexican American." It was the Americano dilemma. In the midst of a political and cultural maelstrom, how did the Chicano movement negotiate this choice and how did it shape it, or fail to shape it, into a national agenda? It is a question that many Chicano scholars have attempted to answer in the last decade or so since the "Decade of the Hispanic" seemingly declared the Chicano generation and its movement dead.[4]

Dissatisfied with the aftermath of *el movimiento's* decline, cultural critics and historians have turned their attention to defining its advances, reversals, and historical impact. Carlos Munoz offers this analysis: "Chicanismo could not even begin to answer the substantive question concerning the ultimate shape of a political ideology and strategy that could take account the diversity of political orientations . . . Nor did it offer a framework for the concrete analysis of the dominant political and economic institutions of U.S. society and how they affected the different strata of Mexican Americans" (Munoz 90).

Munoz highlights the relation of culture to politics, as well as a lack of a cohesive, inclusive vision, and a tendency toward creating a narrow political and cultural subjectivity. These were not problems unique to *el movimiento*. Stewart Burns shows that the same shortcomings limited the effectiveness of the counterculture in general. "In the fluid situation that resulted . . . they [the counterculture] were not prepared to offer a new public philosophy, new programmatic solutions, and a new social charter to replace the old discredited ones, all of which could have percolated upward from the grass roots. Instead, the political and ideological power vacuum was soon appropriated from top to bottom by the New Right and neo-conservatives, who had been methodically gaining ground since. . . . The conclusion to draw is that these movements . . . failed to provide a coherent alternative to [the discredited system] when the terrain was still contested" (177). Both examples of radical *communitas* ultimately failed to refashion national culture effectively.

The Chicano movement limited its efficacy for many of the reasons that Munoz suggests. But explaining the dissolution of the movement as the lack of an effective "framework" for analyzing how U.S. institutions affected the "different strata" of Mexican Americans is a critique that stops short of examining the internal conflict within the Chicano movement in terms of its relation to "America" and "Americanization." Looking at the metaphorical connotations of the choice between "America," "Aztlan," and "América" reveals a great deal about the next leg of the postwar Mexican American journey and the shaping of the democratic debate. An analysis of these "choices" also reveals uncanny parallels between the issues fueling democratic discourse that affected all Americans: the self or narrowly conceived community in relation to a more inclusive notion of the "whole."[5]

The Chicano movement also opted for spontaneous *communitas* that did not seek reintegration, but rather sought schism as a final recourse to societal injustices that were seen as unreformable. Formidable as the obstacles to true and effective social reform might have been, and there is ample evidence of an entrenched, calculating racist and classist resistance to social change, we must now more fully examine the politics of community as articulated and manifested within the Chicano movement. Did an emerging nationalism that tended toward separatism ultimately result in the failure of the Chicano movement at large to create *civitas*? Did the Chicano movement fall short in much the same way as the mainstream counterculture in formulating a long-lasting, far-reaching social agenda?

If one central difference can be found between the Mexican American and Chicano generations, it is a growing awareness by the latter that the character of the U.S. citizen-subject, both culturally and socially, was fundamentally anticommunal. Membership and participation within a "national" culture continued to be a political abstraction. Admittance into the category of full-rights bearing subject was a legal process, one guarded in an arbitrary, capricious manner. America's market logic dictated postwar subjectivity form along the lines of a submissive individualism, authorizing individual liberty through a hierarchical and fixating corporatist structure. Such a logic prefers a consumerist decisionism where market choice replaces open, participatory political choice.

For the Chicano generation, inclusion *en masse* even in such a limited system seemed unlikely due to the need of agribusiness and industry for an even more disenfranchised, cheap, mobile, and docile workforce. Thus a two-tier structure operated: the top one constituted by "citizens" subscribing to the requirements of submissive individualism, and the lower tier made up of disenfranchised "noncitizens" most often marked by race. For the racially marked subject even limited participation within the top tier of the American polity required assimilation. As *El Plan de Santa Barbara*, the founding document of *el Movimiento Estudiantil Chicano de Aztlán* (MEChA), declared in 1969:

> For decades Mexican people in the United States struggled to realize the "American Dream." And some—a few—have. But the cost, the ultimate cost of assimilation, required turning away from *el barrio* and *la colonia*. In the meantime, due to the racist structure of this society, to our essentially different life style, and to the socio-economic functions assigned to our community by Anglo-American society—as suppliers of cheap labor and a dumping ground for the small-time capitalist entrepreneur—the *barrio* and *colonia* remained exploited, impoverished, and marginal.
>
> As a result, the self-determination of our community is now the only acceptable mandate for social and political action; it is the essence of Chicano commitment. (Munoz 191)

The writers of *El Plan* recognized the exploitative nature of capitalism, and implicitly challenged the system by combating the forced movement of conquest and capital with their own communal movement. The communal directives of *El Plan* created a clear-cut agenda for establishing Chicano Cultural Studies in the university and defined the objectives of such academic programs as impacting directly on the *barrio* and *colonia* in a dialectical relationship. Its emphasis on mutual redefinition and a growing political empowerment would mark the highpoint of Chicano movement politics.

Aztlan became for many the symbol of an ideal egalitarian, Utopic space, with a distinctive Mexican culture and identity. However, it also formed a restrictive politics of identity that limited the arena of political and civic participation that ultimately hamstrung the movement. The often strident nationalist message for the Chicano generation was that there were in effect only two forms of political "participation." Mexican Americans either integrated and assimilated within the national culture of capital and Anglo hegemony, or they must commit to *el movimiento* fully and a model of identity that called for a separatism that was unrealistic and undesired by many. Thus, this *communitas* in the limited options that it described for its subject, set a course that would prevent it from achieving a long-range intercultural national transformation.

Victor Turner's typology of three forms of *communitas*— "spontaneous," "ideological," and "normative"—help to explain how the various stages of dissident communal formations act in relation. Spontaneous *communitas* arises as a reaction against perceived structural oppressions and seeks individual freedom and relations. The ideological stage gives conscious formulation and articulation of the utopian goals of spontaneous action. The normative stage seeks to construct a new social system around the ideology of the spontaneous *communitas*. In this progression, "communitas eventually undergoes . . . a decline and fall into structure and law," in the attempted institutionalization of the shared goals (Turner 132). However, Turner points out that in this social drama, one stage of liminality may or may not lead to the next. Thus Aztlan is the ideological stage of Mexican American *communitas* that did not develop into the normative stage.

The fear of a "decline and fall into structure and law," in this case the general perception of an effete gradualist process, kept the separatist and cultural nationalist wings of the movement from setting an agenda that could create a radically new national culture. By suggesting that the only two alternatives for the Mexican American subject were to separate or to assimilate, it doomed itself with the same two alternatives: remain a separate "nation" within the nation-state, or to reduce its disenfranchised Chicano subjects to participating as "assimilated" citizen-subjects (one way of defining the Hispanic generation).

In "Where Have All the Nationalists Gone?" an article that tends to advocate the militant/assimilationist dichotomy, Martin Sanchéz Jankowski seeks to explain the disappearance of Chicanismo. Dividing *el movimiento* into two opposing forces—a nationalist wing and a more reformist, liberal wing—his study claims that the reasons for the dissipation of nationalist tendencies were manifold: young adherents grew out of their commitment; commitment was partially an effect of the "air of the times"; and nationalism became irrelevant as more moderate aims were met. The study, however, focuses almost exclusively on the institutional practice of politics without taking into account the nature of desire.

Jankowski does not consider that the level of commitment by nationalists was "genuine" and deeply felt, but that ultimately Chicano nationalism was inadequate as a response to the complex identity nexus that maps the multitude of Mexican American subjectivities. Dividing "nationalists" into two camps, the "self-interested" and the "cultural," already suggests the "assimilationist/militant" opposition, suggesting that the former were only interested in moving up, the motivation of the so-called Hispanic generation, and that the latter were "truly" radical, committed, and idealistic. His analysis thus replicates the formulation used by *el movimiento* that labels participatarian desire as a form of complicit "Americanization."

In order to understand the shortcomings of the Chicano movement and its eventual dissolution, we must investigate its antipathy to "Americanization" in a deeper and more complex way than simply to mark it as a given, an *a priori* state of opposition. To see the relation between the Chicano and the "American" as a categorical opposition produces a tautology that ignores the dialects of identity formation. In practicing "oppositional identity" politics, cultural nationalism remained incognizant that the loathed American and the process of Americanization were not simply an external threat, but a fundamental element within all Mexican American subjects. This is the exact struggle that Oscar Acosta underwent. So it is critical to ask how "America" and the "American" come to be defined in *el movimiento* and how far this generation of activists, nationalists, and separatists went in order to eradicate these influences from a projected ideal community, and from the ideal Chicano self. In this antipathy lies a conflation of an economic system, citizenship, and the national culture. More critical perhaps, is the automatic assumption that to seek full participation appeared to mean accepting a complicitous integration.

Corky Gonzalez's poem "I am Joaquin" (1967) articulates the conflicted relation of the Mexican American to the United States. Consider a passage that spells out a number of interpretations that would be extremely influential in positioning the emergent "Chicano" subjectivity:

> I look at myself
> and see part of me
> who rejects my father and my mother
> and dissolves into the melting pot
> to disappear in shame. . . .
> Unwillingly dragged by that monstrous, technical,
> industrial giant called
>       Progress
> and Anglos success . . .
> in a country that has wiped out
> all my history,
>       stifled all my pride,
> in a country that has placed a
> different weight of indignity upon
> my
>        age-
>             old
>                   burdened back.
>                           (2)

As Gonzalez explains in his introduction, "writing 'I Am Joaquin' was a journey back through history, a painful self-evaluation, a wandering search for my peoples and, most of all, for my own identity" (*I Am Joaquin* 1). Pondering the strategies of immobilization imposed on his "people," seems to mark a conscious effort on Gonzalez's part to position the Mexican American subject within American history. Discussing identity as a continuing dialectic between the community and the self, Gonzalez distinguishes between a national "white" community from which he (and his people) has been excluded and a local, racialized community that promises release itself from the strategies of containment enacted by American society.

The poem recognizes the price of progress in the United States, the threat of personal and communal erasure; the erasure of the latter constitutes erasure of the former. More specifically, the remedy Gonzalez seeks is located in connection to an ancient past, a communal connection that stretches back to time immemorial. The "melting pot" destroys his Mexican, indigenous past. While these critiques are valid in large measure, the image of absorption into an American identity is too quickly associated with the process of becoming "Anglocized," and the connection to the past suggests the circumvention of an "American" past. Progress is equated with "Anglos success."

The implications for the Mexican American are that a "pure" identity must be forged, free of the dross that is "Anglo" culture—read here as "American." Separatism and a nostalgia for *la patria,* an idealized Mexico, and a nascent indigenism *(indigenismo)* begin to shape the parameters and identity of Aztlan. A form of cultural nationalism, indigenism sought to jettison the European, Spanish side of *mestizo* identity much in the same way that "Chicano" identity freed itself of the "American" influence conceded in "Mexican American." It was a form of countererasure, a strategy that sought to contend directly with the dominance of Western, imperialist, colonial impositions on the "indigenous" subject. Associating with Mayan and Aztec ancestry and folkways, Chicano indigenism created an allegiance with Native American claims of authenticity and created their own national origin mythos separate from, and in direct opposition to, Eurocentric foundational narratives. However, the indigenous movement's recreation of indigenous worldviews was ahistorical, often inaccurate, and uncritical. Furthermore, the formulation of "Aztlan" risked rendering invisible contemporary Native Americans, while displacing Native American claims to the same American space. Both Chicano nationalism and indigenism too readily inculcated the internal colonization model (the Mexican American *barrio* as *"colonia"*), and invested the melting pot with too much power.

Taken together, these elements begin to form a historiographical logic that underpins the emerging ideology of Chicanismo. Gonzalez's historiographical frame ironically posits a notion of "Anglo" success that excludes the Mexican American, "wiping out" *his* or *her* history. So while the poem stands as a condemnation of the hegemonic power of capital, it also constitutes a vision of the all powerful state and its official culture to which the Mexican American subject either stands in direct opposition, or is absorbed by completely, the "I" lost forever. Gonzalez here echoes William Burroughs's fear of absorption in *Naked Lunch,* Ken Kesey's representation of the castrating, homogenizing "combine" in *One Flew Over the Cuckoo's Nest,* and Jack Kerouac's paranoia about the collective's threat to the "self" in *Big Sur.*

The comparison is not as far-fetched as it would seem, for Gonzalez, Burroughs, Kesey, and Kerouac all share an antipathy toward the subjectifying power of a capitalist hegemony. Although each of them characterizes his own particular vision of how this "hegemony" is constituted, they see its machinations in remarkably similar ways. Each of them sees the *e pluribus unum* of "America" as threatening. Ironically, Gonzalez also articulates the power of white hegemony that the Beats furthered. However, none of these writers sees the potential for transforming the national culture in mutually beneficial, egalitarian ways. All four writers ultimately endorse a separatism that places the self (individually or communally defined) in isolation, abdicating one's role in the shaping of a national culture.

Kerouac, Burroughs, Ginsberg, and Thompson ultimately formulated a fellaheen historiography in which the "other" waited in a deterritorialized, dehistoricized "new frontier." Ironically, Chicanismo produced a "counterhistoriography" that was analogous. For the Beats, the fellaheen lands lay in the margins of history, timeless and ancient, separated from the cycle of active, material, and "profane" time of "Western Progress" (as in Ginsberg's "Siesta in Xbalba"). "Aztlan," the mythic territory, bore an uncanny resemblance to fellaheen Xbalba. In its more mythic characterizations, Aztlan was figured as lying outside of American history, in a "timeless" neo–Mayan, neo–Toltec quasi history. The internal colonization model placed the Chicano/Mexican American on the periphery of material history, suggesting a rigid dichotomy that marked the oppressor and oppressed too simplistically. In accepting a model of culture and history that placed the Mexican American subject on the outside, Chicanismo tended to reject the participatarian ethos advocated by the previous generation of Mexican Americans. Thus, even though the Chicano generation rejected capitalist society, neoindividualism, and the imperialist practices of the United States, accepting its marginalization precluded the possibility of using its own communal program in transforming the national culture through transformative communalism.

In its rejection of a narrowly defined American "mainstream" middle-class citizen-subject (Anglo, male, mobile, submissive individualist), the Chicano nationalist created an equally essentialist identity for its own citizen-subject. In rejecting a racist and unfair national culture, Chicanismo opted to create an isolated and exclusive homeland. In this way, Aztlan was in many ways a reimagined *colonia* or *barrio*. In "Tale of La Raza" Luis Valdez articulates this vision of "American" society and "Chicano" identity:

> The pilgrimage to Sacramento was no mere publicity trick. The *raza* has a tradition of migrations, starting from the legend of the founding of Mexico. Nezahualcoyotl, a great Indian leader, advised his primitive Chichimecas, forerunners of the Aztecs, to begin a march to the south. In that march, he prophesied, the children would age and the old would die, but grandchildren would come to a great lake. In that lake they would find an eagle devouring a serpent, and on that spot, they would begin to build

a great nation. The nation was Aztec Mexico, and the eagle and the serpent are the symbols of the *patria*. They are emblazoned on the Mexican flag, which the marchers took to Sacramento with pride.

Then there is the other type of migration. When the migrant farm laborer followed the crops, he was only reacting to the way he saw the American *raza:* no unity, no representation, no roots. The pilgrimage was a truly religious act, a reflection of our past in this country and a symbol of our unity and new direction. It is of no lasting significance that Governor Brown was not at the Capitol to greet us. The unity of thousands of *raza* on the Capitol steps was reason enough for our march. Under the name of HUELGA we had created a Mexican-American *patria,* and Cesar Chavez was our first Presidente. ("Tale of La Raza" 54)

Here Valdez shifts the site of the Mexican American journey to Mexico, expressing a romanticized vision of *la patria,* populating this new history with subjects that are now "purified" of their "American" identity. Valdez also participates in a form of movement discourse that replicates the movement-as-redemptive model that was utilized in the making of the Beat neoindividualist vision.

Moreover, Valdez further narrows the definition of "America," now choosing to cut away all "American" elements from Mexican American subjectivity: "Our *campesinos,* the farm-working *raza* find it difficult to participate in this alien North American country. The acculturated Mexican-American in the cities, ex-*raza,* find it easier. They have solved their Mexican contradictions with a pungent dose of Americanism, and are more concerned with status, money and bad breath than with their ultimate destiny. . . . they will melt into the American pot and be no more. But the farm-working *raza* will not disappear so easily. . . . We are repelled by the human disintegration of people's and cultures as they fall apart in this Great Gringo Melting Pot" ("The Tale of La Raza" 54). I quote the above passages extensively not to condemn Chicano cultural nationalism out of hand. The dissension expressed within both the Valdez and Gonzalez pieces assert a sharp and valid critique of the sorts of immobilizing forms of "progress" that capital sold to labor as "mobility" and that was celebrated by a wide array of cultural producers as personally liberating and culturally redemptive. However, where cultural nationalism and its more extreme separatist form proved shortsighted was in the failure to recognize that self-marginalization was disempowering in the long run.

It was a critical error in effect to encourage Chicanos to isolate themselves further from the political process and the effort to shape a national agenda. Ultimately, separatist and isolationist strategies were blind to the reality that the Mexican American was already profoundly implicated within the material, cultural, political, and social history of the United States. Furthermore, Chicanismo attempted to define the Mexican American as if the latter half of that label did not exist when it so clearly did. It was the synthesis of Mexican and American elements that needed defining and shaping, rather than a denial of that dialectic process that had been in operation for over a hundred years. Rather than rejecting America for Aztlan, they should have been claiming America as their own, a privilege that their Anglo counterparts, through political organs such as Students for a Democratic Society and the Free Speech Movement, showed no hesitancy in asserting.

The effects of a self-marginalizing strategy remain apparent in modern Mexican American historiography. Ignacio Garcia's recent synopsis of *movimiento* tendencies reproduces an operative division between "America" and the outsider status of the Mexican American subject. In his essay "Backwards from Aztlan: Politics in the Age of Hispanics," he writes, "The adoption of American cultural values, integration as a social strategy, and fidelity to Anglo parties and politicians became antithetical to Chicanismo" (166). This formulation of the power and culture structure at work produces the view that the "Anglo" must inevitably construct the cultural values and dictate the content of political identity and agenda. We might trace this social determinism back to the emergence of the ideology of Chicanismo in which the implication is that America is a possession of the "foreign European": "Aztlan belongs to those who plant the seeds, water the fields, and gather the crops, and not to the foreign Europeans. . . . We declare the independence of our Mestizo nation. We are a Bronze People with a Bronze Culture. Before the world, before all of North America . . . We are a Nation, We are a Union of free pueblos, We are Aztlan" (Mexican American Youth Organization, "El Plan Espiritual Aztlan" 402). This declaration suggests that a nationalistic, ethnic purification can take place, that a "European" identity is constitutive of an "American" national culture. "El Plan de Aztlan" as it declares independence, gives away much more than it claims as its own.

In 1975, in a poignant speech entitled "Message to Aztlan," Corky Gonzales gives an impassioned call for a renewed commitment to the movement. However his claim that "the Chicano movement is alive and growing" was a case of wishful thinking (Gonzales 6). It is instead a plea that vacillates between a fiery Che-style, revolutionary leftism and a resigned awareness of a growing participation in mainstream electoral politics. The speech, while earnest in its exhortation to continue the struggle for justice, exposes the lack of a cohesive, national agenda. Rather than giving direction, Gonzales calls for an abstract political moralism. By this point La Raza Unida Party lay in shambles, the Chicano movement had all but dissolved, and even the United Farm Workers union (UFW) was on the wane.

Carlos Munoz suggests that the fall of La Raza Unida Party exposes central weaknesses in the ability of the Chicano movement in general to create effective coalitions. For him, La Raza Unida Party was an example of political organization limited by unresolved dissension between a more internationalist wing of the party (the California group led by Gonzales) and the more electorally oriented wing (the Texas group led by Jose Angel Gutierrez). Munoz suggests that the tension developed around the polarization of Gutierrez's "pragmatic" (read "moderate") brand of politics and Gonzalez's "ideological" (read "radical") emphasis that targeted the raising of consciousness: "The ideological tensions within the party were clearly manifested in debates on the proper emphasis to put on electoral activity and on whether the party should remain exclusively Mexican American or should aim at a broader Latino and third world constituency" (110). But this analysis does not go far enough in explaining why La Raza Unida, and *el movimiento* in general, could not create a more lasting and effective *communitas*.

In fact, Munoz tends to define the two wings of the movement by replicating a dichotomy that subtly denigrates the "pragmatic" brand of politics as "moderate." Ignacio Garcia suggests that the dissolution of *el movimiento* was not caused solely by a divisiveness over political strategies, but by a failure on the part of "both" wings of La Raza (be they moderate, militant, liberal, or Marxist) to understand the deeper psychological needs and desires of the Mexican American.

> The stridency of the Movement alienated many Mexican Americans who sought acceptance and legitimacy from the mainstream. Also those who adhered to the militancy of the Chicano Movement soon found themselves confronted with economic pressures. . . . Other adherents were attracted away from radicalism by the moderate militancy of groups such as the Mexican American Democrats, and the rejuvenated groups such as LULAC and the G.I. Forum. . . . With the cream of the crop once again joining the mainstream, the politics of nationalism and the participation of the barrio declined significantly. The Chicano community because of exhaustion and disillusionment over the slowness of change, turned to spokespersons" (Garcia, "Backwards from Aztlan" 166).

Yet Mexican American concern for the community's well-being was still fully operative. Jose Amaro Hernandez shows in his study, *Mutual Aid For Survival: The Case of the Mexican American*, that there was a centuries-long tradition amongst Mexican Americans in the forming of communal identity and mutual subsistence as demonstrated through the historical presence of the *mutualista*. Cultural nationalism had proven that there was the basis for strong collective identity. In hindsight, these elements could have been used to form a foundation for a well-organized polity in the service of a transformative social strategy based on positive liberty. However, this would have first required an understanding of the

Mexican American's role in American history, society, and politics as well as a revised notion of Mexican American identity.

This reenvisioned Mexican American identity was already beginning to form in the events leading up to the formation of La Raza Unida Party years before. At the heart of the second political takeover in Crystal City, Texas lay a basic desire for recognition and inclusion, not only on the political level, but ultimately on what must be called the human level. The catalyst for the Second Revolution was not directly a political or economic event. Rather it was a result of school board discrimination in the choosing of cheerleaders and the attempt by Anglo alumni to institute its own coronation homecoming queen from within the ranks of Anglo students. Understanding the dimensions of student and parental unrest gave Guttierez an opening for direct action.

The Chicano perception of an attack on their children led to community-wide unity based in familial sentiment and led to an increased polarization between gringo and Chicano. By 1970 control over school and local matters had been seized by a radicalized Chicano *communitas*. However, Guttierez's understanding of the deep desire for equality and inclusion led to the construction of a successful platform: a demand for equity and a voice in school and local governance, as well as an opening up of economic opportunity. The movement to elect representatives to the school board and city council reflected a change in organizational strategy that targeted not only resentment of Anglo politics and economic domination, but stressed pride in ethnicity and organized around the concept of family, invoking a strong characteristic of the Mexican community.

More important, perhaps, Guttierez was able to mobilize an existing participatarian sentiment and demonstrated that the Mexican American community of Crystal City, Texas could effectively participate within the "American" democratic system. The Crystal City Revolution had further implications as well: for if the democratic process was indeed viable for Mexican American at the local level, was it not also viable at the national level? The success of Crystal City provided a direct connection between the shaping of local political culture and national political culture, showing that the postwar Mexican American subject need not cede a national strategy. Although the election did not spell an "egalitarian" revolution, it proved that the desire for equality was a strong motivator for the community, and that an agenda suggestive of radical social alternatives was possible.

## The Chicano Dilemma: Aztlan or América

The refusal to envision "America" as "home" has threatened to hinder direct, political engagement on the part of the Mexican American community. In *American Encounters,* Jose Limon discusses the tendency to disregard the immigrant and migrant desire for "American" inclusion. Limon argues that Manuel Gamio's study of Mexican immigrants exposes a nostalgia on Gamio's part for *la patria,* which Gamio projects onto the subjects of his study. What Gamio failed to realize was that a transformation had occurred in the Mexican immigrants he interviewed. They no longer saw their futures tied to Mexico, although they still longed for their country of origin in many ways. In Gamio's book, *Mexican Immigration to the United States,* he writes, "In short, they had begun to produce another story . . . their own, more territorially grounded version of a well-known American narrative of ethnic mobilization and mobility against adversity" (56). In this sense, the process of "Americanization" was not assimilationist, but rather a self-aware entry into the fray of cultural negotiation and political participation, an evinced desire to live fully within "America."

We might read separatist tendencies in the same way as Limon reads Gamio's nostalgia. This limiting form of Chicanismo misread Mexican American desires for inclusion, and thus failed to ground a realpolitik that might have used this desire to mobilize more effectively. This resulted in a failure to create an agenda that directed the communalist instinct of *el pueblo* in more radical ways that called for the transformation of America and a substantially revised definition of the existent narrow vision of its citizen-subject.

In an emblematic essay written in 1973, entitled "Justice, Deprivation, and the Chicano," Julius Rivera similarly endorses an overly narrow vision of the Chicano subject. While he claims that "there is a striking heterogeneity to the Chicano population that defies generalization and even manageable categorizations," Rivera goes on to suggest that "there is, however, one common denominator: Chicanos are socially, politically and economically deprived: one might say exploited" (123).

In an essay that argues for an agenda featuring economic justice, Rivera replicates a common pattern of *movimiento* activists and scholars. On one hand, he exposes and then objects to exploitative practices of the postwar American market economy; on the other, even while acknowledging a wide spectrum of Mexican American subjectivities, he constructs a very narrow community based on a criterion of "deprivation." The analysis of the "myth of equal opportunity" is valid, but the definition of the community too quickly endorses a dangerously limiting social and political agency. Even a Marxist call for a broad-ranging economic reformation relies too heavily on the *colonia* model, precluding the possibility of a larger, class-based coalition since "the scales of inequality are not identical to . . . the scales of inequality of the Anglo community" (123).

Indirectly, Rivera abandons the possibility of a national agenda, a creation of a *civitas*. *El pueblo* is itself incapacitated, beyond even the possibility of a cultural nationalist identity. Ironically, the concept of "heterogeneity" is overridden by a deterministic economism as class proves to be the determining factor that precludes coalition.

A divisive economic determinism was only one manifestation of an isolationist underpinning that made the formation of *civitas* in the 1960s unlikely. The limiting historiography and sociology of Chicanismo that underwrote much of the cultural production of the period took several symbolic forms. In choosing to construct a symbolic identity around the figure of the colonized subject, many Chicano writers reaffirmed the racist isolating strategies of U.S. imperialism and capital that targeted communitarian projects. It is one thing to point out limiting and circumscribing ideologies, it is another to bolster the resulting hierarchy.

Jose Limon's critique of *indigenismo* points more generally toward the structural limitations of a self-imposed determinism. Used as a source for a new poetics, *indigenismo* produced what was ultimately an opaque and politically limited symbolic construct, a self-subjectifying poetry that "keyed not on social engagement, but on inwardness, indigenous purity, and metaphysical transcendence. All these spiritualist stances are, paradoxically, based on two indigenous societies—Aztec and Mayan—that practiced no small amount of social domination. This set of precursors . . . has not well served Chicano movement poetry in its struggles with past and present" (*Mexican Ballads, Chicano Poems* 110). The figures of *el indio, el pinto,* and *el migro* (the indian, the prisoner, and the migrant) tended to focus on the strategy of immobilization in postwar America in which the subject was constantly forced to move, but ultimately remained fixed within the social and economic hierarchies. While it was a valid critique, it ultimately did nothing to challenge the neoindividualistic, imperialist historiography that has shaped the dominant American imagination, and which has underwritten and severely limited postwar American dissent.

To put it another way, while the Beats wanted very much to play the cowboy on the "new frontier," Chicanismo presented a series of symbolic figures through which the Chicano subject inadvertently played the "Indian." Purifying *la raza* of "America's" pernicious influence and a reterritorializing project that claimed the Southwest as Aztlan in effect left U.S. history to the Anglos to write, and U.S. culture for them to shape. However, the making of Aztlan was a contested project, and the conflict is readable within the work of key figures in *el movimiento.* Figures such as Raulrsalinas, Jose Montoya, and Luis Valdez, all played important roles in constructing and deconstructing the discourse of Chicanismo and its symbolic production and figuration.

Within their texts we find a complex discursive dynamic at work. The stakes are high. On the one hand, we see the Chicano struggles to resist the individualist, imperialist ideology of the American past and present. However, that resistance itself presented different alternatives: Chicanos could read an American hegemony as structurally unassailable, leading to the conclusion that there was only one choice—a wholesale rejection and separation. Or Chicanos could choose to contest an American hegemony by reconceiving and restructuring society through the Mexican American experience. In 1965 Mario Savio, an Anglo countercultural leader, asked the vital question: "are we at the end of history?" The battle could not be fought by retreat into a guise of "resistance" that ideologically and realistically amounted to an ahistorical conclusion. The answer to Savio's query in journals such as *Aztlan, El Grito, La Raza,* and *El Malcriado* was an unequivocal "no."

In article after article, the Chicano academic and artist alike, attempted to prove the relevance of Mexican American participation in "American" culture. Octavio Romano, Juan Gomez-Quinones, Ray Padilla, and a host of other cultural critics strove to show that a mainstream sociology, art criticism, or American history that ignored or misrepresented Mexican American participation was not only seriously incomplete, but that the methodologies that produced these discourses were inherently flawed. However, often within the same articles or journal issues, followed the claim that the solution was either to disengage completely from these discourses, or to trace "our own organic" cultural and artistic production to sources that lay outside of "America." This was a complex set of negotiations with far-reaching consequences. Their conflicting forces are evident in the works of Raulrsalinas, Jose Montoya, and Luis Valdez.

## Form, Content, and Containment: Raulrsalinas's "Poems of (Partial) Freedom"

Raulrsalinas has been described in two distinct ways: either as a Chicano Beat poet, or as a prison poet. Depending on the critic and his purposes, either of the aspects is invoked as "central" to understanding the work. In some essays, both aspects of his aesthetic are commented upon, but no one has yet commented extensively on the significant dialectical relation between *el pinto* and the Beat. Doing so points out the complexity of defining resistance, complicity, and response. Specifically, his work points to competing strategies for mobilizing community and constructing social alternatives and how these are shaped, in part, by the way in which the form, content, and context of "America" is imagined.

Both Tomás Ybarra-Frausto and Louis Mendoza have made a case for reading Raulrsalinas (also known as Salinas) as a Beat poet. In the introduction to Raulrsalinas's first book, *Un Trip through the Mind Jail y Otras Excursions,* Ybarra-Frausto writes,

> Raulrsalinas incorporates into his poetry influences from two distinctly American sources: the music of jazz and the literature of the Beats. Finding close affinities with Ginsberg, Corso, and Kerouac, Raulrsalinas is attracted both by their stance and their aesthetic. Poems like "Jazz: A Nascence," "Epiphany," "Did Charlie Have a Horn," and especially "Lamento," have a free form improvised quality akin to musical riffs. They recall Kerouac's notions in "Essentials of Spontaneous Prose" comparing the writer to a jazz saxophonist in search of language as an undisturbed flow from the mind. Other fundamentals of "Beat" poetry that influence the evolution of Raulrsalinas's style include "a sense of romantic nihilism, exaltation of the emotional dimension of experience and above all, an insistent and voluble celebration of the self." (*Un Trip through the Mind Jail* 10)

In the afterward to *East of the Freeway,* "Barrio Aesthetics, Displacement, and Memory," Louis Mendoza points out that "few people have examined the influence of jazz on his work, an influence that makes him part of the Beat Generation of poets, musicians and songwriters. . . . Lest we forget the collection [*East of the Freeway*] is dedicated to Bob Kaufman, the Beat who epitomizes the melding of calculated protest and improvisational poetics for Raulrsalinas. Other prominent figures from among the Beats—including Kerouac, Ginsberg, Brautigan, as well as Gil Scott-Heron—are present as a force throughout this collection"

(*East of the Freeway* 107). Neither critic, however, goes on to articulate fully the influence of the Beat ethos in Raulrsalinas's work.
Reading Raulrsalinas in the context of the Beat aesthetic suggests
a similar response in the struggle to confront and rework the structural delimitations of a racist, classist society through the appropriation of an aesthetic that experiments with various "antiforms."
Formalistically, there is a shared foundation between this "American" cohort and this practitioner of Chicano poetics—a conflu-
ence of artistic and formal practices that suggests a broader rubric
for reading these two "traditions" simultaneously, perhaps as an
"Americano" aesthetic.

However, another reading emerges that excludes the broader
"Americano" aesthetic. Defining the other characterization of his
work, Ybarra-Frausto writes that Raulrsalinas's "collected verse is
shaped by two primary experiences—his victimization by society
at large and his long experience with incarceration" (*Un Trip
through the Mind Jail* 7). In his essay on the semiotics of *pinto*
(Chicano prisoner) tattoos, B. V. Olguin argues that we should
read Raulrsalinas's entire corpus (both the literary text and the
physical text of the tattoo) as shaped exclusively by his *pinto* persona. For Olguin, Raulrsalinas creates a dialectic of difference
through his work, a narrative that ultimately resists the emasculating and disciplinary techniques of the state as represented by
the penal system and its colony.

This oppositional stance resists the state apparatus while
creating a communal bond with those outside of the prison.
This communal bond is formed because Raulrsalinas's work is
"steeped in the political unconscious of the Chicano community,
and as such involves constant synthesis as various symbols and
icons are troped and embedded with metadiscourses arising from
newer markings that are both visually and metrically rendered"
(Olguin 177). Salinas thus creates an inclusive communal bond
with *la raza,* but in essence assists to create an exclusive *communitas* through its cultural and race-derived "political unconscious." Both Olguin and Ybarra-Frausto argue that this aesthetic should be read through the paradigm of *rasquachismo,* a
Mexican American aesthetic of improvisation: "Through such

strategies of appropriation, reversal, and inversion. Chicano youth cultures . . . negate dominant models and values, [that is], Rasquachismo feigns complicity with dominant discourses while skillfully decentering and transforming them" (Ybarra-Frausto as quoted by Olguin 177). We are left, then, with the figure of the immobilized, incarcerated Chicano figure who represents the closed system's structural limits, while standing in opposition to that closed system.

However, two problems arise from this reading: we are left with defining "resistance" as the opposition of two closed systems, both exclusive in their "memberships." Secondly, we are left with a definition of the dialectical process *(rasquachismo)* that is more suggestive of "subversion" than of "participation."

There is no doubt that *pinto*s are imprisoned, isolated, alienated and comprise a pool for an exploitative economy based on forced labor. This very real position became an important paradigm for reading American society for *el movimiento*. One need only read through the archives of the member newspapers of the Chicano Press Association, to understand the impact of political imprisonment during the 1960s. Prison reform attempts targeted California statutes such as the "Indeterminate Sentence Law" that gave parole boards the power to punish politically active prisoners.[6] Raulrsalinas was himself a victim of draconian efforts on the part of prison officials to curb his dissenting literary output (see excerpted letters in *Un Trip through the Mind Jail*).

Reading American society through the prison model, however, proved to be delimiting because it constructed a purely oppositional relationship between a subjectified noncitizen and an impervious, omnipotent state. This paradigm left few alternatives for those seeking relief from systemic oppression. As one former prisoner wrote in December 1971 in a column entitled "Noticias De La Pinta" ("Notes from Prison") published in *La Raza*, there are only two choices: become a "coconut, sellout, or tio taco," or become a separatist. The Mexican American is either inside or outside of a rigidly drawn communal parameter. The "Mainstream American/Assimilated Consumer-Capitalist" now becomes a "house greaser who is thankful to the penal system . . .

and is lost to the Movement and to countless Chicanos that he might have helped. . . . He has become a part of the problem" (issue 6, 1971, 55). While Francisco Estrada goes on to critique the cultural nationalism of the "Super Chicano" for its lack of class consciousness, he offers a separatist alternative, as the "nacion de Aztlan is a sovereign and free land" (57).

Estrada demonstrates the limits of the prison/*pinto* paradigm, while exhibiting a legitimate critique of American strategies of containment. His and *el movimiento's* communalist strategy was also valid, but I wish to examine how Raulrsalinas attempts to imagine an alternative to the strictures or racism, labor exploitation, and second-class citizenship that gestures toward the possibility of an open system: one that allows for a broader concept of resistance—an insistence on a radical form of participatarian egalitarianism.

Past critical accounts do not go on to analyze in depth the meaning of the influence of the Beat ethos or aesthetic in Raulrsalinas's work. Examining his appropriation of forms that are open, eclectic, and improvisational provides insight into Raulrsalinas's desire to transcend both his personal and his community's systemic confinement by imagining an alternative that avoids a self-marginalizing separatist stance. I hesitate to call this aesthetic *"rasquachismo"* if we are to define it as does Ybarra-Frausto: a strategy of "inversion" that "feigns complicity with dominant discourses." This suggests a form of "trickster" subversion that I want to understand in a more complex way. I argue that his poetry's experimentation with open form reveals a fundamental, but conflicted desire to reconfigure the democratic structure as a potentially open, inclusive, and malleable process. Salinas's conflict occurs between the instinct to reject any possibility of meliorating what has proved through material experience for the Chicano subject a closed system, and the desire to see the possibility of participating in a true democracy.

Raulrsalinas spent fifteen years in prison as a result of his drug addiction and the harsh sentencing laws during the 1950s and 1960s. At one point, he served a five-year sentence for possessing five dollars worth of marijuana. Raulrsalinas was incarcerated

from 1957 to 1972 in such infamous federal penitentiaries as Lea-
venworth, Huntsville, Soledad, and Marion. The mental and
physical torment of his incarceration is evident in a letter written
from Marion Federal Penitentiary: "If forced to continue living
like an animal, soon—very soon—i'll be reacting like one. The
consequences may be fatal, but the debt has been PAID IN
FULL! There's no more to collect . . . they took 5 years of my life
down there for $5 worth of smoke. 15 yrs is PREposterous" (*Mind
Jail* 24). Embittered over an unjust punishment meted out by a
cold, unmerciful legal system that does not recognize addiction as
sickness, Raulrsalinas sees prison as the iron and concrete manifestation of the state. The state is then little more than a structure
of containment.

In "Declaration of a Free Soul," he writes,

> A living nothing
>> in this world of stone
> teeming with loathsome
>> Guardians of the State.
> I'd best prefer upon my back
>> the stinging lashes
> of the dreaded cat-o-nine
>> than to have these lowly curs
> which i abhor
>> constantly gnawing at my tortured mind.
> O' Heinous Gods
>> who stand for LAW!
> to you i shall not bow.
>> i once knelt to my mother's God,
> But NEVER, to the Likes of YOU!
>
> (*Mind Jail* 30)

The "Gods" of "Law" preclude the possibility of freedom. Person-
hood is mediated by sadistic figures that represent repressive
"Law" calculated to emasculate and enslave both body and mind.
The system is figured as deterministic, fixating, and arbitrary.
Thus Raulrsalinas finds his only solace in creating a rebellious
persona who stands in opposition to the conflated God of religion
and state. The decision not to capitalize the "i" posits, however, a

vulnerable self that is tormented on both the physical and mental level by the capitalized "YOU" that recalls the capitalized "LAW." The underlying problem is a power imbalance that subjugates the individual, and restrains the brown subject within a monolithic system here figured as "stone," visually represented by the rigid, grid-like line structure. The connotation of the poem, however, is not purely oppositional, for it suggests the desire for entry into the society that exists outside of the monolithic prison. The persona demonstrates a growing consciousness that recognizes the guardians of the state as only "standing" for law. The implication is that there is a just system of law somewhere, if only in ideal form.

In the poem "In Memoriam, Riche," Raulrsalinas reverts to a deterministic vision of the state and of an exclusive, closed sociopolitical structure.

> And he died
>            2 years later—
> And so dear friend & brother
>            The System
>                       (not God)
>                                  created you . . .
> That system
>            took
>                  you
>                       away.
>                       (*Mind Jail* 49–51)

The possibility of agency was a central issue facing the Chicano movement. Was self-determination possible for the Chicano within American society? Raulrsalinas's view shifts ambiguously. Here he presents the split subjectivity between the socially-imprisoned Chicano subject and Riche, his "dear friend and brother." Raulrsalinas rejects the possibility of the Chicano existing in accordance with a humanist and Christian telos that underlies the modern American democratic state—for it was "not God" who created his "dear friend" Riche—but suggests instead that the ubiquitous "system" has the power to "create" and "take" as it wills its sociopolitically-determined Chicano subject. Since the nation-state, operating as it does as a closed system, impenetrable, and ubiquitous, the Chicano subject has no choice but to separate.

However, in "Declaration of a Free Soul," there is the possibility of an agency derived from the existence of either an ideal system of "justice" or an imagined "outside society" that remains undetermined by the monolithic social logic of the prison house (the guards and prison only "stand" for law). Here the Chicano subject can insist on inclusion and participation. The contrast in visions is critical in understanding the making of a separatist ideology: once defined as a closed and deterministic system, the American democratic sphere is irrelevant to *el movimiento* in critical ways.

Ybarra-Frausto argues that Raulrsalinas realizes that his individual position can be read as a rubric for the Chicano community: "his bondage leads to reflection, analysis, and recognition of how his personal loss of freedom parallels the condition of oppression suffered by the Chicanos within the American society. He further comprehends that as a Chicano *pinto,* he can serve as a representative and spokesman against the repressive reality of America within and outside the prison walls" (7). However, Raulrsalinas does not necessarily read the "self" as purely "determined." In this way he struggles to find a way out of reading Chicano society, and by extension "American" society, as purely determined.

The question of self-determination, social amelioration, and the possibility of transforming the "system" is evident in an early poem "Preguntame." He asks,

> is the problem social/
>     cultural/
>         political/
>             economical?
> is revolution the sole solution?
> or what?
>
> whom do we attack, and must we?
> are the panthers at fault/

the weather underground/
los indios/
or the mexican people?
(67)

Raulrsalinas openly questions the construction of resistance, of social injustice, and of how best to achieve social transformation. Social injustice and its material effects on the community, Raulrsalinas argues, are complex and open to interpretation. Solutions are equally elusive, but there is an awareness that both the problems and solutions are constructed and reside within and outside the Mexican American community.

In essence, the dialectical nature of Chicano identity, its community, and an American society and its politics represents an open system that calls for direct action. Raulrsalinas understands the overlap and negotiation among "social/ cultural/ political/ economical" factors define an overdetermined space that opens the possibility for political and personal agency. Solving the community's problems (the "we" of the poem) invites the reader to enter into a communal effort of investigation, judgment, analysis, and the making of a plan of action. Raulrsalinas assumes that Mexican people and "indios" have agency.

Characterizing Raulrsalinas simply as offering a paradigm of resistance reveals the inadequacy of defining revolutionary political and social participation solely as oppositional: Chicano/*pinto* versus Anglo/jailer. More damagingly, however, this opposition creates the limiting view of a deterministic dominant society that places the Chicano (community) permanently in the margins. In *American Encounters,* Jose Limon points out that "in a recent essay, M. Bell warns us that a myopic focus on resistance . . . can easily blind us to zones of complicity and for that matter, of *sui generis* creativity" (186). We might then read the narrative that Raulrsalinas creates more accurately in terms of an internal debate (both for Raulrsalinas personally, and the Chicano Movement at large) over the viability of twentieth century democratic form, and the possibility of Chicano/Mexican American participation in reformation.

If one reads Raulrsalinas's poetry through its (anti)formal aesthetic, whether we label it spontaneous prose, jazz poetry, or *rasquachismo*, we find a deliberate attempt to create a complex synthesis of elements, symbols, desires, and identities that does not seek simply to "subvert" but seeks to transform. This aesthetic is produced by a political logic that recognizes that an act of resistance in a zero sum game, is ultimately futile. A separatist strategy that ends in isolation is an act of abdication, for it participates in its own exclusion. Using *el pinto* as the embodiment of a "counterhegemony" is a form of exploitative opposition that keeps the figure in constant lock-down.

The institutional form of *la pinta* (the penitentiary) signifies confinement; the open, eclectic, improvisational form of spontaneous/jazz poetry through which much of his poetry is created, containing a multiplicity of roles, themes, realities while creating the potential for unrestricted exchange. I would argue that Raulrsalinas's appropriation of "spontaneous prose" and jazz improvisation is a form of *rasquachismo* intended to act in even a broader, more far-reaching modality than one that acts simply to "subvert." Rather, in poems like "Jazz: a Nascence," Raulrsalinas experiments with forms that resist all structures of containment: institutional, social, self-inscribed, and externally-inscribed. Here Raulrsalinas declares the release of a confined consciousness:

> Late night SHRIEKING Sounds!
>       commence
>   sweeping out the mental cobwebs
>   awakening brains from their torpor
>   tonal (poem) cascades
>           Gently
>   washaway
>   musty/ dust settled within
>   thin lines of genius/ madness.
>           (*Mind Jail* 43)

Through this open form—the poem's water imagery signifying a kind of fluidity—Raulrsalinas suggest the birth of a poetry that "washes" away the "line" that encloses him in mental torment in

"Declaration of a Free Soul." Unlike Kerouac, for whom this practice suggested unmediated articulation and a neoindividualistic rejection of a constricting communality, for the communal-minded Raulrsalinas, and *el movimiento* in general, the aesthetic of open form held out a way of reenvisioning and recreating the processes that collectively make-up "America." For the Beats the open form was a way to escape an encroaching public sphere; for Raulrsalinas, it holds out the possibility of community, here figured in the plural "awakening brains."

His poetic expression does not only resist the containment of penal system, the social system, and the economic system, but also attempts to transcend the delimiting aspects of the *pinto* persona. His resistance does not emanate solely from this confined and confining subject position. Rather, Raulrsalinas is emblematic of a Mexican American consciousness that seeks to reshape the discourse of power between the fixating dichotomy of dominant/subservient by creating a form that turns toward the possibility of transcending all limitation. This discourse, and its resulting hegemony, is not deconstructed symbolically, but rather through an insistence that the democratic process/discourse be open to all. Making this move, sounding these liberating "shrieks," requires that the Chicano insist that participation and liberation is not "madness," but indeed communal "genius."

Raulrsalinas's search for an open, improvisational poetic form acknowledges that the structures of containment that confine him and his community cannot be easily defined. However, the process of confinement and the limitations it attempts to mete out can be recognized. If alternative forms of subjectivity and the "state" can be imagined, the possibility of self-determination is at least possible. This potentiality is pointed to in the deployment of "spontaneous prose."

Raulrsalinas uses his poetry to map the social structure of his environment—the immediate, the past, and the imaginary—and the landscape in which these structures exist. The poetry reflects the relationships among sociocultural-political structures as well as the "nation" that both contains and is comprised by them. The "self" (both personal and communal) must also be understood simultaneously as produced by these structures, contained within them, and containing them. Thus "choosing" how to understand and then project the self is crucial to understanding the Chicano in relation to history, the nation-state, and the position of citizen-subject.

Raulrsalinas makes clear that he aims to deploy this (anti)form to analyze and consider the social and historical forces that have "made" him and his community, and which "they" in turn have made. Witness his "Epiphany" in which he writes

> i heard some cats blow today
>> who spoke of pigs, of being free, of many things
> No Shakespeare/ Keats/ or Shelley, they;
>> no bullshit sonnets of nobility and kings.
>
> Oh, No!
> Theirs was street poetry/turn on poesy
>> of the wake-up kind;
> with snap-to-it-rhythm
>> the type that blows your mind.
>
> (*Mind Jail* 45)

Through the spontaneous, open form of jazz poetry, anyone can take part, can "blow." Participation in this "street poetry," an informal, but politically resonant communal act promises a liberating consciousness necessary for the realization of an effective agency.

The "self" is only inadequately understood as primarily a *"pinto,"* because the figure is defined only through an oppositional stance. A dominant ideology that seeks to disempower the Mexican American subject does so in large part by placing him or her outside of history, outside of "society." It calls for the complicity of the subject in assuming this role, oppositional or not. Prisons are in effect only one way in which the state controls behavior. Ideological control is more pervasive as a form of social discipline.

That is precisely why the figures of *el pinto* and the penitentiary make for an inadequate paradigm of the community and the individuals who comprise it. Control and repression are achieved most widely and effectively through hegemonic and ideological methods that elicit the consent of the oppressed. The Chicano subject, oppressed and socially and economically contained, was not the victim of an unassailable, monolithic authority figure as easily identified as the warden or jailer. Rather, the postwar Mexican American subject is a participant within a complex ethos and worldview that, as Raulrsalinas shows in "Preguntame," can be analyzed, challenged, and changed within the democratic, public sphere.

In an inclusive, improvisational, eclectic poetic, the poet's "shrieks," provide the physically incarcerated Raulrsalinas with the tools for recovering a past (waking-up) that imprisonment seeks to eradicate. In recouping his past, his present, and his potential state(s), he clearly gestures toward the possibility of constructing a unified self/community in spite (and in full recognition) of the fixating systemic structures (both internal and external).

In "A Trip through the Mind Jail," Raulrsalinas sets out to do just that. The (anti)formal aesthetic allows for escaping the "lonely/Cellblocks of my mind," recouping the "Demolished" neighborhood of his youth held "captive," not by physical walls, but by impinging structures erected within the subject. Raulrsalinas revisits "Sunday night jamaicas" and "Fiestas for all occasion" as he reinscribes the landscape that until then has been subject to systemic and personal erasure. Raulrsalinas establishes a connection back to his past, achieving a figurative temporal, geographical, transcendence that symbolically regathers his violently shorn past, present, and future as he discursively embodies neighborhood and self.

> Neighborhood of my adolescence
>    neighborhood that is no more
>       YOU ARE TORN PIECES OF MY FLESH!!!!
>                 (61)

In a poetic reconfiguration, Raulrsalinas gestures toward reconstructing his community:

> Therefore, you ARE
> LA LOMA—AUSTIN—MI BARRIO—
>               i bear you no grudge
>     i needed you then . . . identity . . . a sense of belonging
>     i need you now.
>     so essential to adult days of imprisonment,
>     you keep me away from INSANITY'S hungry jaws;
>                         Smiling/Laughing/Crying
>                               (55–61)

Raulrsalinas's poetry reveals, then, much more than a subjugated, subjectified, or even "resistant," "oppositional" figure. To be sure, his vision and identity are shaped by his incarceration, and his political stance is shaped by a pervasive sense that the unjust systemic and social structures are not easily ameliorated. But rather than give in to an isolationist or separatist position, he looks to defy institutional isolation ("adult days of imprisonment") through active engagement with a past, and possible future, outside the prison walls, a space signified as his "BARRIO." Escaping the enforced isolation foisted on the Chicano subject by the "system," means actively engaging that system by looking to the communal past with an eye toward creating a communal future. Hope lies in participation. Raulrsalinas did so during his incarceration through his poetry and activism and has continued to defy systemic isolation through his political activism in Austin, Texas. He continues to write and has established a bookstore dedicated to Chicano literature, "Resistencia."

The postwar Mexican American subject and the movement faced a similar dilemma. Could a form that opens up to memories of youth, neighborhood solidarity, cultural affinity, physical and spiritual love, and so on be refashioned in the face of immobilizing, constricting forces? To do so requires resisting a deterministic vision in which all is lost or erased through contact with "Anglo" America and mainstream society. To refuse do so by employing a vision of an open, and eclectic, but contested form raises the possibility that "America" as a structure can be reconfigured so that it includes these different, Mexican American realities, memories, histories, and potentialities.

Raulrsalinas later disavowed his affiliation with Jack Kerouac, but not with a "Beat aesthetic" that represented an open form. In "Riff(t)s" he writes:

> Kerouac,
>    you no longer
>          turn me on.
>
> .   .   .   .   .   .   .   .   .   .   .   .   .   .
>          Bore you with some news,
>                Duluoz?
>          Unlike your jug o' booze
>                the struggle
>          Turns Me ON.
>                          (*Freeway* 19)

His break with Kerouac is occasioned by his negation of the apolitical, individualist manifestation of the Beat ethic. However, he retains the combination of "calculated protest and improvisational style" associated with another, more socially committed Beat poet, Bob Kaufman, to whom Raulrsalinas dedicates his latest collection of poetry. Ultimately, Ybarra-Frausto's contention that Raulrsalinas "comprehends that liberty is a sham . . . reflect[ing] his present illusory independence" fails to satisfy (12). While Raulrsalinas is only too aware of the strategies of containment aimed at immobilizing the Mexican American subject, he continues to struggle with an inherent desire to transcend them, and to assist in the first step toward doing so: imagining the possibility of an open, inclusive form that might come to characterize "America." To argue otherwise is to come to the same limiting and factionalizing conclusions that helped to pull the Chicano movement apart.

## Anxiety of Influence: Americano Yearnings and Denial in the Poetry of Jose Montoya

In a 1977 interview with Juan Bruce-Novoa, Jose Montoya discusses his major literary influences in a telling exposition of the making of his literary sensibility. Amongst others, he lists Mickey Spillane, Walt Whitman, William Carlos Williams, T. S. Eliot, Ezra Pound, and most relevant to this discussion, Beat and existentialist literature:

> I had heard the beat poets read. They were so far out that it took the works of Eliot and Pound as well as Whitman and Williams to get me to accept their stuff early on. Now I consider them to have been an influence—especially [Gary] Snyder and [Allen] Ginsberg. I started reading the French poets, the symbolists, Verlaine . . . the existentialists . . . Kierkegaard, Heidegger, Jaspers, Camus, and Sartre. . . . The Myth of Sisyphus blew me away. The same damn problem we all have. I thought that the Chicano really knew how to push that rock up there and let it roll down and enjoy the trip. The dealing with the search became, at that time in my life very real. If existence is absurd, do you cope or commit suicide, and both solutions are legitimate, valid. (*Chicano Authors* 122)

Montoya's statement suggests an affinity with Octavio Paz's controversial depiction of the *pachuco* persona in *Labyrinth of Solitude* that is in keeping with the neoindividualist yearning of the Beat poets. The notion of "the search" to which Montoya alludes, is an articulation of a form of movement discourse that I find both paradigmatic and troubling in narratives of dissent in the America of the 1950s and 1960s. Montoya should not be read as a "Beat" poet, but he should be read "against" the Beats as he operates within the same sociopolitical debate regarding the nature of mobility, community, and democracy in the postwar period. "Dealing with the search" in Montoya's work is not only paradigmatic for the postwar Mexican American, particularly the Chicano subject, but also for the "American" postwar subject in ways that I have described in chapters 1 and 2, and will elaborate below. However, the "search" for the Mexican American subject specifically describes an attempt to mediate between a Mexican, Chicano, and ultimately "American" identity and the politics of "denial" that operated, and continues to operate, in both the formation and obstruction of a fully participatory, and potentially radically egalitarian alternative in the formation of a national culture.

Montoya goes on to define "dealing with the search" as he explains his own Kerouacian road trips during his stint as a high school art teacher in northern California: "That's when Estevan Villa and I started taking trips every summer. The first summer we decided to work in the fields, figuring anything we made on top of our school salary was icing on the cake, but we had been away too long . . . we just couldn't get into the thing any more. After that summer Estevan and I decided to just travel. Every summer we'd take off . . . Those trips even got us here to New Haven. Anyway, I got my M.A. and a teaching credential" (*Chicano Authors* 123). Montoya's movement narrative reveals a perceived causal relation between mobility and progress, as well as an anxious recognition that mainstream success has alienated him from his early migrant roots ("we had been away too long"). At times his poetry is intensely nationalistic, characterized by a class-conscious commitment to *los de abajo* (those at the bottom). At other times his focus shifts to *el vendido* (the sell-out), whom he excoriates for leaving behind the *barrio* and his roots. And still at other times, his poetry is self-parodic, self-critical, and even self-agonizing in its exploration of the distance created between his own past and his entry into middle-class existence as a full professor of art at the California State University in Sacramento.

Like Oscar Acosta, Montoya ponders the meaning of the "American" journey that the Mexican American subject has undertaken. Like Acosta, he rejects the possibility of transforming the "American" national narrative into an "Americano" national narrative. Like Kerouac, Ginsberg, and other Beat poets, Montoya attempts to define mobility, community, and political progress in an era that simultaneously attempts to unmoor the American individual from communal roots as it fixes the individual within a socioeconomic hierarchy.

These issues are at the center of Montoya's poetry, and this is significant for Montoya personally and for what his "conflicted" response signified for the broader Chicano movement. Montoya's cultural production, moreover, participated in American democratic discourse and postwar dissent. The critical response surrounding his work reveals similar tensions and anxieties within Chicano Studies discourse in regards to the nature of participation within the academy and within/outside/beside the framework of American Studies. This demonstrates the residuum of *movimiento* politics that still shape appraisals of Chicano politics and subjectivity in both productive and limiting ways.

*InFormation* collects four decades of Montoya's poetry. The collection juxtaposes his work in ways that call attention to issues of ideological and political identity that have not yet been critically examined. In "El Vendido," a 1969 poem, Montoya develops a theme to which he will return over and over through his career. Although in later poems, such as the 1990 poem "Billy, Billy, el Militante," *el vendido* is the object of the poetic persona's harsh assessment, in "El Vendido" we find that the "sellout" is the narrator:

> Blunt dull pain
> Like nothing
> But, oh, yes
> That lingers and
> Envelopes my soul
>
> Like sack-cloth
>
> Bequeathing penitence
> Upon my sanguine hopes
> Sorry remnants of
> Once regal Dons
> Yet earlier Yaquis
>
> Vestiges fading fast
>
> From the pain
> That hurts my Raza
> Concerned now
> With boats in the
> Driveway, the Boy Scouts
>
> And the World Series
>
> And I
> The weakest

Condemned to bear
It all for reasons of
Betrayal only my father's

Dead father can fathom

And he died for Villa
That year of the
Revolution of pain
So much
Sweeter than

Mine.

(4)

Montoya's critique evokes a personal anxiety that pits mainstream acculturation against revolutionary commitment. By positioning politically meaningless material struggles in America (mere sports contests such as the "World Series") next to the meaningful battles for social justice ("Villa" and the "Revolution of pain") that are now but "vestiges fading fast," Montoya condemns the Mexican American *"vendido"* as betraying patriarchal sacrifice (the "Dead Father" who "died for Villa"). The conflict, however, is internal more than it is social. *El vendido* is "within" the Chicano, and although Montoya alludes to an acceptance of a base consumerism, he seems more disturbed by the Chicano subject's internalization of "American" identity.

Revolution is associated with Francisco "Pancho" Villa and the Mexican civil war that has little to do with economic exploitation in postwar America. "Weakness" is associated more with the betrayal of a masculinist militarism, rather than with the failure to do battle with a base consumerism. Montoya's concern here very closely echoes the recognition that he is no longer in the picking fields. Montoya's poetry, then, is often as concerned—often solely concerned—with a betrayal of Mexicano identity ("Sorry remnants of / Once regal Dons . . . Yaquis") rather than with the workings of an exploitative market economy. In this way, "El Vendido" signals an overriding concern with keeping "American" cultural influences at bay, a concern that ignores the economic question in attempt to purge cultural "intrusions" that Montoya feels are a betrayal of his "Mexican-ness."

It is not that Montoya felt guilty for yearning to join a country club or buy a Volvo and move to the suburbs. Rather, his poetry reveals an anxiety over the influence that "American" culture exerts on his personal and communal identity, which has "enveloped his soul." At times, Montoya paints with too broad a brush, conflating valid sociopolitical and cultural participation as a betrayal, in much the same way separatist and cultural nationalist did in *el movimiento*. In later poems like "El Louie" and "Don't Ever Lose Your Drivers License," however, Montoya's poetry adapted and transformed Beat poetics. Using the theme of movement, mobility, and travel, Montoya calls for both an egalitarian society as well as an individual-centered civil rights agenda.

Like the Beats, this creates a tension between an individualist-oriented program and a communitarian impulse. Kerouac and other Beats decided in favor of creating an isolationist position that protected the individual at all costs and that included sacrificing any communal social strategy. In contrast, Montoya, and Chicano separatists for that matter, opted to suppress "American" instincts by refusing to participate in "mainstream" culture. Ironically, this meant giving up the possibility of a national community in favor of a narrow cultural communalism. However, in Montoya's case, this also results in Mexican American isolation and even dissolution.

In "Los Vatos," it is intracommunity violence that annihilates the Mexican American individual. Community is impossible, and not necessarily because of Anglo oppression, but because of an evinced fear of being absorbed and erased by the community itself, so that the fear of being obliterated by American mainstream culture is here echoed but with the threat originating from one's own *barrio*. The poem describes the murder of a young man at the hands of his own gang. The threat is depicted specifically as culturally internal. In this sense, becoming "American" is not really the problem for Montoya, so much as losing one's individuated "self" is.

His brain, his stomach, his feet—all of him—
was not himself at all and he could stand outside
And look in. He was at once a rock and a lump of jello
Something—a thing but not himself
                              (*InFormation* 9)

The inevitability of a violent end, of the annihilation of self, of a cosmic determinism (in response to which he wishes he could be "born again" of his mother), describes an existentialist worldview. What this suggests is that Montoya shares a good deal with the Beats ethos. However, I would argue that he recognized the isolationist, neoindividualist politics that this form of existentialism breeds, and thus constructed a defensive cultural nationalism that attempted to suppress his individualist yearning, thus resulting in a self-conflicted poetry and a conflation of all things "American" as antithetical to Chicano identity. However, the resulting communality is bound to fail in its restricitve, isolating localization that forms more in reaction to racist, exploitative practices creating a defensive position. The experience of moving outside the parameter of the *barrio,* both metaphorically and literally, thus creates an anxiety for Montoya. This form of mobility (one being encountered more frequently by Mexican Americans in the postwar period) creates an anxiety in which "individual" upward movement is projected as "American," thus locating the challenge to Mexican American solidarity and community as external, foreign, invasive. However this analysis lacks a clear-cut class component and portrays socioeconomic exploitation as a threat of cultural annihilation.

As "Los Vatos" suggests, the threat to the narrator's identity is not cultural, but personal: the self is threatened not by the dominant "other" but by one's own community. That version of "individualism" is too threatening and painful for Montoya to face and so he combats it with an ultranationalism and devastating critique aimed at *vendidos,* an internal force more than an external one.

In "From '67 to '71," Montoya's pessimism over the fate of *el movimiento* takes as its target the effete "revolutionary" self:

Flowers are growing where
      we planted bayonets

Hopelessness provides a respite
And reckless impulses subside

I no longer wait for the rains
Only cold winter evenings

I wince at revolutionary talk-talk
And a tear and a smile confuse
My prodigies

. . . I don't want to recall
when I became ineffective
but I do.

                (*InFormation* 26)

The failure of the movement to produce more lasting results is conflated with his personal failure. Montoya suggests that his community ("My prodigies") have also failed him. The problem seems to reside in an effete "revolutionary talk-talk" that belies deeper systemic and organizational conflicts within *el movimiento*. "Revolution" has failed. But what revolution? Montoya points to the guise of the revolutionary to critique the participatarian democratic movements of the late 1960s.

Yet poems like "Los de Abajo" and "Faces at the First Farmworkers Constitutional Convention," which have a strong class component, are much more enthusiastic about the possibility of the radical democratic project. The latter poem is almost a liturgy sung in praise of the democratic process that the farmworkers have begun to utilize in sophisticated and effective ways. The poem is masterful in its insistence that the "unorganizable" can indeed organize, govern, make decisions, retain their connection to community, and remain uncorrupted while practicing a radical inclusion. Yet, this poem is countered by poems like "The Guard Tower at the Consumnes Correctional Center" in which the penitentiary appears as the most fitting paradigm for Chicano life in America, its guard tower "denuding with every methodical scan," as it stands "Over all that misery, innocuous / for the moment, you stand defiant / sterile erection, symbol / of America" (*InFormation* 80).

For all the progress made by radical democratic organization such as the UFW, the Mexican American subject remains, in Montoya's appraisal, outside the system, an imprisoned, isolated object of surveillance. Of course, neither of these symbolic roles (democratic participant or immobilized prisoner) becomes dominant in Montoya's poetry, for each is constantly undercut by the other in a dialectical dance which points out, amongst other things, Montoya's discomfort with the evidence of "progress" (limited as it might be). Instead, he attempts to stay connected to his "Mexican-ness" by locating its base of operation in the barrio and the prison. Whereas Montoya's analysis is accurate in exposing the effect of an exploitative market economy, it is not always successful in finding the cause or in suggesting effective, political action.

In reading Montoya's best-known poem, "El Louie," both Juan Bruce-Novoa and Cordelia Candalaria read the paean in conventional ways suggesting that it creates in Louie a locus of rebellion and cultural resistance. As Rafael Perez-Torres argues, Teresa McKenna gives an alternative reading. She sees the figure of Louie as a victim of false consciousness: "As McKenna notes, the poem draws on the corrido tradition that celebrates the life of an exemplary individual. . . . The result is 'that he turns to those consumerized images of bravery fabricated by the society which impinge so destructively on his selfhood. By choosing these images, Louie entrenches himself further in the domination which is making him extinct. . . . Louie's link to this center is mediated and ultimately ironic" (Perez-Torres 127). Neither of these tendencies (Louie as rebel or Louie as sellout) are adequate. They fall into the same limiting dichotomy, both readings ignoring the possibility of an "Americano" synthesis.

However, this "blindness" to a possible synthesis seems also to operate within Montoya as well, himself a product and practitioner of a limiting, but conflicted cultural nationalism. In essence, Montoya's content never caught up to his form. The content of his poetry is often pessimistic, accusatory, anticommunal, narrow, and prescriptive, while his form is democratic, pluralistic, revolutionary, inclusive, dynamic. "El Louie" demonstrates this conflict, "Americano" in emphasizing a syncretic poetic, but self-annihilating and anticommunal in sentiment. While critics such as Renato Rosaldo, Juan Bruce-Novoa, Rafael Perez-Torres, and Cordelia Candalaria have argued that "El Louie" is a breakthrough poem in Chicano literature because it constructs a figure that subverts mainstream or hegemonic identity through the creation of the multiplex personality, I find Ignacio Trujillo's reading more nuanced in discussing the poem's conflicted nature: "[When] one places Louie's struggle in historical perspective, one sees that this individual type of revolt was doomed to self-defeat, although it was one of the seeds of the present Chicano Movement" (159). However, this reading does not follow through on its implied critique of the Chicano movement. Thus this dichotomy of interpretive choices seems to construct Louie as either a subversive rebel, a conflicted individualist, or an interpellated subject who has been coopted by the dominant market culture. In many ways, these were the sorts of limiting, mutually exclusive categories that *el movimiento* subscribed to and disseminated. Thus, I argue that Louie is ultimately representative of the *movimiento's* conflicted desire to affect and participate within American society, and the fear that such participation is akin to selling out. Trujillo's comment on Louie's "individual type revolt" is indicative of the Chicano movement's separatist isolation, and its inability to construct an inclusive strategy that could distinguish between participation and cooptation.

"El Louie" is a halting, conflicted step toward the formation of the prototypical "Americano" that ultimately annihilates its new subject. Louie's syncretic character, to disagree with a more poststructural reading, is not simply a liminal function through which the subject is made unsubjectable. Louie's "Bogey-esque" *pachuco* pose speaks to the emergence of an Americano consciousness that refuses to locate itself in one particular space or one particular tradition. This is not an example of oppositional resistance, but of a tentative projection of the Mexican American self within the

"American" sociocultural sphere that has so long attempted to exclude it.

The calo dialect demonstrates a strategic use of language that is as resistant to formal Spanish as it is to a pervasive and colonizing English. It is ultimately Louie's failure to distinguish between the ultraindividualism of the mainstream culture that keeps him from serving as a model for the emerging Mexican American participatory subject. Louie is in fact much closer to Tomás Rivera's Pete Fonseca, a Beat *pachuco* who poses a substantial, but subtle threat to the farmworker community in the story "On the Road to Texas." His appropriation of "American" cinema characters centers around the fantasy world of the antisocial gangster, functioning much in the same way as the western does for Kerouac's Sal Paradise:

> En Sanjo you'd see him
> Sporting a dark topcoat
> Playin in his fantasy
> The role of Bogard, Cagney
> Or Raft
> (*InFormation* 16)

The role-playing is aimed at converting the socioracial outsider role into a "resistant" role through a counterproductive projection into a form based on "American" individualism hostile to communalism. Thus the form of subjectivity Montoya provides (inclusive, syncretic, "Americano") potentially moves postwar subjectivity toward a fuller participation within a shared cultural space, but the content of Louie's persona (individualist, anticommunal, violent, isolationist) is ultimately antidemocratic.

In his "tailor-made drapes" Louie becomes both the icon and hero of neighborhood youth who have little but their own projected fantasies that assert power through his violent, but street-savvy persona. "But we had Louie," confides the poem's narrator. Violence, both literally and metaphorically, defines the systemic and personal dynamic at work, and Louie is always in control: "Va'ver Pedo! . . . Get Louie!" (16). But in this case, and this is not atypical, the violence is channeled intraracially. The pride with which the narrator recalls Louie's bravery in the Korean War ties Louie to the Mexican American generation's desire to enter into the American mainstream. However, the patriotic tone is undermined by the disclosure that Louie was often in the stockade due to insubordination, and that following the war, he hocked his bronze stars.

Louie is ultimately the Chicano Bogart, insubordinate, brave, cocky, idiosyncratic, a character onto which the community may project its own fantasy of resistance without ever finding a true and effective target for its discontent. Louie fails to achieve an "Americano" identity, although he does achieve a tragic, heroic stature, because he does not point toward an insistent inclusion be it within his own community, or within a larger, national community:

> His death was an insult
> Porque no murio en accion-
> No lo mataron los vatos
> Ni los gooks en Korea.
> He died alone in a
> Rented room—perhaps like in a
> Bogard movie.
>                         (*InFormation* 18)

The "insult" posits the value of the heroic persona who acts alone and dies alone, while also suggesting the ultimate disillusion in the inefficacy of this model. However, the reader is left without any alternative for the formation of an effective, communal strategy or an idea of what sort of persona might be most useful in the making of the modern, Mexican American citizen-subject.

In pointing out the paradoxes of the status of Mexican American youth—outside the law, but inside the American dream-fantasy—the poem does serve as an indication of the desire to project the self not simply into a subsuming "American" culture, but to create a new identity and perhaps even imagine a new sort of culture that is partially self-defined. But ultimately Montoya's vision is too closely tied to a neoindividualist American fantasy that does not challenge the status quo in any direct, meaningful way. In the final analysis, Louie does not point toward the more important struggle for inclusion and equality.

Montoya's later poetry reads as a postmortem of the movement. In poems such as "The Movement Has Gone For Its Ph.D Over at the University Or, The Gang Wars Are Back" he suggests that the movement has been undercut by the cooptation of the *movimiento* generation who now walk around in *"corbatitas"* (little ties) and who now live in the "new barrio" in Washington D.C. While Montoya correctly observes the emergence of the conservative and materialistic "Hispanic" generation, he does not move beyond a critique that targets cultural inauthenticity:

> Where do you suppose they've gone,
> All those bad-ass bigotones
> que llegaron shouting RAZA
> y viva EL BARRIO
> and they couldn't even roll their R's?
> (*InFormation* 97)

What's missing from Montoya's critique is a deeper acknowledgment that cultural nationalism was itself an inadequate framework from which to launch a radical national social alternative. In a move that replicates the romanticism of cultural nationalism, the speaker of the poem waits for the Mexican revolutionaries to fan the flames of reform in the United States:

> Meanwhile, to the South a
> gentle wind begins to blow.
> Ojala y tenga paciencia [hope and have patience]
> ese viento de Bolivia
> de Guerrero y Guatemala
> tengan fe en neustra conciencia
> ya nos trea la confusion —
> pero de alli han salir
> los frutos de nuestra potencia.
> (*InFormation* 98)

Revolution is here imagined as external, idealistic, foreign, and violent. Suggestively, the revolutionary zeal Montoya hungers for is most absent in the academy where he serves as a professor. In a scathing indictment of empty theorization and academic practices, he accuses students and professors alike of "searching for those stipends in the sky" (98).

In "Los They Are Us" Montoya concludes that the "system remains the same / But the faces are our faces!" (163). One cannot help but read a projected anxiety in this indictment that advises that we must now contend with the "they" that is now "us." The tension between the *vendido* and the authentic, potential revolutionary subject is thus internal not only to the Mexican American culture, but to the post-*movimiento* subject. In his focus on the need for defending the community from external threats, and the Chicano self from internalizing the enemy's ethos, Montoya continues to reject the necessity of redrawing the parameters of permitted participation so that they might include the national public sphere. Ultimately, Montoya is so wary of participation in "America," that Mexican American inclusion is often portrayed as cooptation.

In some ways, Montoya comes closest to analyzing the exploitation of Chicanos when he concentrates on endemic immobilizing techniques that attempt to fixate not only the Chicano subject, but all citizens—the illusory privileges of "mobility" as incentive are uncovered by Montoya in poems like "Vamos a Dar La Vuelta" and "Gabby Took the 99" and "Don't Ever Lose Your Driver's License." It is in these poems that Montoya voices his clearest critique of the illusory nature of American "mobility" perhaps best understood because of his own Beat-like individualist desire. These are poems that critique America from "within" as a full participant in the American dialogue about freedom, liberty, and inclusion.

In "Don't Ever Lose Your Driver's License," the Mexican American subject rides through the whole of America and is portrayed as surveyor of the sociocultural-political landscape who sees the various dimensions of American existence. Riding the bus in a Kerouacian elegy that echoes and yet counters Whitmanian exhuberance, Montoya leaves behind, at least momentarily, a "Chicano self-consciousness" long enough to use instead a "Mexican

American consciousness" in its most syncretic sense in what is one of his most trenchant moments. I quote this poem in its entirety:

Greyhound riding lonesome blues
Not to mention the turmoil and despair
Of the terminals—pimps and pushers
And frightened grandmas—
Refugees from Middle America
And sadistic cops.

And you ride side by side
old people going on their last journeys
and young people on their way
to new adventures and dreams
leaving their burdens to the mountain
and eventually
visa versa

And the dreams seem nearer
as huge, smiling billboards
Proclaim a grand America
Out there—somewhere—as the
Gloom rolls on, along
Futuristic freeways—
Modern long knives—
Slicers of old barrios

And finally having left the driving
To insulting drivers
A static voice
Crackles a thank you for

Going Greyhound and
You feel grateful
In a hateful sort of way

Knowing you've been taken
For a ride—side by side
Old people going on their
Final journeys.

(99)

In his acknowledgment of "Middle America" Montoya suggests his awareness of being in the midst of America while signaling that "we" are all "refugees" from systemic repression ("sadistic cops"). Like Kerouac *(Mexico City Blues and San Francisco Blues)* Montoya sings his own "lonesome blues" that are here not ameliorated solely by his cultural membership. Instead he rides "side by side" with others different from him in age and prospect, some taking their "final journeys," and others "on their way to new adventures and dreams." Montoya suggests that the American fixation on mobility as a condition for progress affects us all, advertising falsely as it "Proclaim[s] a grand America Out there — somewhere." Montoya here opens up a space in which a unified, and inclusive community can exist. It is a tenuous community, joined perhaps not by culture or race or even class, but still a community that in the final analysis is "American." The Chicano, so long a victim of the market and its profit motive (the "slicer of old barrios") recognizes that his insight is in part made possible by his inclusion within "America," not by a reactionary rejection of narrowly defined "America." Montoya's grudging gratitude given "In a hateful sort of way" is proffered because inclusion can be as enlightening as marginality. The Mexican American becomes Americano through the embracing of both his outsider and insider status.

Within this poem, Montoya creates a syncretic and synergistic space in which the interplay of culture gestures toward an Americano possibility, one that is capable of social critique not simply in a denial of the interstice of "American" influence within "Chicano" culture, but because of it. Rather than rejecting the Beatific influence through a purifying cultural nationalism, Montoya utilizes it as it operates within the postwar Mexican community and within the postwar Mexican American subject (for better and for worse). Through the dialectic articulated between the "Mexican" and "American" self (collective and individual) this poem comes as close to exposing the modes of exploitation alive and well in the U.S. economy and society as *movimiento* poetry does. However, Montoya also demonstrates that this acceptance, grudging as it is, cannot stand for long before a defensive cultural nationalism designed to alleviate the weight that the paradox of Mexican American-ness brings.

In fact, traces of limiting *movimiento* separatism, isolationism, and an underlying anxiety of influence greatly affected the early construction of Chicano criticism, and although there have been strides toward constructing paradigms that refigure the nature and definition of "America" and "Americans," (of which this analysis is an installment), a survey of the criticism of Montoya's poetry shows the deleterious influence of *el movimiento's* narrow identity politics Older appraisals such as Juan Bruce-Novoa's and Arturo Madrid-Barela's readings, emphasize Montoya as a pioneer of "Chicano" literature and underscore his nationalist tendencies: his use of bilinguality, calo, and his featuring of the *pachuco* and *casindio* personas. Both Jose Limon and Jose David Saldivar discuss Montoya's work in its relation to the *corrido*, reading his work as primarily addressing what Limon refers to as the "sustaining tradition" of Chicano social poetry. These mid-eighties readings are in keeping with a second stage of Chicano criticism that moved away from overt nationalist ideology, but not entirely.

In 1990 Renato Rosaldo read Montoya in light of an emerging postmodern Chicano subjectivity, the writing of a "multiplex personality" very much informed by borderlands theory as well as ethnographic theory originating in Victor Turner's concept of the social drama and theorization of liminal play. Rafael Perez-Torres attempts to enjoin a Marxist critique with a poststructural approach that reads Montoya's *pachuco* as a site of resistance that emerges from direct material experience and acts as a central locus for a postmodern localized politics. However, what has often been overlooked in all these readings is the relation of Montoya's work within the broader, national countercultural and democratic debate. This oversight points to an anxiety manifested in an intracultural emphasis that runs the gamut of these readings, which remain informed by the nationalism that shaped Chicano Studies in its nascence.

The following passage from Perez-Torres's analysis of "El Louie" demonstrates this limiting Chicano Studies paradigm:

Certainly "El Louie" stands as an instance of Chicano self-representation. It does so while simultaneously recognizing . . . the limitations of the cultural repertoire upon which Chicanos have historically been allowed to draw in constructing a self-identity. Montoya's poem evokes and complicates the vision of a resistant Chicano culture. Although this culture, embodied by the language and dress of the pachuco, stands apart from mainstream society . . . it simultaneously draws upon the mass cultural products that belong to the very society against which the pachuco stands. The complicitous critique, the curious position of a self that stands apart yet also unwittingly belongs, becomes emblematic of the complexities inherent in articulating Chicano subjectivity. This becomes a place of mestizaje, a place of impurity: the borderlands. (128)

While certainly Chicano self-representation has had a limited "cultural repertoire," less convincing is the suggestion that the *pachuco* or the "Chicano subjectivity" that it represents ultimately articulates a liminal position. The theoretical role of the liminal persona, I have argued, has not been particularly efficacious, and in this case it seems calculated in order to "resist" the intrusion of "mainstream society." The liminal Chicano subject is then placed within the "borderlands" similarly constructed as a place that resists the "mainstream" purity of U.S. hegemony. Rather, the *pachuco*/Chicano culture is already implicated fully as part of "American culture" instead of as *drawing* on American culture. Rather than seeing the open, fluid, unfixed space as the "borderlands," we should consider a redefinition of "American" culture as "Americano" culture, an already syncretic, transformative space. The "Americano" culture and landscape is a space, in effect, in which the Mexican American subject can "arrive," not in assimilationist fashion, but as an agent actively and directly transforming it.

The residue of *movimiento* era separatist politics and the conscious effort to disavow "Hispanic" assimilationist conservatism have resulted in what amounts to a strategy of self-marginalization. I have argued that these same paradigms inform Jose Montoya's work. Examining the way in which his work is constructed to circumvent its participation within the context of a larger, democratic debate, sheds light on the deeply conflicted battle, if you will, for the political and social "soul" of the postwar Mexican American subject. Further, there is an academic, critical parallel in the limited impact Chicano Studies has had on the shaping of American Studies. Isolationism, critical or cultural, has as an unfortunate consequence of forfeiting the shaping the broader sociocritical landscape.

In an early essay on the construction of the Chicano subject and of a Chicano poetics, Jose David Saldivar cites Herbert Marcuse's claim that "ethnic minorities are inherently radicalized and revolutionary by our marginalization and constricted position in the United States" ("Towards a Chicano Poetics" 16). However, this construct of "radicalization" has only been partially successful in effecting "our liberation from tokenism, condescension, racism and oppression." (16). Rather than liberating the Chicano subject, I argue that the current proliferation of "borderlands texts" has effectively coopted liminal reading strategies (the "migrant function"), divorcing its practice from the material history of the border, of migrant experience, and Mexican American desires and aspirations. In essence, Saldivar's caution that "Chicano poetics must not be an alternative technique for deconstructing-interpreting texts," has gone unheeded. This is in part because the "Americano" desire to participate has been displaced in central strain of Chicano criticism.[7]

In constructing a "Chicano sensibility" or a Chicano "poetic," its relation to a national poetic was too quickly abandoned as "American" without questioning why the "American" poetic must be defined as "European" or "Anglo." By suggesting that "the corrido is the central sociopoetic Chicano paradigm," Saldivar understandably argues for the recognition of a literary, cultural, historical collective identity that is historically sustained, resistant, and that results in a praxis rooted in Mexican American material practices. However, where this cultural and literal construction falls short is in omitting the influence of this poetic and politics in the creation of "America" as cultural construct, leaving that for the "Anglos" (it should be noted that Saldivar has worked within the last decade to redefine radically the idea of "America" as well as the definition of "American" in works such as *The Dialectics of Our America* and *Border Matters*).

This early conceptualization of the Chicano narrative echoed the insularity with which cultural nationalism narrowed its own participatory potential. By heralding Montoya as a Chicano writer who "gives the impression of a new, Chicano sensibility . . . [that] dramatizes otherness and . . . bring[s] readers into electrifying contact with social forms wholly different from Anglo-American ones," Saldivar in this relatively initiatory stage of Chicano criticism, implies not only a "wholly" foreign literary, historical sensibility, but also a "wholly" foreign political sensibility.

By emphasizing "resistance" to "the imperialism of Anglo-American forms and thought" as the central tenet of a Chicano narrative, scholars have hastily assumed what constitutes these oppressive forms. They have indirectly conflated the notion of "resistance" with "exclusion," and the phenomenon of "selling out" with the desire for "inclusion," as if there was no radical or progressive potential in direct participation and inclusion. Separatist ideology labeled democratic participation, progressivism, and a national egalitarian concern as assimilationist or as "Anglo-American" political forms, tragically short-circuiting the possibility of strategic interventions. Nascent constructions of the form and reach of the Chicano poetic recreated the same limitations. At this early stage, Saldivar suggests that: "Montoya's vision of the pachuco experience though open to the social, psychological and ideological forces of American society in advanced capitalism is narrated or related to other nineteeth century Chicano perceptions, histories, and its implicit theory of social resistance through its fixity of form" ("Towards a Chicano Poetics" 12). This vision had the effect of centering and fixing Chicano political (re)action and resistance on an "unalien" paradigm that was no longer adequate for positioning the Mexican American subject within the postwar "American" landscape. A resistance based on a static identity and form could not shift as the socioeconomic model changed; nor could it allow entry into a larger American framework that we might have begun to shape through inclusion and dialectical transformation. These early Chicano studies constructs give one the sense that Chicano criticism was itself suffering an anxiety of influence, preferring to keep Chicano poetics as a paradigm that enclosed the Mexican American subject as a particular sort of "Chicano," one primarily related back to the early border subject. Plainly this was inadequate in understanding the evolving forms of exploitation and cooptation, and the resulting forms of resistance that had occurred in Chicano political and social life since the end of World War II.

In discussing "El Louie," Jose Limon similarly suggests that "the corrido is the central sociopoetic Chicano paradigm" (*Mexican Ballads* 90). If this assessment is accurate, how accurate and to what effect? Raulsalinas, Jose Montoya, Tomás Rivera, and Oscar Acosta do not seem to suggest that in their work; add to that list contemporary assessments of Rolando Hinojosa and Americo Paredes's fiction works that have begun to place them within a modernist framework, thus revising our current understanding of modernist racialism and politics. The *corrido* paradigm, in fact, is too narrow for postwar experience. It is an incomplete representation of Mexican American desire and too fixated on a particular notion of "resistance," which posits the same sort of self-marginalizing, self-interpellating move of an older cowboys and Indians paradigm. I have already read the conflict between the *corrido* paradigm and a more open, more participatarian paradigm in Montoya (which he fails to solve in any definitive way). Montoya's conflicts demonstrate a great deal in common with the Beat ambivalence toward participating in "mainstream" culture. Desire for "mainstream" inclusion, and a resulting guilt complex, led to a self-limiting confinement. For Montoya, this spelled isolation in the *barrio* and for the *barrio*. Such "resistance" is a poor response to, and in fact replicates, the more subtle forms of economic exploitation, segregation, and fixating tactics.

Limon's early criticism places "authentic" Chicano poetry solely in conversation with itself. He too quickly dismisses the Beat influence and rejects the poetry of Raulsalinas and Alurista for being divorced from "sustaining tradition." This is telling for it implicitly acknowledges the residue of isolationist politics and ideology inherent in Chicanismo. It is not that the *corrido* is not an important and potent paradigm in Chicano poetry; rather, its dynamic is insufficient for describing the dialectic at work. Seeking a more contemporary and relevant paradigm, I would like to suggest one that focuses on the nature of "mobility" and forced movement that characterizes migrant life on the border and other places. Although it is not limited to Chicano experience, it has specific, historical, Mexican American manifestations while having direct and important relevance to "American" socioeconomic history. The mobility paradigm is in keeping with Jose David Saldivar's contention that any study of Chicano literature must begin with a historical connection of life on the real border. This mobility and fixating dynamic is very much connected to that.

Through a mobility paradigm, we can read Montoya's poetry as deeply imbricated in a larger, broader political and aesthetic discourse that takes part in postwar American literature, and that is connected to Beat literature in important, telling ways. At this early stage, Limon admits that many Chicano poets are influenced by Beat poetry of the fifties, but dismisses them from his consideration because they do not clearly relate back to the "master precursor." However, I would stress that Montoya's work (Chicano literature in general) does not simply relate to the master precursor but engages "American" issues, forms, and politics in particular. Limon's curious dismissal of the poets whose influences are a "collage" is symptomatic:

> Alurista and Ricardo Sanchez are engaged with a collage of influences, none really master precursors, from pre-Hispanic, indigenous poetics to the "beat" poetry of the fifties, to African American culture. The result is an interesting but rhetorically overextended and incoherent poetry in search of a sustaining tradition. Something of this same argument applies to Raulrsalinas's engaging "Trip through the Mind Jail" (its very title and dedication to Eldridge Cleaver already partial evidence), though I find it a more successful poem, one more conscious of a sustaining tradition. But Raulrsalinas's primary precursor is not the corrido so much as, perhaps, the most famous of greater Mexican legends, la llorona (the Wailing Woman), although I am as yet not clear on this. (*Mexican Ballads* 91)

What's clear here is that Limon is discounting some of these poets because of "outside" influences. This dismissal suggests that there is a direct and authenticating "Chicano" genealogy, something that is working off of a tradition, is "focused," and connected to a "sustaining form." This early project construes Chicano literature in a very narrow way, as separate from "outside" influences. He designates this sort of poetry as "Mexican American Social Poetry" (the subtitle of his book). But there is a sustaining connection to material experience that engages its own precursors as well as the culture and society in which material experience and existence is locatable through the lens of culture and tradition. How does Mexican American poetry actually become Mexican American poetry, that is linked, a poetry of juxtaposition that ultimately creates not hybridity, but can be understood to be "American" in the way that "American" must and should be understood as also "Mexican"?

Limon hints at this by arguing with Jose David Saldivar's reading of "Los Vatos" in which he acknowledges a debate on the viability of community and communal identity. However, in painting this debate as largely internal to a Chicano narrative, he ignores the important issues shared in a larger American debate over democratic participation and a potential for egalitarian formation of *civitas* that I have shown the Beats engaged, and was very much central to postwar dissent. Montoya is of interest to me not because he follows or diverges from the *corrido* form, but because he encounters the notion of community and the communal so directly and pensively. His articulations are often ambivalent toward community, violent and sometimes hypercritical of those who "lack" Chicano consciousness, but often he is self-critical enough to demonstrate the complexity of asserting Chicano identity while desiring to act within a larger, national culture.

Like the Beat isolation fueled by communitarian anxiety, Montoya demonstrates a Chicano reticence toward "joining" a larger national culture, whether it is radically transformed or not. However, Chicano critical appraisals of Montoya (and *el movimiento*) have not taken up this question, preferring instead to concentrate on a model of "resistance" that focuses on whether or not a particular poet or critic is effectively oppositional. Witness an early debate on Montoya's poetry between Jose Limon and Jose David Saldivar. Limon writes, "Saldivar seems to want 'Los Vatos' to be as politically and socially affirmative as the Border corrido, a poem as aware of and critically responsive to the politically dominant Other as, let us say 'The Ballad of Gregorio Cortez'. . . . My position is quite the opposite, that both 'Los Vatos' and 'El Louie' are diminished as sociopolitical statements in the comparison to their precursor, and that in this diminishment Montoya is signaling an end to, or at least a severe reduction in the corrido's ability to be transformed for our time, at least in his hands" (*Mexican Ballads, Chicano Poems* 107). While Limon claims that the *corrido* is inadequate as a relevant contemporary social protest and that a new dissenting paradigm is needed as a response to sexism and classism, there is no implication for an intercultural application. Limon chooses instead to focus on a somewhat insular construct of the Chicano community, pointing out that the poem signals an end to community, portraying a world of "intracommunity violence, which, while socially conditioned is nonetheless also self-generated and certainly self-inflicted" (108).

However, as subtle as Limon's argument reads, he too rigidly defines the structure of Chicano poetics as determined by "sustaining tradition" even while pointing to the inadequacy of many of the poetic expressions of Chicano literature. The emphasis is placed, conventionally, on the intracultural literary dialectic rather than on the intercultural struggle so clearly at work during the postwar period. The next step is to consider the implications that Montoya's conclusions had (and have) for redefining "America" and the "Americano."

Renato Rosaldo implies just such an expanded arena of operation. In *Culture and Truth*, anthropologist Rosaldo sees Montoya's poem "El Louie" as constituting a postmodern Chicano identity, one he terms the "multiplex personality" and functions along the lines of an identity nexus: "Figures such as El Louie . . . study more as complex sites of cultural production rather than as representatives of a self-contained, homogeneous culture" (217). Rosaldo offers an alternative understanding of postwar Mexican

American narrative practices. Rather than reflecting a self-contained culture, they depict not *only* a more complex cultural exchange, but they also incorporate and comment on a larger democratic political framework than they have been given credit for by either American Studies or Chicano Studies critics.

However, Rosaldo's reading relies too heavily on "borderlands" theory that would see Montoya's work as primarily speaking to the "liberating" effect of marginality or liminal existence. Borderlands theory too often invokes the same romantic, redemptive effect of "mobility" zeroing in on subject formation as the primary site of Chicano intervention. Borderlands theory also has too readily endorsed a mode of poststructural fluidity and a celebration of ambiguity that it posits as always liberating. While Rosaldo is correct in asserting that Montoya's "distinctive cultural practices personify a certain Chicano gift for improvisation and recombination within an array of disparate cultural elements," I further claim that Montoya's work is also indicative of the limitations of such a discourse of movement in the same way that all "American" movement narratives are limited by the conflict between isolating individualism and communal instincts.

Too often, the hyper "mobility" benefit of the poststructural subject is just another way of denying the possibility of community, thus reconstructing an individualism resistant to any communal impingement upon the subject's liberty. Liberty, in this sense, is construed as "movement" or "mobility." A survey of Montoya's early and later poetry has already demonstrated a conflicted set of desires that ultimately are decided in favor of repressing an incorporative, participatory strategy by too narrowly defining the space in which the "Chicano" can operate. In other words, I don't want to celebrate Montoya's "El Louie" solely as an achievement of "transculturation" and as representing a poetic "postmodernism" before its time as does Rosaldo (*Culture and Truth* 214). Rather, I want to read "El Louie" as part of an *opus* tied more directly to the issues of political efficacy and democratic viability in America, especially in regards to the postwar Mexican American subject. Montoya's work speaks to the desire to effect social justice and to create a space for national community building that attempts to cut across racial and cultural difference, even while that effort in respect to difference does not seek to erase them. Ultimately, Montoya falls short. Understanding why begins with recognizing the limitations of Chicanismo and postmodern and modern fetishism of "mobility."

Montoya's (as well as the Chicano movement's) separatist tendencies narrow the range (and acceptance) of "authentic" Chicano subjectivities as well as their arenas of operation. These reductive characterizations kept *movimiento* activists and participants from asking important, productive questions, severely limiting the scope of intra- and intercultural political debate: Should a national agenda be created? How should "nation" be (re)defined? What is the nature of a "progressive/revolutionary" citizenship and how is it implicated within the context of the (re)defined nation? How should political and civic participation function within a national scope? What are the limitations and benefits of expanding the parameters of "community" outside of its restricted localization? How might the democratic process be revitalized by an infusion of direct, Mexican American participation? Might U.S. culture be moved radically in the direction of a communitarian model in order to effect an egalitarian *civitas*?

These are questions that might have more directly led to a fuller formulation of an "Americano" identity and politics that rebuffed separatism and isolationism while incorporating a Mexican American skepticism grounded in historical experience and current material conditions that underlay a separatist nationalist directive. Montoya ultimately denies multiplex, Americano identity and incorporation even while evoking a desire for it. He constructs too narrow an identity and arena, isolating himself, denying his Americano yearnings to appease his *movimiento* anxiety over "selling out." His work reconstitutes the *barrio* as the location of all resistance, the *pachuco* and *casindio* as the subjects of resistance. His vision of resistance and its object, "American Society," remains mired in the paradigm of the nineteenth century *corrido*—an inadvertantly complicitous analog to the neo-Romantic pinings for nineteenth century imperialism reborn so persuasively in the postwar period. In essence, Montoya, and much *movimiento* rhetoric, unwittingly reinforced the Cowboy/ Indian paradigm it so ardently sought to deconstruct.

At the end of his discussion on Montoya, Rafael Perez-Torres considers the difficult introspection that the postwar Mexican American must undergo: "When dominant society configures the Chicano as an outsider instead of a constituent, a foreigner instead of an American, a labor force instead of a complex human being, an awareness of the limitations and delimitations of social discourses grows" (Perez-Torres 130). Understanding these impositions must include recognizing that the role of the "dominant society" is often played by our own cultural identity politics and that we "allow" for our own status as foreigners as we remain complicit in marginalizing our own community. As we stay ever-vigilant in recognizing classist, racist, misogynistic discursive strategies imposed upon us from "without," we must also be able to recognize self-limiting, isolating discursive strategies that we impose upon ourselves and "our" community. In order to combat such hegemonic impositions, we must insist that we operate within the same social space and same discursive nexus as the so-called "dominant society." This means insisting on our citizenship, or to put it another way, a renewed focus on "insistence" over a less productive notion of "resistance," a recognition that cultural citizenship and national citizenship are not mutually exclusive.

## The American(o) Stage: Luis Valdez's Mexican American Drama

In the ongoing American social drama, the ever-evolving role of the postwar Mexican American has been most thoroughly explored by film director and playwright Luis Valdez. If, as Rafael Perez-Torres has suggested, the central tropes in Chicano social literature revolve around the figures of the *pachuco, el migro* (migrant), and *el pinto* (prisoner), Valdez has given each of these characters life on the stage. Each is given their moment to voice an insistent, sometimes resistant, presence in this most complex sociocultural narrative. On stage or on celluloid, Valdez's dramatic sociology examines the possibilities and limitations of the various masks and roles the Mexican American has worn in his slow, but insistent journey toward inclusion. The third in the triad of writers this chapter will examine, Valdez most clearly sounds the arpeggio of *el movimiento's* identity nexus played to ultimate discord. Valdez finally seems to demonstrate that the disharmony within the movement, as well as between the Mexican subject and American society, is caused, in part, by a narrow emphasis on these inadequate Chicano roles. However, in response, he will sound a note that ultimately finds its place within a somewhat effete culturalist chorus: an acceptance that I argue endorses a consumerist Hispanicization rather than an egalitarian Americanismo.

Beginning in the fields of Delano, Valdez directed *El Teatro Campesino* in its agit-prop work helping the United Farm Workers union to inspire its members during arduous, dangerous strikes. Later Valdez's company would be the first to stage a Chicano play on Broadway. After *Zoot Suit*'s success as a stage play, Valdez would transform it into a feature film, following its substantial success with *La Bamba,* a film that prepared the way for several Chicano film projects in the 1980s and 1990s. Valdez has made the move from staging plays on the back of pick-up trucks, to directing multimillion dollar mainstream film productions. The change in venue, medium, and scope of his projects does not simply chart one man's success, however. Valdez's career self-consciously charts the sociocultural vicissitudes and transformations of the postwar Mexican American subject in dizzying array. Valdez's political and aesthetic evolution coincides with his use of Mexican American modalities, each stage shifting its setting as the character-archetype reaches the limits of its sociopolitical efficacy.

Like the character Richie Valens portrayed in *La Bamba,* Valdez has made the move from farmworker to popular mainstream artist. His work however has had its critics. In *El Teatro Campesino,* Yolanda Broyles-Gonzalez criticizes Valdez as an individualist and narcissist whose self-promotion has overshadowed the group project and the role of women. Most recently, Roy Eric Xavier has insisted on reading Valdez's career as a political narrative, but while he traces the early part of Valdez's career effectively by giving in-depth readings of Valdez's early political commitments, he is less clear on the sociopolitical meaning of Valdez's work in the 1980s and beyond. This has much to do with the less strident political tone of Valdez's work, coupled with an increased emphasis on a culture-as-politics model that has replaced the direct action political model in which he began. An assessment of his recent work, not to mention an analysis of the overall sociopolitical and identity politics of his career, becomes all the more difficult when one also considers the ambiguity of Valdez's neoindigenous philosophy, Mayan humanism, and his later insistence on using the term "Hispanic." [8]

However, to argue that Valdez is either a migrant labor hero (based on his early work with Cesar Chavez) or a Hispanic "sell-out" is much too reductive. Rather, Valdez's career is an important and telling example of the search for an acceptable and successful synthesis for Mexican American identity and sociocultural political participation within America. Yet Valdez's body of work is one of the clearest and most articulate, if ultimately unsuccessful, attempts at creating an effective, inclusive "Americano" identity. His work pushes the boundaries of "acceptable" Chicano participation within the American cultural and political landscape, examines the nature of "inclusion" and "participation."

His journey is interesting for where it starts, how it evolves and where it ends up. From farmworker activism (migrant plays and *actos*), to neoindigenism (new–Mayan metaphysical plays and essays), to a conflicted cultural nationalism and participatarianism (*el pachuco*, Zoot Suiter, Mexican American) and its limitations *(el pinto),* to a final cultural politics (Hispanic identity), Valdez has rigorously displayed postwar Mexican American alternatives and limitations.

Much has been written about Valdez's early association with Cesar Chavez and the Farm Workers union, and I wish only to summarize this part of his career. Valdez started his activism as a student at San Jose State when he and Roberto Rubelcava visited Cuba during the early sixties. Valdez returned from this trip fully convinced that the solution to the racism and classism that afflicted Chicanos could only be ameliorated through revolutionary action. His early *actos* (one act plays) target Mexican American and migrant worker audiences, and even though Valdez centers his critique on the problems of race and poverty, he is clear in his class analysis: agrarian and corporate interests use race as a way of identifying and maintaining an easily exploitable workforce. His early work marks many of the same elements as Montoya's work: an emphasis on cultural nationalism, a skeptical view of "mainstream" education, and a marked paranoia of an infiltrating *vendido* mentality. But viewing farmworker activism as perhaps too limited for broad-based social transformation, Valdez ended this early period in 1967 when he broke his affiliation with Chavez and the United Farm Workers and decided to professionalize his acting company. As the Chicano movement waned, as Xavier suggests, Valdez moved away from a nationalist perspective, attempting to find a broader audience and a philosophical framework that sought to formulate a more universal identity.

Founding El Teatro Nacional de Aztlan (TENAZ), Valdez recognized a broader framework in a romantic indigenous mysticism that utilized "not a teatro composed of actos and agit-prop but a teatro of ritual, of music, of beauty and spiritual sensitivity" that emphasized a spiritual humanism (Xavier 184). Xavier suggests that this form of theater moved Valdez away from calling for direct action politics toward a spiritual politics, a claim that, while accurate in some ways, does not go far enough in examining the implications and dimensions of Valdez's later politics. It is instead useful to read this shift in Valdez's creative program neither as a reaction to the change in political climate nor a change in the definition of "politics," but as part of the change in the post-sixties political climate. In other words, Valdez intuited the limitations of *el movimiento* and began to formulate a more effective, inclusive political identity and participatory forum. We can certainly read this in "Pensamiento Serpentino," which seeks to find a way of reconciling what had become a narrow, nationalist, separatist Chicano identity politics with a more inclusive pluralist model.

This stage has too rigidly been read through the lens of neoindigenism, but Valdez's form of Mayan humanism is really much more syncretic than at first appears. In order to create an inclusive, egalitarian politics he deployed a cultural identity that actively sought to engender a dialogue between neoindigenous metaphysics and American democratic ideals. The neoindigenous rhetoric "justifies" the democratic implications, protecting Valdez, in a sense, from his own anxiety of assimilating, of the charge of becoming a *vendido*.

"Pensamiento Serpentino" ("Serpentine Thoughts") is Valdez's attempt to synthesize the cultural nationalist impulse with a Mexican American desire to participate as a fully recognized citizen-subject, while also laying out a persuasive philosophical argument for the necessity of a communal ethic influenced deeply by the notion of positive liberty. In a nod to *indigenismo,* Valdez calls for a return to the Mayan credo of *tu eres mi otro yo.* The overriding rhetorical strategy of this poetic essay is the reinscription of the concept of "movement" through a communal democratic revaluation that disavows earlier exploitative uses of movement and mobility. The Mayan rhetoric, then, is not simply window dressing. Rather, it gives Valdez an alternative framework for reading through the radical, communal possibilities of modern democracy.

Rather than using "movement" (a stand-in for negative "liberty" in the American imagination) as a method of securing a protective space for the individual or for the purpose of creating an immobilized but mobile subject that is easily exploitable, Valdez insists on a metaphysical understanding of movement that actively constructs a transpersonal connectedness. In essence, it is an "indigenized" revision of Rousseau's *civitas.* By invoking the concept of movement, Valdez attempts to exorcise from the democratic discourse "movement's" historically and ideologically negative connotations. Valdez thus attempts to redeem "movement" from its Americanized uses in constructing redemptive narratives that ultimately justify conquest, selfish neoindividualism, and community-destroying irresponsibility. Instead, movement becomes the basis for empathy, for connection, for a cosmic unity. Metaphysical, historical, and material realms are linked through movement rather than divided or separated. Subtitled "A Chicano Approach to the Theatre of Reality," the piece might be read not only as an attempt to formalize a Chicano aesthetic, but also, as the title suggests, to formulate the underlying ethics of Chicano politics that might transform dominant and exploitative forms of "American" politics.

Valdez's use of the Quetzalcoatl imagery has been critiqued by Chicano theorists such as Jose Limon.[9] However, we might read it as an attempt to place movement discourse in pre-Columbian times, before its connotative value was imbued with the individualist discourse of exploration and conquest. The invocation of Quetzalcoatl is an attempt to place the Chicano within a historical context, to suggest (although problematically in its essentialization of Mayan "spirituality") an origin of philosophical thought that has not yet been colonized:

> but first el Chicano must Mexicanize
> himself
> para no caer en cultural trampas
> and that means that
>
> not Thomas Jefferson nor Karl Marx
> will Liberate the Chicano
> not Mahatma Ghandi nor Mao Tze Tung
> IF HE IS NOT LIBERATED FIRST BY
> HIS PROPIO PUEBLO
> BY HIS POPOL VUH
> HIS CHILAM BLAM
> HIS CHICHEN ITZA
> KUKULCAN, GUCUMATZ, QUETZALCOATL.
>
> (*Early Works* 173)

However, Valdez's call is for a "mexicanization" of the postwar Mexican American, and here he constructs a nostalgic, romantic vision that represses its Americano desire even while it works to constitute a way in which the Mexican American can "live" in the United States. His rhetoric is too quickly undercut by his rejection of "Jefferson" and "Marx," presumably as representatives of Western, Anglo "oppressors" without searching for a way to lay claim to an abstracted vision of a positive liberty. "Nationalist" (Chicano) concerns obscure a national (American) egalitarian agenda.

Yet, as a strategy against forced movement, Valdez does focus our attention on the contradictions inherent in a systemized exploitation that capitalizes on an illusory understanding of "liberating mobility." Like Ernesto Galarza's theory of "organized drift," such migration has cut the Chicano loose in a most debilitating way. Understanding that the unmoored subject is rootless and thus unable to construct a communal space, Valdez provides mythic origins on which to begin to create community. It is a method for making the Chicano aware that the discourse of movement (democratic ethos) does not begin with Columbus or the Constitution. His strongest point is that the "pueblo" is the source of ultimate liberty. Movement must be rewritten as a narrative of connection and not division. Through the essay's neoindigenous cant, Valdez gets as close to suggesting the formation of a national culture as he can bring himself even while he seems to endorse an Aztlan-like separatist community. But as it stands, Valdez fails to suggest that the democratic ethos is "native" to the Chicano, and thus not antithetical to specific forms of "American" radical democracy.

Stopping short of this, Valdez most clearly seems to call for a "neo-Mayan" identity that defines and contextualizes "Mexican American" experience within an indigenous genealogy that obfuscates the place the postwar Mexican American occupies within America:

> We must all become Neo-Mayas
> Porque los Mayas
> really had it together.
>
> (173)

This paradox would ultimately help to unmake the Chicano movement, and to make it an untenable position for Mexican Americans with participatarian aspirations. The nationalist position failed to solve the underlying conflict inherent in finding a way to be Mexican in the United States without donning an assimilationist mask: how to incorporate without being coopted. Here the rhetoric of a "universalized" *indigenismo* works against the possibility of the creation of a national Americano culture,

even while its transpersonal ethic seems to call for it. The poem's
contradictions bring into relief a conflicted desire to create a "Mexican American" identity that is directly connected to an indigenous past, but that locates its particular identifying elements
within a recognizable philosophical discourse that is not exclusive
to the indigenous worldview Valdez specifies. The transpersonal
ethic he focuses on is plainly operative within a Rousseauean
framework of *civitas*.

> just look at their moral concept
> IN LAK'ECH: *Tu Eres Mi Otro Yo.*
> (173)

Ultimately, the poem posits a pluralist ethic, making it one of
the bases for communality:

> Their communal life
> was not based on intellectual
> agreement
> it was based on a vision
> of los cosmos
>
> . . . . . . . . . . .
>
> In Lak'ech: Si te amo y te respeto
> a ti, me amo y me respeto yo;
> si to hago dano a ti, me hago dano a mi.
>
> That carnales, was LEY AND ORDER
> whatever I do to you
> I do to myself.
> (174)

Valdez ultimately suggests that for the Chicano movement to
insist on the institution of social justice, its only recourse is faith.
But the implications of its metaphysical conclusions is troubling,
for Valdez cannot bring himself to locate communal potential
within a national, syncretic Americano culture:

> As Chicanos
> As Neo-Mayas
> we must re-identify

with that center and proceed
outward with love and strength
AMOR Y FUERZA
and undying dedication to justice.
(176)

Ultimately the ethic of *tu eres mi otro yo* attempts to reverse the immobilization and fixity institutionalized in part through an individualistic, imperialist movement discourse. As such, Valdez's Mayan humanism evokes the democratic debate between positive and negative liberty, between communalism and individualism. However, the couching of a burgeoning radical democratic commitment in neoindigenous rhetoric suggests the presence of a limiting cultural nationalist agenda prepared to jettison a material egalitarianism in favor of a spiritualized culturalism. As Xavier writes, "The result was that instead of precipitating an examination and redefinition of concrete issues, Valdez's religious jargon may have obscured social issues and contributed very little to the development of political consensus during the period" (186).

In some ways recognizing this, Valdez's next project, *Zoot Suit,* would define the terms of inclusion, participation, and the nature of democracy in the United States in more direct terms, exploring the viability of an emergent Mexican American identity that might perform fully within the terms of the American sociopolitical contract.

On the writing of *Zoot Suit,* Valdez reflects, "I wanted to write a play that was not just a Chicano play but an American play. I wanted to make a single human statement, to invoke a vision of America as a whole including the minorities—using joy and humor" (Roy Xavier 192). His research for the play focused on a particularly rich period in Mexican American history: 1940s southern California. The play examines the integrationist aspirations of Henry (Hank) Reyna and the systemic obstacles constructed to frustrate those desires.

Preparing to enter the navy and fight in World War II, Reyna is arrested, charged, convicted, and sentenced as part of the Sleepy Lagoon cohort of "gang" members wrongfully imprisoned for the murder of a young Chicano in 1943. Valdez signals the parallel between Reyna's 1940s California, the Mexican American generation, and the contemporary postwar Chicano generation. The Reyna family is traditional, working class, headed by parents with hopes for their children. The children have acculturated, as evinced by their preference for bebop over their father's mariachi music and the clothes they wear. Lupe, Hank's sister, protests that her clothes are not obscene, as her old-fashioned father insists, but are acceptable because they are cut in the "latest American style."

In the same way, the zoot suit signifies a desire to be read as an "American" even while it parodies that which it desires (an example of a pervasive anxiety of influence in Valdez's work). The suit serves the same purpose as does the neo–Mayan garb in "Pensamientos Serpentinos," a device that while deflecting Americano aspirations, reconstitutes them as a symbol of opposition. It is telling that Hank's last night before he reports to the navy is spent in his zoot suit—signifying his need to negotiate his entry into the "mainstream" without "selling out." Yet, the zoot suit also functions as a signal that a hybrid Americano identity is already operative. The wearer of the suit participates within the recognizable national culture while altering its shape and meaning as a method of effective inclusion.

The suit works in a complex way, both implying a desire to be "in" while it also signals a desire to remain "out." Politically speaking, the metaphor suggests participation, but culturally it connotes a wariness that ultimately shackles the political possibilities by positioning the Chicano as an oppositional, easily marked figure for the state oppressive agencies to target. A mainstream America read the suit "correctly," seeing the cultural and political "intrusion" that the Mexican American posed. Paradoxically, even while the suit so offended the mainstream media and its readers, it was extremely useful in identifying the threatening Mexican American figure: one that was not simply assimilationist, but potentially insistent on equal and full political participation, one that threatened to displace their hegemonic dominance by demonstrating an alternative American synthesis. The zoot suit figured as an alternative to the business suit, an alteration that seemed potentially radical, and thus eerily recognizable: a disturbing visage of an uncanny America.

However, as we see in "Pensamiento Serpentino," Valdez (and the Chicano movement's cultural nationalism) does not fully exploit the potential for Americano alternatives that the zoot suit offers. Fearing cooptation, Valdez seems to read the postwar Mexican American choices as limited to either wearing the cultural garb as a mark of pure opposition or to taking the suit off and remaining locked within the confines of the *barrio*. But who is limiting the choices? Most obviously, suggests Valdez, it is a threatened and violent mainstream America. However, I want to focus on the less overt constricting force: a narrow culturalism represented by a number of figures, most prominently the character of *el pachuco*. Through this character, Valdez reveals the self-destructive effects of self-marginalization. *El pachuco* ultimately represents a version of a constricting, narrow Chicanismo. Culturally, and Valdez read this correctly, *el movimiento* used this sort of self-marking not as a new form of progressive hybridity, but as a mark of exclusion, of direct opposition.

Imprisoned by the penal system, but also by his role as *pachuco*, Henry finds himself with an agonizing choice: his desire for inclusion within U.S. society requires him to forego his cultural allegiance; his cultural identity (represented by his alter ego, "el pachuco") requires that he give up any claim to American citizenship and to an Americano identity in order to cope with the systemic violence he has undergone in America. *El pachuco* acts as the voice of escapism, articulating an understandable, but evasive strategy:

> Get up and escape, Henry . . .
> leave reality behind
> with your buenas garras
> muy chamberlain
> escape through the barrio streets of your mind
> through a neighborhood of memories
> all chuckhole lined
> and the love

and the pain
as fine as wine . . .

               (33, ellipses in the original)

Recalling Raulrsalinas's "A Trip through the Mind Jail," Valdez signals the counterproductive isolationist definition of the zoot suit, of Henry's *"buenas garras."*

Like Oscar Acosta, Valdez uses a juridical setting as the proving ground for the Mexican American's status of citizen-subject. Defended by an Anglo "people's lawyer" and a Jewish communist activist, Henry must, in effect, decide to join a multiracial coalition. But the voice of *el pachuco* is hostile: "You're hoping for something that isn't going to happen, ese. These paddies are leading you by the nose. Do you really think you stand a chance?" (51) Attorney George Shearer, as representative of the "citizen's committee," attempts to infuse the prisoners with hope, understanding that he and they must move beyond a purely racial or cultural identity in order to win: "What matters is our system of justice. I believe it works, however slowly the wheels may grind" (42). The theme of deconstructing race comes to the forefront: "The problem seems to be that I look Anglo to you. What if I were to tell you that I had Spanish blood in my veins? That my roots go back to Spain, just like yours? What if I'm Arab? What if I'm a Jew? What difference does it make? The question is, will you let me help you?" (43). The *pachuco's* answer, "Chale!" indicates a deadly isolationist position.

Coupled with the scenes of intraethnic violence (the boys have been charged with killing a fellow Chicano), Valdez points to the anticommunal distinctions made within Chicano culture itself: thus the play can be read both as a critique of *el movimiento's* separatism as well as its increasingly toxic factionalism. At one point, Henry stops short of killing another Mexican American gang leader. "Just what this play needs," comments *el pachuco*, "two more Mexicans killing each other." The moment connotes Valdez's awareness of intraethnic conflict resulting in part from an identity politics. When an uncontested entry into American society seems unlikely, Valdez queries the ability of the justice system to fairly and clearly adjudicate the ability of the Mexican American subject to participate without facing systemic oppression and physical violence.

The result is predictable; the boys are found guilty and sentenced to life in prison after a farcical trial in which the defendants are forced to implicate their own guilt. The overt racist rhetoric used to convict them is on one hand a condemnation of the racism inherent in the political and juridical system in the United States, but it also points to a larger, more abstract realization: race and cultural identity are not the most efficacious strategies for achieving political equality. In effect, Valdez presents the necessity of moving beyond a culturalism that ultimately circumscribes mutualism. The defensive position of *el pachucada* (*pachuco* identity) has within the Chicano community functioned in some very destructive ways. Primarily it has worked to weaken communal progress and commitment. As Joey, a fellow inmate says, "We've learned our lesson . . . Well, anyway, I've learned my lesson, boy. No more pachuquismo for me. Too many people depending on us to help out. The raza here in Los. The whole southwest, Mexico, South America!" (74). It is a statement that critiques the use of *el pinto* as a point of resistance. Valdez suggests that there is a greater responsibility to the community than a "resistant" positionality. The play asserts the need for a more productive understanding of progress, one that insists on a full, direct participation.

In response to *el pachuco's* skeptical claim that Henry must "learn not to expect justice," and that he must "learn to protect your loves by binding them in hate," Valdez counters with Henry's mother's observation when they are released on appeal: "Yes, but if it wasn't for the unselfish thoughtfulness of people like you and this beautiful lady—and all the people who helped out, Mexicanos, Negroes, and all Americanos—our boys would not be home today" (87). Her somewhat sentimental tone notwithstanding, Valdez does use her to suggest the potential efficacy of intercultural, interracial progressive coalitions. What Henry's travail has shown is that a cultural political alliance is viable. The courts may work slowly, but the power of a people's coalition demands action. The victory seems so complete that at the end of the play, Henry makes "peace" with the *pachuco* and says: "Me and the batos have been in a lot of fights together, ese. But we won this one, because we learned to fight in a new way" (88).

However, the play ends ambiguously, for its optimism is undercut by *el pachuco* who tells Henry that "life ain't that way though, Hank." The voice of reality, *el pachuco* points out that Henry is still living in the *barrio*, will continue to be harangued and targeted by the police. More insidiously, *el pachuco* suggests that his life outside of the *pachucada* will be determined by the pressure to be accountable to his family and community. It seems that the oppositional role of the zoot suit is not just aimed at the mainstream, but also at a community that "demands" Henry's participation. Perhaps more troubling, is the closing scene in which Henry must choose between Della and Alice, a distinctly racial choice between brown and white in which the previous temporary transcendence of race achieved in the coalition is quickly forgotten: the play ends by forcing Henry either to commit himself to his "people" or to betray his community by answering to his assimilationist desire made flesh.

In a cacophony of voices that intersperse as they each demand to be heard, Henry must try and understand them all, and respond to them individually. Does he want Alice or Della? Is Rudy, his younger brother, now a man, a marine? Is the *barrio* the same? Does he have a social responsibility as George claims? Each of these questions push Henry toward an anticommunalist direction as Valdez suggests that the ultimate threat may be the prescription of identity that the *barrio* and *el movimiento* demands. The last scene ends with cops trying to lure Henry back out and his family pleading with him stay in. The family seems at this point to pose as much a threat to Henry's personal movement and aspirations as the police and the socioeconomic conditions of the *barrio*.

Ultimately, Henry chooses Della (his Mexican American sweetheart) and even though the press reports that he died a drug addict, *el pachuco* introduces a series of possibilities:

RUDY: Henry Reyna went to Korea in 1950. He was shipped across in a destroyer and defended the 38th Parallel until he was killed in Inchon in 1952, being posthumously awarded the Congressional Medal of Honor.

ALICE: Henry Reyna married Della in 1948 and they have five kids, three of them now going to the University, speaking calo and calling themselves Chicanos.

GOERGE: Henry Reyna, the born leader . . .

JUDGE: Henry Reyna the social victim . . .

BERTHA: Henry Reyna, el carnal de aquellas . . .

JOEY: Henry Reyna, the zoot suiter . . .

TOMMY: Henry Reyna, my friend . . .

LUPE: Henry Reyna, my brother . . .

ENRIQUE: Henry Reyna . . .

DOLORES: Our son . . .

DELLA: Henry Reyna, my love . . .

PACHUCO: Henry Reyna . . . El Pachuco . . . The man . . . the myth . . . still lives." (94)

Yet, imagining the community outside of *el barrio* remains unexplored, as does exploring a post-*pachuco*, postoppositional identity. The play ends, rather than begins, with Henry's move outside the *pachucada*. Outside of the culturalist paradigm (culture as the central stage for political intervention) and outside a mode of violent opposition (Chicano as *pinto*), Henry has little left to say or do, and Valdez cannot imagine the next stage. Henry seems trapped as *Zoot Suit* ends as either a myth, an outlaw, or an assimilated patriot. Thus, despite its opening up of the Mexican American identity and its earlier gesture toward American participatarianism, Valdez seems to articulate an individualist position that stresses Henry's "mythic status" that depends on an oppositional, isolated identity that is antithetical to an egalitarian commitment. This position is as much a reaction to the perceived requirements of a strident cultural nationalism as it was indicative of the influence of American neoindividualism.

The role of *el pachuco* simply allows Reyna (the dissaffected Mexican American figure) to retain a sense of oppositional alterity while remaining aloof from either a communal or national participation. It is in this way that I see a culturalist model of resistance as most regressive for radicalizing democracy in the United States. Unfortunately, it is the direction that Valdez seems to embrace in his most recent film, *La Bamba,* and it is indicative of a consumerist cultural politics that I read as characterizing the decidedly unprogressive nature of the American "Hispanic."

In *La Bamba* Valdez comes to a precarious decision. Deciding not to evade the determinism that both Chicano identity politics and American hegemony have asserted, Valdez articulates a strategy that approximates a post-*movimiento* drift to the right. In *La Bamba* he declines to draw the same socioeconomic determinism he sees operating in *Zoot Suit,* preferring instead to give us the story of Mexican American individual "success" in what amounts to a new *mito* that in essence legitimates the Hispanicization of the political vacuum left by the disappearance of a coherent Chicano/Mexican American agenda. I define "Hispanicization" here in part by referencing the negative connotation given the term by many Chicano scholars.

Part of the Reagan administration's strategy to blur the lines of identification between various Latino ethnic groups in order to cut federal financing of education as well as an insidious plan to remove Mexican Americans from the Voter Registration Act, the term has drawn heavy criticism. Disquieting as well has been the propensity of "Hispanic" politics to work along the lines of what Rodolfo Acuna calls the new political logic of the "power brokers" in which a few, well-placed Hispanic "leaders" speak for a constituency they do not truly represent, offering only token resistance and participation in the shaping of a national agenda affecting social justice. For the Hispanic generation, political activity has largely been relegated to a culturalist/consumerist mode, in which representation and participation is largely measured by how the individual or community of "Hispanics" (from the perspective of marketing, corporate, and media interests) "vote" with their dollars.

In this sense, "Hispanics" feel duly heard and represented if a letter-writing campaign serves to "increase" the visibility of Latino actors on network television. This may be a bit hyperbolic, but not by much. The notion of "resistance" must, and has been separated from a purely "oppositional" definition, but rather than redefining the concept to include an effective civic and political participatory dimension, the term has been imbued with a consumerism. Much as the market logic that emerged in the 1950s in which "liberty" and "choice" were conflated with the ability to choose from a plethora of new products, this revamped understanding of "resistance" ultimately does little than offer marketing strategists new ways of expanding their markets. At the very least, "Hispanic" consumerist politics results in a questionable revision of the cultural nationalism at work in between 1965 and 1975. It fails even more miserably not through a narrow identity politics, but by constructing a very weak notion of community and by jettisoning even the pretension of endorsing and working toward an egalitarian agenda that might possibly achieve some semblance of social justice.

One need not speculate wildly in seeing this logic at work in *La Bamba*. A significant success at the box office, the film generated interest in Hollywood over the largely untapped market of Mexican American moviegoers. The result is that it opened doors, somewhat, for Mexican American-centered films such as *American Me, Stand and Deliver, Mi Familia,* and most recently *Selena* (all critical and box office successes). This should not be downplayed as an accomplishment. Valdez, and a handful of others (Edward James Olmos and Gregory Nava most prominently) have made inroads in an industry that has long ignored Mexican American culture and subject matter. But to suggest that this "awareness" or "increased visibility" is an adequate substitute for insistent, coherent, participatory politics is an equivocation that will do very little in ameliorating not only the lives of Mexican Americans in the United States, but will do even less in affecting the shape of a national culture and broadened political sphere. The culturalist model of politics too quickly assumes that "success" (moderate as it has thus far been) will somehow make itself felt in socioeconomic and civic terms. This is plainly not the case. Capital has long proven that it is willing to forbear "diversity" and "difference" so long as it can profit by its commodification.

And yet, Valdez's (and his character Richie Valens's) success on the cultural front should not be judged as insignificant or as "selling out," for that would be falling into the same bind in which a narrow Chicano militancy found itself. In some ways, I have argued that Valdez's choice to "participate" within the mainstream culture is a necessary "insistence" on the part of Americanos. However, Valdez's "Hispanicization" reflects the narrow choices offered by *el movimiento* and post-*movimiento* politics; Valdez has walked a precarious line between being viewed as a *vendido* for desiring to succeed in America. His struggle is parallel to the Mexican American's struggle to insist on his or her role in the making of America, its culture, its politics, and its economy. The movement's sometimes insistent isolationism and separatism gave Valdez and other Mexican Americans a limited scope for acting on their participatory and inclusive aspirations. Culturalist politics (an easily commodifiable multiculturalism) has given them/us an enticing, but inadequate space in which to enact those desires. This form of "political" activity will not push for a communal, egalitarian transformation of the national sociopolitical culture: it is an abandonment of a loftier goal of creating *civitas* for a mess of pottage. It is the new assimilationism.

Martin Sanchez Jankowski's question (Where have all the nationalists gone?) is not easily answered. I have argued that although the causes of a dissipated *movimiento* are complex, that one area we must examine is the pernicious influence of a separatist agenda in the constitution of Mexican American postwar identity. The movement erred tragically in creating a resistant figure that was not inclusive and did not take seriously the challenge of creating a national culture based in part on a more sympathetic and subtle understanding of their parents' generation. Instead *el movimiento* concentrated on isolating the community, constructing a purely oppositional identity, which as that strategy proved too constricting, created the conditions for a culturalist politics. We substituted this form of activism for a class-based, direct-action, egalitarian, participatory model. Consequently, one important answer to Jankowski's question as we enter the new century, is that we have become Hispanics/Latinos. A "group"

too quickly satisfied with increased "visibility" and product place-
ment—and a modest decisionist impact on local and national
politics. The counter to this effete sociocultural impact can be
found in a strain of Mexican American identity that insists on a
radical inclusion on all levels of the American sociocultural-
political arena: the Americano.

# 6

# Arriving at *el Pueblo Libre*
## *The Insistence of Americanismo*

No task looms larger than the urgent need to say fare-
well to the identity politics of workerism *and* of various
nationalisms and abject identities without surrendering
the radical core of historic demands for freedom.

Stanley Aronowitz

I too
live on this continent
and in this country
I too am an American
and my eyes are brown and my hair
obsidian black.

Leo Romero

Central to this study has been the question of how American dissent, both Mexican American and "Anglo," attempted to remap
the national cultural landscape in the second half of the century.
How did the counterculture redefine "American-ness" and
"America" itself? Answering this question has meant examining
the way in which dissident writers have understood democratic
discourse as they redefined its central elements: the individual,

the community, egalitarianism, participation, civil rights, and *civitas*. If the mainstream countercultural movements were unable to transcend an overriding, decadent individualism, I have suggested that the Chicano movement was unable to fashion an inclusive, open community due to a prescriptive identity, and that ultimately its isolationist tendency abdicated the duty to help shape an "American" national culture. Recognizing how Mexican American dissent has fully engaged within the democratic debate means revising how we understand Mexican American participation in the history and culture of "America."

In Ramon Saldivar's influential study, *Chicano Narrative,* he suggests that the Chicano narrative resists traditional American literature and is formed by its difference in order to offer readers a reformulation of historical and cultural reality as read through Chicano experience in the Americas. Chicano narrative is defined as a dialectical position rather than as a "kind" of literature, that is, a narrative consciously formed through historical tensions rather than as simply a cultural mirror of Mexican American life. This is an important distinction for it argues that we should read the Chicano narrative as directly engaging the American narrative. R. Saldivar argues that the dialectics of this process involve negation, conflict between opposing terms that lead to the creation of a new cultural identity and literature developed "through opposition and conflict—neither Mexican nor American, not yet Mexican-American" (R. Saldivar 8). Useful as this construct is, it envisions a dialectic process that posits a Chicano narrative created in response to a hegemonic American culture rather than a Chicano narrative in full engagement within a national sociopolitical debate. R. Saldivar's formulation does not go far enough in recognizing the full participation of the Mexican American narrative within the heterogeneous and highly contested American democratic debate.

While I am in agreement with R. Saldivar's stress on the dialectical relation between experience, materiality, and narrative, and also the dialectic between American history and Chicano experience, I would relocate the terms of the dialectical relationship between "Mexican American" in reaction/resistance to "hegemonic Anglo capitalism" to a dialectic between positive and negative liberty. The dialectic of Mexican and American narratives leads not to the isolating narrative of Chicanismo, but to a larger narrative, the Americano narrative that positions Chicano/Americano texts as part of a larger democratic debate of insistence rather than the more limited resistance narrative on which Chicano Studies has long focused. Thus I am redefining the third stage of the dialectic between Mexican and American narratives as more interdependent, as part of a common discourse of citizenship. I want to use this final chapter to draw out the participatory aspects of Mexican American writing as part of a larger discussion on social strategy that endorses *communitas* over the individualist prerogatives heralded by the purveyors of negative liberty. In my reevaluation, the narratives of Tomás Rivera and Ernesto Galarza function as commentaries on the price of individualism, the fear of an egalitarian community, and as a direct refutation of the narrow so-called pluralist academia that still ignores the Chicano voice.

R. Saldivar stresses that the Chicano narrative is a group of literary texts that "show how esthetic and cultural production often turn out to be the ideological rewriting of that banished history" (19). I am not interested in particular with ending my discussion of Chicano literature by characterizing it as an ideological rewriting of banished history, which seems to me more of a recovery project, one focused on resisting the ideology of a protestant capitalism that Saldivar identifies as prevalent in a post–Mexican-American War United States. Rather, we will draw out the dialectical relationship of Mexican Americans writing in response to other "Americans" not in a negation of the democratic ethos and its liberalisms, but rather as an exercise in holding the democratic process accountable. The Chicano narrative is a thorough exploration of America's democratic dimensions via the lived and shared experience of the community under pressure from an economic ethos that is used to subvert the will of the people, to manipulate the public sphere and make it irrelevant. Mexican American literary and political insistence does not create an alternative to an "American" system, but insists upon its ideals to bring the democratic potential into reality.

R. Saldivar's interpretation of the Chicano narrative depends heavily on the borderland and migrant quality of the Mexican American: "positioned between cultures, living on borderlines, Chicanos and their narratives have assumed an unique borderland quality, reflecting in no uncertain terms the forms and styles of their folk-base origins" (25). It indirectly relegates the Chicano to the margins, but the Chicano narrative is central to understanding the shape of the twentieth century democratic debate. Whereas R. Saldivar correctly emphasizes the communal nature of what he calls the "folk base of the Chicano narrative," he does not fully investigate the connection of its communality to the tension between *civitas* and neoindividualism at the heart of the democratic debate, the tension between negative and positive liberty. A full engagement of this connection would pull Chicano narrative into the heart of American sociopolitical discourse. Rather he characterizes Mexican American cultural production primarily as social resistance, positing a unified American program of repressive capitalism and imperialism. While it is true that both of those forces remain operative, Mexican Americans do not simply respond or react to those forces as such, but create narratives that seek to critique the ways in which a repressive capitalism subverts true democratic *civitas,* a critique that is relevant not only to the Mexican American community, but to the American polity in general. It is telling that R. Saldivar characterizes the nineteenth century origins of Mexican American cultural production as the "folk base of Chicano Narrative," for it marshals Mexican American democratic and material desire in the service of a much later Chicano movement that did not, as I have shown in the previous chapter, always desire inclusion. Such a reading too quickly dismisses migrant and Mexican American participatory aspiration in favor of a form of resistance more appropriate to the more nationalist-oriented writers of the Chicano generation. Although the Mexican American created "self-consciously crafted acts of social resistance" (42), to focus the discussion there is to leave out the most important dimension of a Mexican American narrative, one fully engaged within the "American" experience that might lead to an understanding of Mexican

American participation within an inclusive, although fractious, Americano narrative.

As Jose Limon has argued in *American Encounters,* there are many parallels between what American writers in the 1920s and 1930s (the southern agrarians such as Tate, Ransom, and Warren in particular) were doing in response to capitalist modernity and what Mexican and Mexican American artists were doing in the same cause. Both try to imagine a viable social strategy that could create community and cohesion rather than give into a politically and socially ineffective dissolution.

Limon's work in *American Encounters* is important because it sets up a nonantagonistic relation between Mexico and the South, as well as possible areas for mutual cooperation with Anglos pointing to a Mexican-Anglo entwinement and solidarity that has been operational on certain fronts against the common enemy of capitalist modernity. Perhaps more significant, Limon's work suggests that Mexican Americans have long been participating in a larger national debate: "We can see a comparable set of responses to the expanding hegemony of a "Northern" and capitalist modernity, responses often couched in ambivalence, paradox, and contradiction. . . . I have also placed these cultural experiences, contradictions, and affirmations within the more mundane and instrumental context of political economy, so as to demystify any essentialist and stereotypic reading of culture and thus better gauge their range and depth as responses to the crisis of capitalist modernity. The erotic, the sexual, and the sensual, I submit here are important considerations in charting the movement and the critical limits of modernity" (Limon, *American Encounters* 33). Limon treats the Mexican American narrative as part of a larger American narrative, of the Americano narrative. Here, the Mexican American and Mexican writers are responding alongside Anglo writers in defense of a communal logic of positive liberty, who see the common enemy as a capitalist modernity that endorses a toxic negative liberty. In this vein, I want to turn to a strong tradition of an egalitarian, Mexican American, participatory dissent that cuts through the second half of the century and offers a model for achieving a radically democratic agenda.

Americano social criticism and literature has most successfully been practiced by Mexican American migrant writers and activists, and the legacy of this model of citizenship is most recognizable in projects such as the Latino Cultural Citizenship Group.

The migrant experience has been crucial in providing a counternarrative to an American mythos of progress, exposing the uses of movement and mobility in the exploitation of labor, and provided a material basis for the "Americano" desire to "arrive." The migrant figure is not simply a "function" of a poststructural reading, destabilized through the liminalized critical space migrancy "provides," as has been most common in a recent (mis)appropriations of borderlands criticism. Instead we must begin to read migrant desire as valid, material, and grounded in the practice of *civitas*, located not in the borderlands, but in América. As early practitioners of "Americanismo" these writers and activists demonstrate the necessity that we think of ourselves as full participants in the American economy, culture, political structure, and civic arena. I prefer to think of these figures as articulating a need for an "insistence" rather than the now almost meaningless concept of "resistance." The Americano dialectic plays itself out within the discourse of citizenship. Recognizing this is the first step in insisting that postwar Mexican American dissent and social analysis are inseparable from a larger American debate on the shape and function of the democratic state, participatory and communal politics, and cultural and national membership. Thus "Americanismo" demands that we think of ourselves as fully participating Americans refusing to abdicate our position to the Anglo "Americanos" (as my grandmother, and many of her generation, referred to white, first-class citizens). This may seem somewhat of a moot point to make, residing in the post-*movimiento* period as we are said to be. But it is a claim that should have resonance in academia and society at large. Mexican American scholarship and Mexican American political participation should be seen as fully deserving and crucial, not only to a Mexican American identity, but to a revised American identity (yet another connotation of "Americano"). Borderlands critiques have proved to be useful in describing liminal process, as well as the ways in which intercultural spaces are formed and give a certain freedom or liberty in subjectivity formation. This study does not satisfy itself with locating the Mexican American culture and its struggles at the periphery or the margins. Rather, this is a study of American culture and society that seeks to claim the centrality of the Chicano narrative as it has shaped issues of citizenship, reform, local and national politics, social justice, and egalitarian participatory politics.

In Tomás Rivera's novel, *Y no se lo trago la tierra (And the Earth Did Not Devour Him)* we hear the voice of a woman who has been standing in the back of a truck trailer as she and a group of other migrants travel north to Minnesota: "When we arrive, when we arrive. . . . I really should say when we don't arrive because that's the real truth. We never arrive" (145). Her observation might be aimed as much at a poststructural or borderlands theoretical practice as it is at the obscured economic forces that keep the migrant on the move. What this plaintive voice should serve to remind is that Mexican Americans, by and large, have consistently sought to find a place within the American social, cultural, and political landscape. Though that search has proven elusive and the strategy for inclusion has by no means been unified—a Mexican American constituency itself being difficult to isolate or define—one desire is representative: full participatory rights and equal access within an American homeland. It is not my intention either to construct or deconstruct the notion of "nation" within these pages, but rather to suggest that such a project, while illuminating and necessary in the wake of nativist activities, does not adequately address the issue of practical, material inclusion. While I argue the necessity of deconstructing still-operative versions of cultural nationalism, I question the wisdom of deconstructing the possibility of achieving a national culture.

In a recent debate over the possibility of a national progressive agenda, Jeffrey Isaacs has argued that the emergence of 1960s ethnic and gender liberation movements dispersed the polity necessary for constructing large-scale populist, progressive politics. Isaacs further argues that what holds sway in postwar American democratic practice is an issue-specific, local brand of politics that foregoes a national agenda.[1] However, as my critique of the Chicano movement has shown, not allowing for the creation of syncretic American identity, the movement failed to generate a broader constituency for its agenda, and because of its narrow identity politics was not able to create a wider coalition that might have impacted national politics more permanently. However, while I too critique the growing fractiousness of 1960s counter-cultural movements, I see that activity as much more than politi-cal discord. The permutation of viable political and cultural iden-tities was a necessary stage in developing the legitimacy of a more effective and inclusive definition of the civic sphere. At the end of the sixties, there existed a more responsive political process than was imaginable at the beginning of that decade. However, I argue that this permutation of individual civic identities can be har-nessed through an active redefinition of American culture—as a multiplicity of fully participating, legitimate citizens in the service of a national agenda centering around the issue of social justice. Thus, I do not bemoan the "fractiousness" so much as I reject the conclusion that this multiplicity of interests cannot be channeled into a wide-scale, progressively imaginative coalition. This means that the Left should not see the multiplicity as "hopeless dis-persal" of its traditional constituency (the old Democratic bloc). Rather, the Left should busy itself in forging a representative agenda that will incorporate the vast set of interests operating in contemporary America—material, egalitarian concerns—by op-erating under the awareness that the "left" is in fact "out there," willing to participate in the shaping of a progressive political agenda.

Thus far, this act of political construction has not been possible for several reasons. Rather than seeing race, gender, and sexual identity movements as a stage in a potential progressive, egalitar-ian project, liberal critics such as Isaacs have given up in the face of a supposedly permanent fractiousness brought on by insur-mountable "difference" exploited by "identity politics." In a simi-lar move, various forms of poststructural, postliberal, and post-colonial criticism have also painted themselves into a corner by deconstructing the possibility of a viable, coherent, and multiplex political agent that might serve as the basis for an inclusive, progressive, and coherent political movement. The idea of "national culture" is viewed with extreme skepticism or even rancor taking as it does in poststructural and postcolonial discourse, a neoimperial or authoritarian shape. "National culture" is conflated with an authoritarian vision of the state or a too simplistic definition of "hegemony." That leaves little room for forming a coherent coalition. A focus on the "resistant" nature of fluid, shifting "subjectivity," central to an antifoundationalist, antiessentialist, counterhegemonic project, has left the minority subject with no place to "arrive." Likewise, a deconstruction of the notion of "nation" has helped to limit the political arena to the local stage.

What is becoming clear, however, is that a localized politics without a national, political agenda will not result in large-scale social transformation or ameliorate social injustice. Just as in Rivera's story "Zoo Island" (in *Harvest*)—a boy paints a sign outside of a set of chicken coops labeling the "compound" as a "City"—a strategy of localized, isolationist politics that continues to deny the possibility of creating a national constituency is futile. Likewise, a strategy that embraces a purely "cultural" model of progress—that is, participating within commodity exchange as a form of "resistance" or "identity formation"—ignores the nature of economic and political power. Buying Selena posters or wearing Los Tigres Del Norte T-shirts might make "us" feel more visible or resistant, but it is not likely to counter the effects of post-Fordism or the increasing gap between the poor and the rich in America. Thus whether the idea of national culture was rejected by separatists in the 1960s or by disenchanted postliberals in the 1990s, the result has been that the American Left has abandoned the making of a national agenda and culture. The Right has stepped in, successfully capturing the imagination of many voters and citizens, and succeeded in moving the national political discourse into a "centrist" mode using a rhetoric that belies that it's far right of the middle agenda.

What the Left, or what's left of it, must heed is the message inherent in the yearnings of Rivera's migrant worker: material conditions, full political and social participation, and egalitarian ideals are valued highly (and thus viable) in the Americano imagination. Whereas the migrant figure has been used as a liminal, deconstructive "process" in much borderlands criticism (at times for very useful purposes), I would like to focus on the critique of American economic and sociocultural practices and realities that migrant experience has engendered, as well as unpacking the political ramifications that "arrival" signifies for American politics: the construction of a progressive, egalitarian national culture that is truly inclusive. Rereading the Mexican American narrative in this light might radically reshape both the disciplines of Chicano and American studies.

Ernesto Galarza's search for *el pueblo libre,* is not just a metaphorical and illusory search for an organic utopia. It is instead a search for the American ideal in its egalitarian, inclusive fullness that while evasive and difficult to constitute must remain central to our understanding of how Americanos have sought to shape America. Rivera, Galarza, and Cesar Chavez serve as prime participants in the efforts to shape the national culture in this way, "insisting" (rather than "resisting"—a term that has become so pervasive in a form of cultural studies critique as to mean virtually nothing) on their rights to access and power.

Americano participation has insisted that the most effective way to combat sexism, racism, and classism in American society is to challenge the assertion, in whatever form, that Americanos do not or cannot participate in the national arena. Thus, the central focus of Americano intervention is in the area of citizenship in postwar America.

## Citizenship, Forced Mobility, and the Migrant Experience

The political and geographical definitions of citizenship attempt to make membership concrete through the invocation of "legality," and nowhere are these arbitrary lines traversed as in the practice of immigration. However, "transgression" as such is not the ultimate or even secondary concern of the undocumented immigrant. Rather, the practice of immigrating has as its aim to find a place or home within a particular national body. Defining that "body," however, is the central challenge for Americanos—a contemporary, but permanent project. Thus, "nation" remains a useful paradigm and a viable concretizing discursive space and ideological formation. Rather than deconstructing it, I want to argue, we might be better served to recognize that aside from its abstracted manifestations (juridical, textual, mythic), it retains a material presence with "real" effects and ramifications. The nation exists geographically, politically, and metaphorically. To replace the "nation" with a plethora of overwrought theoretical localized spaces that give primacy to a version of "culture" limits the political struggle to the realm of identity/subjectivity formation. The market logic of late capital is only too ready to accept (and profit from) the proliferation of alternative identities so long as they do not challenge profitability, capital flight, or economic injustice. In essence, capital itself no longer "believes" in "nation" either. And yet the only alternative to right-wing, racist, classist activity is to challenge its activity on a national scale. This means insisting on the materiality of a functioning national community.

The struggle of migrants to create community suggests how much of a challenge this sort of activity poses to an older, restrictive, capitalist notion of "nation." In many significant ways, the migrant broadly represents the alienated, displaced American citizen-worker whose ultimate "value" is as currency. It is the worker's "fluidity," the ability to be exchanged not only for his value as labor, but for his political and cultural value that defines his history and his present state. As a contemporary issue, immigration is a debate over the power of the dominant society and culture to control "movement" within its own boundaries. As Houston Baker has written, "Fixity is a function of power. Those who maintain place, who decide what takes place and dictate what has taken place are power brokers of the traditional" (202). However, I would add that "movement" is also a function of power. The power to create and fix a hierarchy (discursive, political, social, or cultural) is the domain of the dominant. Thus "place," while suggesting a sort of authoritarian or dominating force, should also be seen as an important and desirable effect of empowerment. Working diligently to further dislodge the "essen-tialized" or fixated subaltern or disempowered minority figure, is thus counterproductive and even self-destructive. The debates have risen in California most recently since 1986 with the passing of Immigration Reform and Control Act of 1986 (IRCA),[2] the overwhelming passage of Proposition 187 in 1994,[3] President Clinton's Operation Gatekeeper that doubled the number of Bor-der Patrol officers, and California's efforts to sue the federal gov-ernment for the costs of "illegal immigration." These are only the past decade's more reactionary attempts to use divisive issues in order to reaffirm the power to control movement. They ensure that the disenfranchised, the poor, the undocumented, and the people of color are kept "on the move."[4]

The events at Green Valley, a shantytown in southern Cali-fornia's La Costa, provide an example of the dominant culture's need to disperse the potentially communitarian community of color by forced movement, all the while enjoying the benefits of its own secure, stable space. Trapped between neoconservatives who use them as a symbol of an "infiltration" of undesirables who must be "checked" and expelled, and liberal forces that, while at-tempting to protect them, also use them as a rallying point to counter the backlash of white discontent, are migrants attempting to maintain a community. As a resident of Green Valley said as he found that the camp was to be destroyed: "Why do the Amer-icans detest the Latin Americans, the Mexicans? The North American invaded all of California. They colonized it. . . . [Now] we come here to look for a job in what you could almost call our native land. . . . We come in search of dollars. Your precious com-modity. With one of your dollars we've earned our living for the entire day. . . . You treat us like dogs. And that's what hurts be-cause we're human, and hard workers because we're determined. We come here honorably" (Leo Chavez iii).

An analysis of the economic exchange of which the migrant quoted finds himself a victim lies within his rhetoric. He is aware that he is living in a colonized space and makes the case that the "precious commodity" of dollars, still a form of pure exchange, is not something that his search will net. Rather, he is put in the position of being apprised at much less than the "precious commodity." His place is to be chased away, moved at will, equivalent to the dollar only in the sense that he can be spent, saved, hoarded, or used.

After an article published by the *Los Angeles Times* on July 17, 1988, the residents of La Costa begin calling in complaints even though prior to the article, "Home Cooking Among the Hooches of La Costa: Two Restaurants Provide Familiar Flavors for the Residents of Hidden Migrant Camp" many living in the area had not even been aware of the camp's existence. Even though the camp was on private property (it was owned by a rancher who used the workers in his fields) the locals were able to close the camp by using the Health Department when the Immigration and Naturalization Services (INS) was unable to do so (many of the residents of Green Valley were legally in the country).[5] The camp was more of a community than a campsite: "In its early years, the Green Valley campsite differed little from other camps of makeshift shelters. Mostly single men lived there. That began to change, however, in the mid-1980s, as women and children also began to live at Green Valley. What developed was a community with a distinctive ambiance. I was struck by its village-like appearance. There were two restaurants, a soccer field, and relatively neat and unlittered campsites. . . . It was surely the most developed camp in all of San Diego County" (Leo Chavez 89).

The crime committed by the Green Valley residents was that as a "transient" labor force, they attempted to create a community, a ramshackle realization of a permanent communal space. The surrounding community decided that the people must be moved. The goal of the demolition of Green Valley was to destroy the communal efforts of the migrant, not to destroy a shantytown. Chavez explains the faulty logic of displacing the Green Valley residents as a failure of the La Costa, California residents to understand that the Green Valley migrants would only go to other less-developed shantytowns. What Chavez fails to emphasize is that it was the formation of community by the migrants that was ultimately threatening to Green Valley's dominant neighbors. The purpose in this exercise of displacement was the reassertion of authority over one's jurisdiction; Green Valley's destruction re-asserted the power to reify the migrant as a currency, a currency held by the dominant culture. What Green Valley "residents" as-serted was their "arrival," a transgression that amounted to a claim of cultural and civic "citizenship." This was an act that their "American" neighbors could not allow.

Efforts to immobilize, displace, "control the flow," "halt the traffic," and "keep the gate" continue to gain momentum in San Diego County where even now self-styled "INS helpers" patrol the San Diego airport in ridiculous-looking jackets keeping an eye out for people who look "foreign" and "undocumented." These "citizens" attempt to regulate movement through forced movement: an effective mode of dispersing any communalist ef-fort practiced by Americanos who have dared to imagine or enact egalitarian communities. At stake are two very different forms of citizenship as well as two competing notions of the American na-tion. Most important however, is the effort of the immigrant to claim a stable communal space from which to practice subse-quently full participation. If these efforts are being actively perse-cuted by nativist and reactionary forces, it is urgent that rather than deconstruct the language and the very possibility of stable identity and place, that those of us desiring to participate within an Americano project rehabilitate the notion of community, na-tional identity, and civic participation. Doing so gestures toward a recognition of social justice and equal access.

This project in part requires that we recognize that a certain valorization of mobility that I have critiqued in Beat movement discourse has a counterpart in borderlands and poststructural the-ory, which valorizes a kind of fluidity that in effect displaces the necessity and desire for stable, communal identity and space. Such theoretical valorizations of displacement render the migrant's ex-perience as an abstracted phenomenon, as merely a migratory reading strategy that ultimately replicates the same discursive ex-ploitation with which I have charged the Beats.

Practicing such theoretical displacements creates an ahistori-cal, essentialized "migrant-function" that the critic then appro-priates for its double-consciousness-giving alterity. The critic performs the same rhetorical violence of an ethnicity-shifting Kerouac who presumes to see through the eyes of the "other" but neither knows nor suffers the experience of his or her subject. The migrant becomes a "disguise," allowing the interloping critic entry into the liminal space of the "marginal." Rafael Perez-Torres eloquently states the problem: "From those who can least afford to be exploited, a migratory reading steals strategies from the lived practices of the dispossessed. This intellectual exploitation tries to profit from the improvisation and negotiation born of necessity in the hard and hostile world of transnational survival. . . . [Yet] the profit born out of this exploitation is meant for those from whom it steals" (170). And yet this is unsatisfactory, for the migrant of the past cannot receive any such "profit." Nor can a decontextualized, abstracted application of migratory reading practices, the "migrant function," be productive in exploring the dimensions and avenues of late-twentieth century Americano political action. Rather, what should be understood as central to the migrant experience is the desire for arrival. We must also incorporate the migrant's social awareness and the political action that emerges directly from material experience. This social awareness and its political dimensions suggest a model for constructing a progressive Americano politics.

In this critique of neoindividualistic movement discourse, I have looked to the experience of the migrant as a direct repudiation of the romantic constructions of progress-and-liberty-through-movement, which inhabit certain liberal and countercultural articulations. In keeping with this critique, I wish to keep migration from becoming merely metaphorical.[6] Perez-Torres rightfully contends that, "one must insist upon the fact of deterritorialization as a historically grounded, painful, and often coerced dislocation" (151). The "gain" of such forced movement may in the end be the acquisition of a tool for deconstructing master narratives that serves perhaps as a poststructural strategy for "the dissolution of ordering systems," but before such effects can be exploited, we must recognize that the migrant desires above all "to arrive," and that this need must be given credence.

This "arrival" is as much denied by a postmodern criticism that trumpets the impossibility of such arrival,[7] as the *patron* who keeps the migrant in a constant state of immobilized mobility. It denies the migrant judgment, observation, transmuting his or her experience into a value-neutral operation that is capable only of deconstructive decentering. Perez-Torres's use of the migrant-function evinces this reductive abstraction: "we return again to the multicultural as a migratory condition . . . [that] moves between, among, and toward two or more cultural practices simultaneously without negating the positions and contradictions of power embedded in those practices" (157). However, as even a cursory reading of migrant literature demonstrates, the migrant's articulations do indeed contradict social practices and make judgments. In Spanish, *repélan,* in the sense of complain, but also in the English sense, "to repel," to contradict, to refuse to accept what passes for normative. If the multicultural or postmodern theorist does not do so, that is because the migrant's experience has been reified.

To make the experience of the migrant merely a theoretical space of fluidity and "antihierarchical" travel is to deny the very material confrontations that the migrant makes and is exposed to in surviving; it is to keep the migrant in constant motion, rootless, moving in the borderlands without rest. The migrant desires above all to arrive, to get home, to make roots. My critique cannot grant the migrant his or her desires, but it can acknowledge them and it can draw out the powerful critique of systemic forces that kept the prospects for arrival at the horizon's distant and unreachable end.

To this purpose, I will focus on the migrant's material experiences and their context, in order to confront directly the mythos that has imbued "movement" with a redemptive and progressive aura in America. Migrant observations and their attempts to articulate their experience do not need to be reduced to a theoretical function, but speak coherently and trenchantly to direct physical and spiritual effects of exploitation, as well as to the making of ameliorative strategies. Read in this way, migrant discourse, in part, helps to define an Americano desire that constructs a complex critique of the ideologies inherent in countercultural and other "American" narratives of dissent.

As the victim of a market logic that has sought to immobilize the Mexican American migrant subject,[8] the migrant writer knows only too well the differences between mobility, movement, and progress. It is through this material experience that a vision capable of remaking and reforming "America" is articulated. The plight of the migrant is to move constantly while in a state of immobilization, or what we might call a state of fixed unfixity. The migrant subject in the Southwest has been the historical target of such strategies of immobilization.[9] What this experience has produced is a counternarrative to the optimistic, individualist, naïveté of American progressivism and the individualist mainstream counterculture. Neoimperial desire inherent in neoindividualist countercultural narratives is countered in the figure of the migrant, forced to move while remaining unchanged and immobile like slightly reenvisioned Beckett characters, who rather than waiting for Godot, are always waiting to go. The migrant writers' challenge to other writers who have pictured only open sky and uninhabited land, and for whom progress is a noun, is to redraw the map of the American landscape. This migrant cartography represents the myriad pitfalls, impassable borders, and ideological spaces in which progress is always a verb, "to progress," to move on, but never to arrive. Their narrative thus stresses directly and indirectly the imperative of arrival, of finding a place in what we might begin to think of as América rather than America.

While challenging the redemptive narrative of "mobility" so common to the American imagination, this migrant-informed Americano criticism also calls sharply into question the positive value of "unfixity" and "fluidity" that borderlands criticism posits as the condition of the unsubjectifiable Chicano or Chicana subject. I propose that this lauded poststructural fluidity might be valid as a final effect, but to valorize and then utilize it as an end in itself largely ignores the direct and specific material and historical context of the American conflict. This material history should remain primary and accessible even as "migrant subjectivity" is deployed through poststructural theorization for various sociopolitical agendas: Renato Rosaldo's "multiplex personality," or the radically heterogenous, discursive subject suggested by Gloria Anzaldua's "New Mestija," or the subject of the radical hegemonic strategy advocated by democratic theorists Laclau and Mouffe.[10]

We must consider the critique and desire that emerges from material migrant experience, how it informs Americano identity and social criticism, and the way in which in its transformation from "migrant" to "Americano" we may begin to speak to the material desires that migrant discourse expresses: finding a stable place, social justice, and a malleable, inclusive identity. All of these desires are capable of shaping the national culture. An understanding of migrant experience will provide a much needed corrective to the "function" of the unsubjectifiable subject that has become assumed in borderlands and poststructural criticism, as well as challenge the prescriptive, narrowed identity that certain aspects of *el movimiento* promulgated. In the journey from experience to meaning, what has been left behind is the migrant's own *testimonio*.

If we listen we will find that the migrants speaks well for themselves. The migrant exposes the destructive formulations of movement: fragmentation, anticommunalism, neoindividualism, movement as a redemptive narrative, the mythos of liberty as a function of laissez-faire capitalism. Most important, the migrant articulates a political and social vision that insists on communality, endorses direct political action, and has given shape to his own moral and ethical system: *dignidad.* This egalitarian imperative forms an important intervention in the remaking of "America" and in the discourse of citizenship. Three figures emerged from the migrant experience and helped shape what we might see as uniquely "Americano": Ernesto Galarza, Tomás Rivera, and Cesar Chavez.

In their work, the ethic of an egalitarian citizenship emerges as a defining characteristic of an Americano politics. Americanismo is an attempt to do away with the most damaging aspects of both the Mexican American and Chicano generations' movements and subjectivities: a Mexican American propensity for an anticommunal individualism, and a Chicano isolationism and narrow identity politics. Americanismo, however, incorporates the best of both: a demand to participate fully on the national scale with a keen sense of reformist politics (Mexican American), and a pride in Mexican cultural heritage and being a person of color (Chicanismo). Each of these aspects operate in the service of creating an egalitarian society, or as Ernesto Galarza termed it, *el pueblo libre*.

## Ernesto Galarza's *Pueblo Libre:* Radical Democracy and the Mover and the Moved

In 1963 yet another accident involving migrant workers took place in California's agricultural backroads. Ernesto Galarza undertook a year-long investigation as to the causes of the deadly event and published it as *Tragedy at Chualar.* The report, among his lesser-known works, is important for what it suggests about the grievous disregard for the safety of migrant workers in California's agricultural industry. However, *Tragedy at Chualar* is much more than a published report to a safety commission. In approximately one hundred pages it manages to convey several levels of meaning in its condemnation of a system that exploits workers and has created a mechanized system in which the Mexican worker is simply the fuel. *Tragedy in Chualar* refuses to allow the migrant to be used; the ugly incident forces us to look at the migrant in his material existence, not as a currency to be used as labor or a liminal and theoretical function. On the contrary, Galarza's introduction begins with the phone call that alerted him to the tragedy. The voice tells Galarza that he'd "better come and look. This town is full of dead Mexicans" (Galarza 1). The statement acts as a command and a warning to the reader. The history of the migrant revolves around the images of the crushed and mangled bodies of its subject.

The accident was indicative of the treatment of bracero migrants in the United States.

Approximately at 4:25 p.m. with emergency brakes set, the train bore down on the bus, which was rolling slowly into crash position. The coupling of the leading engine struck the bus at a point 10 feet from the rear. Before the front of the train could come to a stop 3,050 feet north of the intersection, 56 men lay dead, dying, or injured on the right of way. . . . California highway patrol called it "the biggest single fatal vehicle accident in the history of California." Later the National Safety Council was to rank it as the worst of its type in the history of the United States. In the files of the California State compensation fund, the resulting death and injury claims were classified under the subject "Farm Labor Catastrophe, Chualar, September 17, 1963." (Galarza 10)

Galarza's investigation found that the Chualar accident was caused directly by the negligence of growers who made a practice of converting flatbed trucks into illegal buses. They disregarded all safety recommendations and allowed inexperienced and poorly trained drivers to operate vehicles carrying dozens of passengers. Galarza uncovered apathetic legislators and safety commissions that did nothing to bring agricultural transportation into line even after several deadly accidents had occurred on California's agricultural roads.

In what eventually becomes a reality-fueled allegory, Galarza portrays the accident as inevitable due to the machinations of industry that grind-up and consume dispensable and a cheap and easily replaceable workforce. The long abused bracero is sacrificed by an industry that does not care, and is in fact willing to write off such "losses" as long as they do not outweigh the gains.

Placing Galarza's work within the scope of movement discourse produces a direct refutation of movement as progress. In a materialist demythologization of the conception of the economy as self-regulating, and of a laissez-faire system that produces a highly desired "fluidity," Galarza's report suggests most stridently that the migrant worker is always in danger of being written off. For Galarza, the tragedy of Chualar is that even in the face of the terrible loss of life and limb, it remains only emblematic of an ongoing process.

The riders of the doomed bus, unlike the travelers on Kerouac's road, are not liberated or freed. The promises of an individualist liberty are not even a consideration. The hopes of financial advancement have long been extinguished. As Galarza describes the converted bus, he points out constriction that the riders endured: "For farm laborers on the road, minimum essentials, as laid down in the official regulations, tend to emphasize the minimal rather than the essential. . . . The minimum required aisle space between benches was 24 inches. A man of medium height in a sitting position needs more or less 22 inches of room between the back of his seat and the knee. The benches . . . were eleven inches wide. This left 11 inches of aisle space for each man. Two passengers sitting face to face filled all but an inch or two of the available room in the aisle" (26). The packing of braceros into a homemade bus points to the industry's use of the bracero as a product. No different than the fruits and vegetables they pick, the men are loaded and moved from field to field as needed, in much the same way which water is diverted for irrigation. It is a fluidity that did not serve to liberate, to say the least. The bus is a parody of community: coercive, constrictive, and prohibitive of agency. Yet, Galarza prevents us from contemplating the metaphorical issues for too long without being confronted with the image of the torn body of the bracero.

Galarza highlights the trial of Francisco Gonzalez Espinoza, the driver of bus 197. In what amounted to an exercise in cynicism, Espinoza was charged with vehicular manslaughter and acquitted. His defense, and the defense of the growers who were responsible for the conditions that caused the accident, was that "things happen." Galarza details the conditions of the accident: an illegally constructed "bus" disintegrated when a train collided with its back end, at a crossing that had no lights or railroad warning, on a backroad that permitted very little visibility and that was used many times on a daily basis. Lastly, the vehicle was driven by a driver who was not trained, could not read English, but was given a license all the same. The fault lies not with the driver but with the system for which he drove and which drove him: "If the question is asked again: Why? and if the answer is looked for, not in the narrow focus of one man's failure, but in the broader scope of a system's operation, other factors remain to be considered about the Chualar tragedy.

"Generalizing, it is suggested that the transportation in California of Mexican braceros is accident prone. It is so because it takes place in the course of a very extensive operation of manpower supply and distribution which is lax rather than tight, a medium in which loose interpretation and permissive compliance with the law has been too common" (Galarza, *Tragedy at Chualar* 50–51).

What Galarza makes explicit in his investigation is that the bracero's mobility is not a personal choice. The bus in which he is driven is constructed in order so that the migrant may be *moved*. The very mobility that describes the concept of supply and demand, the fluidity of "liquid assets" is redefined. Systemic operations function for the benefit of the few while putting the many, the worker, the bracero, the migrant, at risk.

Galarza exposes the defining dichotomy as such: the Mover and the Moved. The mover creates the system of transportation and profits from its cheapest operation: "With respect to transportation, the Growers Farm Labor Association and its members were responsible only for carrying the braceros to the area of employment. The growers, as individual operators, were expected to provide the facilities and service necessary for daily travel to and from the fields" (*Tragedy at Chualar* 55). The Moved is stripped of all agency: "No bracero was in a position to make or defend a point in dispute over the conditions of his employment because its terms, written and signed, were not available to him" (*Tragedy at Chualar* 60). The worker is placed in a system that he does not understand and has no need of understanding: "braceros were often loaned on an informal basis. . . . It represented an illegal draft on the local labor pool and shifting from field to field without regard to proper clearance by the State or Federal agencies concerned" (*Tragedy at Chualar* 67). Galarza suggests a system that is configured for maximum "efficiency" in which "efficiency" is defined as swiftest and cheapest. Logic that has perhaps not gone mad, but grown callous and cynical. What emerges is not the image of a tragic accident, but of a systemic mobility that transforms its subjects as it transports them for profit: 'Farmworkers are classified in the vehicle code within the category of "types of loads.' . . . Farm laborers should be promoted in the law from category of things to that of persons" (*Tragedy at Chualar* 92).

This call for fair and equal treatment under the law arises from the specific aftermath of the Chualar tragedy. It constructs the problem as one of movement, in which the Moved are constantly put at risk in a system that depends on quick, cheap, and efficient transportation. However, Galarza's report had the practical results of making it possible for widows and injured braceros to file and collect on demands for state compensation benefits. There was a visible improvement in the quality of transportation in the Salinas Valley. For Galarza the Chualar tragedy is emblematic of the position of the migrant, a vulnerability linked to the lack of full citizen-subject status. The problem is, in part, constitutional, for the legal status that they endured parallels the situation of Mexican Americans in the United States: both make vital contributions to American social and economic systems, but without the benefits of a full and equal political participation. In both cases, the Mexican and Mexican American subject suffered from various forms of disenfranchisement that were manifested in myriad ways, but that ultimately resulted in a lack of stability.

The Bracero Program, in place between 1942 and 1964, was a long-standing practice of worker importation and deportation, which the United States has implemented since the nineteenth century. It began after the United States entered into World War II, when the nation's agribusiness leaders found themselves "short" of workers and lobbied Washington to strike a labor deal with Mexico. However, the 1930s had seen Immigration and Naturalization Service (INS) launch massive "repatriation drives" that indiscriminately deported over one million people to Mexico. The anti-Mexican hysteria invoked in the 1930s was responsible for horrific miscarriages of justice in which citizens and their children were stolen away from their homes and spirited across the border without regard to the toll extracted from individuals, families, and communities.[11] The pattern of deportation and importation of

Mexican workers would continue throughout the bracero era. Even as hundreds of thousands of workers were recruited from south of the border, the federal government launched crackdowns, the most infamous of which was "Operation Wetback."

When the Mexican government complained of the mistreatment suffered by their citizens in the United States, the response by the federal government was to open the border, a practice that the INS had first instituted in 1917. This weakened the Mexican government's leverage in enforcing the rights of their citizens in U.S. fields, and in March of 1954 Mexico relented and agreed to allow the Secretary of Labor determine the prevailing wage. This further undercut the position of labor in the United States and the AFL-CIO joined a national outcry against Mexicans taking American jobs. As a result, the federal government began Operation Wetback. Between one and two million Mexicans were detained, jailed, or deported. As James Cockcroft writes in *Outlaws in the Promised Land,* this revolving door policy has always had deliberate aims:

> The result of enforcing the "legality" of the U.S.-Mexico border by means of the bracero program was not merely an increase in the number of Mexican immigrant workers legally and illegally crossing into the U.S. each year—it was, in effect, the creation of an internationally mobile pool of inexpensive surplus Mexican labor power sufficient not only for U.S. agribusiness's survival and expansion but also for a sudden increase in the tempo of Mexico's industrialization, unprecedented since the turn of the century. This in turn made possible what has become known as the "silent integration" of the Mexican and U.S. economies. . . . The porous common border became a convenient "legal fiction." . . . Both governments, their rhetoric to the contrary, make use of the border for the mutual advantage of a wealthy minority of Americans and Mexicans who dominate the two increasingly integrated economies. (Cockcroft 86)

In the context of controlling the flow of workers, unilaterally opening up the border to destabilize union activity as well as to create labor gluts, is only possible through the regulation of movement. The "revolving door policy" supplied a steady flow of workers both "legal" and "illegal," which was used strategically to keep wages low and the labor market glutted. The "illegal" work force was used to undercut wages while the bracero was used to impress upon the undocumented worker that his or her position was tenuous. Read against Kerouac's *On the Road*, Galarza's *Merchants of Labor* succeeds in creating a movement narrative that demythologizes any romanticized versions of migrant existence. In Galarza's hands, the migrant's unfixity is a deliberately destabilizing strategy related to agribusiness's need for a "fluid labor pool."

With the introduction of the provision of the McCarran-Hartley Acts of 1950 and 1952, the deportation of braceros and undocumented workers became even easier under the grounds of being a suspected "communist" or "subversive." The McCarran Act of 1952 went so far as to authorize the building of six detention camps for those suspected. The fear of deportation or detention made it very difficult for farm workers to unionize or even demonstrate for better working conditions and wages. Protesting was dangerous and opened the worker to being labeled as an agitator or communist and subject to arrest and deportation. Galarza's *Merchants of Labor* is thus an indictment of American capitalism, of its human rights violations, of the cynical use of the power to "fix" and "unfix," to detain and set free, and ultimately to enslave: "Is the state's agribusiness so competitive that its very survival requires a permanent alien contract labor force? Is this indentured alien—an almost perfect model of the economic man, an 'input factor' stripped of the political and social attributes that liberal democracy likes to ascribe to all human beings ideally—is this bracero the prototype of the production man of the future?" (Galarza, *Merchants of Labor* 16). While voicing the concerns of earlier "liberal" social critics such as David Riesman, William Whyte, and J. Kenneth Galbraith, Galarza deals directly and devastatingly with the meaning of institutionalized "mobility" in America. His work presciently recognized the emergence of a post-Fordist economy, in which labor would become more destabilized and would be stripped of many of the elements necessary for communal and civic stability.

Galarza's foundational premise is that movement for the migrant is not a choice. Tragically, the liberating movement to the United States is quickly transformed. Leaving the "caste-bound, immobile society molded on Spanish colonial traditions" the migrant merely trades an agrarian-organized hierarchy for an industrial-organized hierarchy. In recounting the serf-based economy of Mexico, Galarza sets up a comparison with the laissez-faire system in the United States, leaving the reader to draw the conclusion that the serf-migrant is exploited by both systems.

Having immigrated from Mexico in the aftermath of the Revolution of 1910, Galarza presents the uses and exploitation of immigrant labor as the organization of movement. He equally understands and conveys the necessity of finding a stable *place* that will allow for substantive and meaningful civic and cultural inclusion. In *Barrio Boy,* the autobiography of his early youth, as Ernesto moves north to escape the escalating violence, he begins to note the increasingly complex organization and categorization that characterizes the towns and cities as they approach the United States. Galarza establishes that such migrant drift is undertaken solely to establish the conditions that will allow for a stable communal and familial existence.

Throughout *Barrio Boy,* there is a palpable sense of loss and nostalgia for a life that revolves around the security of a homestead, where schedules are determined by the crowing of a rooster and the position of the sun. One's physical position is determined by topographical locality, a cognitive mapping that in a preideological state is functionally organic. The roads and buildings are insignificant in marking space. Rather it is the forest, the arroyo, the mountains that give direction to the village's people. This idealized place of Ernesto's past is in effect the *pueblo libre* for which the Galarzas search. *El Pueblo Libre* thus becomes the idealized community that is searched for by the migrant in the new U.S. homeland: for Ernesto that community is not a narrowly constituted Aztlan, but an egalitarian American national space that makes room for its diverse communities and allows for civic and socioeconomic participation (illusory as this will prove to be).

As Ernesto moves north, he finds that the organic space he left existed only in an insulated way, but like a spoke of a wagon wheel, it revolves around a hub. The center's centrifugal force, the revolution setting events in motion, controls the speed but allows nothing within its pull to remain unaffected. What Ernesto finds is that to escape the revolution and the centrifugal force of the hub, one must enter the influence of another hub. We find that the *patrones,* the *autoridades,* and the military that inevitably encroach upon the space of *el pueblo libre* and force movement are ubiquitous. These forms of exploitative authority simply reappear, replicating the same systemic forces: circular, centralizing, centrifugal. Migration is always already doomed to move within the sphere of influence of both industrialization and colonization, repelled, but always fixed at the periphery of power by the center.

The migrant soon learns that stability is counterproductive for an industrialized market economy. Mobility is harnessed and scheduled as is the burgeoning railroad system in which Ernesto's uncles find work. As Ernesto and his family move north, transportation systems become more advanced and complex: from *burro* to stagecoach, to train and finally to the auto. Ernesto observes that the more complex and industrial the economic organization of a city, the more segregation and alienation he experiences. As a child he begins to find that he can exchange his labor for small wages. His job as a courier and errand-boy indicates the shift from producing or growing, to an economy based around exchange and the movement of products.

The migrant, like the bracero, facilitates movement of products, but he is never allowed to forget that his personal mobility is circumscribed. His "organized migration" is plotted out carefully and forcefully by a market economy he does not fully comprehend. Galarza presents a metaphor on this state of fixed mobility in his description of the railroad roundhouse:

> The roundhouse and the shops, as I viewed them from the guard-house, were remarkable. . . . Everyone seemed to be pushing or

lifting or dragging or carrying tools or hammering on something. On lucky days I could watch a locomotive move slowly
into the yard and on the turntable, an enormous circular platform with a single track down the center. The track was maneu-
vered so as to stop flush with the rails on which the engine
moved in. Once the engine was in position, the turntable circled
no faster than a snail until the track was locked into the rails
that pointed to the stall into which the locomotive was to be
moved. The place was called La Casa Redonda. . . . When the
overhaul was finished, the locomotive was backed onto the
turntable and switched out of the yard to the main line. (*Barrio
Boy* 124)

This organization of labor not only facilitates, but mirrors the
circumscribed and tightly controlled movement of the railroad.
Ironically, its riders—like Ernesto, who watches from the train
window as the "scenery flies by"—lose their agency as they gain
speed. All interaction with nature is lost as it is transformed into
scenery, background, glimpsed but never touched, seen but not
apprehended. It foreshadows the transformation of the migrant
picker whose connection to the earth will be alienated through its
commercialization. Like the railroad that moves only on prescribed rails, La Casa Redonda describes the position of the laborer and migrant whose labor is simply a function of circulation.
La Casa Redonda's purpose is to distribute and redistribute cargo.
Its workers are part of that machinery, and the passengers are
cargo.

Ernesto learns that as the mode of transportation grows more
advanced, and as townships become more intricately organized,
that complexity leads to restriction. The class divisions on the
train are replicated in the industrialized cities Ernesto moves
through. Like elements caught in the spokes of a spinning wheel,
the motion quickly forces things into their places. The migrant
moves toward the hub and once within its influence, is kept away
from the center of power, yet controlled and fixed permanently by
its influence. Ernesto learns that in order to stop migrating (and
thus remain permanently fixed within a system of impoverish-
ment), he must find a place in which to settle. However, this

means confronting directly a system of economic destabilization thinly disguised as "mobility" in American culture.

In *Merchants of Labor* Galarza devotes a good deal of space to outlining the complex bureaucracy instituted for organizing braceros, which by 1946 had in California alone given rise to seventy-four separate labor bureaus. These offices represented the interests of growers in every major crop in all the important production centers: from the concentration centers Hermosilla, Chihuahua, and Monterey, to the contracting centers across the border in the United States, the organization of labor contracting had reached an exact science. The efficiency of mobilizing and distributing labor produces a sense of rigid organization, which belies the extraordinary fluidity and flexibility that worked for the benefit of the growers, to the immediate detriment of the bracero, and the ultimate disadvantage of all agricultural workers. "The labor pool, so constituted, was supposed to be, ideally, frozen at the periphery and completely fluid at the center. It was the common resource of an entire industry, not of a single enterprise. No particular worker was committed to a given employer; and all employers . . . could dip into the pool. This was an important condition, for it made the immigrants the concern and responsibility of no one employer. . . . The pool, at its best, was insulated from the general labor market. American workers would not normally be willing to enter it; the immigrants could not easily leave it" (*Merchants of Labor* 36).

What Galarza proves is that fundamentally, and ironically, fluidity works for the benefit of the movers and not for the moved. The organization and exacting compartmentalization of the agricultural workforce has as its ultimate purpose the enforcement of strategies of containment in regards to wages, workers, and markets. Galarza realizes that such strategies of containment are organized into several apparatuses: the legal, the ideological, the technological, and the violent. "The containment of wages worked smoothly enough over the long run, but it was a standing grievance among workers, who also blamed the employers and contractors for encouraging wetbacks and pitting one racial group against another in the fields. Occasionally passive resistance turned into angry protest and when there was leadership to direct it, the labor associations responded with systematic violence. . . . To organize such violence was, among others, one of the purposes of the Associated Farmers, constituted in 1934 "to foster and encourage respect for and to maintain law and order, to promote the prompt, orderly and efficient administration of justice" (*Merchants of Labor* 38–39).

The use of such "efficient administration" produces a fluid labor pool through divisiveness and violence. The stratification that young Ernesto notes on the train—division of first, second, third, and fourth class—is strategically implemented. The divisions of neighborhoods that isolate and insulate his barrio *(colonia)* in Sacramento abound with statues of Coronado and Columbus, powerful representations of the center of power that symbolically enforce the periphery. The organic organization of his pueblo and agrarian society gives way to human-made, capitalistic market organization. As the young Ernesto learns from a mentor at the end of *Barrio Boy,* such organization can only be fought with a strategy that does not divide, but unites. The organic community is forever lost and the migrant must counter with formidable organization of his own making. However, as Galarza suggests, this means creating a unified Americano insistence on full representation. This also points to the need to reconfigure the national economic and political structure.

The methods devised by growers' associations to keep the labor pool "fluid," transformed the migrant into a form of currency. Galarza tells of the common form of self-reference the migrant in the field used: *"yo soy prestado"* ("I am a loaned-one"). The association succeeded in their making of a labor pool partially through the interpellation of the migrant: the migrant begins to think of himself as currency. Galarza's explanations of the association's practices are rife with the rhetoric of monetary and commodity exchange: the loan, furloughing, job rotation, the creation of sub-pools (renting to unauthorized farmers), and transferring. "Transferring became one of the more reliable methods of making the bracero pool even more fluid. There had been from the beginning a loose sort of transfer system between individuals and associations. . . . Still another way of keeping the bracero plastic was the loan. Men interviewed in the fields and in camps often described themselves as *prestados*" (*Merchants of Labor* 179–80). The end result is the use of movement and transfer as forms of manipulation, of creating "elasticity" in order to keep abreast of changing market conditions.

However, as Galarza is quick to point out, a simultaneous re-sult of such elasticity is the restriction of communality. The braceros' most valuable attribute was that proper deployment pre-vented a stabilized domestic workforce in the agricultural fields. Galarza makes clear that this possibility was to be prevented at all costs. "What disqualified the domestic laborers was the fact that they tended to become stable. While they could undoubtedly carry the burden of production, they were also discovering the possibilities of community life, experimenting with economic or-ganization and talking of collective bargaining. Emerging slowly out of the flux of the labor pool these were the first footings of a countervailing force that might some day face the associations on even terms. In the campaign of a century waged by commercial agriculture to postpone such a day, the bracero system had played an important part. It held the line for twenty years" (*Merchants of Labor* 253).

Actively contesting such a system, Galarza argues, must involve the stabilization of community. The search for *el pueblo libre* is found not in a utopic space, but in the very real mobilization of *co-munidad,* one that insists not so much on the formation of Aztlan, but on the transformation of America into América, an egalitarian national culture that unites within a community, workers, domes-tics and internationals alike. The idealized pueblo of his past, nat-uralized and monolithic in its makeup, broken-up and dispersed by the forces of "revolution," must be reconstructed, stabilized, and organized for the purposes of unity in the new U.S. homeland. This understanding is garnered through the material experiences of a migrating boy and the observations of a young man who di-rectly experienced the cruelties of organized movement.

Like so many of Ernesto Galarza's projects, *Merchants of Labor* had a direct political impact. Passed out to every member of

Congress as they debated the extension of Public Law 78 (the Bracero Program), the book influenced enough members to defeat the resolution. His work deconstructs the national/local political binary so that local action is required but not at the expense of jettisoning a national agenda. In effect, he proves that local intervention has a direct impact on the national arena. Galarza rejects a separatist vision, seeing instead a community that must extend nationally, beginning with Mexican American migrants and braceros, but incorporating the "new migrant" American labor force. His form of activism insists on a Mexican American place in the community, nation, and hemisphere. It exposes the divisive manipulation of movement-as-fluidity, and encourages movement-as-community: a change of movement to *movimiento*. Galarza challenges the moved to recognize the methods of the mover and to subvert them by organizing.[12]

Contextualizing Ernesto Galarza's Americano social critique within the democratic debate gives us a way of rethinking an American studies framework that has thus far not acknowledged Mexican American social criticism in any significant way. Galarza's early intervention pointed out economic trends and labor practices that went unobserved by other social critics. He spoke to the same concerns, but did so from an experience that was simultaneously applicable to both the migrant and the American worker-at-large.

Chicano social criticism, as represented by Galarza, points out the problem of an American individualism and an economic system imbricated in fundamental, and sometimes invisible ways. What Galarza's intervention shows is that Chicano material experience and its brand of organic sociology provides a vital critique. Focusing attention on Chicano/Mexican American participation within the discourse of democracy and citizenship asserts a history of participation in public and national debates with which Chicano social criticism has not been credited. This is in part due to a form of Chicano criticism that has not asserted its Americano critique clearly enough. Galarza's work is one clear example of a broadened, revised practice of American Studies: an Americano studies.

## Tomás Rivera's Americanismo: Mapping the Arrival

When asked by Juan Bruce-Novoa if Chicano literature "reevalu-
ated, attacked, or subverted the value system of the majority society," Tomás Rivera answered, "Now, what part of the value system
are we talking about, intellectual liberation? No. That's one of the
ideals of the North American intelligentsia, that we be liberated
intellectually. I don't think it's subverting the great ideal of North
American thought, which is exactly that: intellectual liberation"
(*Chicano Authors* 157). At first glance it seems a naïve answer by
one of the most important Chicano writers. He seems to accept
the tenets of an abstracted "North American" form of liberalism
that has been effectively deconstructed in the past two decades.
However, as an individual all too familiar with the oppression and
racism inherent in "democratic" America, Rivera would not have
been blind to the material suffering engendered by a benign liberalism. On the contrary, his work bears sharp witness to the hard-
ships endured under the auspices of liberalism. Rather, Rivera's
response is calculated to highlight the difference between American constitutional protections and guarantees of equal access and
participation, and its reality. Rivera's comment imparts the need
to insist that America in practice live up to its written promises.
Insistence over resistance, suggests Rivera, is the course of action
for the postwar Mexican American subject.

But what exactly is the nature of such a system; what is it in
particular that the Mexican American citizen should insist upon
according to Rivera? In the shorthand of Rivera's rhetoric, we
might recognize it as "arrival." Its systemic elements can be defined as egalitarian (expressed as *dignidad*) participatory, and
communal; ultimately they come together in what I would call an
Americano *communitas* that has the potential for envisioning a
national culture that is inclusive, material, and radically democratic. Taken with Ernesto Galarza's work, this Americano communitarian program, if you will, means dispensing with an illusory mobility in the many forms that I have shown in operation in
"countercultural," individualistic, and theoretical formulations. In
order to progress, the Americano subject must *stop*.

Movement becomes stabilized as interaction within community, localized but figured as part of a national community in which race, class, and gender issues are part of the same struggle for equality. "Equality" should be understood, however, not as an abstract juridical term, but in its full material, affective sense. It is here, where migrant and Mexican American experience (and where the experience of being black, Chicano, Asian, a woman, poor, and so on) comes into play. Living on the "margins" means living in exclusion and in deprivation, and the abstract concepts of "equality" and "access" take on substance in the face of that lived experience.

Rivera's remark makes it clear that his answer to past and present national, political, and civic exclusion, "arrival" is material and specific: "I've only written about people who existed in the migrant stream between 1945 and 1955. Right away it's a historical documentation that I want to deal with" (Bruce-Novoa, *Chicano Authors* 148). Those dates are mapped carefully by Rivera. Covering roughly the same period as *On the Road* and other early Kerouac fiction, his collected work documents the other side of American mobility: one that exposes exclusion as the objective of "fluidity" and "movement." Within his work both Galarza's study of the bracero movement and John Kenneth Galbraith's theorization of the affluent society's penchant for the false promise of overproduction come alive in direct, sharp focus.

In a similar appraisal of the Chicano narrative, Ramon Saldivar has argued that the Chicano cultural critic not only renders a vision of hardship, but creates a material vision of solutions: "[The] Chicano narratives seek systematically to uncover underlying structures by which real men and women may either perpetuate or reformulate that reality" (Saldivar 6). Perhaps this is what Rivera means when he says that "This [*And the Earth Did Not Devour Him*] is a positive image of the migrant as opposed to the negative one of him as lost in the stream of labor. Well, that's the point: to be able to document his strength, to show that he really was not lost" (Bruce-Novoa, *Chicano Authors* 152). Replying that his poem "The Searchers" is a paean to the Mexican American who "never stay[ed] in one place to suffer or be subdued," Rivera bears witness to the effort not only to find *el pueblo libre,* but to construct it through hard labor, self-sacrifice, and communal and civic duty.

Connecting work, family, and community that transcends simplistic racial, gender, and class divisions, Rivera comments further on this Americano "spirit": "They always kept searching, that's why they were 'migrant' workers. The word worker is very implicit there, they were travelers. If they stayed where there was no work they would die, and they didn't die. I see that same sense of movement in the Europeans who came here. . . . I've written a poem called 'The Searchers.' To me they were people who searched and that's an important metaphor in the Americas. My grandfather was a searcher; my father was a searcher, I hope I can also be a searcher. That's the spirit I seek" (Bruce-Novoa 151). Searching for the postwar Mexican American's proper "place" is for Rivera part of the development of "the concept of justice so important for the American continent." In his interview with Bruce-Novoa he explains, "I wanted to treat the idea of mental and intellectual liberation and where it fits into the spectrum of the Americas. Can it be achieved here, and if so, can it be done?" (Bruce-Novoa 151).

Rivera seeks to answer his own question through charting the postwar Mexican American subject's journey through the affluent society. In "The Searchers," Rivera's epic poem, he creates a cartographic journey that locates the migrant desire to find a place in which to build "a new life / a new dream." Place, however, is not to be found in an idealized "America," but is clearly a mixture of physical geography and the intellectual, cultural conceptualization of "arrival." It is the will to transform the sociopolitical landscape in the face of hostile or indifferent Americans.

> Other beings?
> We,
> One,
> the very same flavor
> the very same
> We looked behind heads
> At the back of heads
> The back of white heads

was less dangerous
Sometimes we turned the
heads around only to find
eyes that didn't see
who dared not see
who dared not be
within our own
(*Searchers* 60)

The poem's language interrogates the rhetoric of inclusion, the *e pluribus unum* of the republic's purported inclusion. Rivera points to the divisive racism that has come partly as a result of competition in the marketplace, and partly as a defensive exclusion on the part of Anglos who "dared not see" Mexican Americans as full members of the "We" promised in the Constitution. Insisting on being heard, on being seen captures the attention of the "citizen" ("sometimes we turned the heads around"), but the effect is temporary and often does not produce even a tacit acknowledgment of Mexican American participation.

In this sense, the Mexican American creates an Americano narrative, what Julian Olivares has called Rivera's "achievement in the American grain," that documents the existence of the Mexican American within the Americas and within the history of the United States. Insisting on the deconstruction of racist divisions that view the Mexican American as "other beings," Rivera points to the collective failure of nerve of the American public.

The poem ends by cataloging the places where migrants have been and where they have suffered—Utah, Iowa, San Angelo, Italy during World War II, Minnesota—as a way of showing not only how far migrants have traveled, but as a way of insisting upon their presence in historical America. His discursive, material strategy invokes a political imagination that rejects isolation, looking instead to create a manifest arrival of the Mexican American within the idealized and practical "We" of a reimagined American homeland: América. It is an act of *actuatis,* or as Rivera describes in an early essay as "an exact, pure desire to transform what is isolated in the mind into an external form" (Rivera "Chicano Literature" 439).

If the United States became a "place" through a discursive act (the Declaration of Independence), and Mexicans became Americans under the Treaty of Guadalupe Hidalgo, and undocumented workers became citizens under IRCA (Immigration Reform and Control Act of 1986) then America can become América through a discursive act. Acknowledgment of place begins first in the political and cultural imagination of the searcher, on which an insistent sociocultural strategy of inclusion is founded. Arrival is then not an exercise in idealistic utopianism, but an historical intervention on the part of the Americano who recognizes his or her rights, juridical subjectivity, and understands well the resistance to inclusion in all its guises and manifestations.

In *And the Earth Did Not Devour Him (y no se lo trago la tierra,* hereafter referred to as *And the Earth)*, Rivera uncovers the effects of perpetual movement. "The Lost Year" begins the novel with the image of the self-subjecting subject. "It always began when he would hear someone calling him by his name but when he turned his head to see who was calling, he would make a complete turn and there he would end up—in the same place. This was why he never could discover who was calling him nor why. . . . One time he stopped at mid-turn and fear suddenly set in. He realized that he had called himself. And thus the lost year began" (*And the Earth* 83). Rivera's migrant boy is caught in the trap of cycles. Constantly turning, he finds that he never progresses, but always ends up "in the same place." Defining where this "place" is, involves locating the caller, who like Galarza's "Mover," remains invisible in order to function unimpeded.[13] Rivera's migrant "stop[s] at mid-turn" when he realizes that the movement that directs his life also seeks to manipulate his identity. The fear he feels emanates from the sudden awareness that the "voice" of the mover has been internalized. It is at this point that the recouping of the "lost year" can begin. What the migrant-subject learns, Rivera suggests, is that the invisible mover takes the form of any figure that would fix his position by denying him arrival. "Mobility" as such, denies progress while creating a fixed restricted area of agency, so that it excludes from membership in the larger community, in this case the national, civic sphere.

Rivera's work prompts the migrant/Mexican American to refuse to be confined to the *barrio* or the *colonia*, arguing that the proper arena for the Americano is much larger. In "The Night Before Christmas," Rivera decries the limits imposed by the Anglo elite, the labor market, and finally, the Mexican Americans themselves. Rivera's story is in fact an argument for the necessity of a "map" that must be used for navigating within the mainstream of the public sphere (the civic, the political, and the market). In "The Night before Christmas," Rivera portrays the lost migrant, describing the disorientation of a women's first trip downtown.

In what is a direct challenge to a movement narrative that would limit the arena of participation, Rivera's story argues that without a map, directions are meaningless. The town becomes representative of systemic vagary, opaque and strange. The downtown indicates settlement and permanence, the proper realm of the "citizen" in which the migrant wishes to enact agency. As a marginal subject whose purpose is to labor, and thus not participate directly in the infrastructure of the market or other segments of the local and national society, her position is relegated to the outskirts of the town. As she makes her way downtown, she senses the danger of leaving her designated space: "I just pray that the train doesn't come while I'm crossing the tracks and catches me right in the middle . . . I just hope there's no dogs . . . I hope there's no train coming down the tracks" (Rivera, *And the Earth* 132).

By crossing the train tracks into an area beyond her barrio, she has committed a transgressive act, symbolically and socially. The train tracks act as the border between the "fluid" but delimited realm in which the migrant is allowed to move and the off-limits space of full rights-bearing citizenship: "Upon arriving at the crossing she was suddenly struck by intense fear. She could hear the sound of moving trains and their whistles blowing and this was unnerving her. She was too scared too cross. Each time she mustered enough courage to cross she heard the whistle of the train and, frightened, she retreated and ended up at the same place" (Rivera, *And the Earth* 132). It is clear that the woman will not find the base for civic inclusion within the liminal space of her *barrio*. Rather, the border marks the space of full inclusion and is patrolled by the forces of repressive industrial organization (the train) as much as by a self-imposed fear of moving outside the *colonia*. Rivera claims that the latter repressive force—a theoretically and culturally-imposed barrioization—must be uncovered as debilitating.

Once inside the downtown area, she begins to panic. Unaccustomed to the "liberated space" of the marketplace, she is truly lost. Thus Rivera does not fall into the same trap of an earlier Mexican American assimilationism that would see inclusion as an automatic effect of entering the "middle class," or entering more fully into the market economy, or emerging higher in the division of labor. Rather, the "center" of social and cultural power is in need of radical reformation. Rivera brilliantly uses a form of synecdoche to merge the movement of the marketplace with fragmentation and reification: "She only saw people moving about—their legs, their arms, their mouths, their eyes" (133). The barrio represents a delimited sphere of action even though it offers a metaphorical space for cultural self-determination, while the "downtown" suggests that its "citizens" are themselves isolated and fragmented. The answer is then not a retreat into assimilation, but a synthesis that combines the strong communal identity located within the Mexican American's local culture and the national political community—a synthesis capable of creating a national culture shaped by a strong egalitarian, communal political sensibility and commitment.

Retreating to the migrant's insulated, but isolated space is not an option, argues Rivera. For the migrant/Mexican American who does so is destined to remain within that fixed position reserved for the marginal subject: "Just stay here inside the house and don't leave the yard. There's no need for it anyway. I'll bring you everything you need," the woman's husband suggests at story's end (134). Providing a way out for this woman means mapping the different spaces and borders that have been constructed to keep her within her space. The Americano critique sees this constriction as a form of interpellation, one that she carries, feeling its fixating effects on the migrant trail. Ironically, this mobile confinement is enforced as much by her own community (in the guise of the patriarchal as well as the borderlands critic) as by the forces of capital.

Rivera is thus not so much interested in exploiting the "potential subversion" of liminal or subaltern subjectivity, as he is focused on creating a political consciousness that resides in the first-hand knowledge of what it means to live outside the decision-making democratic sphere of influence. He is interested in what it means not to be counted as a full right-bearing citizen. In his interview with Bruce–Novoa, he says, "the migrant worker was living without any kind of protection. . . . There was no legal protection, and without legal protection there is nothing. It was a lot of suffering and much isolation of the people. Yet they lived through the whole thing, perhaps because they had no choice. . . . That's one role, to document all this" (*Chicano Authors* 149). "Americano" then marks this desire for inclusion in a particular political and participatory way, not simply as a designation marking participation within some abstracted "universal" notion of "America."

Specifically and materially, the shape of an Americano national culture is present in Rivera's fiction. In one of his lesser-known stories, taken from his posthumously published collection, *The Harvest,* Rivera refutes the Kerouac-championed neoindividualist form of libertarian democracy and the noncommunity that it foments. While "On the Road to Texas" has been interpreted as Rivera's parody of the *pachuco,* it is more accurately a response to an individualist American democratic ethos that has proved itself exploitative. Although the character of Pete Fonseca uses *pachuco* lingo, he so clearly represents many of the aspect of the Beat ethos that he may be Chicano literature's first, and perhaps only, Beat *pachuco.*

Fonseca's character revolves around the act of leaving, and his figure represents a clear danger to the formation of a migrant, Americano communal ethic. In an opening line that could have easily been about Dean Moriarty, Rivera writes: "He'd only just gotten there and he already wanted to leave" (*Harvest* 91). The contrast between the migrant who longs to leave, but is forced to move, and the beat *pachuco* who desires only to keep moving jux-taposes two connotations of movement that frame the debates in-herent in movement discourse: the tension between individual liberty and *civitas,* between a faith in negative liberty and a faith in positive liberty. Described as a "shadow," Fonseca is most dan-gerous because the threat that he poses is attractive. The young narrator expresses the fear of the migrant camp at the intrusion of the slickly dressed Fonseca until "we remembered there was more of us so we weren't so scared" (*Harvest* 91). As the tale unfolds, the significance of the security that the communal provides against the threat of neoindividualism becomes more apparent.

Fonseca captures the imagination of the young narrator and the young boys of the camp. His violent reputation ("I think it's him who stabbed that wetback in Colorado") and his use of drugs ("He also likes to smoke marijuana") make him an outlaw of sorts within the community of workers. Fonseca begins to make over-tures toward a young woman called "La Chata" (a cruel name sig-nifying her malformed nose). Her husband and the father of her two young boys had gone: "Her last husband had left; he didn't even get mad at her or anything. Just left" (94). Rivera constructs a story in which mobility is associated not with "liberty" so much as an escape from responsibility, an escape that destroys the fam-ily and erodes the community itself.

Preying on La Chata's vulnerability, Fonseca declares his love and marries her. The narrator is quick to point out that the nup-tials had the potential to benefit the family as a unit, but that Fonseca quickly turned the benefits toward himself. "Why, him and La Chata and the two boys could save a lot. He'd also have someone to cook his gorditas for him and his nice hot coffee, and someone to wash his clothes and according to Pete, she could handle at least one john a night. He'd start calculating: at four dollars a throw, at least, times seven nights, that was twenty-eight dollars a week. Even if *he* couldn't work, things'd be pretty good. He also said he liked La Chata's boys. They could buy a jalopy and then Sundays they could take rides, go to a show, go fishing or to dump and collect copper wire to sell" (97-98). In prostituting his wife and stepchildren for his personal mobility (the jalopy),

Fonseca's cynical use of family betrays any sense of responsibility. Inevitably, the family's potential for real progress and security is defeated. Fonseca's real criminality, suggests Rivera, is in his willful destruction of the communal ethic: "They were real happy. There started to be more and more work. Pete, La Chata and the boys always had work. They brought a car. Sundays they'd go driving a lot. . . . They worked together, they helped each other, they took real good care of each other, they even sang together in the fields. We all really like to see them because sometimes they'd even kiss in the fields. . . . They really had it good" (99).

However, Fonseca abandons his family and takes the money they have saved and makes his escape in the car earned by prostituting his wife. The effect of his duplicity on the narrator is to expose the illusion of community and to illustrate an alienation that causes the young boy to remark, "I guess we weren't [mad] too much. I guess because nothing had happened to us" (101). Rivera's condemnation of Fonseca's callow self-interest centers on the damage done not only to the family, but to the ethic necessary for establishing a lasting, significant sense of community: common respect and dignity for all responsible members, as Rivera explained in an interview. "*Dignidad.* It was also implicit in their etiquette, too, the idea that it was the way you taught respect for people. Everyone in society, no matter what he does . . . has dignity within the structure. That was something very important" (Bruce–Novoa 147). *Dignidad* is thus the basis for an egalitarianism necessary for not only the migrant community, but necessary for the reformation of a national culture: the Americano ethos requires active, full, and equal participation by all in the service of a what is recognizably *civitas*. In this way, Rivera maps the pitfalls to a necessary, revitalizing communal instinct.

In the second half of *And the Earth* Rivera uncovers the modes of exclusion practiced by those most interested in keeping the migrant on the margins. In "It's That It Hurts," a young migrant is expelled from school, ruining his chances to succeed. Relegated to the picking cycle, the child dreams of becoming a phone operator (ironically representing a marginalized position that functions as a conduit). Depicting the school as a site of systemic immobilization in much the way which Galarza used the Growers' Associations, Rivera's migrant does not learn the three r's, but rather undergoes a socialization that teaches him that his subjectivity is a construction of white surveillance. "It's always the same in these schools in the north. Everybody just stares at you up and down. And then they make fun of you and the teacher with her popsicle stick, poking your head for lice. It's embarrassing" (*And the Earth* 92). The migrant body is held up to observation by the dominant society's standards and is always found wanting, and thus "outside": "Mother you won't believe it. They took me out of the room. I had just walked in, and they put me in with a nurse all dressed in white. And they made me take off my clothes and they even examined my behind. . . . After a while they let me go but I was so ashamed" (92). Shame functions as a control system. The migrant subject is isolated and examined. Like the vagrancy laws and prohibitions on Mexican ownership of automobiles, controlled mobility is the ultimate end. The boy's selection for examination is based on his just having "walked in."

The migrant boy absorbs a sense of immobility. Rivera portrays this interpellation as an acquiescence to the racially constructed subjection:

> "Hey, Mex . . . I don't like Mexicans because they steal. You hear me?"
> "Yes"
> "I don't like Mexicans. You hear, Mex?"
> "Yes."
> "I don't like Mexicans because they steal. You hear me?'
> "Yes." (*And the Earth* 93)

The messages of systemic oppression and stereotype combine in the voice of the accuser. The affirmative answer "yes" suggests that the characterizations of the past have been absorbed. The school has served its purpose for the migrant has learned what a migrant must learn. Like the system of passes and licenses that were instituted to keep migrants attached to fields, institutional immobilization seeks to keep the child in a state of migrancy.[14] The solution, however, is not to resist this "subjectification" through a further decentering or deconstructive strategy, but rather to recognize of the *ends* that this excluded subjectivity serves. Rather than participating in the zero-sum game of "anti-essentialist" identification, the migrant Americano must focus on insisting on *inclusion*.

Rivera suggests that the moved must recognize the mover and the reasons for a forced instability. In "Under the House," the final story in *And the Earth*, the boy hides under a house in order to consider what he has learned during the course of the lost year. He hides to collect his thoughts, but also to escape the persecution at school. The migrant is trapped between the dirt that is his life's work and the superstructure of an edifice that symbolizes the infrastructure of the market he supports but cannot enter. The image powerfully registers the effects of exploitation: "He was lying face down and whenever he moved he could feel his back brush against the floor of the house. This even gave him a feeling of security. But once the fleas started biting him he had to move constantly. And he started to worry that the people who lived there might find out that he was there and make him get out. But he had to keep moving constantly" (*And the Earth* 148). The image masterfully conveys the paradoxical state of "unfixed fixity" through which the migrant is forced to move, to roam or migrate, to remain mobile, all the while "fixed" within a subaltern subjectivity. What is needed is not a full abandonment of stable identity or of the idea of the "nation," but rather a strategic, malleable, but focused reidentification as citizens and a reconfigured notion of nation.

Rivera suggests that only the construction of a communal identity can move the individual and community from underneath the house. This vision concerns not only the Mexican American or migrant, but is applicable to all "Americans," that is, all Americanos. As the boy's mind acts as a compendium of all the voices he has heard and all the people he has met, he is able to assert a secure selfhood that resides in a specific communal membership that models a reenvisioned American community. "I would like to see all of the people together. And then, if I had great big arms, I could embrace them all. I wish I could talk to all of them again, but all of them together" (151). In "When We Arrive," a woman "speaks" for the group as she thinks about the absurdity of migrant life:[15] "When we arrive, when we arrive, the real truth is that I'm tired of arriving. Arriving and leaving, it's the same thing because we no sooner arrive and . . . the real truth of the matter . . . I'm tired of arriving. I really should say we don't arrive because that's the real truth. We never arrive" (*And the Earth* 145). Rivera's solution is to get out of the truck, to stop, to unite along the lines of a shared material existence. "The people were becoming people. They began getting out of the trailer and they huddled around and commenced to talk about what they would do when they arrived." (*And the Earth* 146). Utopic strains aside, Rivera expresses the desires of the road-weary migrant. For Rivera, the migrant desires to find a home. He has come to the United States to do so. The migrant's movement is a search with a definitive end in mind. The "end" is not simply assimilation, but a transformative and participatory agenda with revolutionary potential.

The Americano, like José, the boy in "Zoo Island," undertakes to create a "town" for his fellow camp dwellers. Materially, they are deprived. "See here, in that little town where we buy our food there're only eighty-three souls, and you know what? They have a church, a dance hall, a filling station, a grocery store and even a little school. Here, we're more than eighty-three, I'll bet and we don't have any of that. Why, we only have a water pump and four out-houses, right?" (*Harvest* 117). José's answer to declare a township in the midst of the state of Iowa.

It is an insistence on the right to exist, to participate, to desire what the "other," the "movers" has claimed for themselves: "The following Sunday just about all the people on the farm had their picture taken next to the sign the boys had made on Saturday afternoon and which they had put up at the farm gate. It said: Zoo Island, Pop. 88 ½. One of the women had given birth.

And every morning José would no sooner get up than he would go see the sign. He was part of that number, he was in Zoo Island, in Iowa, and like Don Simon said, in the world" (119). Rivera's solution requires direct action, solidarity, and a brazen insistence on place *within* a very real national space. Liminal, subaltern, marginalized personas and communities prove themselves effete and regressive. In this sense, the Americano takes up the clarion call of an earlier civil rights agenda while sidestepping the narrow, exclusionary identity prescriptions that prevented a unified, cross-cultural, multiracial front. The migrant, so long the victim of a forced movement, redeems movement by reinscribing it with a communal ethic, one that enables, rather than inhibits political, communal, and ethical progress within an Americano landscape so long divided by spaces unbreached by its constantly perambulating, yet frozen subjects.

The legacy of these Americano activists and critics can be felt in work such as the Latino Cultural Citizenship Group, a collection of activist-scholars who have begun to redefine the way in which citizenship and "resistance" might be considered by examining "how various Latino groups are claiming membership in this society as they struggle to build communities, claim social rights, and become recognized as active agents in society. Our approach to cultural citizenship represents an ongoing dialogue . . . on how Latinos are incorporating themselves in U.S. society, while simultaneously developing specifically Latino cultural forms of expression that not only keep identity and heritage alive but significantly enrich the cultural whole of the country" (Flores 2). This focus on local, cultural practice and participation within a larger framework of national membership and national culture has important ramifications for reconsidering the way in which we as Mexican Americans might bring about an Americano reality that carries into practice the egalitarian national agenda that *el movimiento* envisioned early on, but allowed to dissipate. Like Cesar Chavez, another Americano visionary, the postwar Mexican American subject citizen must strive for social justice that cuts across gender, race, ethnicity, and even class as it provides leadership and not an ineffective "resistance" to a set of participatory desires that are valid and fair. It is left for this generation of Americanos to insist upon our relevance to the democratic experiment, and our important contribution past, present, and future to the shaping of the equitable and just society. To do so, we might begin with rereading the longings articulated in our migrant literature as a cry for arrival. Truly understanding that *grito* might pave the way toward realizing the Americano dream.

Notes

Works Cited

Index

# Notes

## Introduction

1. See Stephen Macedo's *Reassessing the Sixties*, and Frederic Jameson work in Sohnya Sayres et al, *The Sixties, without Apology* for contrasting views on the lasting significance of the decade. Both readings fail to recognize the underlying common ideological ground between the left and the right due to a framing of the decade's political conflict as simply a liberal versus conservative battle.

## 1. "No Fear Like Invasion"

1. Chuck Workman's film *The Source* credits the Beats with making social and cultural conditions possible for the feminist, civil rights, antinuclear, and pro-choice movements to exist. At the film's end a multicultural assemblage of poets are given voice, visually asserting that all American dissent finds its source in the Beat Generation. Ed Sanders suggests just that when he says, "Whenever I hear a kid say 'how come the fifties and sixties had to end' I feel like laughing. Those kids don't realize that they can think and say what they want because of us. They are us."

2. See Gerald Nicosia's *Memory Babe* and Barry Gifford and Lawrence Lee's *Jack's Book*.

3. See Burroughs's *The Job*, Bruce Cook's *Beat Generation*, and Barry Miles's *Ginsberg* and *Burroughs*, all of which claim that there was no unifying beat vision.

4. For examples of the Beat as noncomformist see Ann Charters's introduction to *On the Road*. Also see Cook's *Beat Generation;* John Tytell's *Naked Angels: The Lives and Literature of the Beat Generation;* and various essays in Lee

Bartlett's *The Beats: Essays in Criticism* (Bartlett, Cook, Tytell). A spate of new books on Kerouac continue this view of the Beats into the new millennium: Ellis Amburn's *Subterranean Kerouac*, Paul Marion's introduction to Kerouac's early writings, *Atop the Underwood*, and the *Rolling Stone Book of the Beats*, all published in 1999.

5. See Darby's *Necessary Fictions* for an excellent survey of 1950s bestsellers and what they suggest about the complexities of the reading public during the Red Scare.

6. Both C. Wright Mills and Ernesto Galarza wrote early critiques of the naïveté they saw in placing faith in a self-regulating pluralism. In Mills's 1956 critique, *The Power Elite*, he contends that political scientists and politicians have an outdated faith in plurality and checks and balances. Ernesto Galarza's critique of the theory of "countervailing forces" *(Merchants of Labor)*, which Galbraith developed in American Capitalism, focuses on the failure of labor to wage effective, organized opposition to agribusiness.

7. John Wayne's movie *Big Jim McLain* (Ludwig) has him portraying a heroic HUAC agent who finds communist sympathizers and anti-American union organizers. See also *Invasion of the Body Snatchers* (Siegel), *On the Waterfront* (Kazan), and *Invaders From Mars* (Menzies).

8. Galbraith endorsed reform as a prerequisite to advances in production, rather than the method of using increased production as an artificial cure for inequality: "Reform is not something that can be made to wait on productive advance. It may be a prerequisite to such advance. In the advanced country, in contrast, increased production is an alternative to redistribution. And, as indicated, it has been the great solvent of the tensions associated with inequality. Even though the latter persists, the awkward conflict which its correction implies can be avoided. How much better to concentrate on increasing output, a program on which both rich and poor can agree, since it benefits both" (96).

9. In 1948 control of the Bracero Program was given to the U.S. Secretary of Labor. Critics charge that collusion between the growers and the Secretary resulted in further lowering of the wage scale with the importation of large numbers of "illegals" during harvest time. A common practice of deporting the workers shortly after the harvest kept wages in the growers' pockets. Powerful grower's interest groups formed to keep the profitable system from being reformed. Groups like the Imperial Valley Farmers Association and the San Joaquin Farm Production Association convinced the government that they could not abide by the stipulations of the bracero agreement, claiming that it "favored" the braceros' interests above theirs. By 1951 the Mexican government had tired of the widespread exploitation of the braceros and insisted that the U.S. government take tighter control over the growers and supervise recruitment directly. The United States responded with the institution of Public Law 78, which gave the Secretary of Labor the right to recruit Mexican workers and "illegals" who had lived in the United States for at least five years and to set

their wage levels unilaterally. This increased the migratory flow from Mexico, thus enlarging the labor pool, eroding wages even further, and giving growers even more power to hire workers on their own terms, while stripping Mexico of its remaining power to regulate the flow of labor from its own workforce. The passing of the McCarran-Walter Act of 1952 made the importation or harboring of "illegal" aliens a federal crime, but did not make it a crime to hire an "illegal alien." This became known as the "Texas Proviso" and made the undocumented worker even more powerless, while giving the growers de facto authorization to hire and import as many undocumented workers as they needed to harvest crops cheaply. This undermined the position of the hapless braceros even further, giving them no legal recourse. For further reading see: Rodolfo Acuna's *Occupied America*, Henry Anderson's *The Bracero Program in California*, James D. Cockcroft's *Outlaws in the Promised Land*, Richard Craig's *The Bracero Program*, Ernesto Galarza's *Merchants of Labor*, George Kiser's *The Bracero Program*, and Stephen Sosnick's *Hired Hands*.

10. Isaiah Berlin's *Four Essays on Liberty* presents an excellent consideration and development of the interrelatedness of positive and negative liberty in democratic theory. See John Gray's *Liberalisms*, for an in-depth explication of Berlin's distinctions and use of his concepts in a critique of "presumptivist" tendencies in modern liberal political theory. Gray points to the inherent but hidden conflicts in liberal thought that create the illusion of an unbroken liberal-democratic geneology, which obscures the very different constructs of state, citizen, and rights: "The liberal theories all falter around the issue of conflict between competing and sometimes incommensurable liberties and human goods" (261). Gray objects to "liberalism" as dogma and its more "naturalistic" and "inevitable" interpretation, which covers up the very real contingency of plural and multiple subject positions, the need to negotiate, and the reality that some conflicts are insoluble.

11. The concepts of "positive" and "negative" liberty need further definition. Political historian Anthony H. Birch describes it as a necessary opposition between protecting the rights of the individual from interference, and asserting the right of every individual to expect and receive the full benefits of social association. But this somewhat facile opposition requires further explication. Consider the conflict between a Rousseauean concern with the *civitas* and a Lockean championing of the rights of the individual and property ownership.

In the making the case for unlimited private property, Locke conceives of society as a mutual pact of noninterference that is upheld and facilitated through government. In the Lockean formulation, isolation and society are thus not mutually exclusive, but actually provide for the maintenance of isolation and noninterference. The classic opposing view is Rousseau's notion of civic virtue, which relies on two political wills. Groups and individuals are "conscious of their own individual or group interests, leading to a set of 'particular wills' to promote measures favourable to those interests. On the other hand, they could, in the right conditions, be led to think in terms of the interests of the community as a whole, leading to a 'real will' to promote measures that would protect these shared interests" (Birch 57).

Lockean and Rousseaun democratic theory differ in the degree of emphasis put upon the nature of the individual's rights to self-determination, as well as the nature of society and, by extension, the role of government. A central question, still embedded in modern democratic debate is whether the state's first priority is to protect the individual from individual, or whether it is to be proactive in creating a "common good."

12. Essentially negative and positive liberty differ ontologically: "In the lower, more literal, sense liberty is taken to mean simply the absence of restraint (the negative concept). In the higher sense, which is metaphorical but yet deeply meaningful, liberty means an individual accepts his or her real will, as a rational being, to make the best of him- or herself. In an ideal state, the conditions of self-realization would be established through political institutions, so that citizens would be free, in this higher sense, when they conformed to the requirements of society expressed through these institutions" (Birch 104).

Public and discursive debates over the balance of positive and negative liberty in a given democratic state are never settled. Rather, it is central to the nature of democracy that this tension never be "solved," but that it be held in constant abeyance, as an unreachable horizon. The act of negotiation and debate keeps it so. However, it is my contention that emphasizing the necessity of one type of liberty over another produces very different views of what "society" should be while making the failure of other models a foregone conclusion.

13. See Todd Gitlin's *Years of Hope, Days of Rage,* and George and Starr's essay "Beat Politics: New Left and Hippie Beginning in the Postwar Counterculture."

14. For a good example of the general assessment of Beat literature see Frederick R. Karl's *American Fictions: 1940–1980* (198–214). In this "comprehensive history and critical evaluation," Karl, in titling the section "Beats and Burroughs" also makes a distinction between John Clellon Holmes, Jack Kerouac (whom he claims never found his "voice"), and the superior work of Burroughs. See also Jennie Skerl's *William S. Burroughs: At the Front* for a useful collection of critical responses on Burroughs's work between 1950 and 1989.

15. See Horsman, Montejano, and De Leon. For an interesting example of this attitude in nineteenth century fiction, William Dean Howells's *The Rise of Silas Lapham* presents a conclusion in which the move south into Mexico becomes redemptive and is manifested as an expansion of new markets. A stagnant capitalism is reinvigorated through the marriage between old and new money, which unites in its foray into Mexico (feminized in the person of Lapham's daughter). At novel's end the "virgin" territory south of the border will become the new breeding ground for American capitalism.

16. Horsman describes the nineteenth-century views of Mexico and how the necessity of annexing its lands was justified in racial terms: "The whole of Latin America, like Mexico, was viewed as an area that had been ruined by racial mongrelization and by subsequent misrule. 'The law of progress—of national growth, of very necessity—that has carried us to the Gulf of Mexico and to the Pacific Ocean, will continue to impel us onward,' wrote Northerner John Van Evrie in his defense of slavery in 1853, 'and to restore the rapidly perishing civilization of the great tropical center of the continent'" (280).

17. The last item announced by President Truman in his inaugural address of January 1949, "Point Four," was to be implemented as an integral part of U.S. foreign policy aimed at containing Communism in the third world. It offered technical and industrial aid to underdeveloped nations in Latin America, Asia, and Africa.

18. The nineteenth-century ideas about a new form of imperialism in the South that would deal more with capitalistic market conquest rather than martial conquest are seen in the 1950s faith in expansion and overproduction and are echoed in the work of Whyte and most notably, Riesman. Horsman writes, "A traditional colonial empire had been rejected, but it was believed that the expansion of a federal system might ultimately prove possible as American Anglo-Saxons outbred, overwhelmed, and replaced 'inferior' races. This time was to be hastened by commercial penetration of the most distant regions of the earth. The commercial endeavors of a superior people were confidently expected to transform the world while bringing unprecedented power and prosperity to the U.S." (297). Stressing a new form of imperialism, the parallels to the prophets of overproduction in the 1950s are uncanny, as Galbraith records in *The Affluent Society.*

19. I quote most often from the original letters written to Ginsberg and collected by Oliver Harris. The letters edited by Ferlinghetti were "cleaned-up" for publication, omitting several passages which the publisher must have felt were racist or offensive. For example, Ferlinghetti strikes the frequent use of the word "nigger," substituting "Nigra" or omitting the references altogether.

20. See Ginsberg's interview with William F. Buckley, Jr., recorded on *Firing Line* in 1968 (published in *Spontaneous Mind: Selected Interviews, 1958–1996*). Ginsberg articulates his positions (the Hippie New Order, as Buckley calls it) on the legalization of drugs, ending the Vietnam War, censorship, and racism.

21. Although my discussion of Ginsberg focuses on his early writing and youthful travels, a trajectory of his thought can be seen in two excellent collections: see *Deliberate Prose: Selected Essays, 1952–94* and *Spontaneous Mind: Selected Interviews, 1958–1996*. These essays and interviews provide insight into Ginsberg's political activities during the 1960s and 70s.

22. Ginsberg's affair with Boucher was one of several attempts to live as a heterosexual. See Miles, *Ginsberg: A Biography,* 151, 171–75.

23. For more on Ginsberg's struggles with mental health as well as his eventual coming to terms with his homosexuality, see Miles's *Ginsberg*. In it he describes the actual cost of transgression: "First time I let my imagination and desire dominate over what, in the mental hospital, I had been taught to accept as an adjustment to reality, to limit my demands of the external world to what could be workable so as to avoid excess suffering" (153).

## 2. "With Imperious Eye"

1. See Tim Hunt's *Kerouac's Crooked Road: The Development of a Fiction*.

2. See Karal Ann Marling's *As Seen On TV: The Visual Culture of Everyday Life in the 1950s* for an in-depth discussion of the force of television on defining a mass culture that transformed American culture into a society of "watchers." Marling makes the case that the Western genre suggested a nation obsessed with returning to a reified agrarian/frontier past in an increasingly suburban landscape.

3. See Jane Tompkins's *West of Everything* for an in-depth analysis of the western genre. She argues that the western acts as a counternarrative to the sentimental novels of the nineteenth century and the cult of domesticity that had grown in power and influence. The western rejects progressivism, Christianity, and temperance by creating an ideal space free from such "feminine" influences. The west functions as a masculine region in which ethical questions are reduced to the fight against death. Tompkins points out, however, that the western generally elides the forces of conquest and exploitation on which its action is predicated. My claim is similar, in that in escaping suburbanization and the conformity of postwar society, the Beats create an idealized west (which includes Mexico).

4. The idea of the frontier was so prevalent that it soon appeared in the rhetoric used by those in the highest political offices. John F. Kennedy made it the main theme of his inaugural address: "We stand today on the edge of a New Frontier—the frontier of the 1960s—a frontier of unknown opportunities and perils—a frontier of unfulfilled hopes and threats" (Farber 26).

5. See Robert Fishman's *Bourgeois Utopias: Rise and Fall of Suburbia*, John Stillgoe's *Borderlands: Origin of the American Suburb*, David Thorns's *Suburbia*, Barbara M. Kelly's *Suburbia Re-Examined*, all which deal with the effect on the family unit and male/female identity. Kelly argues that the rise in white family stability caused a crisis in masculine identification, hence the need to portray the white male exerting control in the work place, the home, and the "frontier" despite the frontier's disappearance at the close of the nineteenth century.

6. Marling's *As Seen on TV* provides a fascinating study of the phenomenon of Disneyland in the 1950s and what she suggests was the manifestation of a national desire for the suburban family to escape the settled familiarity of the suburbs into a space that promised adventure and danger, a colonized space

that provided the illusion of stepping into the wild, as depicted in the work of the Beats. The emphasis on covert marketing of Disneyland's "Main Street U.S.A.," with its promise of colonized adventure in Adventureland, the connection of technological greatness seen in Tomorrowland to the glorious past of Frontierland (along with the smash hit, Disney's *Davy Crockett,* as seen weekly on NBC), celebrates the conflation of capital, adventure, and progress in America's past, present, and future.

7. See Nancy F. Cott's *Women in the Labor Movement.*

8. This is not to suggest by any means that the counterculture phenomenon of the 1960s was in anyway monolithic or progressive. I wish to suggest that Kerouac's fears and the conflict and paradox of his political/apolitical positions, far from being "solved" through the 1960s counterculture in some concrete communal agenda (as Kerouac feared), was fraught with the same indecision, tension, and paradoxical positions as Kerouac's work. Furthermore, I suggest that Kerouac's movement (and I wish to call this term into constant question) as documented in his extraordinarily honest and perceptive "fictive" chronicles is more than creative autobiography: it is a documentation of the transmutation of American romantic imperialism into a neoromanticism that flourished in the 1950s primarily in the work of the Beats, and which inspired and informed the movement culture of the 1960s and transferred incompatible ideological and political impulses that would render the progressive advances gained during that period short-lived and largely ineffectual, as seen in the relentless conservative fever which has dictated American politics in the decades following. Kerouac's legendary memoirs provide a journalism of sorts, which dramatizes some of the reasons for the failures of left, perhaps because it did not recognize the resonance of its ideology in earlier imperialistic and subjective American modes.

9. Whyte provides an excellent example of the climate of mistrust in suburbia and its encroaching nature as a deindividualizing community that imprisons the male character's need to move, supplanting it with a sort of illusory "roots": "In suburbia . . . organization man is trying, quite consciously, to develop a new kind of roots to replace what he left behind, and to understand the nature of his quest we need to know what it is he did leave behind, why he left it behind, and how he looks back upon it" (268). Whyte suggests that the rootlessness of the organization man is not the kind of movement that the individual thrives upon; it is an artificial, forced movement that makes him a nowhere man, and thus malleable. The suburbia that he lives in is not a real community but an artificial one—dangerous, conservative, illusory in its unity and supposed classlessness. While the critique is valid, it nonetheless exhibits the same fear of encroachment and a feminizing, absorbing suburb because it has replaced a more masculine, exploration-based movement.

10. A letter written to Neal Cassady regarding his impending trip west, gives an enlightening catalog of Kerouac's reading and how it would be reflected in his work of a Whitmanian literary mapping of the United States:

"My own development in the directions above . . . center around a new interest in things rather than in ideas. For instance, all my reading in the past few months has been of a very practical nature. Here's a list: Parkman's *Oregon Trail,* another book concerned with that trail and also every other important trail in the country . . . , a history of the U.S., a biography of Washington, a history of the Revolutionary War, and last but not least I have begun a huge study of the face America itself, acquiring maps of every state in the U.S.A. . . . My subject as a writer is of course America, and simply, I must know all about it" (*Selected Letters: 1940–56,* 107).

11. This section of the novel is based on Kerouac's real life affair with Bea Franco and the events are closely substantiated by the letters written during that period.

12. See Ann Charters's biography, *Kerouac.*

13. See also Joyce Johnson's *Minor Characters: A Young Woman's Coming-of-Age in the Beat Orbit of Jack Kerouac.*

14. See Ellis Amburn's *Subterranean Kerouac.*

15. Kerouac's religious dilemma, as demonstrated in an earlier novel, *Desolation Angels,* and seen throughout his later life, is constructed as an opposition between an activist Catholicism and a passivist Buddhism. However, the passive indifference of Christianity at the end of *Big Sur* suggests the end of Kerouac's hope to merge Bhuddist indifference with Christian activism and participation. Here, Christianity takes on the role of the visual, of passivity, of illusion—giving way to viewing the here and now through the Buddhist tenet of "samsara" (that is the present life which is counted as "reality" but is only illusion): "the x-mystery mark on the surface of Nirvana" (*Desolation Angels* 238).

The tension most clearly manifests itself in competing religious systems which Kerouac attempts to reconcile: Buddhist indifference and Catholic activism, his call for being the void vs. his participation in the lives of his "desolation angels," his desire to isolate himself in the mountain/fellaheen Mexico and to go into the City, shaping culture through his work.

16. See Tom Wolfe's *The Electric Kool Aid Acid Test.* See also Babbs's *On the Bus.*

17. Nicosia writes that Kerouac "must have felt some enmity to find Kesey becoming the anode for a new generation" and that he felt Kesey was "nuts" and "too wild." For his part, Kesey had been inspired to leave Oregon after reading *On the Road* (653).

## 3. Civitas and Its Discontents

1. See Terry Anderson's *The Movement and the Sixties,* and Gitlin's *The Sixties: Years of Hope, Days of Rage.*

2. On February 1, 1960, Ezell Blair Jr., Franklin McCain, Joseph McNeil, and David Richmond sat at Woolworth's "whites only" lunch counter. By the end of 1960, over seventy thousand people throughout the North and South

had participated in sit-ins. See Farber's *The Age of Great Dreams: America in the 1960s* for an account of these protests.

3. See Stewart Burns's *Social Movements of the 1960s* and Stanley Aronowitz's *The Death and Rebirth of American Radicalism.*

4. See Victor Turner's *Rites of Passage* and Clifford Geertz's *The Anthropology of Experience.*

5. Sacvan Bercovitch suggests that transcendental dissent ultimately was incorporated within the larger culture, a more pessimistic appraisal of the liminal process that Turner describes as part of the "social drama." For Turner, the "fall" of a *communitas* (dissenters) into mainstream society revitalizes the social structure, whereas Bercovitch sees such a "fall" as a cooptation that preserves the status quo.

6. See David Harris's *Dreams Die Hard: Three Men's Journeys through the 1960s.*

7. Both Herbert Marcuse's *One Dimensional Man* and C. Wright Mills's *The Power Elite* dealt with systemic forms of indirect persuasion, or interpellation. An earlier example of a sociological study of the power of organization to "channel" individuals to where they were most needed in the corporate structure can be found in William Whyte's *Organization Man.* See the chapter on "How to Beat a Standardized Test."

8. See Schneier's *Shared Dreams: Martin Luther King, Jr. and the Jewish Community;* Salzman's *Bridges and Boundaries: African Americans and American Jews;* Bauman's *The Quiet Voices: Southern Rabbis and Black Civil Rights, 1880s to 1990s;* and Schultz's *Going South: Jewish Women in the Civil Rights Movement* for accounts of Jewish participation in the civil rights movement.

9. See Acosta's *Autobiography of a Brown Buffalo* and the trial scene in Mexico, where Acosta's own liminal experiment fails when he finds that he is not free to return to the privilege of being an "American."

10. See Turner's "Dewey, Dilthey, and the Social Drama," in *The Anthropology of Experience and the Ritual Process.*

11. See *Fear and Loathing in America: Gonzo Papers, Volume II* for a selection of letters in which Thompson writes enthusiastically about the potential of the "freak power vote," his organization of the "Elko Conference" (a democratic strategy workshop), and his consideration of running for the U.S. Senate seat.

12. His platform for the sheriff's election defines many of Thompson's most important political principles:

    a. Sod the streets at once. Rip-up all city streets with jackhammers and use the junk asphalt to create a huge parking and auto storage lot on the outskirts of town.

    b. Change the name "Aspen" by public referendum to "Fat City." This would prevent greedheads, land-rapers and other human jackals from capitalizing on the name "Aspen." . . . What effect the name-change might have on those who came here to buy low, sell high and then move on is fairly obvious . . . and eminently desirable. These swine should be fucked, broken and driven across the land.

c. Drug Sales must be controlled . . . to punish dishonest dope dealers in a proper public fashion. . . . Non-profit sales will be viewed as borderline cases, and judged on their merits. But all sales for money-profit will be punished severely.

d. Hunting and fishing will be forbidden to all non-residents.

e. The Sheriff and his Deputies should never be armed in public. Every urban riot, shoot-out and blood-bath (involving guns) has been set off by some trigger-happy cop in a fear frenzy.

f. It will be the policy of the Sheriff's office savagely to harass all those engaged in any form of land-rape. (*The Great Shark Hunt* 173–75)

13. See Walter Benjamin's "The Work of Art in the Age of Mechanical Reproduction" in *Illuminations*. See also Herbert Marcuse's "Some Social Implications of Modern Technology" in *The Essential Frankfurt School Reader*.

14. See Alan Trachtenberg's *The Incorporation of America*.

15. In its strictest sense, carnival functions purely to defuse social tension in the guise of radical change. The drug-induced perceptions, the fits of violence, as well as the dangerous pushing of the envelope of control all reflect the gonzo journalist's need to maintain a position "outside" the social structure. See M. M. Bakhtin and Frederick Turner in *The Anthropology of Experience*.

16. The failure of the New Left to form a lasting communal movement is taken up by Stewart Burns: "But in the fluid situation that resulted—more favorable than they imagined—they were not prepared to offer a new public philosophy, new programmatic solutions, and a new social charter to replace the old discredited ones, all of which could have percolated upward from the grass roots. Instead, the political and ideological power vacuum was soon appropriated from top to bottom by the New Right and neoconservatives, who had been methodically gaining round since Goldwater's big defeat in 1964. The conservatives rose to power partly by relentless repudiation of the New Left, the black movement, and feminism. The conclusion to draw, however, is not that these movements' alleged "excess of democracy" seeded the right-wing ascendance of the 1980s, but that they failed to provide a coherent alternative to it when the terrain was still contested" (177).

17. See also Thompson's *Hell's Angels: The Strange and Terrible Saga of the Outlaw Motorcycle Gangs*.

18. See Thompson's *Generation of Swine: The Great Shark Hunt*, and *Better Than Sex: Confessions of a Political Junkie*.

## 4. Historian with a Sour Stomach

1. Penalosa pronounces that "existentially there is no Mexican-American community as such, nor is there such a 'thing' as Mexican-American culture"

in "The Changing Mexican American in Southern California," an essay first published in 1967 and later in *Chicano: The Beginnings of Bronze Power* (Rosaldo, Seligman, and Calvert 15). Penalosa gives an assimilationist analysis of what he interprets as an historically stereotyped characterization of Mexican American culture by social scientists as agrarian and migrant: "The type of characterization which is most unsatisfactory revolves about concepts of the Mexican American population as largely engaged in migratory agricultural labor" (18). Therefore, what begins ostensibly as an attack on the predilection of social scientists to characterize Mexican American culture as monolithic, becomes a way of differentiating the middle-class Mexican American from the lower-class "barrio Mexican." That critique aside, the essay also expresses an anxiety stemming from the fear of being relegated to the narrow confines of the barrio or the picking fields.

Penalosa seeks to displace the cultural icon of the migrant worker with the acculturated Mexican American who successfully "moves away from traditional Mexican values and toward the Anglo-American values of achievement, activity, efficiency, and emphasis on the future" (20). Such an overt assimilationist position is disturbing, but understandably conflicted. Penalosa feels the need to create a dichotomy between a Mexican American culture that is depicted as primitive and regressive, and the "Anglo-American" culture that defines success. In many ways this describes the most repressive side of the Mexican-American generation's accomodationist mode. However, there is also in his essay an implicit awareness that to identify solely with the migrant and barrio iconography is too limiting a position, and is in some ways an act of complicity with Anglo-American repression by accepting narrow, limiting roles. For Penalosa, the barrio or *colonia* should not be the last stop for the Mexican American.

Penalosa's interpretation of "moving" away from the crippling enclave of the "barrio" toward an "inclusion" within the "mainstream" ignores the role of individualism in the oppression not only of migrants, but also of barrio dwellers. He purposely overlooks any potential subversive or cohesive power created through the experience of forced migratory movement. For Penalosa movement is limited either to an assimilationist "mobility" that "promotes occupational and geographical mobility" resulting in "rigid caste barriers against intermarriage and equality of employment and housing opportunities" (19), or to the shiftless, rootlessness as personified in the migrant and borne out, ironically, in the lower-class barrio dweller. For him, a communal *movimiento* is not possible; only an individual can "move" away from the "crippling enclave" of the barrio. The possibility of an inclusive, communalist, but fully participatory Americano identity does not occur to him.

2. See David Gutierrez's *Walls and Mirrors: Mexican Americans, Mexican Immigrants, and the Politics of Ethnicity.*

3. In fact, Mazon argues that the exact opposite response occurred. Anglo-Americans made the outsider status of Mexican Americans central to a "ritual of annihilation" aimed at destroying the "enemy within."

4. Arnoldo De Leon's study suggests that in the movement west, Southern colonialists carried over their racial views of blacks, so that Mexicanos in the conquered lands, in the eyes of Southerners, were in fact colored. His work points to several instances of the conflation of all ethnicity, particularly Mexican and African American, as Negro.

5. Just how much of an inspirational role Acosta played is evident in the correspondence the two exchanged in the aftermath of the publishing of *Fear and Loathing*. Acosta claimed a good deal more credit than Hunter Thompson was willing to grant, although in other correspondence Thompson acknowledges Acosta's central role in the events depicted. See Thompson's *Fear and Loathing in America*.

6. Acosta's work is cognizant of a nostalgia (common in the Beat narrative) that John Gray has defined as presumptivist liberalism. Gray's definition of presumptivism critiques a political essentialism that limits the effectiveness of liberalism by relying on closed teleologies and a static version of the "citizen-subject." See John Gray's *Liberalisms*.

7. For a legal assessment of Acosta's legal strategies, see Michael A. Olivas's study, "'Breaking the Law' On Principle: An Essay on Lawyer's Dilemmas, Unpopular Causes, and Legal Remedies."

8. See Anthony Birch's *The Concepts and Theories of Modern Democracy* for a discussion on the limitations of decisionism. See also C. Wright Mills's *The Power Elite* as a critique of "soft" pluralism.

9. See Victor Turner's "Dewey, Dilthey, and the Social Drama" in Bruner and Turner's *The Anthropology of Experience*.

10. Corky Gonzales had echoed the same mistrust in his resignation from the Democratic Party. See Hunter Thompson's *Fear and Loathing on the Campaign Trail* for a sharp critique of party politics, including McGovern's.

11. In his *Second Treatise of Government*, Locke writes, "He that conquers in an unjust war can thereby have no title to the subjection and obedience of the conquered. . . . Over those then that joined with him in the war, and over those of the subdued country that opposed him not, and the posterity even of those that did, the conqueror, even in a just war, hath, by his conquest, no right of dominion: they are free from any subjection to him, and if their former government be dissolved, they are at liberty to begin and erect another to themselves" (97).

## 5. Mapping *el Movimiento*

1. The Chicano Press Association (CPA) was an extensive "confederation of community newspapers" that included papers from all over the southwestern United States. Some of the more important ones: *La Raza,* Los Angeles, California; *El Malcriado,* Delano, California; *La Raza Nueva,* San Antonio, Texas; *Basta Ya!,* San Francisco, California; and *El Machete,* Los Angeles, California. However, Mexican Americans had a long history of publishing

community papers. More than five hundred newspapers were published by Mexican Americans in the Southwest prior to World War II, seriously dispelling the claim that Mexican American writing is a new (postwar) phenomenon.

2. See issues 3–9, 1970–72 of *La Raza* for a review of one of the liveliest debates in Chicano/Mexican American political history.

3. Segade's analysis of Marxist missteps is based on case history. He examines the politics of Chicanismo at San Diego State, 1970–74 and the attempt of the Marxist contingency to destroy Mexican American Studies. For a lengthy discussion on Chicanismo's rejection of liberalism, see Ignacio M. García's *Chicanismo: The Forging of a Militant Ethos among Mexican Americans.*

4. See Jose Limon's *American Encounters,* David Montejano's *Chicano Politics and Society and the Late Twentieth Century;* the third edition of Rodolfo Acuna's *Occupied America;* David Munoz's *Youth, Identity and Power: The Chicano Movement;* Juan Gomez-Quinones's *Mexican Students Por La Raza;* Armando Navarro's *Mexican American Youth Organization: Avant-Garde of the Chicano Movement in Texas;* and Ignacio M. Garcia's *United We Win: The Rise and Fall of La Raza Unida Party.*

5. See David Hollinger's *Postethnic America* for a discussion of how ethnic and class micropolitics have too quickly endorsed a postnational dismissal of the civic nation. He argues "that the value of civic nation-state in protecting rights and providing basic welfare is undervalued by proponents of postnationality" (14).

6. See "Noticias De La Pinta" in the November 1971 issue of *La Raza* on the fate of Alfonso Alvarez.

7. For an extensive debate on this issue see *Globalization on the Line: Culture, Capital, and Citizenship at U.S. Borders,* edited by Claudia Sadowski-Smith. See my article, "Telling the Difference Between the Border and the Borderlands."

8. For more on Mayan Humanism, see the videotaped interview, "Bettina Gray Speaks with Luis Valdez."

9. See Jose Limon's *Mexican Ballads, Chicano Poems.*

## 6. Arriving at *el Pueblo Libre*

1. See Jeffery Isaacs's "The Poverty of Progressivism," *Dissent* (fall 1996).

2. Immigration Reform and Control Act of 1986: see James Cockcroft's *Outlaws in the Promised Land: Mexican Immigration Workers and America's Future* and Frank Bean, Barry Edmonston, and Jeffrey S. Passel's edited volume, *Undocumented Migration to the United States: IRCA and the Experience of the 1980s.*

3. For the implications of Proposition 187, see the Tomás Rivera Center's *California School District Administrators Speak to Proposition 187: A TRC Survey.* For a discussion of the overall implications of anti-immigration legislation see

Nicolaus Mills's edited volume, *Arguing Immigration: The Debate over the Changing Face of America.*

4. See Charles Gallagher's article, "White Reconstruction in the University," in which he describes a renewed emphasis on reconstructing "whiteness" as an ethnicity based on a "persecutionist" model that dehistoricizes as it attempts to protect Anglo economic interests.

5. For a full discussion on the ramifications of Green Valley see Leo Chavez's *Shadowed Lives: Undocumented Immigrants in American Society.*

6. Perez-Torres cites an example of this sort of theoretical reduction of the migrant to a metaphor in Lisa Lowe's use of the migrant-function in her analysis of Peter Wang's film *A Great Wall:* "[Wang] performs a filmic 'migration' by shuttling between the various cultural spaces; we are left, by the end of the movie, with a sense of culture as dynamic and open, the result of a continual process of visiting and revisiting a plurality of cultural sites" (Perez-Torres 151).

7. The debate between multiculturalism and postmodern criticism in regards to the "end of the subject" is a longstanding one. See Kirstie McClure's "On the Subject of Rights: Pluralism, Plurality, and Political Identity" in Chantal Mouffe's *Dimensions of Radical Democracy.* See also Frederic Jameson's conclusion in *Postmodernism: The Logic of Late Capitalism.*

8. In *Mexican Ballads, Chicano Poems* Jose Limon describes a two-pronged effort to subjectify the migrant: "As the Anglo-American capitalists reorganized the economic life of the border Mexican and imposed a new political order, they also began the systematic effort (almost completed) to culturally assimilate this population even while maintaining it as socially subordinate. This new cultural reeducation entailed a two-front strategy and a host of weapons. First, it was necessary to delegitimize native culture. . . . These efforts included the institutional purveyance of denigrating stereotypes; the disciplined expulsion of Spanish from public life . . . most effective of all, the socially produced construction of 'Mexican' as synonymous with 'poor' and the socially ostracized" (33).

See also David Montejano's *Anglos and Mexicans in the Making of Texas,* James D. Cockcroft's *Outlaws in the Promised Land: Mexican Immigration Workers and America's Future,* and Mario Barrera's *Race and Class in the Southwest: A Theory of Racial Inequality.* .

9. I am of course playing off of Frederic Jameson's "strategies of containment," but I use "immobilization" because, although the end effect is similar to Jameson's containment theory, I am most interested in ways in which the migrant is kept from moving, while paradoxically being forced to move, thus creating movement without mobility. In this sense, Jameson, Althusser, Foucault, Marx, Marcuse, Lukacs, Adorno, and Gramsci all deal with the subject of false consciousness, the victim of ideology, and so on. What the migrant discovers in exposing these strategies of immobilization are the material and thus practical ends that such false consciousness works toward.

10. See Renato Rosaldo's *Culture and Truth,* Gloria Anzaldua's *Borderlands,* Rafael Perez-Torres's *Movements in Chicano Poetry,* Hector Calderon and Jose David Saldivar's *Criticism on the Borderlands: Studies in Chicano Literature, Culture, and Ideology.*

11. See Balderrama and Rodriguez's *Decade of Betrayal: Mexican Repatriation in the 1930s* for an in-depth analysis not only on the individuals who fell victims to the repatriation drives, but also to the damage inflicted on Mexico's fragile social and agrarian reforms then being instituted by President Lazaro Cardenas. See also Rodolfo Acuna's *Occupied America: A History of Chicanos.* James Cockcroft's work also contextualizes the cycle of importation and deportation within the scope of the international labor market. Juan Garcia's *Operation Wetback: The Mass Deportation of Mexican Undocumented Workers in 1954* investigates the economic and political motivations behind the deportation of Mexican and American citizen during the 1950s. See also Douglas Massey's *Return to Aztlan: The Social Process of International Migration from Western Mexico.*

12. In *Youth, Identity, Power: The Chicano Movement,* Carlos Munoz says that "the origins of student activism among youth of Mexican descent in the United States, however, can be traced to 1929 when Ernesto Galarza, then a 24-year old first year graduate student in history at Stanford University, spoke out in defense of Mexican immigrant workers" (21).

13. Renato Rosaldo's concept of "invisibility" is most useful here. It is Rosaldo who has theorized that the culturally dominant is naturalized through making invisibile its own existence. See Rosaldo's *Culture and Truth: The Remaking of Social Analysis.*

14. Mexicans especially lost power both politically and economically in Texas during the 1930s. "From a broad historical view, the agrarian development of this period can be seen as the last in a series that eroded the centuries old class structure of the Mexican ranch settlements. By 1920 the Texas Mexican people had generally been reduced . . . to the status of landless and dependent wage laborers" (Montejano, *Anglos and Mexican's in the Making of Texas* 114). The move of midwestern farmers to the Texas valley and Winter Garden area gave rise to the need for a large migrant force that would not be able to leave the state: "It was sufficiently bothersome to move the farmer to devise ways that would immobilize the Mexican worker" (Montejano 178). Various methods were devised: school segregation; underfunding those schools that, rare as they were, served the migrant community; and "dissuading" workers from unionizing. The feeling was that this was more effective than modernizing. However, in a market economy, the labor force moves to the area of highest wages, so the Texas farmer had to think of more direct ways of immobilizing the migrant worker. Counties enacted antivagrancy laws, attached cars, used local law enforcement to prevent migrants from going north to search for higher wages in the Midwest. Debt was also used, most prominently through

the company store method. Pass systems were devised, as well as licensing and taxes, which prevented the migrant from traveling. The Emigrant Labor Agency Laws were directly aimed at restricting recruitment of Mexicans by out of state recruiters. See Montejano, *Anglos and Mexican's in the Making of Texas.*

15. See Pierrette Hondagneu-Sotelo's *Gendered Transitions: Mexican Experiences of Immigration* in which she finds that the migrant desires above all a home and a communal setting. Francisco Balderrama and Raymond Rodriguez's research shows that the importance of family and the networks created all through North America are signs of migrant emphasis on familial and communal spirit: "Alvarez's research and analysis during an extended period of time revealed the power and vigor of the family. Rather than diminishing in scope, the family actually grew in stature and strength. Family solidarity increased and experienced a new maturation. This occurred rather naturally because, in order to survive, members had to depend upon one another. The concept of rugged individualism, so revered in American literature, was the antithesis of the Mexican experience. In Mexican society, who and what a person is determined by family status and affiliations" (31).

# Works Cited

Acosta, Oscar. *Autobiography of a Brown Buffalo.* New York: Vintage, 1972.
———. *Oscar "Zeta" Acosta: The Uncollected Works.* Edited by Ilan Stavans. Houston: Arte Publico Press, 1996.
———. *The Revolt of the Cockroach People.* New York: Vintage, 1973.
Acuna, Rodolfo. *Occupied America.* 2d ed. New York: Harper, 1981.
Alarcon, Norma, et al., eds. *Chicana Critical Issues: Mujeres Activas en Letras y Cambio Social.* Berkeley: University of California Press, 1993.
Allen, Steve. *The Ground Is Our Table.* New York: Doubleday, 1966.
Althusser, Louis. *Lenin and Philosophy.* Translated by Ben Brewster. New York: Monthly Review Press, 1969.
Amburn, Ellis. *Subterranean Kerouac: The Hidden Life of Jack Kerouac.* New York: St. Martin's Griffin, 1999.
Anaya, Rudolfo. *Bless Me, Ultima.* Berkeley: TQS Publications, 1972.
Anctil, Pierre, et al., eds. *Un Homme Grand: Jack Kerouac at the Crossroads of Many Cultures.* Ottawa: Carleton University Press, 1990.
Anderson, Henry. *The Bracero Program in California.* New York: Arno Press, 1976.
Anderson, Terry. *The Movement and the Sixties: Protest in America from Greensboro to Wounded Knee.* New York: Oxford University Press, 1995.
Anzaldua, Gloria. *Borderlands/La Frontera: The New Mestiza.* San Francisco: Aunt Lute Books, 1987.
Arato, Andrew, and Eike Gebhardt, eds. *The Essential Frankfurt School Reader.* New York: Continuum, 1995.
Aronowitz, Stanley. *The Death and Rebirth of American Radicalism.* London: Routledge, 1996.
Babbs, Ken, and Paul Perry. *On the Bus: The Complete Guide to the Legendary*

*Trip of Ken Kesey and the Merry Pranksters and the Birth of the Counterculture.* New York: Thunder's Mouth Press, 1996.

Baker, Houston. *Blues, Ideology and Afro-American Literature.* Chicago: University of Chicago Press, 1984.

Bakhtin, Mikhail M. *The Dialogic Imagination.* Austin: University of Texas Press, 1981.

Balderrama, Francisco E., and Raymond Rodrigues. *Decade of Betrayal: Mexican Repatriation in the 1930s.* Albuquerque: University of New Mexico Press, 1995.

Barrera, Mario. *Race and Class in the Southwest: A Theory of Racial Inequality.* Notre Dame, Ind.: University of Notre Dame Press, 1979.

Bartlett, Lee, ed. *The Beats: Essays in Criticism.* London: McFarland, 1981.

Bauman, Mark K., and Berkley Kalin, eds. *The Quiet Voices: Southern Rabbis and Black Civil Rights, 1880s to 1990s.* Tuscaloosa: University of Alabama Press, 1997.

Bean, Frank, Barry Edmonston, and Jeffrey S. Passel, eds. *Undocumented Migration to the United States: IRCA and the Experience of the 1980s.* Washington, D.C.: Urban Institute Press, 1990.

Benjamin, Walter. *Illuminations.* Translated by Harry Zohn. Edited by Hannah Arendt. New York: Schocken Books, 1973.

Bercovitch, Sacvan. *The Rites of Assent: Transformations in the Symbolic Construction of America.* London: Routeledge, 1993.

Berlin, Isaiah. *Four Essays on Liberty.* New York: Oxford University Press, 1970.

Birch, Anthony H. *The Concepts and Theories of Modern Democracy.* London: Routledge, 1993.

Bixler-Marquez, Dennis J., et al., eds. *Chicano Studies: Survey and Analysis.* Revised ed. Dubuque, Iowa: Kendall/Hunt Publishing, 1999.

Broyles-González, Yolanda. *El Teatro Campesino: Theater in the Chicano Movement.* Austin: University of Texas Press, 1994.

Bruce-Novoa, Juan. *Chicano Authors: Inquiry by Interview.* Austin: University of Texas Press, 1980.

———. *Chicano Poetry: A Response to Chaos.* Austin: University of Texas Press, 1982.

———. "Fear and Loathing on the Buffalo Trail." *Melus* 6, 4 (1979): 39–50.

Burns, Stewart. *Social Movements of the 1960s: Searching for Democracy.* Boston: Twayne's Publishers, 1990.

Burroughs, William S. *The Adding Machine.* New York: Seaver Books, 1985.

———. *Interzone.* New York: Penguin, 1989.

———. *Junky.* New York: Penguin, 1977.

———. *Letters of William S. Burroughs.* Edited by Oliver Harris. New York: Penguin, 1994.

———. *Naked Lunch.* New York: Grove Weidenfeld, 1992.

————. *Nova Express.* New York: Grove Press, 1992.

————. *The Place of Dead Roads.* New York: Henry Holt, 1983.

————. *The Soft Machine.* Revised ed. London: Calder, 1968.

————. *The Soft Machine.* New York: Grove Press, 1992.

————. *The Ticket That Exploded.* New York: Grove Press, 1992.

Burroughs, William S., and Allen Ginsberg. *The Yage Letters.* San Francisco: City Lights Books, 1963.

Burroughs, William S., and Daniel Odier. *The Job.* New York: Grove Press, 1970.

Calderon, Hector, and Jose David Saldivar, eds. *Criticism on the Borderlands: Studies in Chicano Literature, Culture, and Ideology.* Durham: Duke University Press, 1991.

Camarillo, Albert. *Chicanos in a Changing Society.* Cambridge: Harvard University Press, 1979.

Campa, Arthur. *Spanish Folk-Poetry in New Mexico.* Albuquerque: University of New Mexico Press, 1946.

Candelaria, Cordelia. *Chicano Poetry: A Critical Introduction.* Westport, Conn.: Greenwood Press, 1986.

Carranza, Elihu. *Chicanismo: Philosophical Fragments.* Dubuque, Iowa: Kendall/Hunt Pub. Co., 1978.

Carroll, E. Jean. *Hunter: The Strange and Savage Life of Hunter S. Thompson.* New York: Plume, 1993.

Cassady, Carolyn. *Off the Road: My Years with Cassady, Kerouac, and Ginsberg.* New York: Penguin, 1993.

Cassady, Neal. *Grace Beats Karma: Letters from Prison, 1958–1960.* New York: Blast Books, 1993.

Casteneda, Carlos. "The Rhythm of History." *Man* (February 1946).

Castro, Tony. *Chicano Power: The Emergence of Mexican America.* New York: Saturday Review Press, 1974.

Charters, Ann. *Kerouac: A Biography.* San Francisco: Straight Arrow Books, 1973.

Chavez, Cesar. "The Organizer's Tale." In *Chicano: The Beginnings of Bronze Power.* Edited by Renato Rosaldo, Gustav L. Seligman, and Robert A. Calvert, 57–63. New York: William Morrow, 1974.

Chavez, Leo. *Shadowed Lives: Undocumented Immigrants in American Society.* New York: Harcourt, Brace, Jovanovich College Publishers, 1992.

Clifford, James. *The Predicament of Culture: Twentieth-Century Ethnography, Literature, and Art.* Cambridge: Harvard University Press, 1988.

Cockcroft, James D. *Outlaws in the Promised Land: Mexican Immigration Workers and America's Future.* New York: Grove Press, 1986.

Coles, Robert. *The Migrant Farmer: A Psychiatric Study.* Atlanta: Southern Regional Council, 1965.

Cook, Bruce. *The Beat Generation.* New York: William Morrow, 1993.

Cott, Nancy F., ed. *Women in the Labor Movement.* Munich: New Providence, 1993.

Cowley, Malcolm. *Exile's Return.* New York: Viking, 1934.

Craig, Richard B. *The Bracero Program.* Austin: University of Texas Press, 1971.

Daniel, Cletus E. *Bitter Harvest: A History of the California Dream.* Ithaca: Cornell University Press, 1981.

Darby, William. *Necessary American Fictions: Popular Literature of the 1950s.* Bowling Green: Bowling Green University Press, 1987.

Davis, Mike. *Prisoners of the American Dream.* London: Verso, 1986.

De la Garza, Rodolfo O., Robert R. Brischetto, and Janet Weaver. *The Mexican American Electorate: an Explanation of Their Opinions and Behavior.* The Mexican American electorate series. Occasional paper, no. 4. San Antonio: Southwest Voter Registration Education Project; Hispanic Population Studies Program of the Center for Mexican American Studies University of Texas at Austin, 1984.

DeLeon, Arnoldo. *They Called Them Greasers: Anglo Attitudes toward Mexicans in Texas, 1821–1900.* Austin: University of Texas Press, 1983.

*El Grito.* 7 volumes. Berkeley: Quinto Sol Publications, 1967–1974.

Emerson, Ralph Waldo. *Essays and Lectures.* Edited by Joel Porte. New York: Library of America, 1983.

Estrada, Leobardo, et al. "Chicanos in the United States: A History of Exploitation and Resistance." In *Chicano Studies: Survey and Analysis.* Eds. Dennis J. Bixler-Marquez, et al, 3–21. Revised ed. Dubuque, Iowa: Kendall/Hunt Publishing, 1999.

Farber, David. *The Age of Great Dreams: America in the 1960s.* New York: Hill and Wang, 1993.

Ferlinghetti, Lawrence. *A Coney Island of the Mind.* New York: New Directions, 1958.

Fishman, Robert. *Bourgeois Utopias: Rise and Fall of Suburbia.* New York: Basic Books, 1987.

Fitzgerald, F. Scott. *Tender Is the Night.* New York: Charles Scribner's Sons, 1962.

Flores, William V. and Rina Benmayor, eds. *Latino Cultural Citizenship: Claiming Identity, Space, and Rights.* Boston: Beacon Press, 1997.

Foley, Barbara. *Radical Representations: Politics and Form in U.S. Proletarian Fiction, 1929–1941.* Durham: Duke University Press, 1993.

Foucault, Michel. *The Archeology of Knowledge.* New York: Pantheon, 1972.

———. *Discipline and Punish.* New York: Pantheon Books, 1979.

———. *History of Sexuality.* Vol. 1. London: Lane, 1978.

Frank, Robert. *The Americans.* New York: Grove Press, 1959.

Freeman, Joshua, et al., eds. *Who Built America?* Vol. 2. New York: Pantheon Books, 1991.

Galarza, Ernesto. *Barrio Boy.* Notre Dame, Ind.: University of Notre Dame Press, 1971.

———. *Merchants of Labor.* Santa Barbara: McNally and Loftin, 1964.

———. *Tragedy at Chualar.* Santa Barbara: McNally and Loftin, 1977.

Galbraith, John Kenneth. *The Affluent Society.* Boston: Houghton Mifflin Co., 1958.

Gallagher, Charles A. "White Reconstruction in the University." *Socialist Review* (1996): 165-183.

Gamio, Manuel. *Mexican Immigration to the United States.* New York: Dover Publications, 1971.

Garcia, Ignacio M. "Backwards from Aztlan: Politics in the Age of Hispanics." In *Chicano Studies: Survey and Analysis.* Edited by Dennis J. Bixler-Marquez, et al, 163-70. Revised ed. Dubuque, Iowa: Kendall/Hunt Publishing, 1999.

———. *Chicanismo: the Forging of a Militant Ethos Among Mexican Americans.* Tucson: University of Arizona Press, 1997.

———. *United We Win: The Rise and Fall of La Raza Unida Party.* Tucson: University of Arizona Press, 1989.

Garcia, John A. "The Chicano Movement: Its Legacy for Politics and Policy." In *Chicano Studies: Survey and Analysis.* Edited by Dennis J. Bixler-Marquez, 151-61. Revised ed. Dubuque, Iowa: Kendall/Hunt Publishing, 1999.

Garcia, Juan Ramon. *Operation Wetback: The Mass Deportation of Mexican Undocumented Workers in 1954.* Westport, Conn.: Greenwood Press, 1980.

Garcia, Mario T. *Desert Immigrants: The Mexicans of El Paso, 1880-1920.* New Haven: Yale University Press, 1981.

———. *Mexican Americans: Leadership, Ideology, and Identity.* New Haven: Yale University Press, 1989.

Geertz, Clifford. *Interpretation of Cultures.* New York: Basic Books, 1973.

George, Paul S., and Jerold M. Starr. "Beat Politics: New Left and Hippie Beginning in the Postwar Counterculture." In *Cultural Politics: Radical Movements in Modern History.* Edited by Jerold M. Starr. New York: Praeger, 1985.

Gifford, Barry, and Lawrence Lee. *Jack's Book: An Oral Biography of Jack Kerouac.* New York: St. Martin's Press, 1978.

Gil, Carlos B. *The Many Faces of the Mexican-American: An Essay Concerning Chicano Character.* Working paper series / Centro de Estudios Chicanos, no. 1. Seattle, Wash.: Centro de Estudios Chicanos University of Washington, 1982.

Ginsberg, Allen. *Collected Poetry, 1947-1980.* New York: Harper & Row, 1984.

———. *Cosmopolitan Greetings, 1986-1992.* New York: Harper Collins, 1993.

———. *Deliberate Prose: Selected Essays, 1952-1995.* Edited by Bill Morgan. New York: Perrenial, 2002.

———. *Journals: Early Fifties, Early Sixties.* Edited by Gordon Ball. New York: Grove Press, 1977.

———. *Journals: Mid-Fifties, 1954-58.* Edited by Gordon Ball. New York: Harper Collins, 1995.

———. *Spontaneous Mind: Selected Interviews, 1958-1996.* Edited by David Carter. New York: Perennial, 2001.

Gitlin, Todd. *The Sixties: Years of Hope Days of Rage.* New York: Bantam Books, 1993.

Gómez-Quiñones, Juan. *Mexican Students Por La Raza: The Chicano Student Movement in Southern California 1967-1977.* Santa Barbara, Calif.: Editorial La Causa, 1978.

Gonzalez, Rodolfo. *I Am Joaquin: An Epic Poem.* New York: Bantam Books, 1972.

———. "Message to Aztlan." *La Raza* 2, 6 (1975): 6-9.

Gramsci, Antonio. *Selections from Prison Notebooks.* Translated by Quention Hoare. Edited by Quintin Hoare and Geoffrey Nowell Smith. New York: International Publishers, 1971.

Gray, Bettina. *Bettina Gray Speaks with Luis Valdez.* KQED-TV: San Francisco, 1993.

Gray, John. *Liberalisms.* London: Routledge, 1989.

Griswold del Castillo, Richard, and Arnoldo De León. *North to Aztlán: A History of Mexican Americans in the United States.* Twayne's immigrant heritage of America series. London: Twayne Publishers/Prentice Hall International, 1996.

Gutierrez, David G. *Walls and Mirrors: Mexican Americans, Mexican Immigrants, and the Politics of Ethnicity.* Berkeley: University of California Press, 1995.

Halberstam, David. *The Fifties.* New York: Villard Books, 1993.

Hall, Stuart. "Cultural Studies: Two Paradigms." *Media, Culture and Society* 1, 2 (1980): 57-72.

Harris, David. *Dreams Die Hard: Three Men's Journey through the Sixties.* San Francisco: Mercury House, 1982.

Hererra-Sobek, Maria, and Helen Maria Viramontes, eds. *Chicana Creativity and Criticism: Charting New Frontiers in American Literature.* Houston: Arte Publico Press, 1988.

Hernandez, Jose Amaro. *Mutual Aid for Survival: The Case of the Mexican American.* Malabar, Fla.: Robert E. Krieger Publishing, 1983.

Hollinger, David A. *Postethnic America: Beyond Multiculturalism.* New York: Basic Books, 1995.

Holmes, John Clellon. *Go.* New York: Thunder's Mouth Press, 1988.

Hondagneu-Sotelo, Pierrette. *Gendered Transitions: Mexican Experience of Immigration.* Berkeley: University of California Press, 1994.

Horkheimer, Max, and Theodor Adorno. *The Dialectic of Enlightenment*. New York: Continuum, 1991.

Horsman, Reginald. *Race and Manifest Destiny: The Origins of American Racial Anglo-Saxonism*. Cambridge: Harvard University Press, 1981.

Howard, Gerald, ed. *The Sixties: The Art, Attitudes, Politics, and Media of Our Most Explosive Decade*. New York: Marlowe & Co., 1995.

Huncke, Herbert. *Guilty of Everything*. New York: Paragon House, 1990.

Hunt, Tim. *Kerouac's Crooked Road: The Development of a Fiction*. Berkeley: University of California Press, 1996.

Isaacs, Jeffrey. "The Poverty of Progressivism." *Dissent* (fall 1996): 40-114.

Jameson, Frederic. "Cognitive Mapping." In *Marxism and the Interpretation of Culture*. Edited by Cary Nelson and Lawrence Grossberg, 347-57. Urbana: University of Illinois Press, 1988.

———. *Postmodernism: The Logic of Late Capitalism*. Durham: Duke University Press, 1992.

———. "Reification and Utopia in Mass Culture." *Social Text* 1, 1 (1979): 130-48.

Jankowski, Martin Sanchez. "Where Have All the Nationalists Gone?" In *Chicano Politics and Society in the Late Twentieth Century*. Edited by David Montejano, 201-33. Austin: University of Texas Press, 1999.

Johnson, Joyce. *Minor Characters: A Young Woman's Coming of Age in the Beat Orbit of Jack Kerouac*. New York: Anchor Books, 1983.

Jones, Hettie. *How I Became Hettie Jones*. New York: Grove Press, 1990.

Jung, Carl. *Modern Man in Search of a Soul*. Translated by W. S. Dell. New York: Harcourt Brace, 1933.

Kammen, Michael. *The Origins of the American Constitution: A Documentary History*. New York: Penguin, 1986.

Kaplan, Amy, and Donald E. Pease, eds. *Cultures of United States Imperialism*. Durham: Duke University Press, 1993.

Karl, Frederick Robert. *American Fictions, 1940-1980*. New York: Harper & Row, 1983.

Kazan, Elia. *On the Waterfront*. Columbia Pictures, 1954.

Kelly, Barbara, ed. *Suburbia Re-Examined*. New York: Greenwood, 1989.

Kerouac, Jack. *Atop the Underwood: Early Stories and Other Writings*. Edited by Paul Marion. New York: Viking, 1999.

———. "Beatific: The Origins of the Beat Generation." In *The Portable Jack Kerouac*. Edited by Ann Charters. New York: Viking, 1995.

———. *Big Sur*. New York: Penguin, 1992.

———. *Book of Dreams*. San Francisco: City Lights Books, 1961.

———. *Desolation Angels*. New York: Perigee, 1980.

———. *The Dharma Bums*. New York: Penguin, 1992.

———. *Dr. Sax*. New York: Grove Press, 1959.

————. *Good Blonde & Others.* Edited by Donald Allen. San Francisco: Gray Fox Press, 1993.

————. *Lonesome Traveler.* New York: Grove Weidenfeld, 1989.

————. *Maggie Cassidy.* New York: Penguin, 1993.

————. *Mexico City Blues.* New York: Grove Press, 1959.

————. *On the Road.* New York: Penguin, 1991.

————. *The Portable Jack Kerouac.* Edited by Ann Charters. New York: Viking, 1995.

————. *Pull My Daisy.* New York: Grove Press, 1961.

————. *San Francisco Blues.* San Francisco: Penguin, 1995.

————. *Satori in Paris/Pic.* New York: Grove Press, 1985.

————. *The Scripture of the Golden Eternity.* San Francisco: City Lights Books, 1994.

————. *Selected Letters, 1940–1956.* Edited by Ann Charters. New York: Viking, 1995.

————. *Selected Letters, 1957–1969.* Edited by Ann Charters. New York: Viking, 1999.

————. *The Subterraneans.* New York: Grove Press, 1981.

————. *The Town and the City.* New York: Harcourt, Brace & Co., 1950.

————. *Tristessa.* New York: McGraw-Hill, 1978.

————. *Visions of Cody.* New York: Penguin, 1993.

————. *Visions of Gerard.* New York: Penguin, 1991.

Kesey, Ken. *One Flew over the Cuckoo's Nest.* New York: Viking Press, 1962.

Kiser, George Claude. "The Bracero Program: A Case Study of Its Development, Termination, and Political Aftermath." Ph.D. dissertation. University of Massachusetts, 1974.

Knight, Brenda. *Women of the Beat Generation: The Writers, Artists and Muses at the Heart of a Revolution.* Berkeley: Conari Press, 1996.

Krim, Seymour, ed. *The Beats.* Greenwich: Gold Medal Books, 1960.

Laclau, Ernesto, and Chantal Mouffe. *Hegemony and Socialist Strategy: Towards a Radical Democratic Politics.* London: Verso, 1985.

*La Raza.* Los Angeles: El Barrio Communications Project, 1967–70.

Lewis, Sinclair. *Main Street.* New York: Harcourt, Brace and Howe, 1920.

Limon, Jose E. *American Encounters.* Boston: Beacon Press, 1999.

————. *Mexican Ballads, Chicano Poems.* Berkeley: University of California Press, 1992.

Locke, John. *Second Treatise on Government.* Indianapolis: Hackett Publishing Company, 1980.

Ludwig, Edward. *Big Jim McLain.* Warner Brothers, 1952.

Lukacs, Georg. *History and Class Consciousness: Studies in Marxist Dialectics.* Translated by Rodney Livingstone. Cambridge: MIT Press, 1968.

Macedo, Stephen, ed. *Reassessing the Sixties: Debating Political and Cultural Legacy.* New York: Norton, 1997.

Madrid-Barela, Arturo. "In Search of the Authentic Pachuco: An Interpretive Essay." *Aztlan* 4, 1 (1974): 31–60.

Mailer, Norman. "The White Negro." In *The Portable Beat Reader*. Edited by Ann Charters. New York: Penguin, 1992.

Marcuse, Herbert. *One-Dimensional Man*. Boston: Beacon Press, 1964.

Mariscal, George, ed. *Aztlan and Viet Nam: Chicano and Chicana Experiences of the War*. Berkeley: University of California Press, 1999.

Marling, Karal Ann. *As Seen on TV: The Visual Culture of Everyday Life in the 1950s*. Cambridge: Harvard University Press, 1994.

Martinez, Manuel L. "Telling the Difference between the Border and the Borderlands: Materiality and Theoretical Practice." In *Globalization on the Line: Culture, Capital, and Citizenship at U.S. Borders*. New York: Palgrave, 2002.

Massey, Douglas S., Rafael Alarcon, Jorge Durand, Humberto Gonzalez. *Return to Aztlan: The Social Process of International Migration from Western Mexico*. Berkeley: University of California Press, 1987.

Mazon, Mauricio. *The Zoot-Suit Riots: The Psychology of Symbolic Annihilation*. Austin: University of Texas Press, 1983.

McClure, Kirstie. "On the Subject of Rights: Pluralism, Plurality, and Political Identity." In *Dimensions of Radical Democracy: Pluralism, Citizenship, Community*. Edited by Chantal Mouffe. London: Verso, 1992.

McKenna, Teresa. "On Chicano Poetry and the Political Age: Corridos as Social Drama." In *Criticism on the Borderlands: Studies in Chicano Literature, Culture, and Ideology*. Edited by Hector Calderon and Jose David Saldivar. Durham: Duke University Press, 1991.

McWilliams, Carey. *Factories in the Fields: The Story of Migratory Farm Labor in California*. Boston: Little, Brown, 1939.

———. *North from Mexico: The Spanish Speaking Peoples of the United States*. New York: Praeger, 1948.

MEChA. "El Plan de Santa Barbara." *Youth, Identity, Power: The Chicano Movement*. Edited by Carlos Munoz, 191–202. New York: Verso, 1989.

Mendoza, Louis. Afterword to *East of the Freeway*. Austin: Red Salmon Press, 1995.

Menzies, William C. *Invaders from Mars*. Fox, 1953.

Mexican American Youth Organization. "El Plan Espiritual de Aztlan." In *Aztlan: An Anthology of Mexican American Literature*. Edited by Luis Valdez and Stan Steiner, 402–5. New York: Vintage Books, 1972.

Michaels, Leonard, ed. *West of the West: Imagining California*. New York: Harper Perennial, 1991.

Miles, Barry. *Ginsberg: A Biography*. New York: Simon and Schuster, 1989.

———. *William Burroughs: El Hombre Invisible*. New York: Hyperion, 1992.

Mill, John Stuart. *Utilitarianism*. Indianapolis: Hackett Publishing, 1861.

Mills, C. Wright. *The Power Elite*. New York: Oxford University Press, 1956.

Mills, Nicolaus, ed. *Arguing Immigration: The Debate over the Changing Face of America.* New York: Touchstone, 1994.

Montejano, David. *Anglos and Mexicans in the Making of Texas.* Austin: University of Texas Press, 1987.

Montejano, David, ed. *Chicano Politics and Society in the Late Twentieth Century.* Austin: University of Texas Press, 1999.

Montgomery, John, ed. *The Kerouac We Knew.* Kentfield: Fels and Fern Press, 1982.

Montoya, Jose. *InFormation: 20 Years of Joda.* Sacramento: Chusma House Publications, 1992.

Mouffe, Chantal, ed. *Dimensions of Radical Democracy: Pluralism, Citizenship, Community.* London: Verso, 1991.

Munoz, Carlos. *Youth, Identity, Power: The Chicano Movement.* New York: Verso, 1989.

Nabokov, Peter. *Tijerina and the Courthouse Raid.* Berkeley: University of California Press, 1970.

Nachbar, Jack. *Focus on the Western.* New York: Prentice-Hall, 1974.

Navarro, Armando. *Mexican American Youth Organization: Avant-Garde of the Chicano Movement in Texas.* Austin: University of Texas Press, 1995.

Navarro, Joseph. "The Condition of Mexican American History." In *Chicano: The Beginnings of Bronze Power.* Edited by Renato Rosaldo, Gustav L. Seligman, and Robert A. Calvert. New York: William Morrow, 1974.

Nichols, Mike. *The Graduate.* Embassy Pictures, 1967.

Nicosia, Gerald. *Memory Babe: A Critical Biography of Jack Kerouac.* 1994. Reprint. Berkeley: University of California Press, 1983.

Noriega, Chon A., ed. *Chicanos and Film: Representations and Resistance.* Minneapolis: University of Minnesota Press, 1992.

Olguin, B.V. "Tattoos, Abjection, and the Political Unconscious: Toward a Semiotics of the Pinto Visual Vernacular." *Social-Critique* 37 (fall 1997): 159-214.

Olivas, Michael A. "'Breaking the Law' On Principle: An Essay on Lawyer's Dilemmas, Unpopular Causes, and Legal Regimes." *University of Pittsburgh Law Review* 52 (1991): 815-57.

Ortega, Carlos. "Chicano Studies as a Discipline." In *Chicano Studies: Survey and Analysis.* Edited by Dennis J. Bixler-Marquez, x-xiv. Revised ed. Dubuque, Iowa: Kendall/Hunt Publishing, 1999.

Paredes, Americo. *Between Two Worlds.* Houston: Arte Publico Press, 1991.

———. *George Washington Gomes.* Houston: Arte Publico Press, 1990.

———. *With a Pistol in His Hand.* Austin: Arte Publico Press, 1958.

Pena, Manuel. *The Texas-Mexican Conjunto: History of a Working-Class Music.* Austin: University of Texas Press, 1985.

Penalosa, Fernando. "The Changing Mexican American in Southern California." *Chicano: The Beginnings of Bronze Power.* Edited by Renato Rosaldo,

Gustav L. Seligman and Robert A. Calvert, 15–23. New York: William Morrow, 1974.

———. "Recent Changes Among the Chicanos." *Chicano: The Beginnings of Bronze Power.* Edited by Renato Rosaldo, Gustav L. Seligman and Robert A. Calvert, 23–27. New York: Morrow, 1974.

Perez, Ramon T. *The Diary of an Undocumented Immigrant.* Translated by Dick J. Reavis. Houston: Arte Publico Press, 1991.

Perez-Torres, Rafael. *Movements in Chicano Poetry: Against Myths, against Margins.* Cambridge: Cambridge University Press, 1995.

Phillips. Lisa. *Beat Culture and the New America, 1950–1965.* Flammarion, New York: Whitney Museum of Art, 1995.

Popper, Karl. *The Poverty of Historicism.* London: Routledge, 1991.

Raulrsalinas. *East of the Freeway: Reflections de mi Pueblo.* Austin: Red Salmon Press, 1995.

———. *Un Trip through the Mind Jail y Otras Excursions.* Houston: Arte Publico Press, 1999.

Riesman, David. *The Lonely Crowd: A Study of the Changing American Character.* New Haven: Yale University Press, 1950.

Rivera, Julius. "Justice, Deprivation, and the Chicano." *Aztlan* 4, 1 (1973): 123–36.

Rivera, Tomás. "Chicano Literature: Fiesta of the Living." *Books Abroad* 49, 3 (1975): 439.

———. *The Harvest.* Edited by Julian Olivares. Bilingual ed. Houston: Arte Publico Press, 1989.

———. "Into the Labyrinth: The Chicano in Literature." *New Voices in Literature: The Mexican American, a Symposium.* Edinburg, Tex.: Pan American University, 1971. 18.

———. *The Searchers.* Edited by Julian Olivares. Houston: Arte Publico, 1990.

———. *. . . y no se lo trago la tierra (. . . And the Earth Did Not Devour Him).* Houston: Arte Publico Press, 1995.

Romano, Octavio. "The Historical and Intellectual Presence of Mexican-Americans." *El Grito* 2, 2 (1969): 32–46.

Rosaldo, Renato. *Culture and Truth: The Remaking of Social Analysis.* Boston: Beacon Press, 1989.

Rosaldo, Renato, Gustav L. Seligman, and Robert A. Calvert, eds. *Chicano: The Beginnings of Bronze Power.* New York: William Morrow, 1974.

Rosenbaum, Robert J. *Mexicano Resistance in the Southwest: The Sacred Right of Self-Preservation.* Austin: University of Texas Press, 1981.

Ross, Dorothy. *The Origins of American Social Science.* Cambridge: Cambridge University Press, 1991.

Rousseau, Jean-Jacques. *The Social Contract and Other Discourses.* London: Everyman, 1993.

Sadowski-Smith, Claudia, ed. *Globalization on the Line: Culture, Capital, and Citizenship at U.S. Borders*. New York: Palgrave, 2002.

Saldivar, Jose David. *The Dialectic of Our America*. Durham: Duke University Press, 1991.

———. "Towards a Chicano Poetics: The Making of the Chicano Subject, 1969-1982." *Confluencia* 1 (spring 1986): 10-17.

Saldivar, Ramon. *Chicano Narrative: The Dialectics of Difference*. Madison: University of Wisconsin Press, 1990.

Salinger, J. D. *The Catcher in the Rye*. New York: Bantam, 1964.

Salsman, Jack, ed. *Bridges and Boundaries: African Americans and Jewish Americans*. New York: Braziller, 1992.

Sanchez, George I. *Forgotten People*. Albuquerque: University of New Mexico Press, 1996.

Sanchez, Rosaura. *Telling Identities: The Californio Testimonios*. Minneapolis: University of Minnesota Press, 1995.

Sayres, Sohnya, et al., eds. *The Sixties, without Apology*. Minneapolis: University of Minnesota Press, 1984.

Schneier, Marc. *Shared Dreams: Martin Luther King, Jr. and the Jewish Community*. Woodstock, Vt.: Jewish Lights, 1999.

Segade, Gustavo, V. "Identity and Power: An Essay on the Politics of Culture and the Culture of Politics in Chicano Thought." *Aztlan* 9, 1 (1978): 85-99.

Selvin, David F. *A Place in the Sun*. Golden State Series. Edited by Norris Hundley and John A. Schutz. San Francisco: Boyd & Fraser, 1981.

Shockley, John Staples. *Chicano Revolt in a Texas Town*. Notre Dame, Ind.: University of Notre Dame Press, 1974.

———. "Crystal City: La Raza Unida and the Second Revolt." In *Chicano: The Beginnings of Bronze Power*. Edited by Renato Rosaldo, Gustav L. Seligman and Robert A. Calvert. New York: William Morrow, 1974.

———. "Crystal City: Los Cinco Mexicanos." In *Chicano: The Beginnings of Bronze Power*. Edited by Renato Rosaldo, Gustav L. Seligman and Robert A. Calvert. New York: William Morrow, 1974.

Schultz, Debra. *Going South: Jewish Women in the Civil Rights Movement*. New York: New York University, 2001.

Siegel, Don. *Invasion of the Body Snatchers*. Allied Artists, 1956.

Skerl, Jennie, and Robin Lydenberg, eds. *William S. Burroughs: At the Front, Critical Reception, 1950-1989*. Carbondale: Southern Illinois University Press, 1991.

Sosnick, Stephen H. *Hired Hands: Seasonal Farm Workers in the United States*. Santa Barbara: McNally & Loftin, 1978.

Spengler, Oswald. *Decline of the West*. Abridged Edition ed. London: Oxford University Press, 1991.

Stavans, Ilan. *Bandido: Oscar "Zeta" Acosta and the Chicano Experience*. New York: Harper Collins, 1996.

Steiner, Stan. *La Raza: The Mexican Americans.* New York: Viking, 1973.

Stillgoe, John R. *Borderlands: Origins of the American Suburb, 1820-1939.* New Haven: Yale University Press, 1988.

Tocqueville, Alexis de. *Democracy in America.* New York: Everyman's Library, 1994.

Tomás Rivera Center. *California School District Administrators Speak to Proposition 187: A TRC Survey.* Claremont, Calif.: Tomás Rivera Center, 1994.

Thompson, Hunter S. *Better Than Sex: Confessions of a Political Junkie.* New York: Random House, 1994.

———. *Curse of Lono.* New York: Bantam Books, 1983.

———. *Fear and Loathing in America: The Gonzo Letters.* Vol. 2. New York: Simon & Schuster, 2000.

———. *Fear and Loathing in Las Vegas.* New York: Vintage Books, 1971.

———. *Fear and Loathing on the Campaign Trail.* New York: Warner Books, 1973.

———. *Generation of Swine.* New York: Summit Books, 1988.

———. *The Great Shark Hunt.* New York: Ballantine Books, 1979.

———. *Hell's Angels: The Strange and Terrible Saga of the Outlaw Motorcycle Gangs.* New York: Ballantine Books, 1966.

———. *Songs of the Doomed.* New York: Pocket Books, 1990.

Thoreau, Henry David. *Walden.* Philadelphia: Running Press, 1987.

Thorns, David C. *Suburbia.* London: MacGibbon & Kee, 1972.

Tompkins, Jane. *West of Everything.* New York: Oxford, 1992.

Trachtenburg, Alan. *The Incorporation of America.* New York: Hill and Wang, 1982.

Trujillo, Ignacio. "Linguistic Structures in Jose Montoya's 'El Louie'." In *Modern Chicano Writers: A Collection of Critical Essays.* Edited by Joseph Sommers and Tomás Ybarra-Frausto, 150-59. Englewood Cliffs, N.J.: Prentice Hall, 1979.

Turner, Steve. *Jack Kerouac: Angelheaded Hipster.* New York: Viking, 1996.

Turner, Victor W. *The Ritual Process.* New York: Aldine, 1969.

Turner, Victor W., and Edward M. Bruner, eds. *The Anthropology of Experience.* Urbana: University of Illinois Press, 1986.

Tytell, John. *Naked Angels: The Lives and Literature of the Beat Generation.* New York: McGraw-Hill, 1976.

University of California Los Angeles Chicano Studies Center. *Aztlán.* Vol. 1 (spring 1970). Los Angeles: Chicano Studies Center University of California Los Angeles.

Valdez, Luis. *Early Works.* Houston: Arte Publico Press, 1990.

———. "The Tale of La Raza." In *Chicano: The Beginnings of Bronze Power.* Edited by Renato Rosaldo, Gustav L. Seligman and Robert A. Calvert, 53-57. New York: William Morrow, 1974.

———. *Zoot Suit and Other Plays.* Houston: Arte Publico Press, 1992.

Vigil, Ernesto B. *The Crusade for Justice: Chicano Militancy and the Government's War on Dissent.* Madison: University of Wisconsin Press, 1999.

Villareal, Jose Antonio. *Pocho.* New York: Anchor Books, 1959.

Whitfield, Stephen J. *The Culture of the Cold War.* Baltimore: Johns Hopkins University Press, 1991.

Whitman, Walt. *Leaves of Grass.* New York: Modern Library, 1993.

Whitmer, Peter O. *When the Going Gets Weird: The Twisted Life and Times of Hunter S. Thompson.* New York: Hyperion, 1993.

Whyte, William H. *The Organization Man.* New York: Simon & Schuster, 1956.

Wilentz, Elias, ed. *The Beat Scene.* New York: Corinth Books, 1960.

Williams, Raymond. *Culture and Society: 1780–1950.* New York: Columbia University Press, 1983.

Wolfe, Tom. *The Electric Kool-Aid Test.* New York: Bantam Books, 1968.

Wolin, Sheldon S., and John H. Schaar. "The Abuses of the Multiversity." In *The Berkeley Student Revolt: Facts and Interpretations.* Edited by Seymour Martin Lipset and Sheldon S. Wolin. New York: Doubleday/Anchor Books, 1965.

Workman, Chuck. *The Source.* Fox Lorber Films, 2000.

Xavier, Roy Eric. "Politics and Chicano Culture: Luis Valdez and El Teatro Campesino, 1964–1990." In *Chicano Politics and Society in the Late Twentieth Century.* Edited by David Montejano. Austin: University of Texas Press, 1999.

Ybarra-Frausto, Tomás. Introduction to *Un Trip through the Mind Jail y Otras Excursions.* Houston: Arte Publico Press, 1999.

# Index